HOWARD HUGHES WAS BOB HOPE IN MAKE-UP

JOSEPH POLILLO

"I brake many of the biggest mysteries of the world and the United States within this book"

ISBN: 978-1-63950-057-4 (sc)
ISBN: 978-1-63950-058-1 (e)

Writers Apex

Gateway Towards Success

8063 MADISON AVE #1252
Indianapolis, IN 46227
+13176596889
www.writersapex.com

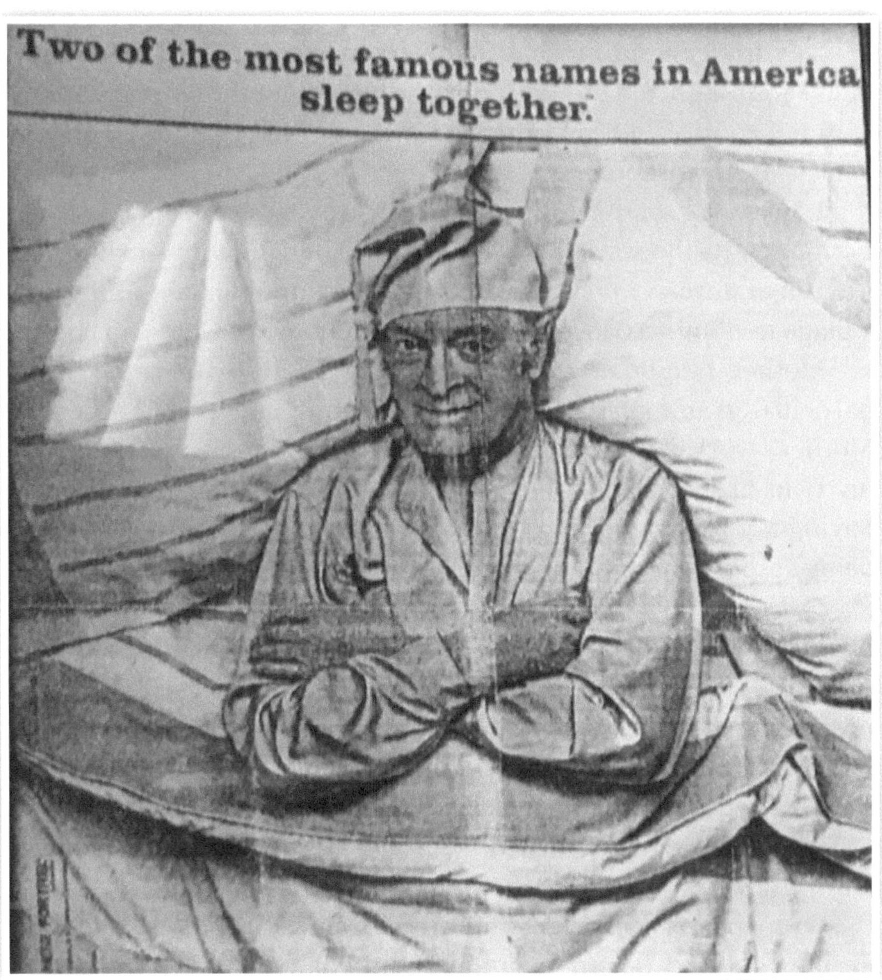
Two of the most famous names in America
sleep together.

AUTHOR'S INTRODUCTION

Joseph Polillo

It is my understanding that if you truly love God in Jesus' name, follow your faith and the 10 Commandments, not the ten suggestions, gain self-control and stop sinning, blessings will be bestowed on you. That's My Inspiration.

I grew up in Atlantic City, New Jersey. My Mother, Alice Loughney Polillo, raised three boys as a single parent working her way out of poverty and public housing, the Pitney Village and Busby Village to obtain a Mortgage and build a home in Chelsea Heights.

Mother taught us about everything, along with providing a parochial grammar school education at our Lady Star of the Sea. Mother's work ethics set an example for my older brother, Anthony, my twin brother John and myself leaving a lasting impression of having a job working hard and saving money for a rainy day, and being responsible is the way to a prosperous, safe, and happy life.

I was blessed to have been taught the basics of the world, to have learned the alphabet, how to spell words and know their definitions, to speak properly and to read and to even reading between the lines, noticing how things were said, not just what is said.

I learned a lot through tough times and had a turbulent youth until I was about 22. These experiences help get my priorities in order. This knowledge was inspirational. God offers discernment and right-thinking, which leads to happiness.

Over the years, I've read and research both the Old and New Testaments and began to understand their meanings. One day on television, I noticed Herbert W. Armstrong, Founder of the Worldwide Church of God. I began studying his teachings which led me to right-thinking and study Prophecy and world events. That Inspiration only strengthens my belief in the First Resurrection, Eternal Life in the kingdom of God through the Philadelphia Church of God.

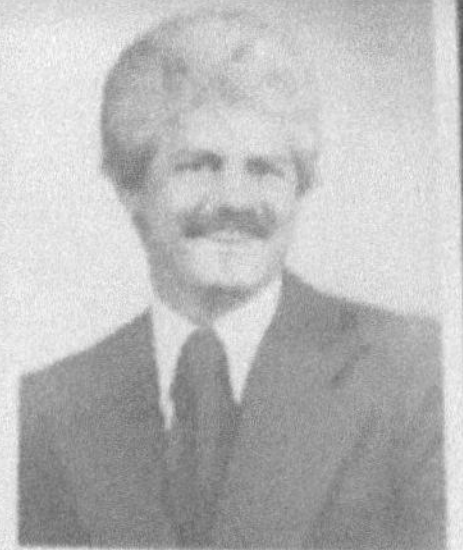

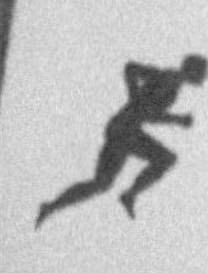
Joseph Polillo
652 Bella Terrace
Chelsea Heights
Atlantic City, N.J.
08401-1115
Phone/Fax: (609) 347-0974

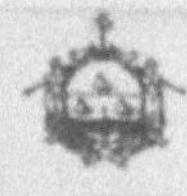
ILLINOIS & PACIFIC AVENUE
ATLANTIC CITY, N.J. 08401
609-347-5660
BUREAU OF INVESTIGATION
DIVISION OF CONSTRUCTION & INSPECTIONS
JOSEPH J. POLILLO
INSPECTOR/INVESTIGATOR

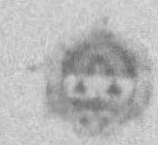
BUSINESS TELEPHONE
Atlantic City Fire Department
JOSEPH POLILLO
License Inspector
DIVISION
OF CONSTRUCTION
ATLANTIC CITY, N.J. 08401

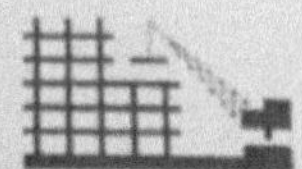
CITY OF ATLANTIC CITY
DIVISION OF CONSTRUCTION
RM 101 CITY HALL
ATLANTIC CITY, NJ 08401
JOSEPH J. POLILLO
LICENSE INSPECTOR
609-347-5660
609-347-5681
FAX: 609-347-6437
ACWCPA
Atlantic City White Collar Professional Association
JOSEPH POLILLO
Vice President
(609) 348-5137
(609) 348-5147 (Fax)
P.O. Box 7877
Atlantic City, NJ 08404

The President, Professors, and Trustees of

New York University

To all persons to whom this writing may come, Greeting:

Be it known that we in recognition of the successful completion of the requisite course of study in our

Washington Square and University College of Arts and Science

by virtue of authority granted us by charter of the State of New York do confer upon

Joseph John Polillo

the degree of

Bachelor of Arts

with all the rights, privileges, and immunities thereunto appertaining.

In witness whereof we have caused this Diploma to be signed by the duly authorized officers of the University and sealed with our corporate seal, in the City of New York, February, Nineteen hundred seventy-five

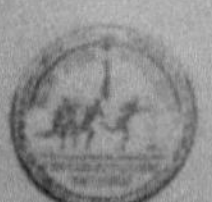

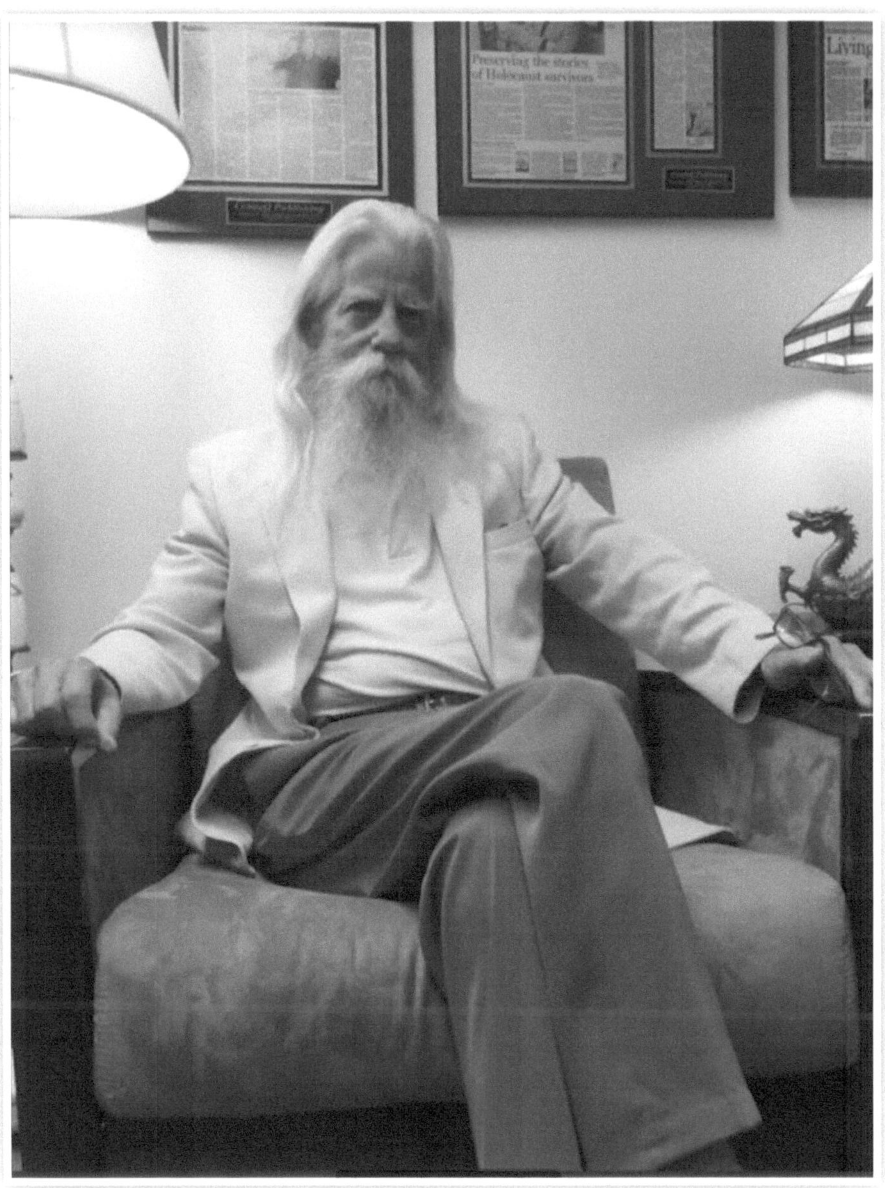
Preserving the stories
of Holocaust survivors

I ALWAYS KNEW TA BUL A ROSA BLANCA

If you know nothing, and you don't know anything at all to begin with, there is nothing there to connect with.

One fact cannot lead to another because you do not have the other. You do not have the knowledge! Nothing with Nothing is Nothing.

I knew something. I found out, and I used it as a constant variable. A controlled variable. I ran My Theory through 266 TV shows, 62 Movies, and many books and radio shows, All by Bob Hope. My constant Theory proved true.

I found out that the clues were in the movies since the 1930s and in books, movies and TV and radio shows right before the eyes and ears of the people.

IT'S CALLED THE JOKE
THE JOKE.... MY THEORY.

My Theory is that Howard Rupert Hughes went underground, disappeared so to speak, alone, behind the scene, and reappeared, made up as Bob Hope.

I know you're laughing right now. I mention My Theory and you laugh and kill it immediately. Why? Did you listen and watch all the Bob Hope Television shows (266) and his (62) Movies? Did you watch them? Did you read all Bob Hope books? Did you read his first book? The title of Bob Hope's first book was titled.

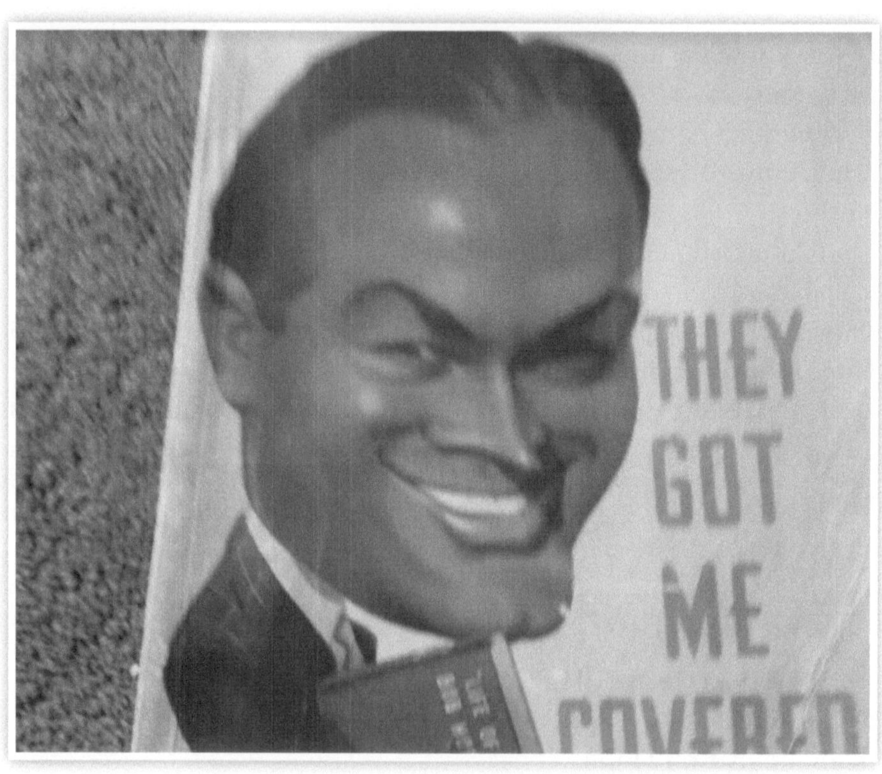
THEY
GOT
ME

CONTENTS

BOOKS

CHAPTER 1

THEY GOT ME COVERED

If you would've read Bob Hopes first Book, THEY GOT ME COVERED, and its PREFACE, you would have noticed that the preface was written by Bing Crosby. If you did not here it is! One sentence of Bing's introduction tells The Joke. Bing to write preface to this autobiography of Bob Hope's ALLEGED LIFE.

Bing wrote the preface of Bob Hope's Alleged Life. A Made-up Actor!

Did you get it? Of Bob Hope's Alleged Life. A Character in a movie and on stage. The M/C.

Bing saw the FACE for the first time. Yes, make-up, costumes and special effects on a new Alleged Face. Before 1941.

It was Bob Hope's Books and Movies and TV Shows that I picked up on where quotes right out of Bob Hope's mouth tells you who he is. Like when Bob Hope was in a Photo AD in a major Magazine. Bob is in bed sleeping. The title above his head says this.

Two of the most famous names In America sleep together. The two most famous names in America at that time were Howard Hughes and Bob Hope. So, Bob Hope and Howard Hughes are one and the same. That's what I am saying!! Nothing but the Truth. Two heads are better than one.

There were so many Movies, 62 in all and I watch them all on TV first. I was looking to get more clues. I zeroed in on the dialog, the words said and how it was said. I watched to see if there was a message beyond the theme and there was, and I found It.

So many movies. I watched, and I listened. I put My Theory to work. I put My Theory to work on the dialog and kept My Theory right on it. From these empirical observations I found out more and more. My Theory proved true as each fact connected the dots. Connect the dots.

I always knew Howard Hughes was someone else. Why else hide and disappear at times. I found out an knew it and I knew it in the 60s. The television show I led three lives hit me in the head. I made the connections.

My Theory is that the mysterious secretive billionaire movie Mongol Howard Hughes is Bob Hope and Bob Hope is Howard Hughes, and that's the joke on the American people. You can fool all the people all the time. Bob Hope said he disagreed with Lincoln. You can fool all the people all the time and he did. They had him covered.

HERE IS THE LINCOLN QUATE

"you can fool all the people some of the time and some of the people all of the time, but you can't fool all of the people all the time". Abraham Lincoln said that.

Bob Hope and or Howard Hughes disagreed with Abraham Lincoln. Meaning, you can fool all the people all the time. That's the joke that Bob Hope played on the people of the United States and the World. They fooled all the people all the time!

Here's another Bob Hope quote. Let me know what you get out of it? Bob Hope says "the names of the innocent have been changed to protect the joke.

Every actor in the movies, every movie star changes their name and takes on a stage name. My Theory is that Howard Hughes took on a stage name. That name being Bob Hope. With being an actor comes the costumes, the makeup, the special effects, the Wigs, The Mask. Howard Hughes was making all the movies and those as Bob Hope. Who was that masked man??

I always knew who Bob Hope was! I always knew who Bob Hope was since the 70s. I put it all together and between the two, Bob Hope and Howard Hughes I began gathering the facts and profs that I would use to prove that I knew what I was talking about.

That Howard Hughes was in disguise as Bob Hope. That's the JOKE. Get it.

And I can prove that Bob Hope is Howard Hughes in disguise with the facts I have researched throughout the past five decades.

1941, Bob Hope writes his first book. THEY GOT ME COVERED, Life of Bob Hope, with Introduction by Bing Crosby.

Whose THEY? The life of Bob Hope is a cover story. Do you remember what a cover is? What's a cover? Whose they? The first wild guess is in my opinion it's the Government. But my not so wild guess is that they are his make-up-men, second, everyone who is paid off, which is everyone who is in on it. And somewhere the Government of the United States. Who could it be? All the above. Could such a trick be kept so secret??

Notes of fact, there was an early television show titled "The Millionaire", where people were paid not to reveal where they got the Money, or the Money would be cut off.

Notes of fact, there was an early Television show titled "I led three lives", What does that tell you? Does it tell you anything? Could anyone live three lives??

Notes of fact, there was an early Television show titled "The Beverly Hillbillies". Listen to the opening song. The song depicts the personal History of Howard Hughes of Texas, of Oil, of Money, of Hollywood, of Beverly Hills that is and of the life Howard Hughes. Bob Hope's Life is similar, with the same History.

Back to Bob Hope's first book, 1941, titled THEY GOT ME COVERED. The Introduction is by Bing Crosby. On page 3 Bing Crosby says, "I started to write a preface to this Autobiography of Hope's "Alleged Life". Hopes Alleged Life? The character of Bob Hope is an Alleged Life. You mean like an actor's life.

Still, page 3, Bing, after coming to his senses says, "the first thing I saw when I came too was "a ski jump made from flesh, this could be a Nose. I came upon a face to face at a forehead, eyebrows, eyes and nose, a mouth and a chin. What a chin. It made the rest of the features look like accessories". Could it all be a Mask, like make–up? The Lone Ranger wore disguises. Like Superman was disguised as Clark Kent, like someone in Vaudeville would have worn? A Mask like the movie Mask. Could it all be make-up? Hollywood make-up? Like Halloween Masks?? Like all Actors.

Later, Bing says, with all that "the owner of the face and I met, that's how we met". When? Read it, page 3, THEY GOT ME COVERED.

The owner of the face and Bing met before Bob Hope became famous, (1932). Bing at the time was the most well known and most beloved Singer in all the World. Everyone knew Bing. Hook up with Bing and you become well known all over the world. Reading further the face, and the owner of the face have a screen test.

Right here Bob Hope tells you that he's doing a screen test under the hot lights, the bright hot lights. He made the test and it worked, and he says afterwards "I made the test and took the test, the Producers got together, and they decided to develop it". THEY!

Direct quote of Bob Hope "After I made the tests I went into the Studio Production Room to watch myself for the first time, the first thing to appear on screen was my Nose, followed by more Nose and my Chin". You mean a Nose and Chin were attached as make-up on the movie screen. The test was to see if it would work. It worked.

Bob Hope…. Or Howard Hughes? "Quote" "with the Nose and the Chin as make-up there was hardly room for me". Who is me? The owner of the face? Howard Hughes! Page 37. Acting!

Quote, Bob Hope!! "THEY stopped the test three times to find out if there was any rubber burning anywhere". Now what do you think that means? You don't think he meant that the fake Nose and the fake Chin were hot. Very hot under the lights. The test to see if the make-up could get over in movies. If it would stay on right….

Were they worried that the Mask was melting?? Made from rubber maybe!!

Notes of fact, there was a Movie titled "The man of a thousand faces." there was also a Movie Titled "House of wax."

Knowing that the test worked, and it worked! The program and the script are ready. Bob Hope says, "he has one writer, one writer with two heads". Is he a writer?

Many years later Bob Hope appears in a Magazine Ad, Bob Hope lying in bed, the ADS header saying TWO OF THE MOST FAMOUS NAMES IN AMERICA SLEEP TOGETHER. WHAT do you think that means? See the Ad for yourself. If Howard Hughes is acting with Make-up as Bob Hope, if he is both, when anyone of them go to sleep, two of the most famous names in America sleep together!!!!!!! Get the JOKE?

Don't forget there was a TV show Titled "I led three lives". One Life, Two Lives, Three Lives. How many lives did the Actor play in the movies?? Also remember he has one writer with two heads. Himself.

Remember HRH was The Oil man, The Billionaire, The Industrialist, The Test pilot, The Movie Producer, Writer, Director, Actor, Photographer, Inventor of Satellites, Lasers, Builder of Ships and Planes. HRH also had many Hollywood Stars under contract. Bob Hope was also a STAR. You can trust your car to the man who wears the Star. Isn't Bob Hope a Star? He did those Ads. There's a Star on his dressing room door.

CHAPTER 2

IN THE BEGINNING

It's in the beginning on page 7 of THEY GOT ME COVERED, Bob Hope's Autobiography. Bob Hope states "that you will find out all about how I change my name on page 37. I don't know what it's doing back there on page 37, but that's what happens when you write a book and are not careful."

In the beginning, Bob Hope says he went around town dressed up in a costume like Charlie Chaplin waddling around and acting like Charlie Chaplin. Later he talked about being in Vaudeville and putting make-up on his Face. He talked about putting black face on. That's make-up.

On page 32, Bob Hope states that he had a clever act. He danced, sang and did a blackface act. You could say putting on blackface is like putting on a mask.

On page 44. Hope says it is the ambition of every actor to get a star on his dressing room door. He states he remembers his first dressing room Paramount assigned to him. 'It's easy for me to remember that first dressing room I'm still in it, it was small, but I made the best of it". He's still in the make -up room. Still disguised.

On page 61 of THEY GOT ME COVERED, Bob Hope talks about some of the guests he would have on his Television Broadcast Show. He starts talking about make-up and questions everyone as too who is YAHOODI??

This is where he reveals the cover-up and the procedure he uses to put on and take off make-up.

He states that Basil Rathbone and Nigel Bruce, famous in radio as Sherlock Holmes and Dr. Watson came on my broadcast to help me find Yahoodi.

Yahoodi. Who is Yahoodi??

Everybody wondered who Yahoodi was.

Sherlock Holmes tracked down Yahoodi. Here's the next quote.

Quote "and now for the first time, for the first time, we can tell you who he is. He's the little fellow who pushes up the next piece of Kleenex". Kleenex to do what? To remove make-up. Maybe? Maybe! Must use a lot of Kleenex to put on and to take off make-up. Who's the "little Fellow"? Shorty. Get Shorty.

Talking about make-up, Hope says he "must have lots of cotton for protection". In the wind on a movie set he states, "They told me I ran around trying to catch my ears". Could those ears, just like the nose, just like the face, just like the chin be make-up? Parts of a Mask. Could the owner of the face with all the make-up on have his ears blow off in the wind?

On Page 69, Bob Hope say's I stoled four scenes and a saucer of milk". While making a movie he had four parts in the movie where he had four changes of make-up, in the movie from the cat. Who's the cat? Is he describing himself or his make-up man?

Same page 69 Bob Hope say's "The Cat and I got along very well together". TOGETHER? Is the cat, the cool cat Howard Hughes or Bob Hope or is the cat his make-up man? He continues to say, "we two use to get there at the studio and hour earlier each morning. We Would get there before everybody else". But why? Because no one else was around. Because he was putting make-up on and being someone else. And no one knew who he really was or is. He further states on page 69 that he, the cat (who put on the disguise) and his make-up artist would go in early when no one was around". Now what does that mean? Is he looking in a mirror? putting makeup on! Cosmetics.

Is Howard Hughes doing Bob Hope? I think so!! On page 71. He say's "if he doesn't act well, the Government will hang up this nose".

Wait a minute, the Government will hang up his nose? He also says that Paramount Studios spared no expense in making the movie. To me that means they spent nothing. The Government spent the money. He was a front man for the Government. That's the cover. A salesman for The American Way. The American Way of LIFE.

On page 74, in one of the battle scenes of a motion picture "the scene was so realistic that it took our director David Butler, 20 min., to convince me (Howard Hughes or Bob Hope] that I wasn't dead". Wasn't it a rumor through-out the years that Howard Hughes was dead? Is this Howard Hughes's way through Bob Hope to state that Howard Hughes is not dead?

On page 83, Hope talking about the Movie NOTHING BUT THE TRUTH, "I play the part, I play the part of a fellow who is always truthful". Plays the part! He doesn't always tell the truth. Sometimes he does. Most times he does not. Yea, in a joke. "Only last week THEY wanted my profile put into a can of cold cream". (1940)?

On page 95, at the end of the book, THEY GOT ME COVERED, Bob Hope says, "I hope you have enjoyed this scant resume of my life and career". Yeah, cause Bob Hope's life and his side of the story is this scant resume compared to the giant resume of Howard Hughes. They got him covered.

So, what does the title THEY GOT ME COVERED mean?? Who are they? A cover story, a fake story! Is it the Government? Howard Hughes? the Movie Studio's? his Writers? or everyone who is paid good money to keep their mouths shut? You tell me! What does the title of Bob Hope's AUTOBIORAPHY mean? Don't forget one thing Crosby wrote in the introduction' to Bob Hope's AUTOBIOGRAPHY about Bob Hope's ALLEGED LIFE. I did not say it Bing Crosby said it. Hope being the owner of the face or as HOWARD HUGHES putting on make-up. FALSE FACES. Anybody smell rubber burning here??

Who was that masked man? Did the Lone Ranger ware disguises? Yes, he did! As Grandma, as the old Prospector, and more. Did the Lone Ranger wear a Mask? Was the Lone Ranger from Texas? Was Howard Hughes from Texas? Howard Hughes first boat was called the Ranger!

IN THE BOOK THEY GOT ME COVERED on page 78 shows Bob Hope? Howard Hughes? With his actors and actresses in a scene from the picture, NOTHING BUT THE TRUTH, with their names printed on to them. Above Bob Hope's head is a question mark? [?] A question as to who that Individual with the? question mark above his head really is. There is no name printed on Bob Hope. What does that tell YOU? Who is he?

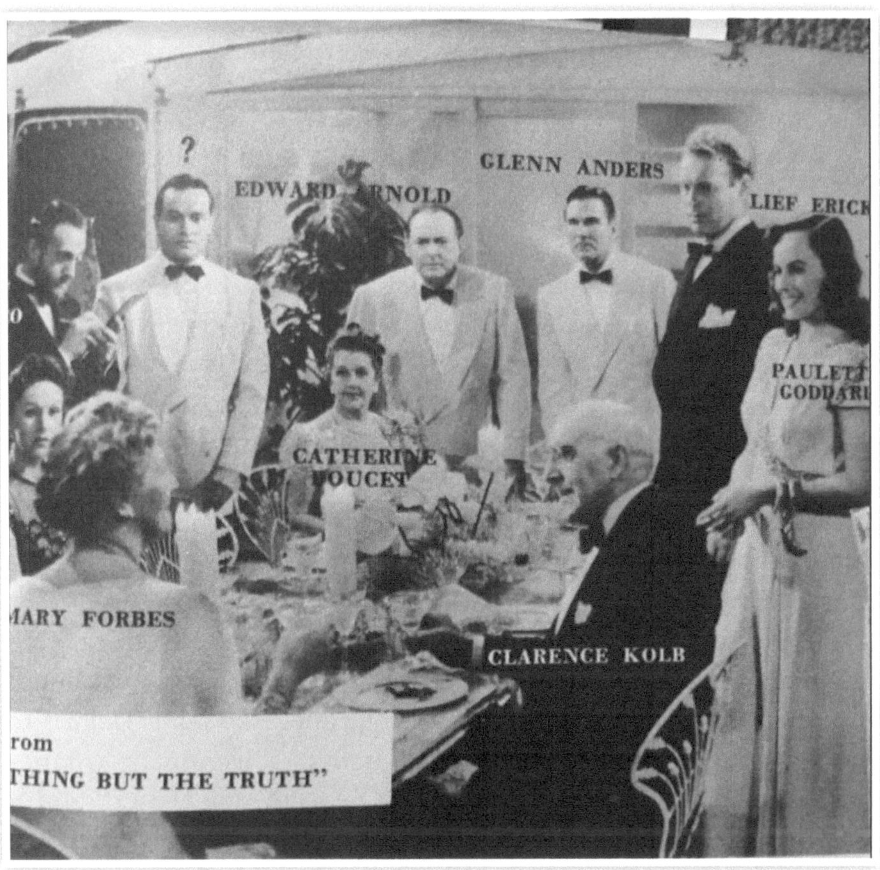

CHAPTER 3

MORE CLUES

I have clues to prove from Bob Hope's own story, in his own words, HAVE TUX WILL TRAVEL. How a regular baby grew up to look like this. This book was written by Bob Hope. His quotes are his. HE wrote the things I quote.

HAVE TUX WILL TRAVEL meant that you were ready to go anyplace at any time. It meant you were "available" for one- night stands or extended engagements. Sounds like an endorsement for Patriotism to me. If you're in the Military, you are available anytime anyplace anywhere.

In chapter 1, where the previous statement came from, Bob Hope talks about his travels. He names many cities and talks about his wife Delores being left home all the time. Bob takes Deloris to the Friars Testimonial Dinner in his honor. "Given many tributes as a Show Business Pro it was nice to hear all that flattery and it was glad that Delores was there to hear it, because up to then she thought I was a pilot for United Airlines". Possible clue?

Wasn't Howard Hughes said to be actually missing for years in the 1950's? Way back. Wasn't he found disguised as an air pilot for a commercial airline? Is this a joke? If Delores thought he was a pilot for an airline did she know he was Howard Hughes, because Bob Hope wasn't a pilot. Or was he? Did they both know? Why would Bob Hope state another fact of Howard Hughes Life. Does Delores know who he is or who he was? Or what he had done! Isn't it a fact that Howard Hughes was missing for a year back in the 50s and found in disguise as an airline Pilot? Why would Bob Hope make a crack about the possibility of him being a commercial airline pilot. Maybe that was his second head running out a fact of his other life. Not the life of Bob Hope but the life of Howard Hughes intertwined in all his jokes. Always throwing it in. Knowing the people won't get the Joke. Stay tuned!

Does that knock your socks off?

The next clue comes on page 10, paragraph 2. I suggest you go there. Get a copy of the book, go to these pages that I have stated, and I'm not finished; and read this for yourself. Prove it to yourself! Before you condemn It. Bob Hope writes; "It is not true My nose is the way It is as the result of having been broken in an accident". It is not true that his nose was the result of an accident? Are you ready for this?

"It came the way it Is from the manufacturer'. Who said that? Bob Hope just wrote that in his book on page 10, paragraph 2; that his Nose isn't the way it is from an accident, but that it is the way it is because it came from the Manufacturer!!!

Really; a Manufactured NOSE!

Hey, wait a minute. Isn't it in 1938 History that Howard Hughes was a jet pilot, a test pilot and crashed into a bunch of homes in Beverly Hills? Wasn't his face crushed, and wasn't he hospitalized for long time. See how Bob Hopes writings told you of two of his life's experiences in the same paragraph. All about his nose, all about his face, all about who he really is! He is one person. But he tells you one of his writers has two heads.

On page 37, "more than anything else, my story, the story of Bob Hope is the story of show business" Move on to page 45. Bob Hope talks about the blackface follies opening. He and George got a hold of a can of black greasepaint instead of the burnt cork to be used in the blackface theater. We lathered it on. That's make-up isn't it. After the show, we tried to remove the stuff. It sank in instead of coming off. We stayed in the theater working with wash basins and cold creams. Cold Creams are used in circuses, theaters and movies to help put it on or helping take it off. Make-up that is.

Like to turn your attention again to a photo, a cartoon on Chapter 13, page 144. The cartoon is of a make-up man doing make-up on Bob Hope's face and Nose with an entire palate of paste paint and creams are in the artist hand. Look at the photo yourself.

On page 50 Bob Hope talks about going into Washington DC in 1953 to the Costume Department in the Pentagon where he relates that he started "to be walking on stilts". On page 64 he states to himself that "you two could at least put on make-up as other actors". On page 68, (are you sitting down)? Page 68. This is Bob Hope writing. "I stuck my jaw even further out then nature had stuck it out". Page 74. Bob Hope, speaking, writing, he says "I'm Bob Hope, I had this name and I had another name. I'm Bob Hope. And I'd change it again". Page 75. "I don't need money". Page 82 "I ran out on stage precious paint". I think that would classify as make-up. Page 87. "When I came to Paramount seven years later still had the very same head". Page 89. A clipping out of the Newspaper the New York Telegraph said Hope came out of the West by Airplane. Airplanes? HRH have anything to do with Airplanes?

SIDEBAR

Page 98. Still in the Theater Bob Hope states that he is on stage in a play titled Ballyhoo. Bob Hope and Vera Marsh opened in Atlantic City. In the History Museum in Atlantic City. There's a short film called BALLY HOO about Atlantic City. On page 109 writing about February 1933 Bob Hope remembers being in Atlantic City, helping Jack Benny celebrate a $6,600 a week contract for a radio show. Stayed at the Amsterdam Hotel, formerly known as the Almanac, then The New Amsterdam and then The Mayflower.

In this sidebar it should also be noted that Bob Hope while he was in Atlantic City was the first person to be arrested for going shirtless on the beach. There was a law that you could not bear your chest on the Beach just as there was a law that women had to wear their suits completely covering them. Bob Hope was in Atlantic City a lot because Atlantic City was a place where Vaudeville and Theater were large. Many Broadway shows were broken in and rehearsed in Atlantic City. On the Boardwalk in Atlantic City years ago as of today all the stars, all the big names are in Atlantic City.

On page 20, still in Theater, Bob Hope writes, "you feel that you ought to get up early and drop in early at the make-up Department before going to the office". Stop into the make-up department before you go to the office? The office is the set is it not? Make-up before you go on the job? Howard would show up as Bob Hope. He told you that earlier with you got me covered. Don't forget him and the cat would get to the studio early. For make-up to make up as someone else.

On page 128, there's an off the wall comment. Bob Hope writes; "if Hope wasn't acting right he was told "If you don't do better you are in danger of joining the Faceless army of the unemployed."

Same page 128, being introduced by an announcer. The announcer mispronounces Bob Hope's name. Bob Hope makes this statement. "It made no difference to that audience because most of them didn't know my real name anyway". Nobody knows his real name, he's changed his name often. You tell me what he's talking about.

Remember the picture cartoon from page 144 chapter 13. Bob Hope writes this, "making road pictures makes me think of MY MAKE-UP MAN SINCE 1939. He could FACELIFT a rusted and dented jalopy in 1939. 36 yrs. old. "There was a lot of need for a lot of corrective work on my nose as well as other places and in 1939, for the most part the make-up men at Paramount were very glad to see me, they could use the money". Meaning there was plenty of make-up work on his face. Corrective work on his Nose as well as other places. Made up to look the way he looks as Bob Hope. Who is that Masked man? Then he says and writes "there you are on TV with your FACE hanging out". Don't forget everybody knew his face. Everybody drew his face off the match-book covers. On page 148. he says, "I remember another one-man audience". Could be talking about himself. "I remember another one-man audience a synthetic or self-made one". There he says he just made himself up with a synthetic something, self-made one. He said he's the one-man audience of himself and he's a synthetic self-made one along about 1939. He further goes on to say that he was doing a personal appearance at a Theater in New York city and the Movie was The MAGNIFICENT FRAUD. He talks about walking outside, looking up at the marquee and the marquee says, "THE MAGNIFICENT FRAUD, BOB HOPE. The Magnificent Fraud Bob Hope. Did you get it? The whole Bob Hope thing is a magnificent fraud played on the world. Howard Hughes is Bob Hope in make-up. He just told you so. Back in the 1950s, the 40's, and even the 30's. GET THE JOKE.

On page 196, Bob Hope writes "I wake up one night to go to the bathroom, as I sat up I heard a noise. Looking through the window was the night guard, the night guard. I smiled. He smiled, should I get up, I asked myself, can I get to the bathroom safely or will the guard take a shot at me as he thinks I'am a spy? Does he know who I am?? Page 197. I look out the window and smiled again. Once more the "character" outside the other side of the window smiled back. The character reflecting in the window smiled back in a sinister way. I kept looking. There was something about that face and smile that seemed familiar. They were mine". Two faces have I. The character reflecting in the window was him again. Him and his character.

On page 250 Hope states and writes that "in pictures I work with broader material and USE MY FACE ALOT. I have a pretty FLEXIBLE FACE". And right here... Now is the time for you who are reading this to grab your socks. He says he has a flexible face and he writes and says, "part of my flexible face was put out by the Goodyear people, and I can mug it up with anybody". Goodyear people? They are the rubber people right, they make rubber right! What's a mask made of? Part of his face was put out by the Goodyear people!!!! Accessories!

There's another clue on page 282 "I Bob Hope grabbed the chair and I asked Jane Russell to get me a glass of water. She looked at my "pasty face" [pasty face?] and ran for the water."

On page 294 Bob writes that his remodeling of his house set them back 10 times the cost of the original. "Very expensive with the tax situation, I had to go into hock". Here's where he throws in the truth sometimes. Remember that? mark over his head in the picture, no name next to his body, but a question mark above his head. Here he writes "One of my heads kept asking me, do you know what you're doing, my other head would ad lib back, you only live once". The first head is the Howard Hughes head and the second head is the Bob Hope head. Remember he was the writer with two heads. Who was that masked man?

So how many times in just a few pages, in just a few chapters, have I showed you, have I proved it to you. Did you get it? Did he say it? Did he write it? Recall that Howard Hughes was never seen and never met with anyone. I read the book, The Secret life of Bob Hope. It's very similar to the life of Howard Hughes the Secret life. Both have money, both are in real estate, both are in oil, both play golf, both make movies, both make it with many women! Both live in Beverly Hills California, both Fly a lot. Are you connecting any dots while you read? This is only chapter 3, and I certainly connected some dots did not I?? The reason Howard Hughes never met face to face with anyone and never kept a lot of appointments is because he could not physically be in two places at once......

Keep reading. There's more coming. Do some research on your own. Get the book. THEY GOT ME COVERED. Get the book HAVE TUX WILL TRAVEL. Look into it. Two books, one 1941, the other 1954.

It's all there!

CHAPTER 4

LET'S LOOK INTO JOKES

Bob Hope writes another book, 2003 with his daughter, Linda Hope. The book is titled "My life in JOKES from the guy who plays the part of a guy who always tells the truth. The opening note to the readers is a Disclaimer.

"The names have been changed to protect the innocent, well, in this case, the innocent names have often been changed to protect the joke". What joke? The joke that's being played on the American public. The joke being played on the world. The real joke is that Howard Hughes, ownership of the movie studios and all filmmaking through Paramount, with the Government paying for it all, is with a fake FACE pulling the wool over the people's eyes. That's THE JOKE!

In Bob Hope's descriptions of his family members, those in his Alleged Life he states their occupations. Each family member has a different life occupation. One is a Butcher, one is a Manufacturer, 0ne is a TV Producer, another is in Real Estate, another is a Writer and one as a Salesman, and he's just a Comedian. The salesman he is. Anyone of those occupations could be put in the lap of Howard Hughes and in the lap of Bob Hope.

What if Bob Hope in his Alleged Life just rattled off every occupation that can be attributed to Howard Hughes. The Butcher, Murder Inc. the Manufacturer of Planes, Trains, Automobiles, Jets,

Tankers, you name it. TV Producer, no doubt about It. Real Estate, California. Most of it. A Writer, Radio, TV, Movies. A salesman of the American way. And a Comedian. If one is both and both are one, Bob Hope is Howard Hughes. Howard Hughes is Bob Hope.

Remember, two of the most famous names in America sleep together. No, I'm not referring to Cannon Mills, towels and sheets. I'm referring to Bob Hope in that ad where he is sleeping alone. Right, two famous names sleep together? What do you think? don't forget Bob Hope is a writer and you know the writer has two heads, He told you so.

You know this guy Bob Hope has been acting, acting his whole life. Everybody's acting. They're all in on the joke. The theater people, real actors, real theater people, who can really play a part in a Mission Impossible. And don't forget all the people in the movies and theater change their names. In each movie every actor plays a part.

Here's a little side note about Howard Hughes as a 12-year-old. His nickname was Sonny and Sonny began to grow into acting, had theatrical ambitions and was growing in the trade. He would go up to see the shows at The Keith's theater, 105th St., Cleveland, Ohio. Bob Hope says Cleveland Ohio is his hometown. Here we have Howard Hughes as a child going to the Theater of Vaudeville to watch acting. To be in the environment of the theater as a young boy.

Also, as a young boy in Cleveland, Bob Hope started to imitate Charlie Chaplin. He would put on an imitation outfit of Charlie Chaplin. He was acting and looking like someone else. Like make-up, the mustache, the derby, the disguise.

As Bob Hope gets older and into movie making, producing and acting. He says, "I spent all day with the cameraman trying to figure out from which angle I like best, but the sponsor wanted you to see my face". Who's the sponsor? Sponsor of the Movie or the TV show or the owner of the face. They, the sponsor of the face. Who's that the Government, Paramount studios, Howard Hughes? Wasn't the Government of the United States footing the bill for all Paramount Bob Hope productions. He said it didn't cost Paramount, anything. Who owned the face?

On page 82 Bob says he likes TV so far, but my profile is causing some confusion". Confusion as to who he might be? On page 92 he states that about the same time my autobiography was published. Have tux, will travel, 1954, that the title is one from my Vaudeville days. Actors used the saying on their business cards or in ads. HAVE TUX WILL TRAVEL. Talking about the book he says, "think about seeing your life flash before your eyes. Little did I know that that book written in the 50s "would cover only half my life". 50 years of life or two lives, one half of the life of two heads, you know the two most famous names in America sleep together.

Only half his life. His is Bob Hope, the other half is Howard Hughes. One is the scant resume of Bob Hope and the other a very large resume of Howard Hughes. One very large resume.

Bob Hope says that his Charlie Chaplin imitations made him show business conscious. "I'd put on my Chaplin make-up and walk ducked legged down to the corner. I was good at it". So, it was good. Putting on the disguises, putting on make-up and acting. And he was good at It.

On page 46. Hollywood went to war and the biggest stars enlisted. Didn't Bob Hope and Howard Hughes go all in for the war effort? Would you think that the guy who made all the military contracts, and all the movies could put himself right out front on stage laughing at the people. What a joke.

A few weeks before Christmas I got a call from my friend Stuart Symington, Truman's Secretary of the Air Force. The Air Force. See any connection there? Bob Hope's friend is the Secretary of the Air Force.

On page 78. He says he took his first plunge into Television in 1950. In that first Television show, Bob Hope says, "we had a tremendous cast in this show. They really had to rush to get all our make-up on". They had to rush to get our make-up on. For the show!

On page 123 Bob says, "he doesn't mean to call Pres. Nixon a pigeon, that would be disgraceful. I won't even say who won the loot but if you look through the President's Budget of $200 Billion I'm in there somewhere". Why would Bob Hope be in the President of the United States budget? I know Howard Hughes and the Military are in that budget. What loot? Does Bob Hope get a lot of loot out of the Government's budget? Is he getting a lot of money from Pres. Nixon's budget? Why would Bob Hope get money from Nixon's budget if he's in there somewhere? Bob gets the money or Howard Hughes gets the money.

Years ago, I got a quote from Howard Hughes, he said "my father won World War I, I won World War II and my equipment is working in Vietnam". Here is a bigger clue, and it is said as a joke. "It appears that the President tapes all his conversations in the Oval Office. I just hope that the 18 min. gap of missing tape included some of the bad jokes I told Nixon". Bad jokes. You mean the truth. It could be Bob Hope as Howard Hughes on the tape. Read for yourself in the book. The Secret Life of Howard Hughes by Charles Higham and the Gemstone book about a White House secretary who knew and heard what was on the 18 min. gap of Nixon's tapes. She was found dead. See the Howard Hughes book where it says that they destroyed the tapes of Watergate because it was Howard Hughes talking to Nixon, about JFK, about Cuba, about O'Brien, about the break-ins, possibly even murder! Bad jokes. Jokes? Remember, Bob Hope says in jest that the gap on the tapes would've been some of his bad jokes, is another joke by Bob Hope.

On page 140 Hope states that "some time Hoffa talks other than politics". Yeah, maybe he does talk too much. Maybe he was talking about the Assassination of John F. Kennedy. Maybe? So now here's a Bob Hope joke. "I don't think Hoffa is missing at all. I think he is just playing a game of hide and seek with Howard Hughes". Yes, Hoffa was involved In the Assassination of John F. Kennedy. Yes, Hoffa is missing. The lesson is don't get involved in the Assassination of The President of the United States or you will die like Hoffa, like Johnny Rosalie, and many others.

No, and that's not the first time that Bob Hope has mentioned Howard Hughes name. At a USO show for the soldiers in Vietnam, Bob Hope, carrying his golf club states that "the show will continue until we find Howard Hughes. That he is there in search of Howard Hughes". Why such a wise crack? He's in search of himself. Get the joke!

President Reagan was an Actor out of Hollywood, California and he decided to honor Bob Hope as an Actor to give him an award. Bob goes on to say that "I'd love to get anything in Washington that's not taxable". And you can also read in History that Howard Hughes was always trying to avoid taxes. The Government was paying for everything tax free.

Back to show business as an Actor Bob says, "he went to the Philippines islands, and he says he gets so hot and so humid here that I am wearing special make-up."

Bob Hope say's "in show business a lot has changed when they used to do my face before a show it was called make-up, now it's called Special Effects". His face Is Special Effects. His face, the owner of the face is Special Effects? Make up. He's playing a part. As Bob Hope.

Remember Bob Hope says before he goes to the office as Bob Hope he first goes to the make-up department. He goes to the make-up department first before he goes to the office. Bob Hope is an Actor in Disguise.

Now, on a side note, I was watching a Bob Hope NBC special about NBC being sold to Westinghouse, when a Westinghouse executive walks onto the stage looks at Bob Hope and ask who are you? of course, the audience laughed. They knew it was bungled. That's all they know. But the Westinghouse exec was asking a real question, who is he? You know, it's not what you say. Sometimes it's how you say it. I guess you're saying that the Westinghouse guy didn't know Bob Hope. Is it Bob Hope?

Bob Hope goes on to say that his secret for staying so young is good food, plenty of rest and make- up man with the spray gun.

All this talk about make-up in every book. All this talk about his Nose in every book, in every movie, on every matchbook, on TV, all this blabber about make-up. Telling the people right to their faces that the Masked man is right in front of them and they don't know it.

Bob Hope says George and Barbara Bush were like family. He knew George HW Bush's father, Prescott Bush, Senator from Connecticut, and he says that I always played golf with him and I always played golf with George HW during his eight years as Vice

President of the United States. I became very close to George and I played golf with him. Bob Hope played golf with every President, Vice president and power connected person in the history of United States.

My opinion is... That if the Billionaire Industrialist with all the connections like Howard Hughes has was playing golf with all US Presidents and Vice Presidents since Truman it would be outrageous. People would be screaming conspiracy that something was going on. But if it's Bob Hope and you're playing golf with the Comedian, the joker of Radio, TV and Movies, it doesn't amount to much, it's like a frivolous golf game. If Bob Hope is Howard Hughes or Howard Hughes is Bob Hope they both are very close all the time to all the power and everyone thought nothing of it. What a joke on the people. It's like having secret meetings a way to meet without being suspected of anything.

Bob says, "that at this age I am getting to spend more time with the Dolores, at least I think it's Dolores. She looks familiar". Is she someone else? Could Dolores be Amelia Erhardt? Both Howard Hughes and Amelia Erhardt are missing. Both had disappeared.

And at the very end of the book Bob Hope writes, "this is my 60th year with NBC, which proves that Abe Lincoln was wrong". He says, "you can fool all the people all the time."

What was that?

You can fool all the people all the time!!!!

I think he did, no matter who he is. Stay tuned.,

Here's another connect the dots. Bob Hope says one infantry man couldn't figure out why his brother would send him a toy balloon until he blew it up and it turned out to be an inflatable woman toy doll. Strange joke. Does it make any sense? I can connect the inflatable woman toy doll balloon to Howard Hughes and Bob Hope both. Are you ready?

Back in the day Howard Hughes was caught at a girl friend's house having sex with an inflatable woman toy balloon. One, page 95.

In the book the Secret life of Howard Hughes, author Charles Hingham writes this.

Howard Hughes is dating a very pretty and famous actress of that time. And here in paragraph 1. You can read in this book that Howard Hughes` ask her to come into the bedroom. She declined. To her amazement he walked into the bedroom, leaving the door open and she saw on the bed a life- sized rubber copy of herself with breast and a virginal. She watched as he mounted the figure, stroked It, thrust deeply into it, and after a few minutes climaxed. Strange connection aah? Seems like Bob Hope and Howard Hughes know about inflatable life-sized women toy doll balloons. They have both been documented as total womanizers. Here, here you see Bob Hope and Howard Hughes connected to toy dolls.

Here is an example to prove my hypothesis. In the movie THE CAT AND THE CANARY, Bob Hope and a woman actress are entertaining onstage to a rowdy bar with a lot of people drunk and disorderly. Can you see it.

Bob Hope and the actress in the dressing room are getting into costumes and make-up to go on stage. Bob Hope comes up with a full tray of noses, Rubber Noses. All the Noses are on a painter's palette with many different noses for make-up. A change in identity. FAKE NOSES. Bob Hope puts a fake rubber nose on his nose and ask his actress partner "do you think this nose will fool the public?' She says, "No not that one". Bob Hope puts another Nose on his face and ask again. 'Will this Nose fool the public?? She says "Yes"!

You can fool all the people all the time.

Bob Hope then goes out on stage to a drunk and rowdy crowd and says.

'I am the best impersonator of people in the whole wide world. That quote recalls a television program such as I led three lives. With that said, Bob Hope turns around and puts the phony nose on and turns back to the audience and says "I do my best impersonations right in front of all the people and they don't get it". (That's the joke! Get it?)

WELL I DID!!!!!!

Joseph Polillo

Remember, recall Bob Hope's first movie screen test with all the sponge rubber, the phony nose and that the Hollywood Lights were so very hot on the screen test that people on the set said they smelt rubber burning. Interesting. Smelt rubber burning.

Remember, recall that Bob Hope said that he didn't get his nose by accident. He got it from the Goodyear Family. I think that means rubber. Bob Hope made this crack joke in one of his books.

'people think I got this nose by accident, but I really got it from the Goodyear family.'

Speaking of an accident. Howard Hughes crashed his jet into the Beverly Hills in 1946. Broke his face, broke his nose, broke his body. An accident, hospitalized, maybe a new nose? Plastic Surgery? Possibly a rubber nose? A prosthetic. How about a new face? How about a different FACE, under make-up, as it's called, cake, years later stucco? The new face, like the one that Bing Crosby saw. The Alleged Life. 1941.

Here's a fact and some proof in the movie the Cat and the Canary. Bob Hope as an actor in the movie makes news by catching a ghost in a weird haunted house. Bob Hope is interviewed by the Paramount news crew and ask how did you catch him?? And Bob Hope says'

'I found this piece of sponge rubber, and I know all about sponge rubber, I am an actor and I use it all the time" as he points to his cheeks.

That's right, he got it from the Goodyear family. Hollywood make-up and Special Effects. Don't forget Mr. Westwood, the best make-up artist in the Movie Business. Howard Hughes as Bob Hope uses Sponge Rubber all the time. Bob's alive and Howard's dead. Another joke on the people of the world.

Remember, recall Bing Crosby on Bob Hope's Alleged Life; the New Face. Who was or is the owner of the new face? Howard Rupert Hughes (HRH) is the owner of the new face!! In the new face is Bob Hope. Bob Hope is and was the phony nose and the new face. Sponge Bob Square Pants. Love that Bob. HRH owned Paramount News Reel. They filmed WWII.

Here's another quote said by Bob Hope (HRH) in the dialog of the 1951 Movie. The LEMONDROP KID.

The movie opens to a drawing of a Christmas tree and the only ornament hanging on the tree is gun. A LUGAR. In the movie, Bob Hope owes the mob $10,000. Which he must pay back to the Gangster by the name of Sam. (Sam Giacona?). To get the money Bob Hope is running a Santa for hire business. Hope has all his Santa's lined up in a roll call. The Santa's will collect the money on the sidewalk so that Bob can pay back the Mob the money he owes them. Hope is addressing one Santa and telling the fake Santa the many names that Santa is known by around the world like St Nick, Chris Kringle and as he's telling them that, a fake Santa looks up at Hope (HRH) and says, "I know another guy who won't tell his real name either."

Now who could that be?? Do you think that could be Howard Hughes and that Bob Hope is Howard Hughes and will not tell anyone his real name? Hope changes his name often.

Howard Hughes as Bob Hope doesn't tell his real name either. Bob Hope is Howard Hughes and Howard Hughes is in disguise as Bob Hope. Right in front of the World. Their lives and their MOs are identical.

Money, Real Estate, Movie Makers, Womanizer's, Golfers', The writer with two heads. The man playing two parts. The greatest impersonator. There I proved It again. Keep reading and I'll prove it the more. 'Two of the most famous names In America sleep together'. When Bob Hope sleeps, Howard Hughes sleeps, when Howard Hughes sleeps, Bob Hope sleeps. They sleep together. They are one and the same person. Somebody Is playing two parts as two different people.

Mission Possible?

Remember, recall Bob Hope is or has a group of writers and reveals that he is one of the group of writers and that he is the one who has two heads. One head is Howard Hughes and the other head is Bob Hope, living two lives, a real split personality. 'You can fool all the people all the time." He's both. Howard Hughes as Bob Hope pulled it off, hence the name of the movie. The Greatest Show on Earth (1952). The greatest impersonator of people as an actor. Bob Hope had a cameo moment in this movie, and the camera zeroes in on Bob Hope sitting in the bleachers. A cameo with Bob Hope in the movie and the camera goes right to Hope. Watch the movie. The camera pans over the bleachers showing all the people watching the Circus. If Howard Hughes is or was Bob Hope in disguise, and I believe he was, he pulled the wool over everyone's eyes. He was then and is the greatest show on earth. Don't forget HRH himself was a great show on earth. Both men had the same mo. from Women to Movies to Money the Military, The Navy, the Air Force and the Army.

I can say here that I broke the biggest story and mystery of the world. Breaking News, Bob Hope is and was Howard Hughes all the time in disguise. Each one covered the earth with US Presidents and Generals from Roosevelt, Truman, Eisenhower, Kennedy, Johnson, Nixon, Ford, Reagan, Bush, playing golf all the time. Howard wanted to be the greatest golfer and played golf all the time. Bob Hope plays golf all the time. The Desert Inn Golf classic. Howard Hughes hid out at the Desert Inn, or did he?? Was HRH ever in the Penthouse?

Interesting!! So, I looked, and searched and I researched, and I found out that in action and dialog and on statements said in Bob Hope's books, Radio Shows, TV Shows and Movies, right out of his own mouth that he is Howard Hughes. Remember he himself is one of the writers, the one with the two heads who sleep together. Convinced yet? Bob writes the cue cards!

Read Arthur Marx's book, The Secret life of Bob Hope. Read it. Get the secrets, the women, the same MO as Howard Hughes. Both living in the same area. Southern California, Moviemaking where Howard Hughes owned and operated all the movie studios, controlled all the Actresses and Actors, all the Writers, Producers, Directors, and ALL the Studio's and locations since 1932. Let's look at Bob Hope as Howard Hughes and listen and see what comes out of his own mouth in those Radio, TV shows and Books and Movies, on the screen and in the dialog. Reading deeper into this book and each Movie, TV show and Books I analyzed them and critiqued them, and I found out more and more each time.

Look, and listen closely to all Bob Hope's words, his cracks and his jokes. The words in his dialog and you will see as I did that Bob Hope (HRH) tells you who he is in disguise and is playing a part for the United States Government (Have Tux Will Travel) and that he is Howard Hughes. HRH is playing the part as the character Bob Hope. The Lone Ranger and the Beverly Hillbillies Tv shows are more proofs.

So, the joke was on the American people, on everyone. "You can fool All the people all the time." Howard Hughes as Bob Hope did just that, He fooled all the people all the time, all the time. With the help of the United States Government, its Presidents, the Army and Navy, the Air Force. The Movie Industry, Hollywood Stars, especially the Make-up Artists. Remember Bob Hope's first book, 1941. They've got me covered. BING!!

Bob Hope (HRH) writes an opening note to his readers as a disclaimer in his book, My Life in Joke's. Bob writes,

'the names have been changed to protect the innocents. Well, in this case, the innocent names have often been changed to protect the joke."

THE JOKE!

Did you get that? To protect "THE JOKE" What was the Joke?? The joke is that Howard Hughes in make-up is Bob Hope. In his own words he said it, he wrote it. He has changed his name many times. Remember he is the Greatest Impersonator of people with Fake Face's like Mission Impossible and he does his impersonating right in front of the people with the fake nose, ears, cheeks and chin. And the people don't get it. And they didn't see it. The Joke is on the people of the United States and the World that Howard Hughes changed his looks and name to act as Bob Hope. Are you still laughing? Are you getting It? Keep laughing!

Who ever saw Howard Hughes?? No one! If Anyone knew who he was they were paid big bucks to keep their mouths shut. Bob Hope has said himself that "nobody has ever seen my face". What? (Howards face).

(TV) The TV show the Millionaire. If anyone receives this money and says where it came from they would be cut off.

Noah Dietrich said he never saw Howard Hughes and Robert Mayhue said the same thing. Howard Hughes was never seen but you saw Bob Hope all the time in every medium on the earth. Also, with Planes with Movies with Women with Presidents with 0il with War with the USO with the Theaters, Radio, Television and Books and Films, but we never saw Howard Hughes. Strange. No one ever saw Howard Hughes. He was said to be dead. In a sense he was dead because he was Bob Hope all the time.

Watching a Bob Hope NBC special Hope's out front as always Master of Ceremonies. (MC) a Westinghouse CEO walks on and looks at Hope, then asks... Who are you? That's a good question. Yeah. Who is he? While the audience laughs because they all know that's Bob Hope. It's an open question. "Who are you?

Who is he? "You can fool all the people all the time" and he did! No matter who he is...He did!

Near the end of Bob Hope's career on NBC Bob Hope said this.

'this is my 60th year with NBC, which proves that Abe Lincoln was wrong."

'you can fool the people all the time."

"two of the most famous names in America sleep together" the writer with two heads.

Years ago At first I looked at Hope, I couldn't see what his jokes and wisecracks were about, nor what his comedy was about. I started to look and listen a little closer in the early 60s. I was a Howard Hughes watcher. I followed America's History and they were one in the same. I followed all of it on all the news. The news about Howard Hughes, especially his disappearances and the other names he went by. HRH went by other names.

I was following Howard Hughes news. His Biography. Many Books and Documentaries. BANG.!!!

In the early 60s I was on the trail of the Lone Ranger, and how the West was won and in search of Jed Klampet, who represents Howard Hughes Biography.

Interesting. Connect the Dots First let's look at the Lone Ranger its Theme and its Dialog. The Lone Ranger Television show and series ran from 1949 through 1957 – a story of a MASKED MAN and his Indian companion Tonto. A strange story about a Texas Ranger. The masked man hiding his identity. Tonto called him Khemu Sabby, which means Trusted Scout to the Indians of the South West territory of the United States. More on the story line and theme a bit later. The dialog in the shows by the writers is telling. Hundreds of episodes. I reviewed mostly all of them. Currently I want to give you my thoughts on the opening statements of the Television show. With a Fiery Horse and the Speed of Light and a Cloud of Dust. Those terms show and have indications as to who the Lone Ranger is and was in this modern era.

1) A fiery horse equals horsepower or engines. 2) speed of light equals the laser. 3) Cloud of dust equals liftoff as thrust from rockets.

Sounds like a few industrial terms to me, engines, lasers, rockets, the Lone Ranger, a Maverick. The masked man Howard Hughes. Who was that Masked Man?

Here's another indication of what's up. Connect the Dots. In the Movie the Barefoot Contessa, starring Ava Gardner the opening dialog says this.

"See that guy over there, he's the Movie Producer, he already owns Texas and he's buying up California". Well isn't that the information about Howard Hughes. In real life Ava Gardner was Howard Hughes girlfriend. Howard Hughes is from Texas and owned Paramount Studios and lived in Southern California. I'm sure he dabbled in Real Estate.

Here's another proof and a quick look at the Beverly Hillbillies opening theme song which is indicative of Howard Hughes life story. The story of the TV show is about Jed Klampet going out, shooting a gun to get some food. He shoots the gun hit's the ground and up popped Oil, black gold, bubbling crude.

Howard Hughes inherited Oil. With all that Oil and all that Money people told Jed, he better run for the hills, Beverly Hills that is. Well isn't that exactly what Howard Hughes did? He went out to Beverly Hills. Well JED struck Oil, Black Gold and Ran off to

California, owned Texas and bought California. Howard Hughes did that. He Owned Standard Oil, Texaco, etc. and settled In California, buying land and running the movie studios at Paramount and every other studio, with his Uncle, who was a screenwriter for the Industry and helped Howard Hughes Learn film Cinematography to make movies. Howard Rupert Hughes was oil and is Oil. Check out HRH's bio. Jet pilot, Golfer, Movie maker, Rocket man. Bob Hope matches those professions. Movies, Golf, Real Estate, all in California. Bob and Howard have the same life timeline 1903, 1905, up through the 70s and 80s. I connected the dots. The dots were everywhere. I continued to look even closer into Bob Hope and Howard Hughes life's as to what was said and shown in the Movies, in TV shows and in the Books. I found my answers in the dialog. Howard Hughes and Bob Hope are one in the same.

In all and most of Bob Hope's words and facts can be attributed to Howard Rupert Hughes and that he was both men. Over the decades I gathered all my facts from the many Books, Tapes, Movies, and TV Shows and Newspaper reports and as I read and watched and listened and read about Howard Hughes and Bob Hope. I pinned him.

It took years for me until 2014 or 15 to review it all again and again and gather the facts anew to advance my discovery and bring to light The Greatest Show on Earth. The biggest trick ever played out on the entire world.

I put it all together and I always looked for my proofs. I wrote down my research. I had to tell the world what I discovered over 50 years. No one would listen. I broke the Biggest Story in the History of the World and proved it only to myself. No one would listen.

Moving forward I read Bob Hopes Books and watched all his Movies and Shows. Read on and as you do think of optical illusions such as Masks, Props, Costumes, Special Effects, Sponge Rubber, Stucco, False Ears, Fake Chin, you name it. For instance, here's a couple TV skits that prove that Height can be an illusion and that Sponge Rubber from the Goodyear family continues through TV, movies and film and in public. There is a story in one of Bob Hope's books where he is at an outing and he is asked to do a show within a couple of hours upstate California. Bob's answer was that he could not do that show because he did not have enough rubber with him at that time. Love that Bob.

Kind of like mission impossible right. well, Mission possible. People impersonating other people with masks and make-up. Every story is about a masked man. The Lone Ranger, Batman, Spiderman, any man, a Mask. Bob Hope was in the comic book business and in the Publishing Business.

Here's an example from a Lone Ranger Television Episode titled "High Heels". A story about a Real Estate guy who is sensitive about his Height in a cowboy town. He is sensitive about his Height. Being short the man wears stilt high cowboy boots, high heeled cowboy boots to appear taller, to look tall. Yeah, like Mickey Rooney had to stand on a box or where high heel shoes. Here is another example from an I love Lucy show. An Actor shows up wearing high heeled stilt boots. Lucy, on the same show is wearing a rubber nose an accidentally on purpose sets the nose on fire. A Phony Nose. Bob Hope was all about his nose from the Goodyear family. You can get taller, but you can't get smaller. You can put on rubber noses and change your appearance. It's called Special Effects and you can fool all the people all the time. Well, can you really trust the man who wears the star, the big, bright Texaco Star. Bob Hope represented Texaco. Bob Hope is the Star. A Star is on his dressing room door. The movie Star. The Lone Star from Texas. The Star on the dressing room doors since the 1920s. Hope is the man who is the Star. Hughes is Texaco. Bob Hope did Texaco advertisements on Television. The big bright Texaco Star is the inventor of the laser. With a Fiery Horse and the Speed of Light, and a Cloud of Dust. With Engines, Lasers, and Rockets. Texaco Oil is Howard Hughes Texas and The Barefoot Contessa's man.

Here's another movie that says something. We all know that Resorts Internationals parent company is the Mary Carter Paint Company which has been exposed as a CIA front company. First the United States Government is the Company. The CIA works for the Company. Follow this movie scene from this Bob Hope movie.

Resorts International was the first Casino in Atlantic City, New Jersey. There is a book about the Company that bought the Boardwalk.

Put the Title of the movie here.

Five Shots ring out in a Penthouse suite at the top of a Hotel. A Woman, Bob Hope and Rochester are waiting for Bellhops to come and take their luggage to the Cruise Ship for a Cruise to Cuba. Someone was shot. Sirens and Alarms are going off and here come the police. As this is occurring, Bob Hope takes the woman's luggage trunk empties it and gets in the Trunk himself and the Bellhops take the trunk off to the Cruise Ship. Meanwhile, as the Police arrive, they huddle in the hallway outside the Penthouse door at the top of the building and say to themselves "We searched this Penthouse all the time and there is always no one in it." Does that sound familiar? Know anyone that hid out in a Penthouse in Las Vegas at the Desert Inn?

Now doesn't that sound familiar to those who know the history and the facts about Howard Hughes said to be hiding out in the Penthouse. The Penthouse of the Desert Inn Casino in LasVegas, Nevada. Howard Hughes probably was never in the Penthouse. He was too busy being Bob Hope...........

As the ambulance arrives and the medic's carry out the victim of the shooting on a stretcher the cops are right behind them yelling that the man on the stretcher from the Penthouse is dead. Does that sound familiar? As they all pass by the camera the guy on the stretcher sits up and says into the camera. "No, I'm not dead", as he is whisked away.

The Woman Mary Carter and Rochester are looking for Bob Hope and seeing all their clothes on the bed realize that Bob is in the trunk and that he's missing. The Trunk had been taken to the Cruise Ship. They realize that Bob Hope is in the Trunk and on the Ship. They know that Bob hid in the trunk and is on the ship.

They head to the ship and Rochester is told to go to the cargo hold to find the trunk. The Women gives Rochester a clue as to finding the trunk and how to identify it. She tells him my name is Mary Carter and my initials M/C are on the trunk. Rochester finds the trunk and finds Bob and are reunited with himself and Mary

Carter. Go watch the Movie an prove it to yourself. They are off to Cuba. Did Howard Hughes have any Casinos in Cuba or any links to the mob running his casinos?

As the ship sets course to Cuba Bob Hope is on deck at the front of the ship standing like Napoleon with his hand in his jacket and as the camera moves in Bob Hope is writing something in a book. As he is doing that Mary Carter comes forward to see him and ask him what he is doing, and Bob Hope says this.

"I am rewriting history. I took this island (CUBA) without firing a shot". Took Cuba without firing a shot? Review the Movie. See it for yourself. Landing in Cuba they go to Mary Carter's Mansion. Bob is still trying to make it with her. Ever the Womanizer.

One scene has Bob with Mary Carter coming down a spiral staircase and Bob notices a large portrait painting of a Woman. Mary Carter tells him it's a Painting of her Mother Mary Carter. Bob Hope looks at the Portrait and says, "what a wonderful name for a company". Google Mary Carter Paint Co and you will find out that Mary Carter Paint Company is a CIA front company and the Parent Company of Resorts International, a Casino Corporation out of Miami which became the first casino In Atlantic City, New Jersey, USA. Casinos have everything to do with Howard Hughes. Watch the movie. Listen to the Dialog. Google Resorts International.

My thing about movies growing up was that there must be messages in all these movies other than just foolishness and entertainment. What is really being said in all these movies? Like in a 1936 Movie titled "Snowed En". Bob Hope is 33 years old in 1936. First you must remember that Bob Hope said, "he is a writer with a group of writers". Hope says, "he is the one writer with two heads". This Movie Snowed En is about a writer hiding out in a cabin trying to get some writing done. Hiding out in a cabin? Hiding out. He is interrupted by past wives and many girlfriends. Wives and girlfriends! A womanizer!

Here's another movie with a clue to support My Theory that Howard Hughes, unseen owner of Paramount Movie Studio and in fact all Hollywood Movie Studios is Bob Hope in make-up and disguise. Using a Sponge Rubber Nose, Fake ears, Cheeks, Chin and Nose plus Stucco.

Sponge Bob Square Pants

Talking about Special Effects and Make-up in the Movie Industry here's an example. Turner Classic Movies Interviewer interviews Orson Well's Daughter about her Father and his roles in Movies Particularly "The Third Man". Orson plays the part of a Writer. She says Her Father Orson Wells did not look like her Father in that Movie. He was playing the part of a Villain. She goes on to say that in the movie The Third Man, her Father did not look like her Father. "Orson had a small nose; a little Nose and that little Nose didn't sit right with him as a Villain with a little Nose, so he built it up!" He built up his nose! He put on a bigger nose! Did you get that? He built up his Nose and put on a bigger Nose in the Movie. Really.?? He put on a bigger Nose! He built his Nose up! He built up his little Nose with Make-up! That's called a Disguise, right? Thanks to the Goodyear Family, right? The Make-up Artists in the Movie Industry used fake Nose's.

Orson Well's also made a movie called "Fake". Go see it. Don't forget to remember that Bob Hope stepped out of a Burlesque Theater to have a smoke looked up at the Marquee and the Marquee said.

"The Magnificent Fraud Bob Hope."

Wally Westwood, a Make-up Artist and Special Effects person, the make-up man at Paramount Studios is the man and the creator of the make-up for the movie the man of 1,000 faces. The man and the creator of "The man of 1,000 faces, a movie starring Lon Chaney. A 1,000 Faces. 1,000 different Faces made up with make-up. Sponge Rubber, Stucco, and whatever. Let's remember a statement by Bob Hope at the end of the Movie.

Bob Hope is asked how did you catch that criminal in that ghostly Hotel? Bob says, "I found this piece of Sponge Rubber and I know all about Sponge Rubber, I'm an Actor and I use Sponge Rubber all the time". He says this while being interviewed by the Paramount News Cameras. Howard Hughes owned Paramount Studios. His cameramen filmed all the Newsreels that were presented to the public throughout all the Movie Theaters in America. Bob Hope uses Sponge Rubber "All THE TIME "All the Time. Yeah, as Bob

Hope. Because Bob Hope is Howard Hughes. Howard Hughes is the owner of THE FACE. The Producer Director and Actor character in the Movies. A Writer with "TWO HEADS". Two people in one. "Two of the most famous names In America sleep together". They sleep together. Howard Hughes is Bob Hope. Bob Hope is Howard Hughes an Actor. Howard Hughes is Bob Hopes "Alleged" Life. Remember Bing Crosby said that in his preface to Bob Hope's first book, THEY GOT ME COVERED. The Alleged Life of Bob Hope.

THE MAGNIFICENT FROUD

Check the Movie Oceans 11 and watch the camera pan all 11 Actors with Beak Noses. Have you seen the NBC symbol? The spectrum of colors. Did you notice that chemical beaker? The Beak. The Beak is a Nose. Bob Hope's whole career was about his Face and about his Nose and he owned NBC for 60 years. Drew his Nose from the Matchbook Cover. The symbol of the Peacock is about Bob Hope himself where Howard Hughes is so proud of himself, so vain, so pretty, so rich. Proud of himself.

How many times in movies does Bob Hope play two people at once? How many times is Bob looking into Mirrors talking to himself? How many times is Bob Hope ask in Movies and TV, "Who are you?" Yeah, who is he?

In a Bob Hope special on TV, Dean Martin says to Bob Hope "How are you.... There' a long pause as Dean tries to recall what name to call Bob. Dean then looks over to a cue card that says Bob. Dean then says, "how are you Bob". At another time in a Movie there is a statue on a table with a large Nose on it. Another time in a Movie is a statue with two heads. Look for it. Review his movies as I did. Those facts will be my footnotes that back-up My Theory which I am proving through this book.

Another Bob Hope USO TV Special to the Troops. Bob list the many City's and Country's he has done his shows from. In one Vietnam show he says, "this show will not stop till we find Howard Hughes". Is that a joke? Bob says this all the time. In many of his TV shows, his first 10 shows or so he says Howard Hughes name many times. Here's another quote from Bob Hope. Under a photo of Bob leaving his plane to do a show there is a statement by Bob that says "I stepped off the plane and disappeared" to do a show as Bob Hope. Who disappeared? Howard Hughes disappeared into the character Bob Hope. I have a photo of Bob Hope, hustling to a plane after a show. Under the photo is a statement by Bob Hope. "After every show I leave quickly under an assumed name." Who is I? Who is who? What Assumed name? What Alleged Name? What Alleged Life? Is Alleged and Assumed the same thing? Same thing.

I have another quote by Bob Hope "the names of the innocent have been changed to protect the joke." That quote is from his book, My Life in Jokes.

At another time, Dean Martin calls Bob Hope Mr. Potato Head. Mr. potato head was a toy for children. You used a Potato as a Head with little plastic ears, nose and eyes, etc. that are stuck into the Potato making It look like Mr. potato head with a NEW FACE. The product was sold in stores and it was a real Potato with accessories. Dean Martin knew something. It was a crack and a joke about a Face that was put together by accessories. They laugh about the joke of putting on accessories like Rubber Noses. He has a protruding chin, large phony ears using sponge rubber and Stucco. Thank the Goodyear family again using make-up. Those in the movie making business knew who he was. Bing Crosby's Introduction to Bob Hope's first book in 1941 about meeting THE FACE and meeting THE OWNER of THE FACE and about Bob Hope's ALLEGED LIFE tells you "Nothing but the truth". Read it for yourself. Read Bing Crosby's preface, introduction to Bob Hope's book, THEY GOT ME COVERED. Yeah, with make-up and a cover story. Like a spy with a new Identity a false story is a cover story. On one TV special Bob and Bing are singing "Thanks for the Memory". Bing sings and as he sings Thanks for our marker ears. In another cut he says CA EARS. Bing points to his EARS, then again and again ask Bob "Who are you.?"

Here's more in Bob Hope's first book. There are cartoon pictures of a make-up artist painting a Nose on Bob and a picture of Bob Hope running and chasing his ears that had blown off. Another incident stated in a book says Bob Hope was asked to quickly do a show. Bob says that he does not have enough rubber to make a show. In one clip video Bob Hope puts his face in a cake. Cake is also a term for make-up. Hope always calls attention to his Nose, and so does everyone else, always, even on match-book covers and he is known as ski Nose. Aside from movies of Bob Hope the studios put out other movies, all with the writers telling Howard Hughes History in an autobiographical way. Like in the movie "O Sullivan," 1941. To me this movie came through as the complete Autobiography of Howard Hughes as Bob Hope. The Dialog, the Plot, and the scenes of this movie is the evidence of the adventures of Howard Hughes aka Bob Hope about a guy who just wanted to make people laugh.

I took the information on this movie off the Turner classic movie website. The following critique of the movie and the background information of the making of the movie is as follows. You tell me if the facts are not associated with Howard Hughes adventures and experiences Here's the information from TCM.

A Hollywood director, (could that be Howard Hughes or Bob Hope,) who made a profitable career making franchise comedies decides to make a movie of a sociological and artistic important movie and dresses like a hobo. Sound familiar, Howard Hughes disappeared once and was found as a hobo bum in New Orleans and put in jail. The hobo takes to the road for research to see how the other half lives. To be a regular person.

My Theory is that the entire movie is about Howard Hughes. It's about being Bob Hope, a guy who just wants to make people laugh as a comedian. Sound familiar? Howard Hughes owned all the film studios and Bob Hope made franchise comedies.

Howard Hughes had an office in every single studio in California, Hollywood. He had something to do with every movie that was made. The O'Sullivan movie has the same plots as Howard Hughes had in his secret life. Like the secret life of Walter Mitty. Howard Hughes disappeared several times and the facts are well documented, and he was arrested in New Orleans as a vagrant. At another time Howard Hughes wandered around Florida as a bum and a Florida woman bought him a breakfast. Another time

Howard was missing and was found to be a Commercial Airline Pilot under an assumed name and later as a newspaper reporter for Metropolitan Newspaper. A mild-mannered reporter. Sounds like Superman to me. How many assumed names is that? Who changed their name many times?

As the character O Sullivan in the movie, he is thought to have murdered someone and takes off and runs from the Law. He jumps on a train and on the train a hobo steals his shoes. O Sullivan had his ID hidden in his shoe. The hobo falls off the train and dies and is found with O'Sullivan's ID and is declared dead. O'Sullivan is declared dead. It is said that O'Sullivan is dead. He's dead. Sounds familiar. Howard Hughes is said to be dead too, right? Dead right. Yeah, sure. Wanted Dead or Alive.

O'Sullivan Is described in the movie as a boss. A director of movies from Hollywood, Beverly Hills and lost. They guess! Sound familiar again. O'Sullivan Is called a phony. Remember Bing referring to Bob's "Alleged Life". Remember Bob Hope wrote in one of his books, that during an intermission of one of his shows he went outside on a break and looked up at the marquee, and it said The Magnificent Freud Bob Hope.

Here's some dialogue from the O' Sullivan movie "He knows everything" "talks about taxes and giving away money" "does the boss have any ID" 'he is said to be dead" "he's dead"...... sounds like the personal History and Characteristics of Howard Hughes and the situations he had in life.

The bum steals O'Sullivan's ID, which is in his shoes. As I said above the bum falls off the train and dies. The authorities believe and think that O'Sullivan Is dead because the ID the bum had said he was O' Sullivan. O'Sullivan Is still on the train. He gets arrested as a bum. Sound familiar. He Is found guilty in court and jailed. O'Sullivan refuses to give his name like someone else we know. The newspapers report that O'Sullivan Is dead and publish his photo. En route the paper reports that the murderer is dead. Let's consider that Howard Hughes could've been linked to the Mob, Murder Inc. and that murdering and waging war during World War II could be considered a murderer. He may have murdered many people in his life. He could've been the CIA. I think that he was the CIA. He certainly was associated with the Mob.

'Sullivan is found alive in the movie and he gets out of jail. He is cut loose and Its big news. He is not arrested.

Found alive and released from jail and back in LA and Hollywood he is asked if he will make a movie about himself and about his story and he says "No" "he just wants to make Comedies". Make comedies? That's all. Bob Hope did. Bob Hope made comedy movies and possibly wrote them. Here are some more dialog quotes.

why not make a movie?

"no" he says. "I just want to make people laugh". Howard Hughes is alive and makes movies as Bob Hope from 1920s onward. Read the TCM review of the movie and of the director that made the movie.

When O'Sullivan with no name was in jail there was a picture show for the Inmates in a church. In the dialog, the jailer says to Hope. "Do you think this is a Broadway Vaudeville show."

O'Sullivan says" they think I'm dead, but I am not dead". Sound familiar? Remember the man on the stretcher. The cops say he's dead, he says he is not! Howard Hughes was believed to be dead, he wasn't.

Did you see My Theory in any of the dialog yet? The team of writers and the one with two heads wrote all the dialog, they also wrote many of the movies produced by Paramount and other studios. Even when TV shows came on many of the themes were of the Old West Cowboys and Texas. Texas and California.

Here is some opening dialog from the Barefoot Contessa again starring Ava Gardner. Howard Hughes girlfriend in real life as I said before, and Humphrey Bogart is the director in love with Ava. Dialog. "That's him over there. He already owns Texas and he is now buying up California real estate". The Movie Producer Howard Hughes and Bob Hope Real Estate tycoon. A citizen could have more money than the Government. Don't forget the words of the Beverly Hillbillies. HRH BIO.

Here's something you can think about. I found a good clue from the lyrics of a song by Ricky Nelson.

GARDEN PARTY

Ricky Nelson's Mother and Father, Ozzie and Harriet Nelson came right out of the big band era of the 30s and 40s. Ozzie was a leader of a big band. His band was also in many movies.

In the 50s the Ozzie and Harriet show was on TV with their two sons, David and Ricky.

Young Ricky Nelson became a teen idol, producing and singing great songs from 1957 onward. When Rick Nelson came to Atlantic City he played the Steel Pier. My Brother John and I were there. My Mother slipped us in the Balcony door. Later he played the Marine Ballroom at the ocean end of the pier. The pier was rocking and rolling and swaying due to the weight of all the people. A great crowd. George Hamid, Steel Pier owner said that that day was the biggest attendance that the Pier ever had.

My twin brother and I had all Ricky Nelsons 45s. They were records and we liked his songs and as 10-year-olds were said to look like Ricky Nelson.

Ricky Nelson lived in Beverly Hills his entire life. His whole family the Nelsons were in the in crowd. Ricky Nelson appeared in many movies with all the great stars of Hollywood.

Many years later, Ricky Nelson did a concert in Madison Square Garden, he had an experience there and he wrote about it in the song. The song Garden Party is about a music reunion. I like the song, and I listen to it. I listen to many songs in my life and I always try to interpret what was being said in songs. I listened to Garden Party. In the third stanza of that song, Ricky Nelson revealed what he knew about Howard Hughes. Here's the quote. "And over in the corner sat Mr. Hughes in his Dylan shoes wearing his disguise". "Ricky Nelson" outs" Howard Hughes, wearing his disguise during the Concert at Madison Square Garden. Hence the Garden Party.

Ever since my youth my eyes and ears were wide open to the news talk about Howard Hughes. Howard Hughes, the mysterious Howard Hughes, the Billionaire Glob Trotting Industrialists. I thought of Howard Hughes as Mr. America, a Superman among men since 1965,66, & 67. "Absolutely nothing was truly known of

Howard Hughes, he mainly HID himself." that quote came from the book written by James Phelan, an author from California with Gordon Margolis and Mel Stuart. Those two were the chief aides of Howard Hughes. The book titled, The Hidden Years.

Howard Hughes vanished from public life in the mid-50s at 55 years of age and became invisible. Remember, it was 1941 when Bing first saw THE FACE.

I had heard that Howard Hughes refused to show in public no matter what and would not answer any subpoenas to Court no matter what the cost. He disappeared from public view, and even from the courts and from the Government. But he would be out there under other names and in disguise. That's My Theory.

People laugh as soon as I mention My Theory and for years just at the mention of My Theory that Howard Hughes was Bob Hope in disguise as an Actor they were laughing. That's not fair. They haven't even heard or read any of my proofs. They rush to judgment. Listen to some of my facts at least, don't kill It right away without hearing My Theory, without listening You cannot disprove My Theory! Howard Hughes was born in December 24, 1905. Connecting the dots, Bob Hope, says he was born in England in 1903, a cover story. They got him Covered.

As a young boy Howard Hughes, about the age between 10 and 12 years old, was nick- named "Sonny" as he was growing up in New York City. Born into a rich family, his Family was High Hat, High Society. Millionaire Oil Rich with Top Hats and Tuxedos and plenty of Money. Bob Hope's second book Have Tux Will Travel is about working for the United States Government and being on call to travel at a moment's notice.

Sonny, Howard Hughes as a young youth of 12 years old would hang out at the Theaters on the Great White Way where he got his first glimpses of beautiful well-built Showgirls, well-built Women. High Hats and High Society frowned down on Burlesque and Vaudeville and Broadway people.

Howard Sonny Hughes was exposed to Broadway shows. MCs, Actors, Actresses, Show Girls, and Stars. This boy had never seen so many pretty Woman.

Later, young Howard was being prepped for Harvard. He went to Fessenden school in West Newton Massachusetts. Later, Howard was sent to California to his Uncle Rupert Hughes on weekends. Rupert Hughes was a Novelist, a scriptwriter, writing movies in Hollywood. Howard was said to be about 17 years old at the time. He attended the Thatcher School in Ojal California. Howard spent a lot of time with his Uncle Rupert at Paramount Studios. How About that? Well Well, Paramount Studios and Howard Hughes. Later in life Howard Hughes would own Paramount Studios. Do you think he could've played a part in a movie as a character actor?

Hanging around the studio at Paramount with so many pretty girls on the sets he loved all the women. At that time Howard got into the intricacies of Moviemaking at age 17. In 1922 he became a Cinematographer, a Writer, a Producer, a Director and an Actor. In 1922 through 1924 Howard Hughes made a Movie Hells Angels. A story about Airplanes at War.

In 1922, his Mother died. He was 17. In 1924, His Father died. He was 19.

At 19, young Howard Hughes jr Sonny, inherits Standard Oil and possession of Hughes Tool Co. and the Invention of the Drill Bit and all the Money, Gold and Oil Companies. At this time Howard Hughes buys out the family to become sole (Lone Ranger) owner. In 1925 Howard Hughes marries Ella Rice. She was the daughter to the founder of Rice University.

1926 and 1927 at 22 years of age, Bob Hope shows up. He has been an Actor since 1921. Remember the Theater Marquee? Bob Hope, The Magnificent Fraud. Bob Hope is not who he pretends to be.

Bob Hope does a Show at The Globe Theater in Atlantic City, NJ. Atlantic City My Hometown.

In a Bob Hope Book it was said that Bob met Lucky Luciano, and that Lucky Luciano, the head of the Five, The Commission of all Mob families in the United States was bank rolling the Broadway shows. Did they hook up? Howard Hughes and Bob Hope. Big money to big money. It was at this time in the 1930s that the Mob moved into the Movie Business.

In 1932, at 29 years old Bob Hope did a one-week engagement at the Apollo Theater in Atlantic City, New Jersey. Bally Ho.

Bob also did shows at the Werner Theater, Atlantic City, Played Golf at the Atlantic City Country Club and opened and owned the Atlantic City Racecourse with Jack Kelly father to Grace Kelly, and Frank Sinatra.

Information from Bob Hope's book, Bob Hope says this. "I got to Make- up before anyone else arrived before going to work". Nobody saw him put on his make-up. They only knew him as Bob Hope. People working with him didn't even know who he was. Make-up before anyone else arrived! They think he is Bob Hope. They only know that he is Bob, that's all they knew. I have a TV skit of a Bob Hope television special. A Skit about a make-up man making up Hopes Face. The make-up man says this to Bob Hope after being questioned as why it's taking so long to get the make-up right. The make-up man says, "first time I ever worked with stucco". Stucco on his FACE. A Plaster Face. Really, from Sponge Rubber to Stucco. A new Face! They had him covered in make-up. Don't forget the Nose. Don't forget the Cheeks. Don't forget the Ears. Don't forget MY THEORY!! Howard is Bob, Bob was Howard! Bob is Howard'! Howard is Bob!

I wonder what the face looks like without THE MASK and what it looks like when the stucco is off. What does Bob Hope look like without the Stucco?? Without the make-up, the Ears, the Nose and the Chin removed do you think he Looks like HOWARD HUGHES?? I DO!!!!!

So, just like all Bob Hope Movies and Books they all basically tell the truth. Nothing but the Truth was one Movie. Many other Movies such as Spies like Us, which was done twice by Bob Hope. One a cameo in Spies like Us in the 80s, and as a spy in the 40s. Is Bob trying to tell us something? Like the possibility that he was a Spy. How about an early movie called Ghostbusters made by Bob way back in the 40s? The modern movie Ghostbusters in the 80s or 90s. Many movies about Spies. My Favorite Spy, My Favorite Brunette. How about the movie Iron Petticoat which is all about Bob as a spy, turning Russian women into American spies as he works as an officer in The United States Air force. Also, the movie Comrade X. The dialog is all about Howard Hughes the spy flipping Russian women into being spies for the United States, being on both sides. Being on both sides, just like Iron Petticoat. The dialog is all Howard Hughes MO.

Lucille Ball sang a song at the Kennedy Center awards. Her lyrics in the song said this, "you all think we are Comedians, but we are all Spies". Don't forget the movie Masquerade. Masquerade means like someone isn't who they say they are. They are masked. Like the Magnificent Fraud. Like the Long Ranger.... Bingo.

Let's take My Theory a step further and bring it to an MGM movie in 1947. Are you're ready for this? The Secret life of Walter Mitty.

My Theory is that the writer's group of Hollywood movie making, which Bob Hope is one of the writers with two heads have all their Movie Scripps based on the activities, the experiences and the Incidence's and life History of Howard Rupert Hughes.

Take Walter Mitty for an example. A guy whose mind is on something else makes up stories from his secret life. Secret life. Anybody you know have a secret life? There are many books out about Bob Hope and his secret life and Howard Hughes in his secret life. Check it out. Walter Mitty is said to be a Cowboy. Howard Hughes from Texas is a Cowboy. The Lone Ranger, a Texas Ranger for instance. Walter Mitty, a Pilot. Howard Hughes was a Jet Pilot, a Test Pilot of Jets for the United States Air Force. Don't forget the movie Hells Angels by Howard Hughes. (1922-24) Also, Walter Mitty considered a Gunslinger and a Killer. Walter Mitty was also considered a Publisher of Books. Bob Hope was a Publisher of Books and Comic Books. In the Dialog of this movie one of the Quotes is the Quote "he's really dead." Wasn't that the rumor that Howard Hughes was dead?

Walter Mitty was said to be in the dialog a "medical genius". In many of Bob Hope's Movies and Television Skits on his Television Shows Bob Hope plays the part of a Doctor doing operations in an operating room with nurses and as he is performing an operation in one skit he refers to his Nurse as Mary Carter.

As a Jet Test Pilot. We all know that Howard Hughes was a test pilot for the United States Air Force. As a killer. We all know that it was all Howard Hughes equipment during World War II that killed millions of Japanese and Germans, 1942 through 1945. That's a killer. Hope has said himself he "had killed nine people."

We also have quotes like this in the dialog of the movie "we only live once, or two" that supports My Theory!! "We only live once, or two." Here we need two. Remember the TV shows I led three lives. Don't forget Mission Impossible. More dialog, an Actor says, "never forget his impersonations."

Remember the movie in the bar scene where Bob puts on the fake nose right in front of the people, and they don't get it. Said he was the best Impersonator of people in the whole wide world. The greatest show on earth. A tray of noses, pick-one.

Mitty sings a song as a German in disguise at an Air Force headquarters with a foreign woman. Dialog says "you have a good face" that's like the Movie the Iron Petticoat. Dialog continues talking about sensational murders. Mitty is acting like a spy. Hope plays a spy in many of his movies. His life was in danger. Check out the movie Comrade X. Mitty's life is in danger. So is Howard Hughes or Bob Hope. Mitty is chased by the Dutch Police and the FBI over World War AI stolen Art. Well, there was stolen Art during World War II. Bob Hope was everywhere. During World War II. First in North Africa, first in Malta, Sicily and the very first to Hitler's office. If you led the war effort and you won and killed off the enemy, you'd be considered sort of a murderer. Not the mention of the connection to the American Mafia and the so-called Mob Wars. Boris Karloff says in the dialog of this Movie "that I know a way to kill someone without a trace". There is also a quote in one of Howard Hughes books talking about where all the bodies are buried.

In the Movie, a Howard Hughes look-alike stands at the door with his hand over his mask to act as a gambler with cards. Did Howard Hughes have anything to do with cards and gambling and casinos?? In this Movie the Gambler states, "I hate women" and then walks off as a Penguin. I think Penguin was the name of a Publishing Company of Books. To walk off as Charlie Chaplin is an indication that it's Bob Hope. Remember Hope started his acting career acting as Charlie Chaplin. Bob Hope did a Movie with a Penguin in a Burlesque Theater. Concerning Howard Hughes's life story, the Penguin is Hope's symbol of High Hats, High Society, Tuxedos and Top Hats which indicated Money. Big money.

The Rich did not like Burlesque Theater Actors. They looked down on anyone in the Theater Business.

Mitty is said to need help. They said he's crazy. They said Hughes was crazy. Bob Hope said he himself was crazy in his Books.

They said he needed psychiatric help.

Well, did I throw enough facts against the wall? Is any of it sticking, this was just the introduction to this book. The rest of My Theory will be put out by pulling out all the Statements and Themes of Bob Hope's Books to prove My Theory that Bob Hope is Howard Hughes. That Howard Hughes is Bob Hope in make-up. Call it Sponge Rubber. Call it Stucco, but that Face is a made-up Face of an Actor playing the part of Bob Hope. You only see him in the Movies, you only see him on the TV, you only see him when he's playing the part, and he played that part, and he was Bob Hope and behind the scenes he was Howard Hughes. The Joke over top of the American people.

BOOKS

The following critiques are from my research of Bob Hope's Books. They got me Covered 1941 and Have tux will Travel 1954. The following are the quotes I pulled from all of Bob Hope's statements, Quotes and situations that prove My Theory chapter by chapter, quote by quote, that Bob Hope is Howard Hughes in disguise, that he is and was Howard Rupert Hughes. (jr. Sonny).

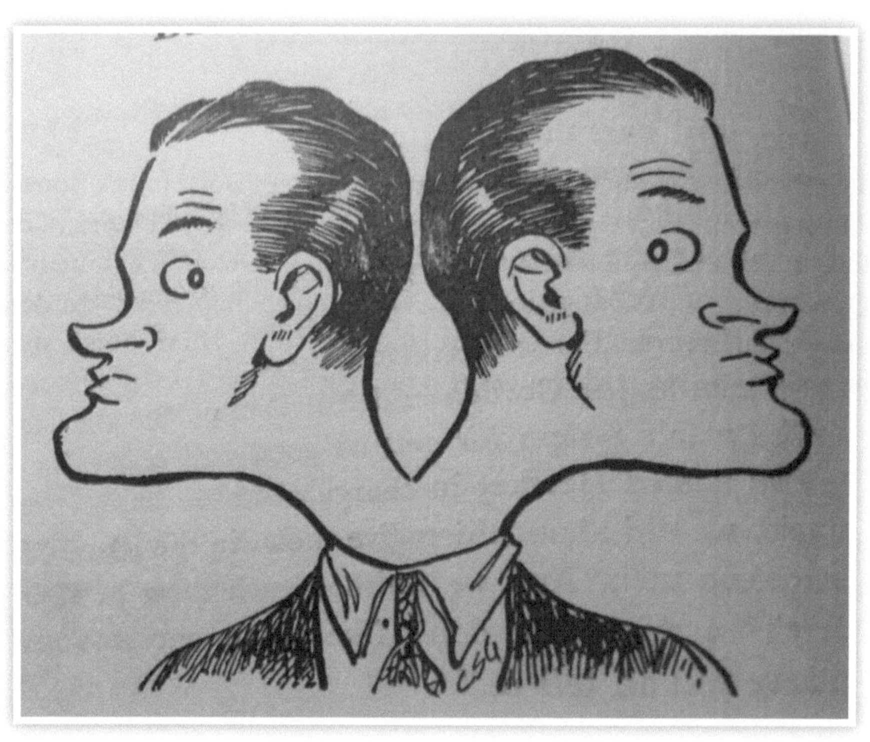

BOOK #1

I NEVER LEFT HOME, BOB HOPE 1944

Chapter 1... Hope Springs Eternal.

Here's a quote from Bob Hope. "It's still a Military Secret or I would be able to explain it, My Broadcasts not only furnished the basic idea, the Military also provided and supplied most of the raw material used in the development of powdered eggs."

A Military Secret? Really? Powdered Eggs. Really, for real? Would that be Bomb Material like the Manhattan Project, like Uranium? "Quote" The Army's doing everything."

Chapter 2... Hope says, "It's nice to know your ACT is going over". What Act?

The Act that your Howard Hughes and playing the character Bob Hope. He goes on to say that his "act is by Airplane" and that "the Military foots the Bill.

Page 18. Bob Hope says, "no blabbing to his cast". He says, "you are a Military Secret, and so are your comings and goings". Top Secret Mission.

Getting ready to go on the USO tour's during the war Bob Hope says "we were mugged by photographers, front and profile, neither of which is the best view of Me." Yeah right, because it was a phony view. The real view of him is Howard Hughes and he then says "our ID papers and passports were given to us before we left. The FBI also gave us a "light" going over. "Fortunately, they did not recognize me". Who wouldn't recognize Bob Hope in 1944? I think he means they didn't recognize him as Howard Hughes behind all the make-up with the new face on. Nobody could recognize that it was Howard Hughes behind the Mask of Bob Hope.

On the plane there were four Mysterious Financiers and a few Generals. It was a special plan. "Must be really important". Hope is talking to Boeing employees in Seattle as the Paramount News men are filming for their news. Bob says it "was like being in Hollywood, like I had never left home."

"Every place I went I met people from Show Business Entertaining or Fighting."

Chapter 4... We played Hamlet.

"The Army figured it would take 11 days and 1306 miles". Page 45... Hope talks about a guy he knew who ran a chain of Movie Houses. He played Hope's Movies.

And Hope goes on to say that "he knows all Presidents and Generals, Secretaries of States, Generals, even Privates in the Army, Navy, the Air Force Intelligence and the Constellation Aircraft Core. Called Maps, The Military Air Transport System.

Chapter 5... Everything was just Great– Britain.

Hope goes on to say that he was with Dr. John Davies. He's a physician an MD. Also, with Frank Freeman, President of Paramount Pictures. Bob Hope states that "Freeman and I lived in the Projection Room". The entire Paramount Studios filmmaking apparatus travels with Bob Hope. "We spent five weeks together. We visited 30 Hospitals and 120 Installations, mostly Air Force installations", filming the entire war. That's what Paramount Studios Newsreel did.

Chapter 6... We left them in the Aisles.

Page 78... Bob Hope says "the Royal Air Force flew us, and the Royal Air Force Pilot let me pilot the Plane for a little bit". "It is not generally known," says Bob "but I have over 1,000 hours of Air Experience. I am an Expert Pilot". There're the words right out of Bob Hope's own mouth. I know Howard Hughes was an Expert

Pilot, An Air Force Jet Pilot, a Test Pilot. Bob says he's an "Expert Pilot" with "thousands of hours in the air" and he flew the plane. Gee I wonder when Bob Hope had all the time to get thousands of air hours as a Pilot. If he's Howard Hughes he's got plenty hours in the air.

Page 79... Bob Hope is always giving information on all the types of planes and shows up at many aircraft plants such as Lockheed and Boeing and shows up at P 38 plants and Submarine bases, UN shows, USO Shows and Navy shows. Just because he's an MC and a comedian?

In Bob Hope's travels he talks about sitting in Winston Churchill's office at 10 Downing St. Who is this guy? He also made statements in his books that he was one of the first to arrive at Hitler's business office and swiped a Lugar and a Nazi Flag. He was in North Africa with Eisenhower and he crossed into Sicily with Patton and all his troops in the invasion of Sicily.

Chapter 7. We're off on the road to Monaco.

In this Chapter Hope mentions Henry J Kaiser. Kaiser was Howard Hughes partner in the construction of the Spruce Goose. The Kaiser was into Aluminum, but they built the plane out of wood. As he was traveling to see Churchill, Gen. Doolittle had a B-17 waiting. Hope was with Col. Wheeler and the 20th Air Force. Page 97.

Chapter 8... Blood and Sand– both real.

In August of 1943 Bob Hope with Gen. Doolittle were flying around in P 40s and be 25s throughout North Africa, Bob Hope and Frances Langford handed out Purple Hearts. That's a Government function Isn't? Bob Hope is handing out the Purple Hearts. Are all these Soldiers Bob Hope's Soldiers? Are they Howard Hughes's Soldiers?

Chapter 9... Heavy, heavy hangs over our heads.

Bob Hope mentions Henry J Kaiser and his Victory Ships. Howard Hughes built Ships, Aircraft Carriers, and Airplane's as an Industrialist.

Chapter 10... Two days on a Sunny Island.

Here Hope flies the B-17 Fortress. He's a Pilot again. Also, Bob Hope states that, "I've handled a 50 mm machine gun". Bob Hope meets Gen. Patton and has dinner with Gen. Patton.

Chapter 11... Africa speaks Hope listens.

Bob Hope meets with Commander Henry C Butcher, Eisenhower's chief Aide. Later Butcher becomes vice-President of CBS.

Chapter 12... Frost in war Frost in peace and Frost in the Hearts of our Countrymen.

In this chapter Hope writes about all kinds of planes, the B26, the C 54 and the A 20. So, Bob Hope knows all about these planes. All about the Construction of the Planes, the functions of these Planes. He flies planes. We all know Howard Hughes built Planes, we now know that Bob Hope flies' planes and that the Military has all these planes and that the Military flies Bob Hope everywhere and anywhere he wants to go around the world. So, this Book, I Never left Home, seems to say that he was everything that he is. He never left home because he was an Actor and a character in a part of which he was, and he never left home because he was always in and around planes and part of the military. The guy who was just in the Movies and makes Jokes is everywhere at the pinnacle of every event that the United States was involved in. and there's a fact that Bob Hopes best friend was Stuart Symington, Sec. of the Air Force under Truman. He provided all the air Transportation for Bob Hope.

There's enough information here to have you wondering.

See you at the next book.

BOOK #2

SO, THIS IS PEACE 1946

Chapter 1... How about another Peace.

Bob Hope says "yes, sir take it from a traveler who from 1941 through 1945 as a Civilian with privileges sometimes got pretty close to war."

"I travel by two Trans Air Constellations and we were always two or three jumps ahead of the FBI." Now what does that mean? Was the FBI always chasing Bob Hope or Howard Hughes. In one of Bob Hope movies he says, "J Edgar Hoover doesn't make a move without him". Was Bob Hope in with J Edgar Hoover? Was Howard Hughes a Canary, telling the FBI all about the Mob. Hope has said he was a "Mole."

Howard Hughes had a lot to do with cameras. Who really had the picture of J Edgar in the Red Dress?

Bob Hope did a lot of talking about the Constellation Aircraft.

It's a fact that Howard Hughes built the Constellation and gave it an Inaugural flight to New York. Hope said he flew the Constellation.

Page 15... While doing shows in France, Bob Hope says "between shows I ran across a guy who had been a make-up man at Paramount. Pfc. Howl Lierile. Naturally I rushed over to him, grabbed his hand and said, how are you fella? He just looked at me blankly and said politely. "Have we met some where before"? "he didn't recognize me with my street face on". Which face? The Howard Hughes face or the Bob Hope face. So, Bob Hope's face is his street face? What face is not his street face? Another face! Two faces!!

The French Press asked Bob Hope, who are you? That's a good question. Hope's response was "this was kind of a tough one to answer so I passed It to Colonna". He didn't answer the question.

Why was it a tough question to answer? Because he was several different people in his head, and it was a tough one, but he wasn't going to tell them he was Howard Hughes. Remember, there was a Television show called I led three lives. By now you know, and I know of two of his lives. Of the third life I'll let you know deeper into this book. Hollywood make-up and Costumes can go a long way.

Chapter 2... It's best to keep moving.

On Page 23 Bob Hope says and writes "imagine flying six hours just to do a show in Denver. Imagine flying five hours from Hollywood to Denver to do a half-hour show". A show. It's just a show'.

Page 24... "As our big new Constellation flew in over the Cleveland Airport", The first flight of the Constellation that was built by Howard Hughes Bob says, "as OUR Plane". Who's Plane? Bob Hope's? Hope is on the Inaugural Flight of the Constellation. Who's talking here? His words seem to somersault. Bob Hope is Howard Hughes talking.

Page 35... At the Birmingham General Hospital Bob Hope was turned down to enter and asked to talk to Sgt. Desi Arnaz. Desi Arnaz.

Page 42... "At the Riviera a four-hour flight down the coast at 10 AM we took off in a motor boat from the coast. We came to a US Destroyer of the Third Fleet. We waved, and we were invited on. We did a show and then cruised onto Monte Carlo the Las Vegas of the Mediterranean with Casinos."

Chapter 3... Old Rocket Planes got us.

Hope talks about using Jet Propulsion Aircraft's and talks about hanging on to a Rocket. I think Howard Hughes was into Jet Propulsion and Rockets and Aircraft's. There's a Jet Propulsion Laboratory in California. Bob Hope has said He had done a Space Flight and a Space Walk. Bob Hope said that!

Page 46... Bob Hope goes on to say, "I know all about Jet Propulsion." This is the same Bob Hope who said prior that he's "an expert pilot with 1,000 hours in the sky." Bob Hope has said previously that he "knows all about jets". This proves My Theory! Every Word out of Bob Hope's mouth speaks of the facts of life of Howard Hughes. How many times in Bob Hope skits have you seen him in space suits? In a certain Movie he's talking about Fuel and Rockets to the Moon. The Road to Singapore to be specific. A movie about spies trying to get US Rocket Fuel information.

When the US landed on the Moon they played Golf. Howard Hughes Invented the Loner Lander that was put on the Moon. Hughes wanted to be the best Golfer in the World. Bob Hope always carries a Golf Club and plays Golf and puts on Golf Tournaments.

Page 48. News flash "Pilgrims came across the Ocean, the Conestoga Wagons brought the Pioneers across the Prairies, the Harvey girls brought the Santa Fe Railroad across the Mountains. Howard Hughes has now brought the Constellation across the sky and made all other airlines look dated. Howard Hughes had to come up with something big like the Constellation. That was a report, a News report in the Newspapers 1946. Read it! BINGO!

So here we have Bob, the Pilot, talking about flying the Constellation, and then News Reports that the Constellation is all about Howard Hughes. Strange?? Connecting the dots?

Reading Between the Lines

Page 49... But back to Aviation. To inaugurate a non-stop coast-to-coast daily run of the Constellation Howard Hughes flew a load of Big Movie Names to New York for the weekend. There's a connection right there. Howard Hughes and big movie names. I wonder who they were? Know any of those big Hollywood names. Howard Hughes owned Paramount. Bob Hope made all his movies at Paramount. Bob Hope was the connection to all the stars in Hollywood. Connecting anymore dots?

Chapter 4... Back to Normalcy.

Yeah, how many times was Howard Hughes considered crazy. I guess Bob Hope was considered crazy also playing the part of two lives. Being the writer with two heads. Two of the most famous names in America sleep together.

Ever hear the expression two heads are better than one.

Page 60... remember, there's a cartoon of Bob Hope showing him with two heads. The cartoon with two heads. Is the cartoon saying anything? Don't forget that famous quote of Bob Hope when he was describing his writers and he was "the one writer with two heads."

He's abnormal, meaning not being normal is that he is not like regular humans. He's using his brain. He uses his mind. You must use your mind to be a Pilot.

Page 64... Bob Hope says "as I came in for breakfast after a fast nine holes in the fog. The two kids were already at the table and as I entered my son, Tony hollered Good morning Bob Hope". "Naturally everyone laughed". It was a joke? Naturally everyone laughed. Was it that the joke was that Bob Hope is just a character? Did he show up for breakfast as Howard Hughes? Did he show up with all his make-up on and that they were laughing because they were all in on THE JOKE. Remember Bob's quote "That the names of the innocent have been changed to protect the Joke. Have you figured out what the joke is yet?

So, "I Bob Hope said, look that Bob Hope stuff is okay when where alone, but when where in public you call me daddy if you don't mind". Linda says, "we know daddy we will let you get the laughs". Who was the daddy? Howard Hughes! And they all knew it! It is Bob Hope who gets the jokes right? The joke was played on the entire World by Bob Hope, The Magnificent Fraud. Howard Hughes was under the make-up.

Page 65... On this page Bob Hope admits to being United States Army Military Personnel. Yes, in a Command Performance. Bob Hope talks about the Kleenex tissue paper. You recall I signaled that that was Yahotti, the Kleenex tissues of which he scrapes off the make-up, acting in his Vaudeville days. this is where Bob Hope says, "when I talk through my Nose my words turn somersaults". Does that mean his words mean the opposite of what he says, and they relate to Hughes when Bob Hope says them? He's talking out of both sides of his mouth, talking out of both sides of his head, talking out of both sides of his life.

Chapter 5... So, this is Peace.

Page 90... Bob Hope says "we hoped over to an airbase where I ran into one of my postwar plans, A Helicopter.". did Bob say he had a plan and the plan was a Helicopter. "I must have one what a plane"! Remember this is Bob Hope talking not Howard Hughes. "What a plane, you can peek in a bedroom six floors up and just hover there". He also talks about "our C- 47" Airplanes. There was a Movie called Blue Thunder where they did exactly what was said above in a Helicopter hovering outside of the Hotel looking in the windows at a female undressing. Hope then makes a comment about Rockets. Bob Hope's talk about all these planes all the time.

Chapter 6... Worn World

It is said here in the book that Bob Hope is "offering Bing Crosby Cheese Factories, Oil Wells, and any amount of Money to go on the air. Bob Hope even offered Bing Crosby a TV Network. Did Bob Hope have all that Money, Oil Wells and a TV Network? Remember from the book They've got me Covered, when Bing Crosby wrote the preface, he stated that before he wrote the preface that he had to check His Oil. What does that mean? He checked the Oil. He wrote the preface. Then says that "he met the owner of the Face and the Face was Bob Hope's New Face. Hughes's New Face. Howard Hughes was the owner of the Face. Howard Hughes made the movies that Bob Hope was in as a character Actor.

Chapter 7... South Sea Island Makeshift.

Here's Bob Hope talking about aircraft again.

On page 173... Bob Hope says "I got a New York style haircut. I think he cut it a little close around the East Bronx. What a clipping I got. I've had my ears sent out before but that was the first time I took them home in a sack". What's that about False Ears. I saw Bing Crosby sing a song. Bob Hopes theme song, Thanks for the Memory. Thanks for my ca ears, as he points to his "ears". It's in the DVDs that are for sale by Time Life Bob Hope right now. See it for yourself. False Ears. Seems like everything in film such as Face features, etc. had to be enlarged so that the camera could pick it up correctly. There's a Cartoon out there in Bob Hope's first book where he is chasing his false ears. They're in the air and He's chasing after them. Fake ears, fake cheeks, fake chin, a fake nose, Fake clothes. In the Airplane.

Make-up. Sponge Rubber or Stucco. A totally NEW FACE. Sponge Rubber -Square Pants. Fancy Pants.

Check out this statement by Bob Hope. "On Bougainville....

A lot of the guys from Ohio were there "who knew me from Cleveland" Who knew who, Bob or Howard? "but I managed to Hush them up before they talked". Talked about what? who he really was? I attach Cleveland to the Mob. The Mob that was called the Butchers. Did he bribe them or kill them? I think he killed them.

Again, in this chapter, Bob Hope is always describing planes and talking about women, talking about pin-ups. Bob Hope and Howard Hughes are known to have the same mo. Womanizing. And playing golf. And a lot to do with the Movie Industry.

Chapter 8... From Bad to Worst

In this Chapter Bob Hope mentions the Dodgers. A lot of the Beverly Hills TV shows said a lot about the Dodgers. The Dodgers moved from Brooklyn to LA. NBC moved from New York to LA. Bob Hope was also on NBC for 60 years. Ears clipped out of Broklyn.

It was made known that Bob Hope was in Berlin after the war that he was at the Potsdam Conference with the Big Three, Roosevelt, Churchill and Stalin, and with Avril Harriman. Bob Hope was In Potsdam! How is it that the MC Comedian is the first at every critical juncture of world history as Bob Hope or as the Billionaire Industrialist War Chief.

Bob Hope says, "I looted a piece of Hitler's desk and a plate from Hitler's bomb shelter and a piece of Eva Braun's corset". Really. Who was Bob Hope to be right there and grabbing memorabilia from Hitler's office? He says he got the stuff on a quick tour of Hitler's Bunker. He also got Nazi Tapestry and a Nazi Flag. Who is Bob Hope to be able to take all this stuff out of Hitler's place? Hope is like first on the scene escorted by the Air Force. I also saw a picture of Bob Hope sitting on the Berlin wall. He was also in on the Berlin Airlift in 1948. One of the first flights into Berlin.

Chapter 9... Deutschland Under Allies.

Bob Hope visits Douchland Concentration Camp an speaks of the horrors of the Holocaust. At that time, Bob Hope says he was pleased to see Texans. He states "you can always tell a Texan" yes, probably because he is a Texan as Howard Hughes.

Page 179. Quote "at Fort Maguire and all over the deserts of Southern California and Texas The Army and the Navy in 1946 are shooting Rockets into the Air, launching molten metal projectiles that will strike like a bolt of lightning (laser) and testing all kinds of constructive devices that are fantastic." How does Bob Hope the Comedian have knowledge of all these things occurring in the United States? Rockets, Lasers and other devices. I think the Lone Ranger theme song comes in here, with the "Fiery Horse and the Speed of Light, and a Cloud of Dust and a Hearty Hi Ho Silver. Not the Horse but the raw material. So, Bob Hope knows all this in 1945, about all these United States Weapons. I think Howard Hughes was involved in a lot of that stuff. So, the United States Military has a projectile that chases its targets in 1945, 46 and flying Bombs that will seek out the heat and destroy targets over 70 and 80 years ago.

Chapter 10... To the Victors belong the Spoiled.

Says here that Bob Hope goes through Germany like he owns it, goes to all the Nazi homes, office's, shelters etc. Really, through tunnels and through all the hideouts, to the living rooms, in the pools an into the Mountains and Hitler's elevator. He also went to the Eagle nest, Hitler's liar. All this for an MC of a Vaudeville Show, for just a Movie Star.

Here's a good quote from Bob Hope. "If some of this book Writing sounds tipsy and dizzy It's only because I wrote it while following My Nose". That's Howard Hughes following the Nose on his face as Bob Hope. That's My Theory. The Comedian right at the front of the European Theater of War operations in Germany and Europe.

BOOK #3

BOB HOPE, 1966 BOB HOPE'S VIETNAM STORY FIVE WOMEN I LOVE

Chapter 1. This is written rilght at the start of the book and is speaking of Bob Hope flying out of California to do his USO shows. It states as follows:

Bob Hope rises from a Southern California Air Base tips his wings in tribute to the USO and the Pentagon Brass and flies West. So, Bob Hopes the Pilot out of Southern California and tips his wings to the crowd. Looks like a Howard Hughes take-off to me.

Aboard the plane, Janice Page, Anita Bryant, Kaye Stevens, Carol Baker and Joey Heatherton. Bob Hope says this book is about "womanizing" and goes on to say: "I had five women every year."

At this time Bob Hope is surrounded by NBC, the Department of Defense, the Army, the Navy, Air Force, Marines, the USO crowd, and all the Professional Entertainers and Special Service Officers just to do a show.

Bob Hope makes a crack about Drew Pearson, a columnist. Jack Anderson worked for Drew Pearson. Jack Anderson was after Howard Hughes *in* a few of his columns.

You must recall My Theory as you read the next quote from Lyndon Baines Johnson, President of the United States spoken in public at in a forum honoring Bob Hope. In his Book Bob Hope writes and quotes LBJ.

"LBJ" "I have come here today to honor a man with two, (2) unusual traits. He's an actor who is not!". Not just an Actor? What's the second trait Billionaire Industrialist. Remember, he did lie on his form for a visa. He said: "he put down Actor and that was a lie". He's an actor, but what's the second trait? I think that says that LBJ from Texas seems to know something about Bob. Love that Bob. Bob Hope says "he's" just a guy standing in a phone booth". That's a statement about Superman right. Superman changed in Phone Booths. Howard Hughes did everything over the phone. Howard Hughes disappeared once, twice, once as a mild-mannered Press Reporter for a Metropolitan Newspaper. Another time as a Commercial Airline Pilot.

Page 21. Hope talks about his audiences and says: "my audiences are like opium to me, book me I need a fix."

Page 22. "I've worked for the last five Presidents" and they would be LBJ, JFK, Ike, Truman and Roosevelt. On the same page it is revealed that Bob Hope is right-handed. I wonder If Howard Hughes is right-handed?

Chapter 2...at another awards banquet honoring Bob Hope he writes:

"they honored me as the Honorary Air Force Recruiter." Upon accepting the award Bob Hope goes on to describe planes again. Talks Aviation.

Page 35. Hope talks about Therapists and says that the 'Therapist and I have to get into Bob Hope's head to show about those services above and beyond the call of duty". That's right, to check out the second head. Get into Bob Hope's head to see what Howard Hughes says.

Page 36, and page 37. "I would no more think of going on a trip without Dr. Miron than I would leave without my caps and eyelash curlers. There you go, talking about his disguise's again. Dr. Miron is Bob Hope's make-up artist. One of many make-up artists who work on Bob Hopes face. That says that Bob Hope has make-up on all the time. Can't leave home without it. Always in the character of Bob Hope. Unseen as Howard Hughes.

Page 36. A picture. Bob Hope has a Pinky Ring on his right Pinky. Page 37 Bob Hope has a Pinky Ring on his left Pinky. Next, Bob Hope talks about having a "Mafia Agent". I told you that Hughes and/or Hope are in with the Mob. The Mob ran all Howard's casinos in Vegas and in Cuba and Atlantic City.

Hope also reveals that he writes a column for the Hearst newspapers. In one column he states that "with the USO, he's had 100 flights across the Pacific."

Chapter 3. "Talking about tripping and falling Hope says: "when I fell, I would've landed on my Nose and would have to shut down show business" he couldn't keep up the joke with a broken Nose or with no Nose at all. He broke that Nose once before, shattered it. What is it Porcelain, Plastic, Stucco? Broken again Hope says that he "is the master of the miracle". Plastic Surgery?

Page 79. Hope refers to himself here in a photo as a Peacock, the symbol of NBC. I get it. The Beak at the top of the Beeker. Check it out. There's a big Beak at the top of the Beeker that is the symbol of a Peacock spreading its colors.

Page 104. Bob Hope is made an official Honorary Lifeguard in Atlantic City. Try to figure this quote out, "so if you're ever in Vietnam or Atlantic City let me know, it's the only place I am Licensed to practice". Practice a Doctor's License? Bob Hope started out in Atlantic City at the Globe Theatre trying out Broadway shows before they went back to New York. (30's) Bob Hope also was arrested on the Atlantic City Beach for taking his shirt off. (30's). Remember all the Bob Hope skits about doing medical operations. Atlantic City during the War years was the Government's Hospitals. Howard Hughes left a fortune to a Medical Foundation. I wonder If Howard or Bob performed operations.? It is known that Howard Hughes invented the modern Hospital Bed.

Chapter 5.

Page 114. Picture this. Bob writes that he's in a crowd and someone from the crowd yells "I don't care whether your Bob Hope or not" Hopes tells that story. There's a hint; why would Bob write that? Is he two people or not?

It's here that Bob Hope mentions a Bob Hope Comic book. I believe Bob Hope was into Publishing. Bob Hope published A Bob Hope Comic Book for years!

Chapter 6, Chapter 7, Chapter 8, writes about secrecy, secret meetings, and mystery. Chapter 9, Page 199, "I have enough trouble keeping track of my chin strap". Fake Chin as make-up.

Chapter 10, Page 209 and 210.

Bob Hope was quoted from Vietnam in this book he wrote: "Mike Miscella my make-up man didn't have any trouble with my make-up. He's been making me up for so long. He knows every Nook, Ridge and Cranny in my face, he just takes a pound of Putty and a Spatula and within 5 minutes. I looked like a reject from Mount Rushmore". Yes, the big Bob Hope Face or Howard Hughes Face with a pound of Putty. You could say a Pound of Putty could sure cover a face completely as a whole new face. You know, in one movie Bob Hope and Bing Crosby put their faces on Mount Rushmore.

Chapter 11. Page 222. There's a Picture or Photo of Bob Hope with his golf club leaving a show. Under the Picture is this Caption written. Bob Hope put the photo in the book. Bob Hope let that Caption be under the Photo. Here it is. "After each show I leave quietly under an "Assumed Name". An Alleged Life. What assumed name? Bob Hope is the assumed name that everybody believes is Bob Hope. You remember what Bing said in the preface to Bob Hope's first book, They Got Me Covered, about Bob's "Alleged Life". Alleged Life! A made-up life. Here's another statement by Bob Hope. You know where his words do somersaults. Here's what he says, "I get off the plane and I disappear". He disappears as Howard Hughes when he becomes Bob Hope.

In his own words, out of his own mouth, written in his book, Hope tells you in a round-about way that he is someone else. But really in a direct way.

BOOK #4

THE LAST CHRISTMAS SHOW BY BOB HOPE 1974

A review and critique of Bob Hope's book, the Last Christmas Show reveals In Bob Hope's own words how well connected The Comedian MC of Stage, Screen, Radio and Television is right there with all the top brass of the entire United States of America.

Right there at the top, Paramount, with men such as Ike Eisenhower, Omar Bradley, Jimmy Doolittle, William Wesley Westmoreland, George Patton and Emmett Rosie O'Donnell and many others.

And of course, Bob talks about all sorts of Planes, Aircraft flying Boats, Bombers, Army, Navy, Marines, Air Force, Coast Guard and Merchant Marines. Sounds like he was running the show.

Bob Hope's own words and the Books he's written indicate that Bob Hope knows about Military training of the Russians to adapt and learn to fly United States Jets. Its History that the United States gave USSR Jet Planes during World War II. A lot of planes out of the West Coast into the back of Russia. To fight in World War II. The United States trained their Jet Pilots.

Hope goes on to tell of giving shows to servicemen, including a lot of Russians, "we were training their Pilots and giving them DC35s & C 40s to fly back to Russia also LCI's to Russia, a landing craft for troops."

Hope says "we ran into the Russians again. The Navy was training Russians crews to handle LCI's (landing craft infantry)". This was all ultra-top-secret and a showbiz guy is right there. There must be a joke in there somewhere. Hope is telling this.

We enter Chapter 2, where Bob Hope has written "it's nice to see your ACT is going over". His ACT Is going over alright and it's going over big. That's the Joke. It states that Bob Hope goes by Airplane all the way and is stated that the Military foots the bill and pays for the entire event.

Page 18. Bob Hope is speaking to the USO, to all his employees and volunteers, to the stars, to everyone. Bob Hope says to all of them "No blabbing You are a Military Secret and so are your comings and goings". It was war time and thereafter.

Page 58. Here we have Bob Hope saying and writing and talking about the Okinawa Christmas shows. He sets up his CONFESSION!! A Confession as to who he is and that he is playing two different roles like an Actor looking in the window and the reflection of looking in a mirror. The reflection every time there's is two of him. That's right! Two of HIM. When Bob Hope looks in the mirror or in a window, he sees two of himself. He sees Howard Hughes and he sees two of himself. Bob Hope and Howard Hughes are one and the same. The writer with two heads. Two of the most famous names In America sleep together! Howard Rupert, SONNY Hughes, Junior!!! Explanation. CONFESSION!!!! Its HIM!!!!!!!

Hope says "he looked out the window (These are all his own words), and there was this trigger-happy guard looking at me. I pointed to my nose in a joshing matter to establish my identity, he pointed to his own. I didn't think that was too funny. So, I stared at him and he stared right back. He was right. He did look like me. He was ME. He was my reflection. I turned off the light and he disappeared."

Well? There you have it, in his own words, in his own story, in his own book, and in all his television skits and movie gags. He tells you who is!

Now I ask you, didn't I Tell Ya?? He's the Writer with two heads. He's the guy with the make-up face. He's the Masked Man! Howard Rupert Hughes.

This Book moves on to 1948, where Bob Hope says that Pres. Truman's Secretary of the Air Force's Stuart Symington called concerned and worried and wants to set up the Berlin Airlift.

Chapter 10 Page 105. We have Bob Hope complaining about his crazy USO schedule to the military and wanted to know from the Military who sets up his travel plans. The Military retorted to him "you can take that up with him in the morning when you're shaving that's Him that you will see in the mirror". Hope continues to write "I have to admit it, I was the guilty lamebrain."

Page 109. Bob Hope writes "he's a man of 42 years old" in 1958. Bob Hope continues to say," that little voice in my head knew my real age"

The Writer with two heads, and even Bob Hope himself says he was born in 1903, in 1958, he would be 55 years old. That little voice knows his real age. The little voice in his head is the Howard Hughes voice in his head.

In this book Bob Hope tells all about his nine years of Vietnam shows, and of all the best entertainers in the world and he is always, always telling all about his connections to the top brass of the United States Military and its Government.................

BOOK #5

BOB HOPE 1985 BOB HOPE'S CONFESSIONS OF A HOOKER

Chapter 1... Bob Hope writes about knowing Ronald Reagan and knowing him for 44 years. Talks about spending New Year's together for a long time. He states that he "likes Ronald Reagan. He's smart, he's honest and he's the only President who has ever called me "SONNY". So, Bob Hope carries the Nick Name "SONNY" and only Ronald Reagan knows that he Is "SONNY". "SONNY". isn't that the nick name that Howard Hughes Junior was called as a 10-year-old by his family? Howard goes to Cleveland and as Bob Hope meets Ronald Reagan. Howard Hughes Junior "Sonny" moved to Cleveland when he was a 12-year-old. Howard Hughes and Bob Hope are one and the same. That's My Theory and I'm sticking to it!! So, Ronald Reagan knew that Bob Hope was Howard Hughes all the time since their youth.

On page 201 of the book The Secret Life of Howard Hughes by Charles Higham, it states that Howard Hughes as a 12-year-old was living at the Biltmore Hotel in New York City, before going to live in Cleveland. December 8, 1915 Howard jr was 10 years old. It states and is written down that Howard jr's Nick Name as a child was "Sonny", and Howard "SONNY" Hughes as a child, as a 12-year-old enjoyed the Broadway shows of the day, which gave "SONNY" a lifelong love of Showgirls, Glamour and Music. It is also written that

"SONNY", Howard Rupert Hughes jr, Dudley and Rush Hughes take off to Cleveland Ohio to stay with his Uncle Felix in his music filled house on Euclid Heights. It was Howard Hughes who went to Cleveland. Hope makes it a point that he grew-up in Cleveland Ohio. Howard Hughes, Bob Hope and Ronald Reagan all grew up in Cleveland. Read it for yourself. Howard Rupert Hughes is "SONNY". Reagan calls him "SONNY". Reagan's from Ohio and was a Radio Broadcaster of Sports. Bob Hope was into Radio from the beginning. Reagan went to Hollywood. Reagan went into movies as a star. Hope has said he grew up with the Reagan's.

Page 43. "I played golf with nearly all the recent residents of the White House. I would Golf regularly with IKE and Gen. Omar Bradley. We played a lot together and it all started back in the 1930s". Say what? the 30s! 10 years, a decade before World War 2. It was later that IKE and Omar Bradley were directing Allied troops in Europe during World War 2. "I was over in England doing shows for the US servicemen during the war they complimented me for all that I was doing". Bob Hope, right in the United States War Room about being and doing Entertainment Shows. Thanked for what he was doing. Just Entertaining?

Page 48. Howard Hughes was the only child of the Hughes. There's a picture on page 60 of which Bob says "who's the guy on the right? The Government? It must've been from the IRS checking our winnings."

Hope points out that he had golf at the Greenbrier Resort in White Sulfur Springs, West Virginia. Isn't that the secret underground shelter for the entire United States Government, it's Congress and Senate, and the Cabinet? Greenbrier was not exposed as an underground Government complex in case of emergency until~1980s. Hope goes on to say good things about his longtime friend and confidant former Air Force Secretary of the United States, Stuart Symington and continues to speak and write about the Air Force, about Planes, about the Navy and Aircraft Carriers, etc. etc.

Bob Hope says "one year I was playing in the Dinah shore golf tour and I was leading after five holes. That's when my WIG fell off." Now he wears a WIG. Add the wig to all the accessories and you got a Wig, Eye brow's, False Eyelashes, False Ears, False Nose, False Cheeks and probably Contact Lenses and his False Teeth (caps). That's an entire False Face!! Don't forget the Mascara and other make-ups.

Page 73 through 75. Hope talks about his relationship with Eisenhower and goes on to say that he played golf with Ike and Gen. Omar Bradley and Sen. Stuart Symington all the time. Talking money changing hands. The next day speaks about golfing with Prescott Bush. Prescott Bush, Sen. From Connecticut and the Father of George H W Bush. Father of George W. Bush from Texas. All from Texas, Houston Texas for that matter. Houston Texas was Howard's Hughes home address when he was said to have died. Howard Hughes was taken to Houston, Texas. George HWBush Texas Congressman, UN Ambassador, head of the Republican Party, Dir. Central Intelligence. Vice President and President of the United States. Called 41. See any connections there.

Page 115. "My friend, Bill Fugazy who is a big transportation man, I think he arranged the last tour for a Amelia Ehrhardt". Recall Amelia was a Pilot trying to fly around the World and was reported missing. I wonder If Howard went underground and if he took Amelia Ehrhardt with him. Could Dolores Hope be Amelia Erhardt?? You know Bob Hope, the family man with the Wife and Children. And all the Children were adopted. The American way. Bob Hope, the American salesman.

Page 129. Bob Hope says, "he first met Bing in 1932". Hope goes on to say, "that in 1937 Bing says to Bob Hope maybe we can get together doing something". In 1937 Bob Hope signed with Paramount. Hope says that Bill Baron, a Producer at Paramount Studios says, "we've got to do something with these two boys."

Page 135. On December 7, 1941, "a day that will live in Infamy", the attack on Pearl Harbor by the Japanese. Bob Hope and Bing Crosby with Dick Gibson met at Elliott Roosevelt's house in Colorado Springs at news of the attack. They plan to join the Navy. Elliott calls Franklin Delano Roosevelt at Fort Knox, Secretary of Air and FDR's friend Mr. Knox said "no. and for us to continue Entertaining the Troops but "yes" to us joining the Navy. Read the Secret life of Bob

Hope on page 133. So, they joined the Navy. You know, there's a lot of TV shows about the Navy as well as movies. One such television show, McHale's Navy another movie of Navy life, Sgt. O Farrell's Navy.

Page 171. This entire page is about Golf with the Presidents. Why so close to all the Presidents and all the Generals in the Pentagon and throughout the World. He plays golf everywhere and names everyone worldwide. Something funny going on, if it was the Billionaire Industrialist somebody would be screaming foul.

Hope goes on the say that it's his "first time home in 12 years." "12 years ago, I started working all the time mainly on projects for the United States of America.

BOOK #6

DON'T SHOOT IT'S ONLY ME BY BOB HOPE: 1996

Bob Hope's, The History of the United States / with Melville Shavelson

* * * *

In this book, Bob Hope admits writing the history of half a century. He starts off talking about "The Lie" that he's "only an adopted son, I was born in England 1903. I come from a family of seven". That statement reminds me of when Bob Hope writes that he was in England and tells a Butler that he was born in England and the Butler retorts. "Okay I'll keep your secret."

As I say, He wasn't born in England. He was Born in an American/English spy factory. I say with six other Covers. He was all 7. They got him Covered. When he put on the Mask-up!

It was 1923 when 20-year-old Hope says he first stepped out onto stage as a dancer in Cleveland, Ohio.

Page 35. Here Bob Hope explains that "In real life (HRH) I am actually irresistible to Women and as strong and as Tuff as Mike Tyson used to be and I throw money around like a drunken sailor and I really am really a liar". So Hope/Hughes is really A LIER. There's the Peacock in real life. Howard Hughes was a strong womanizer. That's Howard Hughes writing. Bob Hope was a strong womanizer and they both put women up in the cottages of the Beverly Hills.

Hope talks about the writers' strike in Hollywood in 1987. He states that "his Q cards went blank. He says that 3,000 Writers went on strike and that "they all work for me". They all worked for Bob Hope? Did he own and operate all the Hollywood Studios? Howard Hughes owned all the studios. Howard Hughes made many if not all the Movies made in Hollywood. All the Writers worked for Howard Hughes. Howard Hughes had his own staff of Writers and Bob Hope says He had the same and they all worked for him. Hope owns all the writers of Hollywood? Hope owned all the studios? I don't think so unless he was Howard Hughes. Howard Hughes owned all the studios and had an office in each one. Hughes owned Paramount. He had writers and Hope was a writer. The Writer with two Heads. Howard Hughes himself wrote his own stuff and made his own Movies as Producer, Director and as an Actor. Right: He became an Actor. He became an Actor, a Character. He became Bob Hope! Hope said he is a Writer. Admitted at one time to writing a newspaper column for Hirsch. He can write.

Page 38. Hope insisted on getting into Costume for his first radio show "possibly as a disguise". He dressed as a Cowboy out of Texas with Boots and Spurs and a Gun. Sounds like the Lone Ranger. Hope says he told jokes and that someday he'll explain all of them.

* * * *

Chapter 9 … 1974 through 1990

Page 295. Bob Hope tells of when he "swiped the Swastika German flag from Adolf Hitler's Bunker". What?

Page 48. Hope says that after the Russians had taken Berlin at the end of World War II and Adolf Hitler had taken his own life Bob Hope says he walked right into Hitler's underground bunker in Berlin after OUR Army assured me Hitler had checked out and is quoted writing and saying, "I was one of the first on the site to visit the bunker when the shooting was over. I went down into the Bunker with some American Air Force Men and we started picking up Souvenirs. I got stationary with Adolf Hitler's AH initials on it". Who is Bob Hope that he gets to walk right into Hitler Office at the very moment shooting stops?? And with the Air Force!! Howard Hughes was very much involved with The United States Air Force. So was Bob Hope!

"Sonny" Jr, also known as Bob Hope did his Charlie Chaplin Imitation in Cleveland at age 12. At age 12 Howard Rupert Hughes Jr, "Sonny" moved to Cleveland. Bob Hope went into Show Business in 1923 as "Bob Hope". An Actor in Vaudeville.

Page 72. Speaks of the term or nickname "Yehudi" it became a Mysterious Personality. "The little man who wasn't there" the little voice disappeared. What I got out of reading about Yehudi I figured it was the Kleenex. The Kleenex Bob first used to take his make-up off. Bob Hope (HRH) is the "little Fellow". Acting, Theater, Vaudeville Radio and Costumes.

About the term called "the little man who wasn't there". Get Shorty. When the make-up was on, he (HRH) was not there. Once the make-up is on he's the other person who is there! Like the Lone Ranger with a Mask.

There is a Lone Ranger episode from the TV series that was titled High Heels. It was about a Real Estate Man out West who was sensitive about his height and he would wear Stilt Cowboy Boots. The Community found out he was wearing stilts and tried to torture the man. There is a great possibility that short Howard Hughes would wear stilt Cowboy Boots to appear tall like a Texan. Like the photos taken at different airports as he flew around the world. And isn't it strange that a group of movies would be about The Thin Man and another one "Shorty."

Page 84. Bob Hope writes he went back to the Military and never left until the war was over because of "Insufficient Rubber". During World War II, Rubber was rationed due to the war effort. The Military needed rubber. There wasn't enough rubber for Bob Hope to put on his face. He stayed inside the Military. Howard Hughes was with the Military as much as Bob Hope, Right! And

Bob Hope writes a book called "I never left Home" means His home was in the Military. He stayed in there to resume his life with the Military. (HRH)

Page 93. Bob Hope is talking about a plane crash and writing on this page that he expected to die and said this.

"My whole life flashed before my eyes. I let it flash by Twice"! Twice? Hope wrote it and you just read it!! Two lives! "Two of the most famous names In America" flashed before his eyes. The writer with two heads. The two famous names! Howard Hughes life flashes by, and then Bob Hope's "Alleged Life" flashes by!

Remember, Bob Hope stated that he himself was an expert Pilot with thousands of hours flying. When did Bob Hope crash an Airplane and almost die? Howard Hughes crashed Jets. He almost died. Howard Hughes was a Jet Pilot. Bob Hope has thousands of hours in the sky. Bob Hope said and wrote that.

Page 97 The Opening Introduction to Bob Hope's radio show The Command Performance opens with this line.

"Here is your Commanding Officer and Master of Ceremonies, Bob Hope."

That's right, the Commanding Officer of United States of America, its War effort against Germany and the Japanese. That's Howard Hughes with all his Armaments, a Billionaire Industrialist. He truly was the Master of Ceremony of World War 2.

Page 98. Bob Hope is over in England and he says to a Butler "I was Born in England no matter how much Paramount tries to deny it". Bob Hope writes and recalls telling a Butler in England that he was born in England and the Butler says back to Bob Hope. "I'll keep your Secret". I've Got a Secret. They got him Covered. Out of England is a lie. The Cover. The Magnificent Fraud. The spy. The Greatest Impersonator. The Greatest Show on Earth.

Page 108. Hope himself says and writes that he calls himself "a self -respecting Spy". "and who would ever wear a nose that obvious". He says and writes that he stole some of Winston Churchill Stationary. What's a comedian doing in the Prime Minister's Office??

Page 136. Bob Hope says his writers "Write False stories about me". That's right all the writers in Paramount's employ some 3,000 writers and use Howard Hughes Biography, Autobiography in all that they write. Everything about Howard Hughes is what is written in many movies. Watch the many movies and you'll see his influence telling you who he is in all Movies and TV. His writers write about him and you'll still have to remember that Hope is always writing about Airplanes and Spies and making movies about "spies like us" twice. Donovan's Brain 1953. The Bad and the Buti full 1952. It's all about him.

Page 150. Hope says that he went to Québec Canada when Roosevelt was meeting Churchill. What's Hope doing there? This is where I add that Hope says and writes over the years that he was also at Hitler's office and Bunker, Churchill's office, Potsdam, and a US negotiator / agent with the North Vietnamese, The Iranians, and The North Koreans! Negotiating for the United States of America as Howard Hughes the Owner.

Do you still think Bob Hope is just Bob Hope?

Page 159. This is strange incident written in Bob Hope's Book.

The Air Force takes a group of Hollywood VIPs on a tour of the Nuclear Military Underground Operations. Really Who would that be? The Owners of all the Studios or a group of Actors. Think it was the guy involved with the missiles.

Page 167. Bob Hope admits he has been under contract to NBC radio and television since 1938, says he likes looking back. Thanks for the memory. The year 1948 Hope says he was 41 years old. Bob Hope said he was born in 1903. That would only make him 45 years old or 44 before off a couple months. Howard Hughes says he was born in 1905 that's 43 years old. How can he say he's only 41?

Page 191 and 192. Hope writes that "Nixon's plans for settling Vietnam is to "let Howard Hughes buy it and move it to Las Vegas". Isn't that funny said like a joke. It was Howard Hughes who was waging the war In Vietnam. The Phoenix project for instance.

Page 205, I was watching the news when I noticed the 1988 Olympics were to be held in Seoul South Korea, and Bob Hope was to be the Master of Ceremonies. At about the same time before the Olympics out of the United States with no Import Export Permits or Licenses 85 Sikorsky Helicopters were delivered to North Korea.

I guess Bob Hope and/or Howard Hughes didn't want any problems disrupting the Olympics of 1988. There was no trouble. A good show for NBC.

Page 209. Hope writes that his "adopted kids thought I was an airline pilot". In one of Bob Hope's earlier Books he writes that he was being Roasted at a Rotary type dinner and receiving an award for being a great Humanitarian and Actor. Bob Hope writes that "Deloris all this time thought I was a Commercial Airline Pilot just like the kids thought". They were all kept in the dark. She didn't even know? He duped them all. He fooled all the people all the time. Remember Hope said and has written that he was an Excellent Pilot with thousands of hours in the sky. Bob Hope and Howard Hughes were both expert pilots with thousands of miles in the sky. The thing is that he faked his family out and they didn't even know who he was.

Page 216. Hope writes that in 1958, Pan Am had just put the first United States Jet in service across the Atlantic and the Soviets were right up there with us. "He writes "I thought the CIA might be able to use any information I could get to them on this new Jet of the Soviets. So, I put my keen mind to work gathering secret intelligence on the TU 104". A vertical takeoff Jet Aircraft. Bob Hope wrote "The CIA ask if I might be able to get them info on an airplane."

So, Bob Hope the Expert Pilot volunteers and is asked by the Air Force to spy on the Russians about a jet plane. During World War II the United States gave Jet Planes and its workings to the Russians to win World War ll. Bob Hope wouldn't have access to or be able to find that information on a Russian jet unless he was Howard Hughes. Hughes could get that information. What do you think Billionaire Industrialist means??

Pan Am was an airline that functions for and by the CIA. Bob Hope said he worked for Central Intelligence. So, Bob Hope the Spy went to work gathering Secret Intel for the United States Military.

Page 229. Hope also writes that "he's very happy working for the State Department". Hope said and wrote this out of his own mouth. This is a book Hope wrote. So, whose talking? Bob Hope or Howard Hughes, out of both sides of his mouth and both sides of his Two Heads.

Page 240. Bob Hope notes that Alan Shepard an Astronaut was the fifth man to hit a Golf Ball on the Moon. So, Hughes was in with Von Braun and Jets and Rocket and The Space Program NASA. Strange... Do You think that's any indication as to who put the golf ball on the Moon?

You know, I have a Theory that I believe that Howard Hughes, John and Allen Forster Dulles along with the Mob eliminated Kennedy. Two things, One, Bob Hope Writes and Jokes that the days of Camelot came to an end of its run, to be replaced by Dallas". Did Dallas take out Kennedy? Yes! Dallas took out Kennedy. Now what kind of joke was that. Was that a joke. A Hope Television show skit opens in a court room scene with Tony Randall Presiding Judge. Hope is sitting in the witness stand. He's a Witness. The Witness to what? Judge Randell asked the Witness to allow the Defendant to enter the court room. Placed at the defendant's table is a puppet looking like John Kennedy. The puppet is going through the mannerisms of Kennedy. Pushing back his hair, ruffling his tie and putting his hands in his suit coat's side pocket. That puppet is considered Kennedy. Judge Randell asked Bob Hope, the Witness "what's the charges"?

Bob Hope says, "I had a deal with him, and he broke it". That's the deal with the Chicago Mob. Kennedy would get the vote and in return lay off the Mob. Randall says to Hope why didn't you talk to him? Hope retorts "I hate him". Why didn't you speak to his family? Hope retorts "I hate him and his whole damn family". Then Judge Randall asked Bob Hope the Witness what he did about it. Bob Hope looks right into the camera and says, "I really turned his head around didn't I". They blew his head off didn't they. Bob Hope said that.

I thought Howard Hughes was behind that!

Is Howard Hughes Bob Hope, is Bob Hope Howard Hughes? Take notice, you got Bob Hope talking all HOWARD HUGHES Words.

Page 242. How can Bob Hope write about the Bay of Pigs fiasco? Hope says it was his fiasco and goes on to say," the Bay of Pigs was written and directed by the CIA". Howard Hughes was the CIA.

Let's recall that Bob Hope told Lana Turner he "worked for the Central Intelligence". A group of Cuban exiles was trained in secret in the late 50's by the Agency to land and capture Cuba for the Eisenhower Administration. The late 50's.

Page 242. Here's quotes by Bob Hope "it turned out to be the biggest fiasco since my first screen test". The Bay of Pigs was a Bob Hope fiasco? First screen test was a Howard Hughes fiasco? Now who's fiasco was it??

Cuba was a hot bed of spying activity. Hollywood made a lot of movies about spying. Bob Hope made a lot of movies about spying and stared in many of them as the spy. Hope told you he was a spy and that he was spying for the CIA and the State Department. Bob Hope is Howard Hughes and Howard Hughes is Bob Hope in Make-up.

Page 257. Here Bob Hope talks about his Air Force shows, doing routines with starlets as the straight man in a comedy duo. It's in the dialog of the movies and in the print in his books. You have Bob Hope telling the truth and writing it. Here's the skit that Bob Hope tells Lana Turner He works for Central Intelligence.

Recall all the words written by Bob are on cue cards at the ready.

Lana Turner "Bob if you're an officer like you say, why don't you wear uniform"?

Bob Hope "well Lana i don't want this to get around that I work with Central Intelligence."

You must recall Bob Hope's second book Have Tux Will Travel. The entire book written by Bob Hope states that "Have Tux will Travel is about being ready to travel at a moment's notice with the United States Government". Hope has said he works for the Government, the State Department, and the CIA.

Page 258. Bob Hope writes that" he wanted to get up to the 38th parallel to the UN truce Headquarters to see if they needed my diplomatic skills". So, here's Bob Hope at 38th parallel doing some negotiating with North Korea. Just prior we had him negotiating with the North Vietnamese. We also have him writing that he was called in to negotiate with the Iranian hostage takers. Hope? Do you think this was the Comedian doing the negotiating? Think it was the Billionaire Industrialist doing Negotiations for the United States? Hope in his writings says, "if he is captured what will happen if they find out who I am"? Right, if they find out he's really Howard Hughes.

Bob Hope says, "I found out that we had a lot in common with the Pentagon and US intelligence". Hope talks about spying and spies. Yes, because he was one of them. That's what he had in common with The Pentagon, Central Intelligence and with all the Presidents of the United States.

BOOK #7

BOB HOPE, 1994 I WAS THERE

Chapter 1... Soldiers in Grease Paint

Greasepaint is make-up, make-up from Vaudeville, make-up on Actors, acting, pretending to be characters in the Movie Industry.

You should know that the Government and the Movie Industry worked together making Training Films for the Military all through WW ll. Made in Hollywood's Movie Industry. Bob Hope headed the USO. He also carried the 10 runners-up to the Miss America Pageant with the USO tours, and he also mc ed all the Academy Awards. Was it Bob Hope or Howard Hughes who gave out all the Academy Awards? Howard Hughes owned the entire Movie Industry. Strange that Bob Hope never got an Oscar and that's because he was The Greatest Show on Earth. Nothing to be compared too. As Bob Hope or Howard Hughes nobody could come close. He was behind the whole thing. Howard Hughes also owned the entire Aviation Industry. And all their Manufacturing of all things Military were made on the West Coast.

A Bob Hope Quote Here, "I worked for Uncle Sam". The United States Government is referred to as Uncle Sam. Working for the Government is working for the Company. The CIA is the Company. Uncle Sam is the USA.

The War Department created the Armed Forces Radio Service (AFRS) through the Entertainment Industry. Every star from Hollywood was a member of the Victory Caravan which was ran right out of the White House during the World War II. Bob Hope was a pioneer of radio in the United States.

Check out the photos on page 25 and 26 in this book. One photo show Bob Hope standing with Eisenhower and Doolittle. Hope is taller than Doolittle, and as tall as Ike. Also, in a photo on page 34 Bob Hope is as tall as Henry Fonda.

Page 36... New Chapter.

The title, The Mosquito Network.

That's what Bob called it. It was radio on NBC with the DDC" I have no idea what DDC means.

A new Chapter

SOS – the real thing.

Bob Hope says: "our Pilot was Lt. Frank Ferguson, I was nagging him forever for me to take over the controls of our new Catalina flying boat. Pilot Ferguson relented and let me pilot "our" new flying boat". So, Bob is into flying boats just like Howard Hughes was into flying boats. Remember, the Spruce goose that was a flying boat. Are Bob and Howard one and the same? so here's Bob Hope flying the plane. Hope the Pilot always talking about and mentioning planes all the time. Hope is a Pilot. He can fly a plane. He did fly Planes. He said he was an "expert pilot with thousands of hours flying and that He's been flying since there were bucket seats in the planes". That would be from the beginning of flight. Bob Hope said, "flying since bucket seats". Like Howards Movie, Hell's Angels. 1922.

A TV special honoring Bob Hope for 75 years of Airplanes by the Air Force landing on Aircraft Carriers. Hope is in an Air Force Helmet and Gear. Why would they honor Hope for Jets landing on Aircraft Carriers? Did Hope have anything to do with that? Was Bob Hope or Howard Hughes involved in building big Ships and Airplanes. How is it that they give credit to Bob Hope for what Howard Hughes had done? Must be one and the same guy. Must be a lot of people in on that secret.

Page 46. Another photo this time Bob Hope is as tall as JFK.

Page 49. Bob Hope says this about himself "When a guy has flown over 300,000 miles, he begins to wonder how much longer he can keep it up". Still on Page 49 Bob Hope says, "I made my first trip on the Constellation". Now I thought Howard Hughes made the first flight on the Constellation. He goes on to say not the flight with all the Hollywood stars. Bob Hope continues to talk about the flying boats. The Catalina flying boat. Hope always talking about planes and all kinds of planes, types of Engines, Jet Engines. Bob Hope knows all about these engines and planes, ships and everything? (I led two lives).

"The war sure did speed up aviation". Howard Hughes tested flying boats on Lake Mead. Here we have Bob Hope talk about the invention of the flying boat, talking about the flying boat test flights. Hope says "it had a motor in each wing and a third motor in the nose. In those days, experts agreed it was safer to have a motor in the Nose, naturally, when this theory was disproved, I had mine taken out too, but it permanently altered the shape of my Nose". Hope had his nose taken out too? There Hope admits to another New Nose. Yes, his Nose was taken out. How can this be, that his Nose was taken, and his face injured? Howard Hughes tested flying boats on Lake Mead not Bob Hope. The boat crashed and as the boat crashed Howard Hughes was crushed again. but you must admit that was Bob Hope talking. Were they both on that boat in Lake Mead? I know Howard was in the Hospital. Got himself a new Manufactured Nose. How many different Noses has he had? Here's a quote from Bob Hope in the movie from the 80s called Spies like us. They're fighting the Afghan war and two Spies are in a tent freezing. A golf ball comes flying into the tent and Bob Hope comes in looking for his golf ball. In the Tent Bob Hope says, "he's freezing in the cold and that he has a cold blue nose" he then states that he "never had a blue nose before." He had many Nose's before and none of them were blue. He had other Noses.

BOOK #8

DEAR PREZ: I WANT TO TELL YA BOB HOPE, 1996 A PRESIDENTIAL JOKE BOOK

As you know Bob Hope had a connection to every American President from Roosevelt, Truman, through Bush 41 & 43. Strange connections playing golf with every President. If the Billionaire Industrialist was playing Golf all the time with the President it would be called a conflict of interest and a Conspiracy. With Bob Hope playing golf with everyone it's considered a joke. A laugh with no questions about it at all. It's just Golf with the Comedian. What do you think they talked about? Golf? IF Bob Hope was Howard Hughes there's plenty to talk about!

Page 10. There's a photo of Bob Hope with Nixon, Ford, Reagan and Bush. I guess they all talked about golf right. I guess they all talked about movies? What could they be talking about?

Page 17. Bob Hope: "Seriously, I've known 11 presidents about as intimately as a man can. I golfed with them, dined with them and told jokes with them, and about them."

Maybe they talked about jokes. Maybe they laughed about "the joke" that Bob Hope's act was going over big time since 1938. That's right that Howard Hughes joke was going over big time.

Here's another quote by Howard Hughes or Bob Hope. I'll let you make the call. Bob Hope says this as a joke. A joke I explained prior.

"Abe Lincoln said you can fool all of the people some of the time, and some of the people all of the time, but you can't fool all of the people all of the time"......Bob Hope disagreed with that quote adding that "You can fool all the people all of the time". You can see right there that he's talking from experience. He has fooled all the people all the time! You'll see in upcoming Chapters that Hope in one of his Movies states that he Is the Greatest Impersonator of people in the whole wide world. Don't forget the Cameo in The Greatest Show on Earth. That Movie wasn't really about the Circus. For what reason would the Camera focus on Hope in the stands watching the Circus? The Circus is like Vaudeville People. Howard Hughes as Bob Hope did just that. Pulled the Wool over the Eyes of the people and with the help of the United States Government and its Presidents he fooled all the People all the time. Throw in the Army, the Navy, the Air Force, the Movie Industry, all the Hollywood Stars, especially His Writers of Radio, TV and Movies. Remember Bob Hope's first Book They got me Covered. Covered with a false Identity or covered up with make-up. (top-secret).

Page 19. Bob Hope: "Roosevelt is the first President I met personally in 1941. Roosevelt had General Hap Arnold of the United States Air Force put me onto an Air Force plane". Hap Arnold was the Air Forces Bomber Leader along with Doolittle during WW ll. Talks all about Aircraft again.

Page 27. Bob Hope "Congress are the people who are funny with your Money. I don't want you to think that I am knocking Congress. I'm not. All I know is they spend it faster than I can make it". That's because they're running on Howard Hughes and Bob Hope's Money. So here we have Bob Hope saying that the Government is spending more of "his money" faster than "he" can make it.

Page 30 "Pres. Truman through Stuart Symington asked Deloris and me to participate in the Berlin airlift in 1948." Here Bob Hope wrote that his friend was Stuart Symington, Secretary of the Air Force who was flying Hope around during World War II. (41-45)

Bob Hope says, "NBC asked me to be the News Commentator at both Conventions in 1952". Bob Hope met Ike in Algiers in 42 in North Africa.

Hope goes on to say that "after Ike left office I spent many hours in Palm Springs on the golf course with Eisenhower". As he did with all the Presidents of the United States.

Page 34. Howard Hughes was into Golf. Howard Hughes said: "He wanted to be the best Golfer, the best Movie Maker, the Richest Man. Bob Hope was into golf, was a Movie-maker, and is a Rich Man. Just a coincidence? Hope always carried the Golf club with him all the time.

Page 34. Bob Hope tells this as a joke, he says "Julia Childs" said to him "if you can't stand the heat get out of the kitchen". What heat? The heat of Spying. A little History here: Julia Child's was a SPY for the United States in France during World War II. Was Bob Hope a SPY. Bob Hope was talking to Julia Child's. Were they both Spy's "like us"? Bob Hope sure made a lot of Movies about Spies, and about Ghost, and about People being Dead? One of Bob Hopes early movies was Spy's Like Us in the 30s. Later, he did a cameo role in 1980s film Spies Like Us. All of Howard Hughes and Bob Hope experiences are in the Movies and written by all his Writers at Paramount. Bob Hope was one of those Writers. Recall that Bob is the Writer with "Two Heads" and he's making those Movies.

Years ago, on one TV special from NBC they open the show (a Bob Hope Special) with this Skit that there's someone running a Spy Agency out of the basement of 30 rocks NBC Headquarters. Bob Hope did 60 years on TV at NBC. Funny Skit. Did NBC just indicate that somebody (Bob Hope) out of the basement of NBC is running a spy agency. So, they tell the truth as a "JOKE" and the people laugh. It was the Truth and "Nothing but the Truth". That was a Bob Hope Movie. Bob Hope was running a spy agency out of the basement of NBC.

Lucille Ball and Bob Hope were great friends. Made many Movies together. Lucille Ball at the Kennedy Center in Washington sings a song with the lyrics. "You all think were Comedians, but we are all Spies."

Page 42. Bob Hope continues to talk about his experiences with Eisenhower. Bob Hope says "one of the most memorable times was the rounds of golf I played with Ike in 1953 at the Burning

Tree Golf Club, the President, Sen. Prescott Bush, (George Herbert Walker Bush's father), Stuart Symington (then, Sen. From Missouri), and I made up the foursome."

Page 45. "Ike and I spent many wonderful hours in Palm Springs on the Golf course". What's Bob Hope trying to say here?

JFK

Page 49. Hope goes on to say, "he was given the Congressional Medal of Honor from JFK". He says he got the metal for "being out of the country". What does that mean? was Bob Hope out of the country in the 60s or even in the 50s. I know Howard Hughes was out of the country hiding out in England, Canada, Costa Rica and in the Caribbean. Who said that? Howard Hughes or Bob Hope?

During the Eisenhower Administration the Bay of Pigs was planned. A plan designed by the CIA to eliminate the Cuban Dictator and take back the Island. We all know that! right. So, what does Bob Hope have the say about that. Here's a "quote" from Bob Hope about the Bay of Pigs Invasion.

Bob Hope says, "the Bay of Pigs invasion was the biggest fiasco since my first screen test". Woooo, what does the failure of the Bay of Pigs Invasion have the do with the failure of Bob Hope in his first screen test? Check the History of Bob Hope's first screen test at Paramount Studios and that failure, that fiasco was about the rubber nose and ears burning under the hot Hollywood lights, somebody smell rubber burning. If Howard Hughes planed the Invasion to take back Cuba and return with his Casinos, then it was Howard Hughes fiasco. Hope indicates the "fiasco" was on him. How's that a failure and a fiasco for Bob Hope? Only if Bob Hope was involved in it. What did Bob Hope have to do with the Invasion of Cuba? Well, it has been written that Howard Hughes trained the invaders on his island in the Caribbean. The Invasion was started in the Eisenhower Administration. Maybe that's what they were talking about on the golf course. I wonder if Bob Hope or Howard Hughes held any disdain for Kennedy because of him not backing up the Invasion with the Air Force. I think so. Listen to the following quote from Bob Hope on Page 57. Concerning the Assassination of Pres. Kennedy. Hope says, "in November of 1963 the thousand days of Camelot ended its run to be replaced by Dallas". Wow, what a wise crack. Does that tell you anything? Maybe that Kennedy was taken out by Texas. Did Hughes hate the Kennedy's? Dallas sure did end Camelot! It happened in Dallas...............

So, one night watching Television, the Bob Hope special has Bob in a Courtroom scene with Tony Randall as the Judge and Bob Hope is in the Witness Stand. The Judge calls for the Defendant to be brought into the Courtroom. The defendant comes into the room and it's a miniature John F. Kennedy Puppet displaying all the characteristics of Kennedy. Pushing back his Hair, flipping his Tie and putting his hand in his right-side Jacket Pocket. Certainly, the mannerisms of John F. Kennedy. The judge asked Bob Hope "What's the charge against this defendant?" Bob Hope chimes in that: "I had a deal with him, and he broke it". Judge ask Hope "why didn't you talk to him and his family"? Hope "I hate him and his whole damn family". Judge asked Hope, who is the witness in the witness stand, "what did you do about it"? Bob Hope looks right into the camera and says, "I really turned his head around didn't I"! Did you get that? Bob Hope admitting that he blew Kennedy's head off! I believe that the deal that Bob Hope spoke about was the deal with the Mob in Chicago, that if Kennedy got the vote he would lay off the Mob. The Kennedy's got the Vote but did not lay off the Mob. In fact, they intensified their Prosecution of the Mob. They broke the Deal and Howard Hughes had his head blown off. That's My Theory and I'm sticking to it! So, Bob Hope had something to do with turning Kennedy's head around? Howard Hughes was in with the Mob. They ran his Casinos with his Money.

That situation reminds me that Howard Hughes in the 20s or 30s would attend house parties. Everybody loved Howard Hughes at the time, but not the Kennedy's. Howard Hughes had tried to wrestle RKO's Television and Movie Studios away from the Kennedy's. Prior to that, he probably tried to take over their Booze and Scotch whiskey business running in association with the Mob. I think the Kennedy's and Howard Hughes hated each other specially when

John and Robert were making it with all the Women in Hollywood, such as Marion Davies, Marilyn Monroe and others.

LBJ

Page 66. LBJ gives Bob Hope the USO's Silver Medal. Page 67. In awarding the medal LBJ says "I have come here today to honor a man with two "unusual" traits. He's an actor." and what's that second trait? LBJ didn't say what the second trait was.

Page 68. LBJ continues to say, "it may come as a surprise to some people with short memories that Bob Hope is more than a comedian". Is that's so? That's what I'm saying. He's more than Bob Hope he's Howard Hughes. Hughes, the Billionaire Industrialist, a United States Air Force Test Pilot, Movie Star and in complete control of the whole United States of America. That's My Theory and I'm sticking to it. "you can trust your car to the man who wears the star."

Page 69. Hope talks about the United States Budget as a Texas Budget. I'm pretty sure that means it's a very large budget. Yeah! and it's all Howard Hughes Money.

Page 70. There's a photo of Hope and Johnson and the Caption under the Photo says this by Bob Hope "LBJ was either consulting me on a Foreign Policy problem or he was playing crossword puzzles". Was Bob Hope running the Foreign Policy of the United States and LBJ was just a no nothing playing crossword puzzles? That's what he said. I think Howard Hughes was being consulted on the foreign policy.

Page 72. "The eyes of Texas are upon you". The writings go on to say that LBJ and RFK were talking to each other. Bob Hope has a comment about that also.

Bob Hope says, "can you imagine a Texan having a conversation with a New Englander."

It's a fact of American History of Politics that the West hated the Northeast.

Page 75. Howard Hughes is a Texan and LBJ is a Texan. LBJ says "remember, I still have the Army and Navy and Texas". Was it Bob Hope or Howard Hughes who controlled the United States Government it's budget and its Military? I say it was Howard Hughes in Disguise as Bob Hope running the whole show. Howard Hughes, the Beverly Hillbilly from Texas, owning Texas and buying up California, making all the Movies, controlling all the Raw Materials, with complete control of Texaco Oil and a great chunk of the Industry of the United States. That's who was running the United States. The Industrialist Billionaire!

NIXON

Page 81. Bob Hope "I had the pleasure of knowing a relaxed Nixon and a smiling Vice President Richard Nixon since 1953 when I referred to him as Ike's caddie."

Page 83. Nixon lost the 1960 Election to JFK. Many attributed the Vice President's lack of humor as a major cause of his defeat. "Nixon's defeat to me you see was my significant Contribution to his 1960 campaign because I advised him to meet JFK face-to-face in a television debate". Turned out to be some bad advice didn't it!.

Page 86. Bob Hope: "Dick Nixon is traveling back and forth to Florida so much we could have a surprise winter capital in Havana". Is that talking about the planning of trying to take Cuba back again. It was Nixon and Rebozo going down into the Caribbean all the time. Was he meeting with Howard Hughes on one of his private Islands? There was something going on between Nixon, Rebozo and Mr. Alpalnap. Don't forget Paradise Islands is down that way. Resorts International had some goings on in that area. Resorts International is a CIA front company titled Mary Carter Paint. Remember in a Bob Hope movie as Bob looks at a Portrait Painting of Mary Carter on the wall in a Mansion in Cuba, he states "that would be a wonderful name for a Company". The Mary Carter Paint Company. The Mary Carter Paint Company is the Parent Company of Resorts International! First Gambling Casino in Atlantic City, New Jersey. I wonder If Howard Hughes and Richard Nixon had anything to do with opening a Casino in Atlantic City? After Public Office Nixon moved to New Jersey and settled in Saddle River probably so he can keep an eye on the skim. I know Bob Hope had a lot to do with Atlantic City.

Page 88. Bob Hope "in December 1968 I was preparing for an overseas Christmas Show and I received a phone call from Nixon inviting all the Cast and the Crew to start their tour with Rehearsals, a Show and a Dinner at the White House."

Page 89 and 90. Bob Hope says "Deloris and I have been fortunate to have a few of the Presidents to visit our home. It was Nixon who made the greatest entrance of them all when he landed by Helicopter In our backyard in Toluca Lake to play golf on January 3, 1970 with four Helicopters."

Page 91. "If you look through the Presidents $200 Billion $ Budget I'm in there somewhere". What does that mean? I believe it means that a lot of the Money is going back to Hope or back to Howard Hughes.

Page 94. Bob Hope says "the Investigation of the Watergate break-in has implicated the Republican Party and its Officers. Watergate proved to the Country how tough it is to find good Plumbers today". What's Bob got to do with Plumbers? The only Plumbers I heard about before were the Plumbers who broke into Daniel Ellsberg's Psychiatrist office. The Burglars into the Democratic Headquarters offices in the Watergate property were called "Plumbers". Did Bob Hope have good "Plumbers" before and how difficult these plumbers were to find at this time since they got caught. Bob Hope knows about hiring Plumbers? Did Howard Hughes know about Plumbers? I would think so. Considering that the Burglars at the Watergate break-in into the Democratic headquarters and the offices of Lawrence O'Brien to find evidence as to whether Howard Hughes was transferring money to Richard Nixon's brother. Any connections? Check the News. Some of the Plumbers who all got caught and arrested were all people who were involved in the Bay of Pigs Invasion. i.e. Howard Hunt, McCord and others who were implicated in the Assassination of Kennedy. Well what do you know. Check it out!

Continuing the quote "here I am on my first television show of the year and I want to thank the Watergate Committee for making room for "me". They made room for Hughes not for Hope. Hughes was implicated in the hearings.

Bob Hope: "it appears that Pres. Nixon taped all his conversations In the Oval Office I, Bob Hope, just hope that the 18 min. gap of missing tape included some of the bad jokes I told Nixon". Now that quote is very revealing. Was Bob Hope or Howard Hughes talking to Nixon? What kind of Jokes could Bob Hope be telling Richard Nixon? Jokes that he was very happy the tapes were erased. Bob Hope says, "I told Richard Nixon to "burn the tapes". Couldn't be just jokes, had to be important and very revealing, plus possibly about the Watergate break-in. Could have revealed that Bob Hope was Howard Hughes.

FORD

Page 103. Bob Hope says: "either I was getting brash in assuming that there was always a spare room waiting for me, the Hospitality of Betty Ford always made me feel at home, but my stays at the Ford White House were more relaxed than visits with previous Presidents" Really? Could that be because Gerald Ford was on the Warren Commission Report that investigated the killing of John F. Kennedy. Most people know the Warren Commission report was a joke and a cover -up. Ford was in on it.

CARTER

Page 118. Carter says: "I've been in office now 489 days and then in three more weeks I will have stayed overnight in the White House as many times as Bob Hope."

The Comedian stays overnight at the White House more than the Presidents? what's going on?

Page 121. September 1980, Bob and Delores with Mr. and Mrs. Clark Gifford and Mr. and Mrs. Stewart Symington, and Alex Spanos's took off on the Road to Moscow to Entertain the American Community in Russia.

REAGAN

Page 127. Bob Hope says: "I bought a cup of coffee for a YALE Student Jerry Ford in the late 1930's but it is Ronald Reagan that I've have known the longest". Since he was fresh to Hollywood from a job as a Sports Broadcaster in Demoise Iowa or as a lifeguard in Dixon Illinois.

Bob Hope says: "I used to call the White House before every TV special was taped to tell my material to Reagan". Pretty close relationship there ah?

Page 144. Bob Hope says, "Delores and I have known Ronald Reagan and Nancy for a long time when he was an Actor and when he was the Head of the Screen Actors Guild and as Governor of California, and as President of the United States". That's a long time.

BUSH

Page 149. September 1988, Bob Hope starts his 39th year on NBC. Well, he is the Peacock and that is their symbol. The symbol with the beak in it. There's a movie out there of Bob Hope where he says that he is the Peacock.

Page 150. Bob Hope says: "it is no surprise to anyone that I jumped on the Bush Bandwagon early in the game. George and Barbara Bush were like family. I knew George HW Bush's father, Prescott Bush and I played Golf with him for many years. I also played golf with George HW Bush his eight years as Vice President to Reagan. I was very close to George and I played a lot of golf with him also". Very close!? George HW Bush, Congressman from Texas, Head of the Republican Party, UN Ambassador, CIA Director, Ambassador to China, Vice President and President. You name it. Very close. I should also add that George Bush owned and operated the Zapata Oil an off-shore Oil Drilling Operation Company in the Gulf of Mexico and owner of a Maj. League Baseball Team, the Texas Rangers. Real close.

Page 151. Bob Hope says, "on October 27 the Victory 88 Campaign came to Toluca Lake where Delores and I opened our Home for a Reception honoring George and Barbara Bush"!

Bob Hope is surely showing the depth of his involvement within the United States Government.

Page 159. Bob Hope says, "the President called Secretary of Defense Dick Cheney and said, "give Bob Hope whatever he wants", so I asked for a plane to go to Saudi Arabia to entertain the troops". He did just that.

Page 159 continuing. Bob Hope says, "on Easter Sunday 1991 I entertained 350 troops who had just returned from Saudi Arabia at our home in Palm Springs". It was Bob Hope's Yellow Ribbon Party taped and aired on NBC. It was also star billing for George HW Bush.........

BOOK #9

MY LIFE IN JOKES BY BOB HOPE AND LINDA HOPE 2003

Bob Hope writes an opening note to readers: He calls it the "disclaimer". Bob Hope says: "the names have been changed to protect the innocent. Well, in this case, the innocent names have often been changed to protect "THE JOKE"! Bob Hope said that to protect "the joke". That's My Theory! And that's what I've been saying all along. Howard Hughes in make-up, in disguise became a Character Actor in his own Movies made by Paramount. That Character being Bob Hope. My Theory has been proven to me. I'm writing this book to prove it to you. It's that a big joke has been played over the whole wide World!

Bob Hope goes on to explain and describe the members of his family. Those in his "Alleged Life" and their Occupations. Each family member is said to have a different life. One member is a Butcher, one is a Manufacturer, one is a TV Producer, another a Real Estate man, another a Writer and one a Salesman, and Hope goes on to say that "I am a comedian"! To me that's Bob describing his own Characteristics and the different traits or actions of his own self as Howard Hughes.

The Butcher, his association with the Mob, a Manufacturer as an Industry, a TV producer of which he was, a Real Estate man buying up California. The Salesman of the American way of life, and a Comedian. That's Bob Hope and each of those occupations he listed above do reflect the many situations that Howard Hughes was also involved in.

Two of the most famous names In America sleep together. Remember the guy with two heads. The writer. One Head being Howard Hughes, the other Head being Bob Hope. "Sonny" has been acting his entire life. Everybody's Acting. Real Theater people with make-up and costumes as other characters.

All Movie Actors change their names. Spies get new identities, their covered. Bob has been acting since he was 12 years old. He did the Charlie Chaplin bit on the streets, and it is written about Bob Hope that he began to grow as an actor to grow in the Trade and had Theatrical ambitions. He would go up to Keith's Theater on 105th Street in Cleveland Ohio, and he says: "I decided that the stage was my dish". He started in an imitation outfit of Charlie Chaplin looking like someone else using make-up, a mustache a disguise. The Greatest Impersonator of people. The Greatest Show on Earth.

Page 82. as Bob is about to enter Television Bob Hope says: "I spent all day with the Cameraman trying to figure out from which angle I look best, but the sponsor wanted you to see "my face". If you recall Bob Hope said the Sponsor of his Act was the United States Government. He told you previously that the United States Government was footing the bill. Bob goes on to say that it "didn't cost Paramount a dime". Paramount didn't Pay anything. Who owned "The Face?

Page 82. Bob Hope says: "I like TV So far, but my Profile is causing some confusion."

Page 92. Bob Hope says: "talking about my Book Have Tux Will Travel the title is one from my Vaudeville days. Actors used this saying on their Business Cards or in Ads". Have Tux Will Travel, meaning they were always ready to go to do their show. In talking about the book; "think about seeing your life flash before your eyes little did I know that book written in the 50s would cover only half my life." Yeah, the Bob Hope Half not the Howard Hughes Half.

50 years of life or two lives. Two Heads sleep together. Out of Hollywood, Out of California, only half his life. Half is Bob Hope

and the other half is Howard Hughes. The book talked about Bob Hope as an MC being ready to travel at a moment's notice for the United States Government.

Bob Hope says: "My Charlie Chaplin Imitations made me Show Business conscious. I'd put on my Charlie Chaplin make-up and walk Duck legged down to the corner. I was good at it."

So, he put on his Charlie Chaplin make-up, and he was good at His Imitations."

Page 46. Hollywood went to war and the biggest stars of Hollywood enlisted. I know Howard Hughes and Bob Hope were all in the war effort. All Hollywood followed.

Page 75. Bob Hope says: "a few weeks before Christmas I got a call from my friend Stuart Symington, Truman's Secretary of the Air Force". Air Force!

Page 78. "I took my first plunge into Television in 1950" Page 80. "We had a tremendous Cast in this Show. They really had to rush to get all our make-up on". They had to rush to get all their make- up on for the show. Interesting! Page 133. "I don't mean to call Pres. Nixon, a Pigeon that would be disgraceful. I won't even say who won the LOOT But if you look through the President's Budget of $200 Billion $ I'm in there somewhere". So, Bob Hope is still getting a big chunk of the United States Budget between 1968 and 1972.? What for? What LOOT does Bob Hope get out of the Government? Who's getting the loot of money from Pres. Nixon's budgets? Why would Bob Hope get a lot of loot from the budget? Loot means to take. Bob Hope is just taking Money from the United States Budgets. Bob Hope is in there somewhere! Bob gets money and Howard gets money.

Page 136. Here's an even bigger clue. Is Bob Hope on the 18 min. gap of the Nixon Watergate tapes or is it Howard Hughes on the tapes?

My belief is that it was Howard Hughes on the tape as Bob Hope telling Nixon all the bad news and probably talking about the break-in at Watergate, about JFK, about Cuba, about O'Brien, about the Assassination of Kennedy. Some bad Jokes.

Here's what Bob Hope says in jest about the gap on the tapes "it appears that the President taped all his Conversations in the Oval Office. I just hope that the 18 min. gap of missing tape included some of the bad jokes I told him". Wow, bad jokes or bad news.

Was Bob Hope or Howard Hughes on the tape? Read it for yourself in the Book the Secret life of Howard Hughes by Charles Higham and read the Book Gemstone, about a White House Secretary who knew and heard what is on the 18 min. gap of the Nixon Tapes. She was found dead the next day. Research it and as you read don't forget about Martha Mitchell. She says she was killed by the FBI. Jack Ruby even repeatedly said that he "was shot up with something he did not want". There both Dead.

At this time i must relate to you two story's that connect Howard Hughes with Bob Hope. The first is about Howard Hughes trying to make it with a Hollywood Starlet. I can connect the dots because of two stories that Bob Hope and Howard Hughes have something in common. The other story comes out of Bob Hope mouth. In the book about Howard Hughes it is written that Howard was caught at a girlfriend's house having sex with an inflatable woman's life-size toy balloon. That would be in the secret life of Howard Hughes by Charles Higham. The story goes this way.

Page 95. Howard Hughes is dating a very pretty and famous Actress of that time. Here's the paragraph I read in the book. "He asked this beautiful Hollywood Starlet to come Into the Bedroom. She declined, but to her amazement Howard walked into the bedroom and leaving the door open she saw on the bed a life - sized rubber inflated balloon Doll, a replica of herself with Breast and a Vagina. She watched as Howard mounted the figure, stroked It and thrust deeply into it, and after a few minutes climaxed.

On page 182. In this book, My Life in Jokes there is the connection between Howard Hughes and Bob Hope about life-size inflatable woman's toy balloons.

At a show overseas to the troops, Bob Hope, says "one infantry man couldn't figure out why his brother would send him a toy balloon until he blew it up and it turned out to be an inflatable life-size toy balloon of a woman. Do you find that strange that Bob

Hope, knows about a life-size toy balloon in the shape of a woman? Seems like Bob Hope and Howard Hughes knew about inflatable life-size woman balloons.

Page 140. Bob Hope says, "sometimes Hoffa talks other than politics". I wonder If that means that Hoffa was talking about his role in the assassination of John F. Kennedy. Like squealing. Hope continues to say: "I don't think Hoffa is missing at all. I think he is just playing a game of hide and seek with Howard Hughes". Get anything out of that? If Howard Hughes was behind the assassination of John Kennedy and Hoffa was a participant in that killing and Hoffa is talking, I think Howard Hughes would be out to get him. Hoffa did wind up dead. So, did Johnny Roselle, so did Howard Hunt, so did Martha Mitchell, so did Jack Ruby, and many others. I think the bottom line here Is don't get involved in the assassination of an American President. You know that's not the first time that Bob Hope mentions Howard Hughes. Many times, Hope mentions Howard Hughes in his many television shows.

Page 170. Bob Hope quote: "Reagan decided to honor me at the Kennedy Center as an actor."

Page 171. Hope says: "I love to get anything in Washington that's not taxable."

Page 175. Bob Hope says, "in the Philippines it gets so humid here I am wearing special makeup."

Page 181. Bob Hope again relates that the Bush's were like family, that he knew the father of George HW Bush, Prescott Bush, and he played golf with him all the time, as was related prior in this Book.

Well, gota tell you this is my opinion. As I said before, if the Billionaire Industrialist with all those connections like Howard Hughes would have been playing golf with all US Presidents since Truman, and all the Vice Presidents it would be outrageous. People would be screaming conspiracy that something was going on; but if you're playing golf with the Comedian, a joke teller for Radio, TV and a Movie Star its kind of doesn't amount to much. Don't you find it strange that Bob Hope would be sleeping in the White House hundreds of times, and if Bob Hope is Howard Hughes, Howard

Hughes and Bob Hope are the two most famous names in America were sleeping together in the White House. Hope was very close to all the power and everyone thought nothing of it, what a joke!

Page194. Bob Hope say's "at this age I am getting to spend more time with Delores at least I think it's Delores she looks familiar."

Is Delores Delores? or is she someone else? Like maybe she's Amelia Erhardt? She was a Pilot just like Howard Hughes. She disappeared just like Howard Hughes. Maybe the two Pilots eloped together and later appeared as Mr. and Mrs. Bob Hope. Just my opinion.

Page 198. Bob Hope talking about show business, says; "a lot has changed when they used to do "My Face" before a show It was called make-up. Now it's called special effects". I think that's because they went from Sponge Rubber to Putty, to Porcelain, plastic and stucco.

Howard's the owner of the face, it's Special Effects and Make-up. Hughes is playing a part as Bob Hope. Just another character in a movie, just another character on stage. The only time you ever saw Hope was in a Movie or on a taped TV show. On film or from a distance. That's the only time the public really saw him.

Bob Hope was quoted earlier "before I go to the office I first go to the make-up department". I think that means before anybody sees him. So, Bob says he "gets made-up at the make-up Department before anybody sees him". Most of them probably only know him as Bob Hope. He gets made up before he goes to work as an Actor, as Bob Hope. It's really Howard Hughes.

Here's an interesting side note. On one of Bob Hope's NBC specials about NBC being sold to Westinghouse, a Westinghouse Executive walks onto the Stage looks and stares at Bob Hope and ask, "who are you"? The Audience laughs. They all know him as Bob Hope. But the question was "who are you"? Really? Who is he? I say Bob Hope is Howard Hughes. I guess the Westinghouse executive didn't know that it was Bob Hope. Everybody knows it's Bob Hope. Why was the question even asked in the first place? Bob Hope was on NBC for 60 years, and a guy ask who he is. (Bob writes the cue cards)

Page 203. Bob Hope say's "my secret for staying so young is good food, plenty of rest and a make-up man with the spray gun". He's always talking about having make-up on. A Fake Face all the time. All this blab about make-up all the time. Remember there is a part in a movie where Bob Hope presents a Tray of Noses to his Actress co-star and ask, "which one of these Noses do you think will fool the Public"? He also said he "does his best Impersonations right in front of the Public, right in front of them all the time, and they don't get it". All the time! An Act! Right in front of them and they don't get it. He also said in a movie that "he's an Actor and he wears Sponge Rubber all the time. ALL THE TIME!

Bob talks about his make-up man and about his Nose all the time. 60 years in the public eye and a guy from Westinghouse doesn't know who is.

Page 199. Bob Hope writes: "this is my 60th year with NBC, which proves that Abe Lincoln was wrong you can fool all the people all the time". What's that? You can fool all the people all the time!! I think he did that no matter who is he! Did his joke fool all the people all the time? The Joke was that he is Howard Hughes and was in make-up and Character as Bob Hope all the time! Howard Hughes in make-up all the time as Bob Hope. Stay tuned. Keep reading. Not to be egotistical but I broke the biggest story in the world. Who's the Joke on? Who's the Joke off? All the people were fooled all the time. HRH/BH JOKED-OFF the people all the time.

Well, by now My Theory has been proven true to me. That is that a big Joke has been played out on the World. As I continue my research to review and critique all (most) of Bob Hope quotes that have been said by Bob Hope and written in his books I have noticed that what Bob Hope says from behind His face are words that somersault his head. He looks like Bob Hope, but he talks like Howard Hughes. I am out to prove that Howard Hughes was and is the 20th Century Fox. You know the Fox is the guy who out-foxed everybody else.

Let's put two and two together. Some of Howard Hughes Bio's say that his nick-name as a child of 10 years old was "Sonny" and that by 10 and 12 years old He was into Burlesque Theaters and watching the beautiful women. Showgirls that is. At 12 years old Howard Hughes, Sonny that is, with part of his family moved to Cleveland Ohio. Bob Hope says he moved to Cleveland Ohio. So, they're both in Cleveland Ohio at the same time. Bob Hope says he met Ronald Reagan in Ohio and that Ronald Reagan was the only person that could call him Sonny. Think that's a coincidence? I don't!

It is documented about Howard Hughes that he had an eye operation. Bob Hope spoke of his eye operations. Think they were at the same time. Coincidence?

Bob Hope in one of his books states that he told Richard Nixon to burn the tapes because he believes he was on the tape telling Richard Nixon some bad jokes.. In a book about Howard Hughes It states that it was Howard Hughes on the phone and on the Tapes. That's why they were destroyed. They were destroyed because the Tapes would have exposed Howard Hughes as Bob Hope. So, they were both on the tapes! H R Haldeman said it was Hughes on the phone, on the tapes. Hope say's he was on the phone. What was that a party line? Bob Hope and Howard Hughes are the same, one and the same person! That's why Nixon had to destroy the tapes. It's true, Howard Hughes was mentioned in the Watergate hearings. So, they both were said to be on the tapes. There's Bob Hope own words somersaulting into his head. You know the writer with two heads. Yes, Bob Hope's Alleged Life.

As I continued to read all the books concerning Bob Hope and Howard Hughes, we find out within Arthur Marx Book about Bob Hope's secret life. They both had "Secret Lives". Bob Hope was making it with all the Hollywood Starlets and put them up in the Beverly Hills Cottages. Howard Hughes was also putting all those Starlets in the Cottages.

Both Womanizers, both Pilots, both Golfers, both Rich, both into Real Estate, both into Oil, both Beverly Hillbillies, both in the Motion Picture Business. Coincidence, right?

Arthur Marx book the Secret Life of Bob Hope: How Bob Hope concealed his "Double Life. The "Alleged Life". What's the Hope Secret? I led Three Lives. Love that Bob.

BOOK #10

THE SECRET LIFE OF BOB HOPE ARTHUR MARKS

The Book starts out by saying that Leslie took on Impersonations as a child. Hope did his Charlie Chaplin impression as a 12-year-old in 1915 in Cleveland. Bob Hope went into Show Business at 16 years old in Cleveland Ohio. Sonny was living in Cleveland Ohio at that time. Leslie Hope or Bob or Howard went into boxing as Packy East. Boxing didn't do too well. Was Packy packing a Gun?

At 17 Bob drops out of High School. He has his sights on a Vaudeville Career. It is said that he first forsook the Cap and Gown for Greasepaint and Haney plates. Remember greasepaint is a make-up. Makeup is used in disguises. They got me Covered.

If Hope was said to be tall and thin as early photographs portray, handsome except for his ski jump nose. If he already had a ski jump nose or snoot, why in the book They got me Covered does he talk about putting on a Rubber Nose. Remember that first Screen Test at Paramount under the hot lights somebody said that they smelt rubber burning. Sounds like the same reason Orson Wells built up his Nose on screen in the Movie the Third Man.

Later in life, Bob Hope was never home for 12 straight years.

Page 109. Hope kept his Nose. He was pressured from Paramount's President to get a Nose Job. He kept it and built it up with Special Effects and Make-up. Hope got an office and a

Dressing Room right next to another one for Script Conferences or Meetings with his Writers and Agents.

"It was also where he got into costumes and was made up". Another room was strictly for entertaining women. In that room he had a "secret backdoor."

Page 128. Hope had women stashed all over town. Howard Hughes had women stashed all over town. One and the same person?

Bob Hope lived in Toluca Lake and Ozzie and Harriet Nelson lived nearby. Their son Ricky Nelson was a teen age Idol and sang songs. One song Garden Party was about Ricky's experiences at Madison Square Garden. The Song Garden Party had these words in the third stanza.

"And over in the corner sat Mr. Hughes in his Dylan Shoes wearing his disguise". Did Ricky Nelson just reveal in his song that he knew Howard Hughes and that Howard Hughes was wearing a disguise? Get the Record, listen to this Song. That's exactly what he said. Mr. Hughes in his disguise.

Page 143. In the1942 film They got me Covered by Bob Hope carries the same title in his 1941 Autobiography. It's a film spoof on espionage, strange spoof on espionage. Bob Hope had so many movies about Spies like us, Ghostbusters and another Movie in the 80s Spies like Us in which Bob Hope has a cameo spot where Bob says that it was so cold that he "never had a blue Nose before" and then says that he's going to play right through the Afghan war. Does Bob have anything to do with the Afghan war or was he talking about Howard Hughes and his weapons not being involved. Road to Singapore was about spies trying to find out from Bob and Bing what the Formula was for superior Rocket Fuel.

By 1941, Bob Hope made 12 Pictures and had five more Pictures to go. Mr. Mark says that 'They got me Covered as a Bio had little information about Bob.

On page 198. Mr. Marx says all of Bob Hope's books despite glaring omissions of truth and accuracy were Hugh best sellers. He then says that Bob in his Books avoids telling the truth about his life. Really, He has told no one who in life he truly Is. Did you get that?

Page 248. Marx says of Hope "Bob was discrete about his outside love affairs. He felt he could count on the people he paid, his Writers, Producers, Directors, his Make-up men, Agents, Actors, Actresses, everyone to all keep their mouth shut about what they saw or heard. Years later it was a Television Show called The Millionaire in which people were given $1 million dollars and told if they said where they got the money they would no longer have any money.

Page 252. Mr. Marx writes Hope would just pick up the phone and call the President of the United States and be put right through to the President.

Page 265. Hope had a relationship with Ike and all future Presidents who afforded him access to almost any important figure in the Government he chose to speak to by merely picking up the phone in his bedroom and calling the White House Switch Board. Unbelievable access. Do you think that Howard Hughes is Bob Hope, yet? Just who Is this guy?

Page 297 & 298. Bob Hope calls President Jimmy Carter and then Iran and he talks to the hostage takers directly. What? Hope negotiated with the Iranians and talks directly to the hostage takers to secure their release.

It is said that all of Bob Hope's Shows were at Government expense from 1954 through 1969. Not to mention all those shows from 1941 to 1952. All the TV Shows, the USO shows, the TV plus NBC specials.

It was also said that Bob Hope flew way too much back and forth and he flew his own planes and the Air Force Flew Bob Hope free all the time.

It is written that in 1954, Bob Hope scored Millions in Oil from his Stocks in Texaco. In 1973 Hope becomes a Spokesman for Texaco and Texaco sponsored many of his Radio and Television Shows. Many of Howard Hughes's own Businesses sponsored Bob Hope shows.

On May 29, 1978, Bob Hope's 75th Birthday @ The Kennedy Center in DC is the event where Lucille Ball sang a Song and the words of the song said this "we are all spies."

As we all know Bob Hope died in 2003. He said he was born in 1903. He lived 100 years. It is also known that the Howard Hughes medical Institute knew how to keep people alive.

BOOK #11

THE BEAUTY AND THE BILLIONAIRE BY TERRY MOORE 1984

Terry Moore says she was with Howard Hughes from 1948 through 1956. She tags Howard Hughes as a creative, charming, caring, secretive, powerful, warm, eccentric, patriotic genius billionaire playboy and great lover.

Howard Hughes lived in Southern California with his father and his uncle Rupert, his father's brother, a screenwriter at Paramount. Howard Hughes went to school at the California Institute of Technology. He later moved back to Houston. In 1924 he Inherited the inheritance of Money, Oil, Gold and Silver. He was 19 and he owned the Hughes Tool Company 100%.

In 1928 at the age of 22 Howard Hughes received his Pilot's License and in that same year he filmed Hells Angels as a silent Movie. There he had his first plane crash and was badly hurt. (bucket seats)

In 1932, age 27, Howard Hughes founded the Hughes Aircraft Corporation. In the following years Howard Hughes broke all the flying records. In 1941 - 1945 he assisted the war effort. In 1944 at the end of the war he disappeared.

Howard Hughes's Factories built Airplanes and made drill bits, owned a Brewery, owned RKO studios and the controlling stock of

TWA. He owned Paramount Studios and many other movie studios and had an office in everyone.

His company built advanced electronic communications and spy satellite systems, Rockets, Aircrafts, Battleships and Aircraft Carriers. He built the spacecraft that landed on the moon and the lunar Lander. He invented the first operating Laser Weaponry know as Star Wars by Texaco, and invented a better Submarine, a Hospital Bed and a Steam Car. He owned Television Networks, (NBC) Radio Stations and Cable Television. He owned land throughout Texas and California, Mines, LasVegas Hotels, Casinos and much of the Raw Materials, esp. Uranium.

It is no secret that the Hughes Empire was intimately involved with the United States Government' including the CIA and the State Department, and the Pentagon. It was said that his men were deeply involved with the CIA. Bob Hope himself said that he worked for Central intelligence and the United States Government. Is Hughes Hope or is Hope Hughes??

Terry Moore says this about Howard Hughes mustache: "if your Nose did not turn up so much you wouldn't have so many problems, besides it's crooked. It veers to the left. Affectionately he'd give it a shot to the right." She talks about a Mustache Howard grew to cover up a scar on His left lip. Bob Hope has a scar on his left lip. She is talking about Howard.

After 1948 when Howard bought RKO. He never showed up on the studio lots again. He was branded with the nick name "Harvey", after the invisible rabbit. "Harvey" was based on a play and two movies. An invisible rabbit. (sex)

In 1949 There was a movie made by Paramount titled "The Great Rupert."

Page 87. Terry Moore writes that she was making a Movie at the direction of Paramount. The Barefoot Mailman. She said she had to work with Alligators in the Florida swamps where she read the book The Sex Life of an Alligator by Ross Allen. The book taught her the Alligator Love Mating Call. She writes She practiced the love call and is best at calling Alligators to the shore line. It worked. She'd growl and the Gators would show up at the shore line.

Howard would call her every night. He was fascinated with the love call and Terry taught him how to do it and at the end of each phone call they would growl the Alligator Mating Love Call to each other. Howard practiced it and became very good at it. Howard practiced it and became very good at it! She taught Howard!

Isn't that interesting. Now here's the connection to Bob Hope. Remember Terry Moore is writing about Howard Hughes and the love call not Bob Hope. Terry Moore was deemed the legal wife of Howard Hughes by a Federal Court.

I watched every Bob Hope Movie and TV show skit and there was Bob Hope doing the Alligator Mating Love Call Growling every time he saw a Beautiful Woman. How about that!! Add the Mating Call to the Projection Room, to Movies, to Paramount, the Golf Club, to the Airplanes, to Flying, to the Woman, to the Beverly Hills, the Television Networks, to the Casinos, to Vegas and it proves that they are one in the same. The two most famous names in America sleep together.

Now here is where I prove that Howard Hughes in any make-up as an Actor would play many parts in movies and that the people in the movie with him didn't even know it was him as another character. Remember Bob Hope said he was "the Greatest Impersonator of People in the World.

The Greatest Show on Earth.

Page 114. Terry Moore says she was going over a script and dialog with Howard Hughes and he knew every word, she says he probably wrote them. There you go. He was a writer. He made four movies early. He's the Writer with the Team of Writers and he is the one with two heads. One head Howard Hughes, the other head Bob Hope. Recall Bob Hope said he's the one with two heads as a writer with his group of writers. Bob Hope previously wrote that the 3,000 writers in Hollywood worked for him. 3,000 writers work for Hope? Or HRH... He then said, "They write many things about me". She says they acted out the script and says, "he was a great actor."

Many nights she and Howard would visit Burlesque Houses. Howard loved Burlesque and Comedians and she says it seemed to be a part of his past he had once known. She is talking about

Hughes. Sounds a lot like Bob Hope's History. Same experiences. If Howard Hughes, "Sonny" that is, loved Vaudeville and if he is Bob Hope who loved Burlesque. It was a part of his past and they both knew it so well.

Terry Moore talks about having new Ids. Howard would be Mr. Grimes in public and they would present themselves with assumed names. Assumed names. She goes on to say that Howard was always testing planes and talking about planes all the time. I say just like Bob Hope talks about planes all the time in books and in the movies and on the TV shows. Remember Bob Hope said that he, Bob Hope was an "expert Pilot and fly's all the time". She says Howard Hughes never wanted anyone to know his true ID nor his age. Then Terry Moore refers to Howard Hughes as James Bond and as 007. She calls him James Bond twice.

She further goes on to state that Howard had number one clearance priority for landing at any airport in the world and that he hid out in large mansions in the Hollywood Hills. Howard called himself Sam. Uncle Sam was known to be the United States Government.

Page 151. Terry Moore says that in observing Howard she says she never saw anyone change personality so fast. "He was some actor"! she says that on the sets Howard would like to play all the parts. Howard Hughes was certainly Howard Hughes as Bob Hope in make-up. The Greatest Impersonator in the whole wide World.

She writes that Howard was advised of all the latest goings on as good as J Edgar Hoover. She would not be surprised if Howard Hughes was hooked up with J Edgar Hoover.

Bob Hope in one of his movies makes the statement that "J Edgar Hoover never makes a move without Me". There was a rumor out there that somebody had a picture of J Edgar Hoover cross-dressing in a red dress and that Hoover was a Homosexual. Howard Hughes had spies all over the place following everyone. The man with the camera was a television show. Hughes was into Photography.

Page 171. Terry Moore talks about doing a Movie with an Actor who looked like and seemed to be Howard. It probably was Howard in make-up.

Page 174. On this page Terry Moore says she had a meeting with Howard Hughes' attorney Lloyd Wright in his office and that Howard was there. She also writes that Noah Dietrich was there as well as others.

As far as I know from news reports Noah Dietrich said he never saw or met Howard Hughes in person. What about that? She continues to write that Howard Hughes saw her more than any other woman in Hollywood from 1948 through 1956. She writes that Howard started bringing Noah Dietrich, his number one man with him when he drove to Glendale. They held their meetings in a car. She says that she was the only woman that Noah Dietrich Ever saw with Howard Hughes and that she saw Noah Dietrich just as much as he saw Howard Hughes. Noah Dietrich says he never saw Howard Hughes in person and only spoke to him on the phone. Bob Mayhue said the same thing.

She talks about hitting Howard with her handbag and cutting him to require stitches and that a plastic surgeon showed up and rendered stitches.

Page 239. Terry Moore had four names, Helen Koford, Jan Ford, Judy Ford, and Terry Moore. She made 70 movies throughout her career.

Page 246. It's stated here that Howard is 47 years old. She rats out Bing Crosby as just as much as a womanizer as Howard Hughes.

Page 253. She writes, "I headed down the studio lot where Wally Westmore the famous make-up artist called down from his studio window. "you can't miss kid you got the Westmore turned up nose." What Was that? I thought she was making it with Howard Hughes. The turned -up nose is Bob Hope or is Howard Hughes the turned-up Nose? I thought Bob Hope was the turned - up nose. Howard Hughes has the turned- up nose. Says it all right there. Howard Hughes is Bob Hope in Make-up.

On the same page She writes that Howard would not be attending the Oscars Academy Awards. She had been nominated for an award and he would not attend with her. He told her to go with someone else and she chose Robert Wagner as her escort. He can't be in the audience at the same time as Howard and be emceeing the awards as Bob Hope. One person cannot be in the same place as another person at the same time. Bob Hope will be there as MC of the event but the guy who owns all the studios and makes most of the movies can't be there. Right. They can't both be there at the same time.

Page 299. It is written that Howard Hughes and Ava Gardner together attended the opening premier in New York City of the Barefoot Contessa. The movie was about him. She is in the movie that he made.

Terry Moore continues to write and tell us about Cuba and spy rings and the CIA. She tells us that Howard was setting up his Medical Center and Institute. She writes that Howard had to have the best Doctors and Nurses in the World, and Howard Hughes was supervising them since the war. That's strange, Bob Hope has stated that he got his doctors license in Atlantic City during the War. It was Atlantic City during the War that the United States Government took over all the Hotels as Hospitals. In Atlantic City the Haddon Hall Hotel was owned by the Lippincott family. The Hotel was titled The New England General Hospital. In Panama there were facilities set up by the Lippincott family to train many Nurses from around the world. Bob Hope was always setting up Hospitals for Eisenhower. There were many skits about being a doctor in Bob Hope's Movies and TV shows.

You must recall that Bob Hope as an Actor in Burlesque and Theater started out in Atlantic City. Bob Hope was arrested on the Atlantic City Beach without a shirt. Bob Hope signed up Jack Benny for radio shows in Atlantic City. The United States Government took over all the Hotels and made them all Hospitals for the wounded soldiers of World War II.

There's been many movies made in and about Atlantic City. Just so happens that in 1980 I happened to be in one. The movie Atlantic City USA. Freeze-frame it an one (1) hour and 18 min. in and you'll see myself and my twin brother at the table.

United States Air Force made Terry Moore the most popular actress at Bob Hope request. She was to do a Christmas show for the USO. What was the connection of the Air Force and Bob Hope? The Air Force said no. She went on other shows and other places for the

Air Force. Terry Moore was an Entertainer. She states that she was also an accomplished Pilot. She's flying with Howard Hughes and knows about the whole thing. She's an Actress, she's a Pilot, She's an Entertainer, and she's flying everywhere with Howard Hughes.

Page 314. It states here that everybody was in Cuba, Rocky Marciano, Robert Mitchum, Eddie Arcaro, Nicky Hilton, and Hemingway the Spy. Cuba, the hot bed of Spy's. The place where spies from around the World met.

Page 360. With Howard She meets Franco of Spain, and King Hussein of Jordan, Ernest Hemingway and Ava Gardner. Talks about meetings and dealing with spies. Terry Moore's book tells a spy mystery. Was Bob Hope the spy or Howard Hughes the Spy in make-up?

Terry Moore says she went underground and reveals that she befriended new friends in France of all Nationalities. She writes that in this crowd she made up herself one day to look like French woman and talk French and dressed French and gave her new make-up tricks like a beauty parlor would and that one day she looked Egyptian and one day she looked Oriental. It was magic land to her. It was a Government make-up room. Hope had said he ran a theater group right out of the Pentagon. Terry Moore was a spy and she loved it, and after the mission she would return to Howard Hughes. Mission impossible or Mission possible?

The 50s: Terry Moore, also known as Helen Koford has been legally recognized as Mrs. Howard Hughes by a Federal Court and as strange as it may seem she wrote at the end of her book of the dream she had about Howard Hughes after his said demise.

The dream about Howard......

I was entering our bedroom, Bungalow 19 at the Beverly Hills Hotel. Howard was lying in bed with a uniformed Guard at his side. The moment Howard saw me he sat up and swung his long legs over the side of the bed smiling at me. As he rose from the bed I could see another Howard, sitting exactly in the very same position, but this Howard, although he was also smiling was transparent and ghostlike and as the TWO Howard's reached out their hands and encourage me to come to them the Dream faded.

Two Howard's!

The epilogue at the end of this book the Beauty and the Billionaire is about a dream of TWO Howard's. That's My Theory. One Howard Hughes the other Bob Hope. Howard being said to be dead is the ghost concept. Remember Bob Hope said he was a screenwriter, the one with two heads. There is a cartoon of Bob Hope with two heads. As concerning Terry Moore, she was always with Howard in Southern California, in the Entertainment Hollywood Movie Industry and traveled the world as a spy in Europe, Cuba and the Middle East and she herself was a Jet Pilot. She could've been "My favorite Brunette" the spy like us. Or My Favorite Blonde.

As Howard was living his early life adventures, He and his writers would put all his experiences and adventures into the movie's and make all of Bob Hope's 62 movies that I researched about Bob Hope. I found my proofs of autobiographical movies.

Watch all Bob Hope Movies and in fact watch all movies and use My Theory as that constant variable and you'll see the history of Howard Hughes played by Bob Hope.

BOOK #12

THE SECRET LIFE OF HOWARD HUGHES BY CHARLES HIGHAM

From the book The Secret life of Howard Hughes by Mr. Higham the book starts out with some information from Raymond Price, a former special assistant to Pres. Richard Nixon in 1976. And here It is….

"There is no inconsistency in trying to earn money from Hughes while serving the interest of the Central Intelligence Agency and the Nation, after all the interest of the Hughes Organization are so intertwined with the United States as to be almost symbolic."

I believe that Mr. Prices statement says that the United States, The Hughes Organization and the CIA are all one and the same!! Howard Hughes and Bob Hope are one in the same! Hope has said he works for CIA and the United States of America.

Page 14. January 10, 1901, Bo Hughes first leases Spindle Top in Beaumont Texas. Spindle Top biggest Oil Hit. Sing the Beverly Hillbillies Song and think who the song was about.

It was about Howards family history.

Page 15 & Page 16. Reveals that family History.

Bo Hughes marries Arlene Gano on May 24, 1904 in Dallas Texas. Bo and Arlene Hughes moved to Humble Texas in 1905 where Howard Junior, known as Sonny was born.

In November 1908 Bo invents the Hughes Tool Co. drill-bit. In 1909 Sonny Howard Hughes Junior was four years old.

December 8, 1915 the family moves to New York City to the Biltmore Hotel. They enjoyed the Broadway shows where 10-year-old, "Sonny" became enamored and in love with the beautiful showgirls, glamour and music.

At about the same time Howard Hughes Junior Sonny went to Scout Camps in West Pennsylvania where he learned Indian signs and secret codes. He lived in an Indian Tepee.

In 1918 Sonny Junior Howard was flying in planes with his father and he fell in love with flying.

By Howard's 15th birthday in September 1920 Junior was in school at Fessenden school. He was sporting his own Invention of an Electric Motorcycle.

Bob Hope has said he was an Inventor. Howard Hughes was the Inventor.

It was at this time that "Sonny" Howard Hughes Jr, Dudley and Rush Hughes took off from New York to Cleveland Ohio to stay with his Uncle Felix in his Music filled House in Euclid Heights. This is Howard Hughes History. Cleveland Ohio is the same Home town as Bob Hope where "Sonny" Howard Hughes met Ronald Reagan (Howard Hughes not Bob Hope!) Bob Hope said Reagan is the only man who could call him (Bob Hope) "Sonny". So "Sonny" is Bob Hope because Ronald Reagan is the only one that could call Bob Hope "Sonny" and "Sonny" is the nick name of Howard Hughes jr! Did you get that? Both in Radio, both in Movies, both in Television, both in Politics! Both in the Projection Room all the time. Does that tell you anything?

Bo Hughes, Howard Rupert Hughes Father founded the Texas Fuel Oil Company in 1903 which later became Texaco. Did Bob Hope have anything to do with Texaco? Wasn't Bob Hope a big Shareholder of Texaco? Hope scored Millions from Texaco stocks in the 50;s. Bob's major sponsor on television was Texaco. Bob Hope did all their Commercials "and you can trust your car to the man who wears the star". Yeah, the Star of Stage Screen and Television.

Bob Hope did a Commercial during the first Gulf War in 1991 to keep those Texaco Oil Tankers coming through the Strait of Hurmuz out of the Persian Gulf. Bob Hope surely was concerned about Texaco. One third of all the World's Oil transport comes out of the Middle East from the Persian Gulf. I might add here that Bob Hope and his 60 years with NBC shows the Peacock as their symbol. Thus, The Shah of Iran, The United States Air Force trained Jet Pilot who became Shah of Iran in a 1952 CIA plot that took over the nation of Iran. Iran's Throne just happens to be titled the Peacock Throne? Isn't that interesting? Can you imagine that the NBC's Peacock Symbol is the same Symbol as the Shah of Iran? The Shah, the Peacock Throne was put in place by a CIA plot. Don't forget that Peacock on the NBC symbol has a Beak. Beak like a Nose. Beak like Bob Hope. Beak like a Peacock. And Bob Hope with The Peacock for 60 years on NBC. Who owned NBC?

Many years ago, one NBC Bob Hope special had an opening about "someone running a spy operation out of the basement of 30 Rock". 30 Rock being Rockefeller Center, the home base of the NBC Network in New York City. Was Bob the Spy? Was Howard Hughes the Spy? How do you run Spy operation without connections? Bob Hope certainly made a lot of Spy Movies. Do you think The Industrialist Billionaire had a lot of connections World Wide? I do!

Here's another Movie Bob Hope made. It's about Bob being an Oil Executive in England and having vast Oil operations in Saudi Arabia. Bob Hope into Oil Investments in Saudi Arabia. Who was into Oil more Howard Hughes or Bob Hope? The Movies are telling you that Hope is Howard Hughes with all the Oil Investments in the Middle East. Bob Hope was not the Oil Executive. Howard Hughes is the Oil Executive. It was also Howard Hughes building all the double hold Tanker Ships to transport Middle East Oil to the United States.

Page 60. Howard Rupert Hughes Born 1905 in Humble, Texas. The Family being Rich moved to New York City. Howard as a boy and living in New York City with his family carried the Nickname "Sonny."

Page 20. "Sonny", Howard Hughes in the year 1915, as a 10-year-old was living at the Biltmore Hotel in New York City. December 8, 1915, to be exact. It is written that Jr Howard Hughes "Sonny" enjoyed the Broadway Shows of the day, which gave 10-year-old "Sonny" a lifelong love of Showgirls, Glamour and Music. Above we were talking about Howard Hughes not Bob Hope. Was "Sonny" going into Vaudeville? Reagan called Bob "Sonny". The above was about Howard Hughes not Bob Hope. Sounds like they both had the same interest.

As I continued to read it came to my attention that prior to 1929 Howard Hughes had made four (4) Movies. Howard made many Movies. He wound up being the Producer the Director and the Cameraman. You may recall that at 17 years of age, Howard Hughes was at Paramount with his Uncle who was a Scriptwriter for Paramount and as a 17-year-old really got Into Cinematography, all under 25 years of age. Imagine that, by the time Howard Hughes was 25 years of age He made four (4) Movies. Before Hell's Angels.

1. Swell Hogan
2. Everybody's Acting
3. The Racket
4. The Mating Call

All made by Paramount, all pre-1929. I never saw these Movies, but I am trying to collect them. If I can find them, I am sure their autobiographical and that Howard Hughes thought processes are in them. You know, "Nothing but the Truth" I bet my Theories are in those Movies also.

Page 65. Back in the day, somewhere in 1929 all the High Hats, the Swells, the Rich People, the People Wearing Tuxedos, the very Rich had Social Parties at their homes. Everybody loved Howard Hughes. Everybody but Joseph and Rose Kennedy. They detested Hughes. That was because Howard Hughes tried to wrestle control of RKO Studios from the Kennedy's. Everybody else in Society was excited to have Hughes as their House Guest, everybody but the Kennedy's.

Page 67. Have Tux Will Travel.

That Book was Bob Hope being ready in a moment's notice to go to work for The United States of America.

Page 67. At this point the discussion is about the Disguises. Page 120. Howard Hughes vanishes and disappears from his Home in Culver City California and disappears from his home in Beverly Hills for eight months to a year. Probably out there as someone else ahh. Let's recall that Howard Hughes disappeared many times. Once as a Bum in Houston, once as a bum in New Orleans, another time as a baggage handler for American Airlines under the name Charles Howard and became an Airline Pilot, then a Newspaper Reporter.

It's also good to note here that Jed, the Beverly Hillbilly was a Millionaire and had to run for the Hills because of his discovery of Oil. Beverly Hills that is. That is Southern California. Let's recall that it was Howard's Father that discovered Oil in Texas. Southern California is where all the Hollywood Movies come from, that's where Howard Hughes comes from, that's where Bob Hope comes from. All from the same place. When Howard went missing he said he was traveling for eight months. He turned up at the Park Plaza Hotel. Found in his closet was men's and woman's clothes and 12 Douche Bags. Must've been about Sex for Pornographic Movies.

Page 190. Howard Hughes continued to use Goldwyn Studios Projection Room. He would allow only the Projectionist to be present. He began seeing pictures alone in stretches of as many as 72 hours straight, movies, old movies, everything. The secrecy of the projection booth. Bob Hope stated at one time that he was in the Projection Room all the time. Hope admitted that in his book they got me covered. Bob Hope made 62 movies himself. History has it, and everyone knows No one met face-to-face with Howard Hughes. Noah Dietrich says he never met or saw Howard Hughes, Robert Mayheu says he never saw him, and they all say they only spoke to Howard on the phone. Terry Moore said the opposite. Bob Hope has said "no one has ever seen his face"'

Page 209, and page 210. Of this book must be read. This book, The Secret life of Howard Hughes is a must read. It's all there.

Howard Hughes was very excited when his first Surveyor landed on the Moon. Mr. Hughes was into Rockets and Moon shots, putting a Rover on the Moon. Here's another hint that Howard Hughes is Bob Hope. This is strange but proves my point. When the Astronauts landed on the Moon, they planted an American flag, and then proceeded to play Golf. Howard Hughes wanted to be one of the best Golfers in the World. Bob Hope was all about Golf. Bob Hope always carries a Golf Club. Bob Hope had the Desert Inn Golf Classic on NBC. Howard Hughes was said to be hiding out on the top floor of the Desert Inn. The Astronauts putted on the Moon's surface. There are also many movies with Bob Hope in Space wearing Astronauts Space Suits in his TV shows. Coincidence?

Page 210. The last paragraph on this page states the Hughes owned the Island of Cay Sal in the Caribbean 30 miles north of Cuba where Howard Hughes planned to launch an attack on Castro before the Kennedy Assassination. The invasion was planned by Eisenhower and Hughes in cooperation with the CIA and the Mafia, Do you think Howard Hughes wanted to take back Cuba to reinstate his Casinos which were operated by the Mob. Strange. All these individuals were involved in the Bay of Pigs, the Assassination of Pres. Kennedy and the Watergate fiasco. Remember Bob said that the Bay of Pigs invasion was the worst fiasco since his first screen test at Paramount. Remember when the rubber was burning under the hot Hollywood lights. How was the Bay of Pigs invasion of Cuba, a fiasco for Bob Hope? My Theory. They're one and the same person.

Page 216. There was an actor who used to play Howard Hughes, dressed in his clothes and was taken out the door of the Ritz Carlton and helped into a limousine as a decoy. The press gave chase allowing Hughes to exit the city unobserved. It's called a double. Howard Hughes used a double look-alike.

Page 225. Talking about Hughes, it was said his ego flourished like some creature in a Science-Fiction Movie. It was also said that he would sit at the Bathroom at the basin rubbing alcohol on his hands and arms for hours at a stretch. Was he removing make-up?

It states that Howard Hughes had another motive for buying the Sands Casino. He still retained his hatred for Frank Sinatra.

Sinatra had been forced out of obtaining a Casino License by the Nevada Gaming Commission so as not to have a Casino because of his links to one of Howard Hughes's Chief Contracts, Sam Giancana. Using a Photo of Frank Sinatra with Mob members. There's a Photo of Sinatra with the Mobster. Giancana was Howards chief contact. Did you get that?

Page 230. Howard Hughes at one time decided he wanted to own more of tax-free Nassau as well. He made a deal with the CIA which owned Mary Carter Paint, a front company, the Parent Company of Resorts International Casino Hotel Resort of Atlantic City to let him buy the operating rights to MCP, Mary Carter Paint's Paradise Island Casino Hotel and Ocean Club. The founders of Mary Carter Paint were Thomas Dewey and Allen Dulles. What!

Remember Bob Hope in a Movie looking at a Portrait Painting on the wall of the Mansion in Cuba ask who the Woman in the Painting was and was told it was Mary Carter. Hope is quoted in the Movie as saying, "Mary Carter What a wonderful name for a Company". That's Bob Hope saying that in a Movie not Howard Hughes. Back in the day if you said you were working for "the Company" it was that you worked for the CIA, The Government. With Resorts International going into Atlantic City Casino Business a book came out Titled "the Company that bought the Boardwalk". Get It!!

Mary Carter Paint is the Parent Company of Resorts International Casino from Miami that put a Casino in Atlantic City. So, Allen Dulles, head of the CIA was instrumental in forming Mary Carter Paint Company. Shortly before Dulles obtained Mary Carter Paint Company Howard Hughes's assistant Robert Mayheu (FBI) set up to kill Castro with Howard Hughes's approval.

Page 230. In 1960 Mary Carter Paint supplied the Money an paid loyal Forces to take back Cuba.. The CIA linked up with the Mob connections of the Mary Carter Paint Company to retake the island of Cuba. A 1961 Fiasco.

Page 231. By 1964, Robert Kennedy, even after he left his post as United States Atty. Gen. was aggressively exploring the Hughes

Sam Giancana link with the CIA, Mary Carter Paint and Nassau connection. (Hughes)

Page 234. The 1968 Election was coming up and the question was who should Howard financially back of the possible Democratic nominee's? Howard Hughes, of course, despised and feared Bobby Kennedy. Probably because Bobby was on the track of the Mob and its Howard Hughes Connections. I believe Howard also didn't like the Kennedy's making it with all the beautiful female Hollywood Stars. The females where all Spies sent in on the Kennedy's by Sam Giancana.

Page 240. Hughes had long been interested in the Dominican Republic from his first visit by Yacht in the 1930s. Recall Howard's first yacht was titled Ranger. That's a connection to Texas. That's a connection to the Lone Ranger. Howard did it all alone. Maverick.

You might recall the opening statements of the Movie the Barefoot Contessa where the dialog points out that the Producer of this movie is the guy who is the one who owns Texas and is buying up California!

BOOK #13

AVA'S MEN THE PRIVATE LIFE OF AVA GARDNER BY JANE ELLEN WAYNE 1990

Ms. Wayne writes that Howard Hughes is one of the most famous man in America. One of the most famous names in America. That recalls to mind Bob Hopes ad in a popular Magazine. Bob Hope is in bed in his night clothes and the title above his head states "two of the most famous names in America sleep together". That's My Theory! They are one and the same person. When Bob goes asleep, so does Howard. Hope has been quoted saying, "My "names" will go down in history."

MS Wayne goes on to quote Ava Gardner.

Page 21. Avis states "the make-up experts will emphasize the good and camouflage the bad. They study every freckle and cover up any blemishes. They measured the space between your Eyes, the length of your Nose, and how far it points to the right or to the left to the millimeter. Teeth will be capped, and your eyelashes matched to false ones, then the team of Hairdressers will decide what color your Hair should be and whether it looks better long or short, or in between."

In one of Bob Hope's books he talks about his teeth being capped, wearing Wigs, false Ears and always talks about the Nose.

Page 25. tells us about Make-up Supervisor Jack Dawn, who was responsible for the many Faces of Lon Chancy. Jack was all about make-up and his major interest was in Facial Masks, Pancake Bases, Rouge, Tints and Powder Puff. Disguises! Jack Dawn was responsible for the many Faces of Lon Chaney in the Movie, The Man with 1,000 Faces. Howard Hughes took one of those Faces home for a lifetime and showed up on the Golf Course with Bing Crosby with the brand-new Face on. Read the pre-face to Bob Hopes first Book, (1941) They got me Covered and you'll understand more. They can make Brand-New Faces and they did! It's as plain as your Nose on your Face.

Howard Hughes owned Paramount and many other studios and Howard Hughes made many Movies. Bob Hope worked for Paramount and made many Movies.

All the Studios have whole Departments dedicated to Wardrobe, Costumes, Make-up, Construction Crews of all Trades and Carpenters of Illusions. Jack Dawn's under study was Wally Westwood. Both make-up artist.

By now we all know that Rubber Masks are used in Movies. The Inventor of using a larger Nose and Beak on Hope was this make-up man working for Hughes, working for Hope.

Bob Hope always calls attention to his Nose. In years past Hope's Face and Nose were on Matchbook Covers requesting people to draw him. I say it's Howard Hughes's Nose and his reconstructed Face and Nose. After how many Test Pilot Plane crashes as a Government Test Pilot had he suffered? How many times was he left in critical condition? Twice or more. Every part of his body was broken one time or another. His Face had been on fire, his Nose was Broken, his Chest crushed. Here's a Bob Hope quote.

"People think I got this Nose in an accident, but I got it from my good friends the Goodyear family". The Goodyear family is all about Rubber. (First screen test) (Fiasco)

That quote recalls Bob Hopes first screen test at Paramount. The test was stopped and halted under the real hot lights of Hollywood when someone yelled they smelt "Rubber Burning". yeah, the Rubber on the Nose, the false Rubber Ears, the Cheeks, on and on.

Don't forget that Bob Hope disagrees with Abe Lincoln's Quote that "you can't fool all the people all the time". Yes, you can! because he did!

Listed in Ava's Book are the Five Plane crashes that Howard Hughes was involved in.

First Crash, at 23 years of age in 1928, filming the Movie Hells Angels. Howard crashed his Airplane and seriously injured himself. He crushed his cheek bone and underwent surgery.

Second Crash. 15 years later at age 38 In 1943Howard Hughes had his Second Crash, two dead. Hughes had burns on his face from a test run of an Amphibious Aircraft on Lake Mead. The test was for the Army. Howard suffered minor Head injuries. The test was during World War II.

Third crash three years later at age 41. In 1946 Test Pilot Howard Hughes testing his new Jet the XF 11 crashes into the Residential area of Beverly Hills, California. From the 1946 jet crash Hughes suffered a crushed chest, Nine Broken Ribs, a collapsed left lung filled with blood, third-degree burns, and many aberrations on the left side of his body and a fractured Nose. Hughes left with a Scar on the left side of his upper lip. I noticed the scar on Bob Hopes left upper lip in a few of his movies. His heart was laid on one side, and he was in severe shock.

Page 86. True to form Mr. Hughes disappeared. You can notice the Scar on Bob Hopes left upper lip in the Movie the Princess and the Pirate.

Here's a little more History of Howard Hughes. "Sonny" was said to have been born on December 24, 1905, Houston, Texas. Humble, Texas. His Father, a Beverly Hillbilly struck Oil in Texas and became a Millionaire and Invented the Oil drill Bit that made The Hughes Tool Company a legend. Drillers came running for the Drill Bit, but Bo Hughes would only lease the bits.

Page 60. Here's some more Biographical facts about little Howard. Howard "Sonny" Rupert Hughes in preparation to be sent to Harvard University was sent to Fessenden School in West Newton, Massachusetts. The young man was very unhappy and then was enrolled at the Thatcher School in Ojal California. His

Uncle Rupert Hughes, a Novelist who had turned to writing for the Movies at Paramount sent a Limousine for Howard on weekends to hang out at the Paramount Movie Studios where Uncle Rupert worked. There is a Movie out there called "The Great Rupert". This was quite a thrill for a 17-year-old in 1922. Even though "Sonny" had seen many Beautiful Women at the Burlesque Shows and Theaters in New York City as a 12-year-old at the studios he saw so many beautiful Women and was infatuated with Women. Howard's visit to the Studios was fascinating. He loved being on the set. Howard studied not only the many scantily clad Women Actresses but studied the intricacies of Moviemaking and all about how to make Movies at 17 years of age. Between the age of 17 and 29 Howard Hughes made 4 Movies on his own. Recall that he took over all the Producing, Writing, Directing and Filming of the Movies. He had done all the above before 1929.

It's a fact that in 1922, 17 or 18-year-old Howard's Mother died. His Father died in 1924. He was 20 years old. "Sonny" inherited the Hughes Tool Company. He also inherited mines of Gold, Silver and Oil and Millions and Millions of Dollars. He inherited Movies. He bought Paramount, and in 1925 he married Ella Rice He moved to Hollywood. He lived at the Ambassador Hotel for three years, 1925 thru 1928, when he produced a Hells Angels silent movie all about Airplanes and Warfare. When talking pictures came he had to re-shoot Hells Angels into a talking picture in 1930. He was 25 years old.

In the 1930s the mob \ gangsters moved into Hollywood. Some of them became Movie Stars, some were shot dead. It took over Hollywood, possibly with Howard Hughes permission. In the meantime, Bette Davis was making it with Howard Hughes, and they were caught by her husband, Ham Nelson. Ham Nelson tried to blackmail Howard for $75,000. Howard then hired a Gangster to kill Nelson. Nelson informed the Police that if he was murdered Howard Hughes would be responsible.

In 1944 Howard brought TWA, a Commercial Airline. In 1948 he bought RKO pictures from the Kennedy's. Howard did all his business deals in cars and over the phone with water running in the bathrooms if the phones were tapped.

As we know in 1928 -1944 and 1946 Howard had three plane crashes that affected him mentally and physically. He became partially deaf.

It was at that time that he met Ava Gardner. Howard and Ava Gardner would fly to Mexico frequently in his Boeing Stratoliner. All Howard had a do is push a button and the plane would be ready and the Hotel would be ready, and Howard would disappear for long absences. He always used a Helicopter to do business. Howard would fly everywhere. Ava states that Howard was very much engrossed in his FX 11 Photo Reconnaissance Plane he was developing for the United States Air Force. He also was involved in space exploration.

Again, here's a list of Howard's injuries from his plane crashes. Six weeks in the Hospital 1946 with a crushed chest, nine broken ribs, a collapsed left lung, a liver full of blood, an third-degree burns, a fractured Nose and his Heart pushed to one side and in severe shock. Just after that Ava and Howard were hiding out in Mexico. Ava states that Howard was never the same after that accident. She states that Howard grew mustache over his scar on his upper lip as stated before. I saw a scar on Bob Hope's upper left lip. Howard said that Ava was just another good lay. In 1949 and 50 Howard met Terry Moore. In 1951 Howard chases Terry Moore and true to form he disappeared. In 1949, Terry Moore and Howard got married on his yacht, the Ranger, but there is no documentation to prove it. Later a Federal Court ruled that Terry Moore was the legal wife of Howard Hughes.

Page 87. It is stated that Howard had his mind on the XF 11 for another test flight. He conferred with the Air Force in Washington. It was stated that Howard was "the Boss."

In my research I found out that Bob Hope was the man who set up all the Entertainment at all the Las Vegas Casinos. Howard Hughes would help Franks Sinatra many times with jobs. Frank Sinatra took Ava Gardner away from Howard and Howard never liked him. In 1951 in September Sinatra depressed tried to use suicide pills. Frank was at odds with Hughes.

Page 155. 1952. Hughes was seeing Terry Moore. He was also dating at the same time Mona Freeman, Mitzie Gaynor, Linda Darnell, Yvonne DeCarlo, Janet Leigh, Liz Taylor, and Jean Peters. Howard Hughes forever the Womanizer Married Jean Peters and then went into seclusion again.

Howard would spy on all his girlfriends. No wonder Bob Hope made all those Spy movies. Howard's Spies were everywhere. Money talks. His Spy Network was Worldwide along with the Over Seas Services, which later became the 40 Committee, which later became the CIA. In January 1957 Hughes sold RKO Studios to Lucille Ball and Desi Arnez. Arnez was a Bandleader in the Hotel Casinos in Cuba. Howard Hughes had been going to Cuba since the 1930s. He then married Jean Peters.

Ava had connections with many Air Force Officers. Ava was in Spain in an apartment with Juan Perone, President in exile from Argentina.

It was at this time that John Kennedy snubbed Sinatra due to his Mob ties while visiting California, instead of staying at Sinatra's home Kennedy stayed at Bing Crosby's house. Remember Bing Crosby was with Bob Hope in the very beginning. Bing was close to Bob and Bob was close to Bing. The feud against Sinatra continued into Vegas. Sinatra drove a Golf Cart through the Sands casino and got in a fight at the Sands with Howard Hughes's people. Howard Hughes bought the Sands in 1967. He also bought the Silver Slipper. the Frontier, the Desert Inn and the Castaway. To me it looks like he was buying it up to get control from the Mob. Remember, he opposed Sinatra getting a Casino License. Sinatra could not compete with the Billionaire. Frank Sinatra was mad all over about Howard Hughes's Spies in the 1950s. Howard Hughes would not talk to Sinatra regarding the Sands Contract. Sinatra said that Hughes should share profits with him. When Sinatra signed with Caesar's he went over to the Sands, got into a fight with Howard's people and lost some teeth.

Howard Hughes with Gov. Laxzalt set out to ban Frank Sinatra from obtaining a Casino License via the Nevada Gaming Commission as was said before. My knowledge is that Sinatra got a Casino License and a Casino in Reno called Cal Nev but not in Las Vegas. Sinatra taped Paul "skinny" D'Amato of Atlantic City as the Manager of the Casino. Skinny D'Amato was the owner of the 500 Club Atlantic City. The five. You get it. The Five. Like the Mob Commission. The Five! It was Skinny D'Amato who gave John F. Kennedy $1 million $ so that Kennedy could win the West Virginia primary to secure electoral votes. When Kennedy won and had a party Joey Heatherton sang a song and her song went something like this "It used to be DC now it's AC". So, the Atlantic City connection to the Mob had taken the Presidency away from Washington. Howard Hughes a.k.a. Bob Hope was Washington DC. At this time Howard Hughes was Globetrotting and hiding out in many many places. Unseen by his Workers and unseen by the Public hiding out in London. In 1971 he was in seclusion in the Bahamas. It is said that Howard Hughes died in 1976. If you believe it?

On page 190 Ava Gardner says this about Howard Hughes. "He was filthy rich of course, he inherited a fortune, his daddy owned Hughes Tool Company, Houston Texas. At 21 when his Father passed, he got the whole kit and caboodle. Howard got the lot". We all know this. Watch the Movies Pale Face and Son of Pale Face. Ava referred to Howard Hughes as "the quiet Texan."

Let's go over the Beverly Hillbillies opening song to their Television Show. Let's talk about the Lone Ranger as in Texas Ranger. Let's talk about The Barefoot Contessa the movie and its dialog "The Producer of this movie owns and operates all the Hollywood Production Studios and has an Office in every Studio. He was the 20th century Fox. He owned RKO, MGM, 20th Century Fox, Independent & Republic, United Artist and possibly many others. Think he had any input in the making of Motion Pictures since he was 17 years of age. Think he could've put on make-up as an Actor and played the part as Bob Hope for the rest of his life. Bob Hope was only seen on film in Movies and on TV and from shows from a distance. I think he was a very good Actor. The Greatest Show on

Earth. The man who was one of the best Impersonators of people in the world. Certainly, buying up California real estate certainly gave a lot of land to the movie industry for their locations..............

Keep reading. There is more facts and information to come. THE RAT PACK KNEW HOPE WAS HRH. Sinatra, The Atlantic City connection to the Mob in the 50's- (500 club). It came out of Atlantic City. Frank Sinatra, Dean Martin and Jerry Lewis all came out of the 500 Club, Atlantic City. All hooked up with Hope, Casino's and Movies. They knew who he was and muscled their way in with Hope/Hughes..

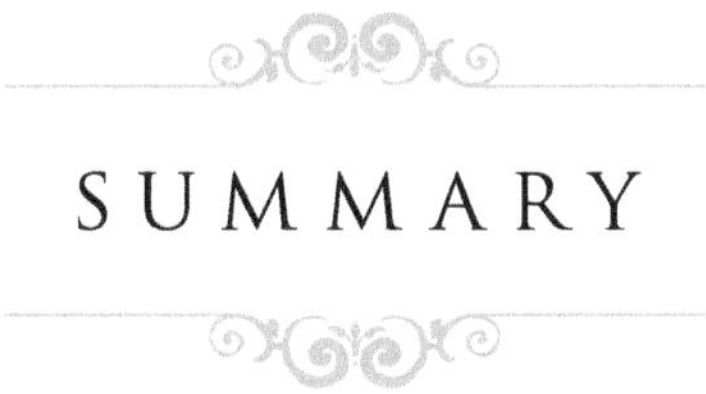

SUMMARY

BOB HOPE BOOKS

I read every book written by Bob Hope and other books about Howard Hughes. My purpose was to pull the statements made by Bob Hope and match them to what I knew of Howard Hughes. I also read many book's about Howard Hughes and followed his History.

Below is the list of the Bob Hope written books that I read and quoted what was said of which you have previously read. The list is in date order.............

- 1. they got me covered - 1941
- 2. I never left home - 1944
- 3. so, this Is peace - 1946
- 4. have tux will travel - 1954
- 5. I owe Russia $1200 - 1963
- 6. five women I love - 1966
- 7. Hope's Vietnam story - 1966
- 8. the last Christmas show - 1974
- 9. Hopes life in comedy - 1982
- 10. don't shoot, it's only me - 1990
- 11. I was there - 1994
- 12. Dear Prez, I want to tell you 1996
- 13. Hope's my life in jokes - 2003

My 50 years of memory and my hard work and research paid off! With Bob Hope's own words in "dialog." Attributed to him! Quotes by him in his books I found out what was going on!!

I prove My Theory! I'm sure you agree that Bob Hope's book's written by Bob Hope would be a bit of an Autobiography. When Bob Hope's words are put up against the History of Howard Hughes they prove My Theory. Bob Hope and Howard Hughes are one in the same person. Two heads are better than one.

I also must note that I have read the many books concerning Howard Hughes as well as following the News and History of his footsteps since 1966. 53 years to date of this writing.

The following is the list of books I've read concerning Howard Hughes.

There is another reading list of books concerning Howard Hughes that I'm still seeking, to be listed forward. All The following Books about Howard Hughes I have read. The Secret Life of Bob Hope by Arthur Marx Howard Hughes, the Hidden Years. James Phelan 1976 Howard Hughes Achievements and Legacy 1984 By Howard Hughes the Beauty and the Billionaire by Terry Moore 1984 Howard Hughes Secret life by Charles Hingham 1993 Inside Gemstone file 1999 by Thomas and Childress.

the Secret life of Howard Hughes boxes... 2015. By Wellman and Musick.

Of all the Bob Hope books I have read I offer a summary of the critiques and review of Bob Hope books. Bob Hope's own words out of his own mouth and written down tells the story.

"Well let me tell ya...."

As Bob Hope would say: "let me tell ya" with his Texas Beverly Hillbilly slang and twang, and he does tell ya.

I believe that through books written by Bob Hope, it's in the dialog that I prove My Theory and that I broke the biggest story, the biggest News story in the History of the World. The joke played out right in front of all the people all the time that Howard Hughes was Bob Hope in make-up.

As I continue my research to critique and review an Investigation with this summary. My research of books below is a list of Bob

Hope's books, of old books that I could not find. Both Hardcover and Paperback. I'm still trying to find them, to possess them and read them. All of them.

The following is a list of books written by Bob Hope that I do not have and that I am in search of.

- Bob Hope collection one and two
- Bob Hope vehicle cargo
- this is my life
- Airport
- radio show audio
- the road to Hollywood
- greater late than never
- we could have finished last
- the road well-traveled
- to be or not to be
- Hope entertainer of century
- thanks for the memory
- the world of Bob Hope
- so, this is Hope
- Minister of entertainment

The above are Bob Hope books that I'm still trying to collect. I'm sure that those readings will support My Theory.

A Reporter is interviewing Bob Hope and Bob Hope says to the reporter that "he should write an autobiography of his real-life" to the reporter. The reporter wonders what Bob Hope could have left yet to reveal about his life.

The alleged life or the real-life? pick one! You must admit that the life of Howard Hughes was certainly mysterious.

Jumping from Books

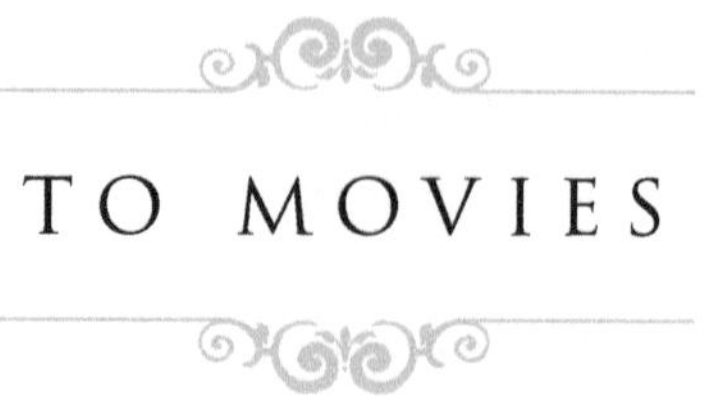

TO MOVIES

BOB HOPE MOVIES THAT IS

I will move forward to review every Movie Bob Hope has made an point out "quotes" and "skits" that prove My Theory. My Theory that Bob Hope was Howard Hughes in a Disguise as a Character Actor in movies for decades, playing a part in the movies that he himself had made. I am not in possession of "Junior's" and "Sonny's Howard Hughes's first four movies that he produced at Paramount, all before 1929. Young Howard was a filmmaker since he was 17 years of age. Research has Howard producing, casting, directing and filming his movies at Paramount. It is noted that young Howard also did a cameo role in one of his own movies. Below is a listing of Howard Hughes's first four movies.

- Swell Hogan
- Everybody's acting
- the racket
- the mating call

Recall at this time Bob Hope's first screen test with all his make-up on and under those very hot Hollywood lights, practicing with the make-up in his first screen test someone yelled "someone smelt rubber burning" What a fiasco!!

I finished proving My Theory through Books. I researched and reviewed and critiqued them. I dissected them in the dialog. I moved on to critique and review the 62 movies made by Bob Hope. I bought all of them through TCM and Bob Hope Enterprises.

I am out to prove again that Howard Hughes is and/was Bob Hope with make-up in movies. The movies he made himself. I bought them because I knew that in those movies that Howard Hughes was playing the part of Bob Hope. I watched all 62 Bob Hope movies and I applied my constant variable, My Theory to the test and wouldn't you know its' in the dialog, and in the skits. I noticed and I found out it was Howard Hughes talking with a Bob Hope face.

HOWARD HUGHES TALKING WITH A BOB HOPE FACE

In these movies you'll be shown and told again and again that Bob Hope is Howard Hughes out of his own mouth. His words will tell you he wants to play dead for many reasons. He will tell you "nothing but the truth."

Knowing that young Howard "Junior" "Sonny" Hughes at Paramount became very proficient at making movies since he was 17 years of age, an expert Cinematographer! As he was making those movies he became an Actor, as a Character Actor in his own movies,

My theory.... As Bob Hope!

I noticed and found out that in every Bob Hope movie, in every movie he speaks of who he is. He tells the people right to their faces, right in front of them, who he is and how he does it.

The Following review of Bob Hope movies, or should I say Howard Hughes movies will reveal who he is right out of his own mouth. Read his books and watch his movies and you will find My Theory proven way beyond any reasonable doubt. No Doubt! There is No Doubt at all! You will see it and you will stop laughing.

Recall, I went through every Bob Hope written book and showed you with Bob Hope's own words by what he said that he was someone else.

As I did books, pulling out his quotes from the dialog and going forward using the same technique to prove My Theory I do the same with movies.

The Movies as Books will prove My Theory that Bob Hope is Howard Rupert Hughes, the Actor, the Owner of The Hollywood Movie Industry, the Writer, writing, along with his 3,000 Writers of his adventures and experiences, and nothing but the truth, all as he ran America and the war effort as a spy in Hollywood make-up, the Billionaire "crazy" Industrialist.

Hughes as Hope admits The JOKE as Hope admits "you can fool all the people all the time". "Two of the most famous names in America sleep together". Read on. Read his books and Investigate My Theory. Read this book twice.

The JOKE heard round the world must be read between the lines and with the facts from your own reader comprehension. Connect the Dots. To Theory or not to Theory, that's a good question? The truth is stranger than fiction. Keep laughing.

I always knew, this is not just my opinion. Try on My Theory as a constant variable and hold it as you watch Bob Hope movies and seek to prove me wrong. Facts are stubborn things in these reviews. I give you many facts to prove My Theory. Please continue reading as the many movies of Bob Hope are dissected. You'll be amaze what you will learn. I was.

Bob Hope is Howard Hughes as Howard Hughes is / was Bob Hope in make-up since he was 12 years old as Sonny, and Junior. Read on.

I got on Howard Hughes tail many years ago. I put the Bob Hope thing together after I watched an NBC Bob Hope special. I was watching TV one night and it was a Bob Hope television show. I started really zeroing in on the dialog of Bob Hope's TV shows as I've done with books and am doing here with movies. I do the same to every television show, but in this show as an example of who Bob Hope really is I saw and heard the dialog in the skit that proved another conclusion of mine that Howard Hughes is and was Bob Hope in make-up because of what Bob Hope says in this skit.

The show opens with the courtroom scene and the defendant is brought into the courtroom. A puppet in the likeness and image of John F Kennedy is brought In and seated at the defendant's table. JFK as a puppet sits in the defendant's chair and Bob Hope sits in the "witness" stand. Tony Randall is the Judge.

I heard Bob Hope say, "JFK is charged with breaking a deal and that he had a beef with JFK."

It is history that there was a deal with the Mob over the Chicago Vote. The Kennedy's broke that promise. The dialog in this skit is out of Bob Hope's mouth. It's Howard Hughes talking in the dialog.

Hope "the witness" says he "hates JFK and his whole family" and the Judge Tony Randall says to the "witness" Bob Hope / Howard Hughes in the witness stand, "since JFK broke the deal over the Chicago Vote what did you do about *It*"? Bob Hope / Howard Hughes says

"I really turned his head around didn't I."

DID YOU GET THAT?

"I really turned his head around didn't I."

They really did turn his head around didn't they

If Howard Hughes is talking out of both sides of his mouth as Bob Hope, he just admitted to his role in the assassination of Pres. John F. Kennedy. You can take it or leave it. I hope you believe it.

How about the television show Dallas, Like Dallas, Texas, where Kennedy was assassinated? I think the last show was titled "Who Killed J R" Who killed John and Robert?

It should also be noted here that Joseph and Rose Kennedy, Mother and Father of John Kennedy, Robert Kennedy and Ted Kennedy, did not like Howard Hughes through-out the 20s and 30s. There is more on that struggle later As I review every movie.

Now back concerning that Bob Hope and Howard Hughes being the same person with the same adventures and experiences. Here's another comparison. I'm reading Bob Hope, A Life in Comedy, 100 years of life. So, I'm reading in a chapter with the Header, Jolly Follies. 1903 to 1928, and it reads before 1928.

Hope's Biography says, "he was once a newspaper man". Hope is saying that "yes" he said "he was a newspaper man and wrote a column, a national column in and for Hersh newspapers."

Its history and as a matter of fact, Howard Hughes went missing for some time. Many time's Hughes was missing more than once. Several times he was missing and once he was discovered as a Reporter under an "Assumed Name for a Metropolitan Newspaper". Sound familiar. We also have Howard Hughes always using phone booths as a mild-mannered Reporter. That's Howard Hughes speaking.

Look up in the sky, it's a bird, it's a Plane, it's Superman, Man of steel. The Industrialist Billionaire to crush the German Volkswagen. Check out the first cover of the Superman comic book. It's also documented that Bob Hope was into Publishing and Advertising and that he may have been Time, Look and Life Magazines.

If you've read the front of this book it has been printed that Hope said at an awards dinner for him that Dolores always believed he was a Commercial Airline Pilot, and to take it a step further it was written an read that the children also believed he was a Commercial Airline Pilot.

Very interesting. History has it written down that Howard Hughes was found another time arrested for vagrancy in New Orleans. History also has it marked down that he disappeared and was found operating under an Assumed Name as a Commercial Airline Pilot. Well what do you think about that? Coincidence?? I led three lives. Howard Hughes and Bob Hope were both Pilots and both flew everywhere in the world.

So, as I see it I pulled the Mask off the Lone Ranger! The theme of wearing a mask, that it is Howard Hughes wearing his Bob Hope mask as a disguise. The masked man Bob Hope is Howard Hughes, writing and making movies and staring in them. Also keep in mind that Howard Hughes and Bob Hope were both womanizers.

The Lone Ranger story was this, The Lone Ranger and his twin brother(2) and other Rangers were ambushed and all except the Lone Ranger were killed. Twin was killed dead. The Lone Ranger survived and was saved by Tonto. To not be recognized in the future the Lone Ranger cut a mask out of his dead Twin Brothers Fest. Which mask he wore for the rest of his life. The Ranger wore many disguise's. Howard Hughes first boat was titled Ranger.

Here's a clue, Terry Moore writes in her book "The Beauty and the Billionaire". that "she taught Howard Hughes to growl like an Alligator, and she taught him an Alligator Mating Love Call. This is Terry Moore telling Howard Hughes how to do the Alligator Mating Love Call and after every phone call they would both sign off their phone calls with the Alligator Love Mating Call.

Now let's look this over. I always saw Hope do that Alligator Love Mating Call in a lot of his movies if a beautiful woman was near. He would growl. He would growl the Alligator Growl on his TV shows. Did you catch it? Bob Hope knows the Alligator Love Mating Call. The mating call that Terry Moore taught only to Howard Hughes. The call for love. I thought she taught Howard Hughes the Alligator Love Mating Call and it looks like Bob Hope is Howard Hughes because he knows the Alligator Love Mating Call.

As I said previously, in the early years of Broadway shows it is written that Charles Lucky Luciano and the New York City Mob financed most of the Broadway Shows. Hope or Hughes knew Lucky since the 1920s.

Check out the Movie "The Lemon Drop Kid". The movie opens with a drawing of a Christmas tree and there's only one ornament on the tree and it's a Gun. Looked like a German Lugar. Have gun will travel. (tv)

The story goes this way. Bob Hope in his Horse Racing Gambling ways owes the Mob $10,000 for cheating and losing at the Horse Races. Hope and the Mob meet in New York City at Charles's Restaurant and the dialog says this "if I don't pay the Mobster Sam the $10,000 I owe him he will have me killed". To anyone who studied American Mob History certainly you are aware of the names Charlie and Sam and their connection to the Mafia. (the five)

The FBI investigates The Mob's infiltration of Hollywood and the Movie Industry in the 1930s. Ironically in the 1930s and most of the decade many mob crime movies were made. Hope had been quoted as saying that "J Edgar Hoover head of the FBI doesn't make a move without him. (Hope) And "Life is different when you have the Mafia on your side"

"I have a Mafia Agent."

In one Bob Hope movie I have a quote from Bob Hope that says this: "J Edgar Hoover doesn't make a move without me". That's interesting. Years later, J Edgar Hoover would testify to Congress that there was no such thing as the Mafia. What?

Bob Hope, any way you like It is Howard Hughes "Sonny" "Junior" and it was Bob Hope who knew Lucky Luciano in the 30s.

In Hopes early years in Vaudeville and Broadway in New York City the Broadway shows were financed by Lucky Luciano. He's a member of "the five" Mob Commission of New York City Families. I received that information in a book about Bob Hope.

Reading Bob Hope's books and Howard Hughes Books I put together a list of similarities, meaning they both had the same traits.

Howard Hughes was very rich, and Bob Hope was very rich. Howard wanted to be the best golfer. Bob Hope was a good golfer and hung out with all the golfers and Bob always carried a golf club. Bob Hopes Desert Inn Golf Classic, as it was titled at the same time that Howard Hughes hides out at the Desert Inn. They are both all about Vegas. Hughes owns Vegas and Hope made the call on all the Entertainment that was to play in the Vegas Casinos. Both very well connected to Hollywood and in with all the Stars and all the Beautiful Women and both are involved in the Paramount movies as well as other studios. Bob and Howard – Howard and Bob, however you want to look at it. They were both holding great Southern California Real Estate and both in the Movie Making Business and in the projection booth all the time. Both pilots. Both involved in World War II and Vietnam. Both from Texas.

Let's recall that Bob Hope had written that he was negotiating with the North Vietnamese to end the Vietnamese War. Bob Hope was negotiating an end to the Vietnamese war. Take it a step further. He also negotiated with the Hostage takers in Iran also with North Korea at the DMZ. Interesting!

Recall that prior to all that he was stealing stationery out of Winston Churchill's office and picking up soveneers at the end of the war out of Hitler's office. So, the Comedian is the first on the scenes and negotiating for the United States Government, and you want me to believe that it's Bob Hope alone doing the negotiating for the United States Government. Bob Hope is Howard Hughes, the Billionaire Industrialist and I am sticking to it! Hughes was the Negotiator!

Here's more information that proves that both Howard Hughes and Bob Hope are connected to Pres. Nixon's 18 min. gap that was erased by Nixon.

Both Howard Hughes and Bob Hope in writing had both said and have been accused of being on the phone with Richard Nixon and they were both said to be involved in the Bay of Pigs fiasco. Hope himself said that he was on the phone with Richard Nixon and that he told him to burn the tapes because he had told Nixon some bad jokes. Hope also said this about the Watergate break-in "it's hard to find good plumbers today". Plumbers means good Burglars. Like the Burglars that Howard Hughes used to burglarize Daniel Ellsberg's Psychologist office. Nixon got caught using his plumbers, Howard Hughes did not get caught using his plumbers. It is funny all of Howard Hughes's plumbers were the same plumbers working for Richard Nixon and involved in the Bay of Pigs invasion of Cuba and the Assination.

Here is another point. Howard Hughes loved ice cream and he would have gallons delivered to him wherever he was. Howard Hughes also set up his ice cream connection in business in Los Angeles, so it's not strange that Bob Hope would talk of ice cream and being an ice cream lover and eating gallons of vanilla. Wherever he was he would have ice cream delivered to himself and to his writers, and to his girlfriend's. Howard Hughes and Bob Hope both loved ice cream.

To tie it all together with the Ice Cream or the Alligator Love Mating Call proves My Theory. Howard Hughes and Bob Hope both had great Dane dogs.

Further, Bob Hope says that he Hope offered to cut a deal with the North Vietnamese to end the war, and that the North

Vietnamese rejected his offer. His offer! What did Bob Hope have to offer? That he'd do a show In North Vietnam?

So, Bob Hope negotiates on behalf of the United States Government. Recall it is also written that Bob Hope also had direct contact with the hostage takers In Iran. Hope talked directly to the hostage takers in Iran?? was he Bob or was he Howard. Bob Hope makes the call where the Billionaire Industrialist can cut the deal. It was revealed in a book that Hope could pick up the phone and get right to the President of the United States. How about that?

Let's throw this Bob Hope quote right in the middle of this. Bob Hope says "the… Innocence names have been changed to protect the joke."

The joke that was played out over all the people. Howard Hughes took a stage name. Howard Rupert Hughes took the stage name of Bob Hope. One reason, because his real name was too long for the marquee. The joke Is that Howard Hughes unseen is Bob Hope in secret, in movies, in make-up, and in life.

Terry Moore states in her book The Beauty and the Billionaire, on Page 143 that "Howard did not want anyone knowing his true identity". How many Identities did Howard Hughes have??

I have a photo of Bob Hope from his book where he is leaving one of his USO shows with the caption under the photo saying this,

"after every show I leave quickly under an assumed name". In his book under his photo He adds the caption. "After every show I leave quickly under an assumed name."

Here's another one, another quote from Bob Hope "nobody's ever seen my face"

Bob Hope said that with his Bob Hope face on. Who's FACE?? The FACE under the Bob Hope Mask. The Lone Ranger. The Beverly Hillbilly. Nobody ever saw Howard Hughes FACE either. Remember Hughes was never seen at the studios. He was never seen and got the nickname of Harvey an invisible rabbit.

J Edgar Hoover, longtime FBI Chief was quoted at a hearing to Congress "there is no such thing as the Mafia". He had to say that. I believe that Hoover was sexually blackmailed. "J Edgar Hoover didn't make a move without Bob Hope". Bob Hope said that Hoover would have been ousted as a young Peeking Tom and that he was a cross-dressing homosexual freak, alleged to be caught in a photo and a dress as a cross gendered dresser'. It was also reported that United States Government also had a gay spy ring.

Hope in one movie says that he Bob Hope "is a mole" that means he was doing some spying. Cuba was always loaded with spies. All the spy's in the world. Howard Hughes owned many of the islands in the Caribbean. It is written that one of Howard Hughes islands was used as a training base for the Bay of Pigs invaders. They were trained starting in the Eisenhower Administration. Trained on the island owned by the Howard Hughes's Medical Foundation in 1959 and 60. The Eisenhower administration trained Invaders via the CIA. Bob Hope's best friend was Eisenhower. Played golf all the time. Going over everything I presume.

Bob Hope said it was his fiasco. The failure to take back Cuba, Bob Hope said it was his fiasco. Howard Hunt trained the invaders to take back Cuba and for many reasons, one being that the American Mafia wanted Howard Hughes to get back his gambling Casinos and Hotels.

Hope and/or Hughes knew Nixon. Nixon was always Boating in the Caribbean with Mr. Alpernape. Howard Hughes was involved as Hope told Nixon to kill and burn the tapes. Nixon erased 18 min. of those tapes. Hope says, "he was on that phone tape and that he had told Nixon some "bad jokes."

Page 93... On June 20th1972, H R Haldeman, Nixon's Chief of staff revealed that it was Howard Hughes on the tape, on the phone with Nixon during the 18 min. gap. They are one and the same. Two of the most famous names in America sleep together.

A few years later it was Treasury Secretary, William Simon, who signed off on Howard Hughes death certificate.

Question remains, was it Howard Hughes that was dead?? Check the DNA of Hughes and Hope.

Watching Casa Blanca, the Movie with Bogart and Bacall, the dialog between the spies is the focus on one Great Guy. As the camera films the profiles of both Boggy and Bacall in a dark shadowy room a beam of light lights up the tips of each of their noses. The tip of the Nose's is an indication of being a spy and of having the make-up on. I also noticed that same light beam hit the nose of the man in the movie the Blue Gardenia. The Nose. Hope admitted he was a spy and that he "wore a funny nose" and "worked for the Central Intelligence Agency and the United States Government". And got the US info on a USSR Russian Jet Plane.(CIA).

What must happen today is that the DNA of Howard Hughes and the DNA of the guy that was buried as Howard Hughes and Bob Hopes DNA be investigated with My Theory Through DNA, that A Bum was buried instead of Howard Hughes. To prove that Bob Hope and Howard Hughes are one and the same.

In the movie the Blue Gardenia, the Beak Nose is silhouetted by a beam of light on the tip of the actors Nose.

It glowed!

In reviewing other movies, I would notice the actors all had nose extensions. I watched Ocean's 11, and Masterpiece of a Murder. Check it out for yourself. They all had nose extensions. Whenever I watch any Movie I look to see if they had fake make-up ears and make-up noses on.

Make-up for Bob Hope or for Howard Hughes was first Sponge Rubber from the Goodyear family. It was Putty later. It was Stucco like Plaster and Make-up. Some of it held together with the Invention of invisible 3M tape.

Through all the years I watched all the Movies. I read all the Books. I watched all the TV shows and I watched all the Biographies and all the advertisements and bought all Hope Tapes and DVDs. Also all recent Movies, the Aviator, Rocket Man, the Lone Ranger, etc..

On August 12, 2016 i caught the Time / Life advertisement for Bob Hope, and The Golden Age of Television by NBC Universal. I watched and then a clip that I had not seen before is showing Bing Crosby, putting make-up on Bob Hope's face with a make-up Feather. Using that feather to indicate that he is putting make-up on Bob Hope. Bob Hope yells to Bing Crosby, "pick it up". To put the make-up on faster, and Bing Crosby tells Bob Hope

"I never worked with Stucco before."

That make-up clip is similar to a skit I found in Bob Hopes TV show. The exact same skit with the make-up man working on Bob Hope's face. Bob Hope demands that he hurry up for He has a show to do, and the make-up man responds to Hope saying "I never worked with stucco before". The make-up man turns to the camera and says,

"I have never worked with stucco before."

There in two clips It has been admitted that Bob Hope has a false face on. Howard Hughes has his Bob Hope face on. (Stucco) Plus all the other accessories.

Another clip in the same Time / Life, NBC Universal sales pitch is a clip with Ann Margaret on stage with Bob Hope. On this USO tour, on film she says out loud on the stage about Bob Hope "that Bob Hope's make-up weighs more than he does". Another indication that Howard Hughes FACE is built up with Stucco as Bob Hope.

You recall The FACE that Bing Crosby identified in his preface to Bob Hope's first book You've Got Me Covered. You remember... The Alleged Life.

Let's go to The Movies. One by one and You will see My Theory develop before your very eyes. Again, i say,

"I broke the biggest story in the History of the World."

MOVIES

Jumping into Movies with My Theory intact. A Review of 62 Bob Hope movies has My Theory on track.

I had to write this book because I got sick and tired over many, many years telling people 'My Theory' to only one or two people at a time, so I wrote this book.

Howard Hughes was Bob Hope in make-up!

* * * *

#1. 1934... PAREE—PAREE a series of seven short comedies.

Bob plays the part of Peter Forbes. Peter is profiled as a womanizer and through dialog He is said to be "a maniac". He is also portrayed as one who goes to the racetrack. Womanizing is both Howard and Bob's MO. In one scene Bob Hope says to a Horse "Hello Texan". and a guy in the dialog says, "He's not a bad guy even if he is rich". So, they are talking about a very rich man. Hope indicates in a way that he Is a Texan. There was also a dramatic scene in a Restaurant. Good acting.

A group of his friends say he is so rich and if he wasn't so rich, he couldn't woman eyes a woman into any engagement, so he puts all his money in his friend's hands and goes off to catch a woman. (Hughes Tool Co). (Noah Dietrich).

This Movie is full of dialog with cracks about himself in the movie where he says things that are facts about his real self and his real-life as Howard Hughes. Viewers don't get it. The maniac rich crazy womanizer from Texas is buying up California and is out to make it with every beautiful woman that he can find. Young Sonny has been chasing showgirls since he was 12.

* * * *

#2. 1934... GOING SPANISH

At the start of this movie Bob Hope is 31 years old and Howard Hughes is 29 years old and in the very first scene Bob Hope is grabbed by the Nose by another guy and Hope knocks the guy out. Bob is in Mexico and talking Gambling and Oil. Talking about Gambling and Oil is very Interesting and very important. Great make-up has large Noses on the Mexicans.

One Actor in dialog says to Bob Hope. "My nose, my ears and my eyes are yours" To Bob Hope. I think the actor is referring to the studios make-up Department, owned by Howard Hughes.

Bob plays the role as a vain show boating womanizer with money and it's all about himself, all about Southern California, Beverly Hills and growing up in an adult life in the LA area. Going to College in the Hollywood environment with Actors and Actresses everywhere.

Howard Hughes a.k.a. Sonny, a.k.a. as Jr. was working at Paramount Studios, where his Uncle was a screenwriter. At 18 or

19 years of age: he inherited Hughes Tool Co. In 1934 in the movie industry he put himself in the movies as a Star. Howard Hughes was very much into mega producing, writing, directing and starring as Bob Hope… "you can trust your car to the man who wears the star, the big bright Texaco Star" And who might that be? Who owned Texaco oil?

Paramount means on top of it all.

Howard Hughes was behind the whole thing. On top of it all!

Only Bob Hope's second movie and it's all about him. There's a couple of clues here. He certainly knows how to make a movie. Good Acting.

* * * *

#3. 1935… The Old Gray Mayor

As the movie opens, THE NOSE, A Nose is silhouetted on glass. Bob is playing Bob Hope. His girlfriend's Father is a Mayor and George Burns is a tough guy and Hope wants to marry the Mayor's Daughter, but dialog says that Hope is "nuts zee crazy". recall they also said Howard Hughes was nut zee crazy.

Bob shows up in a disguise with a long beard as a Doctor. Recall Hope did say he was a Doctor and that he got his license in Atlantic City. In the movie Hope say's "think they recognize me". and at the end an actor in the dialog says this. The actor;

"his face looks very familiar to me". Hope gets away with the girl.

This movie started out with Bob Hope's Face and Nose prominently silhouetted over glass. The Beak. This new ski nose silhouetted on-screen. It's all about the Nose and a made-up face.

This is all happening in the 1930s. Hope is 28. Howard is 25.?

* * * *

#4. 1935... WATCH THE BIRDIE

The Movie opens with Bob Hope aboard a Cruise Ship, and he is again proposing Marriage to the Mayor's Daughter. The Mayor objects.

Hope says to the woman that "she should marry him, so he could get her off his hand". I think he means so that he could stop playing with himself. He's a photographer taking pictures and using a camera saying watch the Birdie, as you do the camera punches you in the eye. Hughes was deeply into Photography.

The dialog has an actor saying that Hope is "a candidate for the Insane asylum". Hope response by saying "don't worry about that. I am an Inventor."

Did you read that. He said that he's Howard Hughes. He said that he's the Inventor. I think you would agree that Howard Hughes is an Inventor. He also is quoted as saying that "I am an American citizen". I think that means he wasn't born in England. Did Bob Hope go through the citizenship program and become an American citizen since he says he was born in England? Bob Hope says he's the Inventor. Since they are both two of the most famous names in America and sleep together, Both Bob and Howard are Inventors. Hughes invented an electric motorcycle, a steam car, and more before 1935. There's Bob Hope again talking his Howard Hughes head-off with his Bob Hope face.

So, they say he's nuts. Didn't they say that Howard Hughes should be in the Insane Asylum! He tells you he's the Inventor. He sure was the Inventor and he is an American citizen at that.

Put My Theory to the test with past facts. Bob Hope said these words in the dialog of this short made by Bob Hope. Bob Hope wrote what he said in this movie. Remember Bob Hope said he has a group of writers and that he's one of those writers, and he's the one with two heads.

* * * *

#5. 1935... Double Exposure

Double means two. Exposure means to show. In Bob Hope movies he shows you and tells you that he is a double person and in the dialog it is exposed.

This movie starts out showing a lot of Press Photographers, Arabs and Arab Dress and an Oil Truck. Bob Hope is dressed like an Arab, and there's an Oil Truck in the picture. Wasn't Standard Oil who discovered Oil in Saudi Arabia in 1922? Who owned an Oil Truck 1935? Hope? (ARAMCO)

Bob Hope is running around taking Photographs. There is a great Profile of his Nose, and large Noses on other Actors. The real Hope puts on a disguise, An Arab Headdress, and again another disguise, as a maid and the photo powder explodes.

So, here's the Character Actor again in make-up in the movies with large noses and disguises and playing different parts. Again.

In future movies and other statements Bob Hope has said he does his Greatest Impersonations right in front of the people and they don't get it. That was in the Movie the Cat and the Canary.

My Theory is correct, and I believe Bob Hope and/or Howard Hughes was the Greatest Show on Earth. The Nose is an indication as to who is making the films.

Howard and Bob, it's all about the ski jump Nose. The Beak is the same because the Beak on the NBC Peacock logo tells you it is him. Howard Hughes with all his money and his beauty is the NBC Peacock. Bob was 60 years with NBC. As Howard Hughes he probably owned the Network.

* * * *

#6. 1936... Calling all Tars

At first I couldn't figure out what Tars meant and what you could call them. Since the movie was about the Navy, and it was made in 1936 I believe it has something to do with Oil, Oil that was running the United States Navy and the tars would be those who worked with the Oil. and back in the day got it all over them.

The film starts out with real Pictures of all Battleships and all types of Cruisers. At least Twenty ships. The Navy. The film Is about Fleet week. Bob Hope And another Actor put on Sailor Suits during Fleet Week to pick up some chicks. Womanizing all the way with a lot of Profile's on the Nose.

Sort of a corny movie. As they return to New York there is a kitchen scene with a big Nose and a Nose on another actor has white powder on its tip.

You may know that the Industrialist Billionaire was in the Airplane and Ship Building Business and built Battleships and all types of ships and did It for The Government of The United States and it was his Oil Company and his Factories of Steel and Motors that powered America and England, Europe and the Middle East and around The World.

So, Hope is a very Rich Southern California Womanizer who is considered a Crazy Inventor. Does that sound like Bob Hope or Howard Hughes? Watch the Movie Paleface and the Movie Son of Paleface after you read my critique in the reviews of those movies. Forward.

My Theory intact! Howard Hughes is Bob Hope in make-up.

* * * *

#7. 1936... SHOP TALK

The Movie is a short Autobiography with true facts. Bob Hope as Howard Hughes could come home from Europe to run Daddy's Business. The Oil Business.

Bob Hope comes home from Europe to run his Dad's Department Store. His position is President Manager of the Department Store. The employees are playing tricks on Bob Hope.

Recall that young Howard inherited his father's company's (USA) 100% inheritance, goes to Beverly Hills and as a youth enters the Motion Picture Business and pushes Movie Production to a Grand Scale, where he and his Screenwriters work off his Memory.

THANKS FOR THE MEMORY!!

Watch the Movie the Barefoot Contessa. On the Film at the very beginning of this movie, Ava Gardner, (which incidentally was Howard Hughes girlfriend) is told by another actor in the dialog that "that guy over there is the Producer of the Movies. He already owns Texas and is buying up California". The Beverly Hillbilly.

Who does that sound like they're talking about? Howard Hughes is buying up California and Bob Hope winds up owning most of Southern California. What's up with that?

End of 7 Short Comedies

FEATURE FILMS

#8. 1938… Big Broadcast of 1938

The Big Broadcast of 1938 is about two Cruise Ships racing across the Atlantic. One ship, The Gigantic, that Hope is on and the other Ship Colossal that WC Fields is on. At the start Hope Is in jail on an alimony charge. Three Woman show up and say their wives of Bob Hope. Sound familiar people claiming to be his wife. Howard Hughes had that problem. There's betting on what Ship will win, and there's gambling on board.

Concerning marriages, Howard Hughes and Bob Hope both had situations over Marriages and License's.

In dialog it states, "did you ever find the marriage license."

I know that was a situation in Howard Hughes life.

In dialog it states, "where did this money come from."

Howard Hughes wanted to be the best Golfer in the world. This movie turns out to be about Golf. Lots of scenes about Golf. To draw the line and connect the dots of Bob Hope to Howard Hughes in this movie, Bob Hope's Golf Cart turns into a Plane. Then the movie is about Electricity, and about Inventions. Sounds like Howard Hughes life as an Inventor to me. Howard Hughes must've stolen Western Electric.

Most of the movie is truly Musical Entertainment. Bob Hope and Martha Ray broadcast over Radio. In the dialog Martha Ray says to Bob Hope "hey boss". Hope carries no money on the ship but in the dialog it states that he "pays all salaries."

The Woman keep mentioning Bob Hope's Nose and that he is a Womanizer. The Electric gets fixed and the Gigantic takes off fast. Gigantic wins the race.

This movie has a lot of details that connect Bob Hope with Howard Hughes. Cruise ships probably built by Hughes. Talk of Marriage Licenses, Money, Planes, Ships, Inventions, Gambling, Women, Actress's, Actors, Bands and all types of Entertainers. Somebody pays all those salaries. Could it be the very Rich Man. Could it be that guy that owns the studios, who Produces the Production; who writes the scripts, who directs the movies. Howard Hughes has been making movies since he was 17 years of age and Bob Hope has been playing a part since he was a teenager, all in Southern California. He never left Home.

* * * *

#9. 1938... College Swing

In this movie, stated to be played out from 1738 to the present, the opening dialog states that in 200 years the WILL of a Rich Grandfather takes place. This Movie is about Wills and rich grandfathers. Sounds like a hint to me. Son of Pale Face. All of Howard Hughes Inheritance came through his Grandfather and his Father.

Google it!! the High Hats, the Swells, the very Rich, The TUX wearers.

The opening shows 1738 Colonial setting with an old-school, it's Bell and a College setting. The Hideout is shown.

This movie is another Showcase of Entertainers, in fact every Entertainer in Hollywood is pretty much in this Movie.

It is in a College setting and about Theater. There's a Variety Magazine and Bob Hope is the Press Agent for that Magazine.

As Martha Ray and Bob Hope engage, the dialog goes back and forth something like this to Bob Hope "You are so phony". Martha Raye taps Bob Hope's Nose. Martha Raye sings a song and Bob, or Howard sing a song.

It becomes a traveling show to all Colleges. Jerry Colonna does his scream song. There are skits, and extra film clips.

Someone "calls for a Fraud Investigation". Dialog says Gracie Allen only sees with her Nose. you know, that may mean she smells money.

Good Camerawork of Pratfalls, a Conga Dance and a great showcase of talent including a Keystone Cop chase. Hope is not in this Movie much at all.

Can you imagine Bob Hope being connected to every single person in the Movie Industry? I thought Howard Hughes had all the movie industry tied up since the 1920s. How early is Bob Hope connected with all the Stars, it's only 1938? Howard Hughes in the 1920s was the Movie Industry! Every Star in the Movie Industry is with Bob Hope and in his movies!

Remember the story in Bob Hope's own book, written by him, where when he was off the Vaudeville Stage at an intermission he goes outside to look at the Marquee and the Marquee reads "The MAGNIFICENT FRAUD" Bob Hope!

Someone called for a Fraud Investigation into the ALLEGED LIFE of Bob Hope.

I did that Investigation. I did that research. I obtained the truth of facts and nothing but the facts.

* * * *

#10. 1938.. Give Me a Sailor

This Movie opens with that beautiful film of all kinds of Battleships and Airplanes. A film about Ships in the Navy.

Then there's Bob Hope (Jim), the Womanizer who seems to be in some sort of a double cross with Spies and is writing a love letter in Code. Writing in Code. Young "Sonny" Howard Hughes studied Indians Secret Codes as a Scout. Tonto always called the Lone Ranger Trusted Scout. Hughes has said he is on the side of the American Indian. Plus the Navaho Indians broke the Japanese War Code in WW 2.

The Movie has Martha Raye in a food contest for best legs. The Movie Scene has Martha in a bedroom as she's preparing to dress. She is filmed with a complete White Clay Pac Mask stuck on her face. Showing you the make-up.

Like I said, from Sponge Rubber to Putty, to Stucco, to False Chins, to Fake Ears, to Wigs, to Fat Clothes and Special Effects.

In dialog it is said to Bob Hope "If you could see an inch beyond that phony Nose of yours". Busted.

In one scene Hope acts like he's producing a movie. A Paramount news crew shows up. That's strange, Howard Hughes was Paramount Movie Producer. Paramount was a newsreel crew. Is Bob Hope telling you he's the Producer of the Movies and that he has his Newsreel Crew working for him?

One main clue is that quote "that Phony Nose of yours". Not many clues, but most Actors were noticed to have Nose extensions.

Here we have the Peacock. The Vain Womanizer. That's both Bob and Howard and here's a quote from Hope "you hit it right on the nose". (Yes, I Did!)

Another quote in the movie, a Woman is to marry Bob Hope at a "Hidden Runway". Bob's a Pilot. he told you that in books. Howard's always hiding. Howard's a Pilot. we know all this from history. Paramount symbol is the Mountain. Terry Moore wrote that Howard as a Pilot had first Landing Rights around the World.

My view again is that I broke the biggest story in the History of the United States, possibly in the entire world.

* * * *

#11. 1938... Thanks for the Memory

The Movie opens with a Song. Bob Hope says something about a Nose in the very first scene. It's about being an Author and a Writer with talk of the Tall Hat relatives. There it is again, early United States of America rich people. The Movie has a lot of scenes over borrowing money and a man describes Hope as "eyes and nose". The rest of the movie is about the concern about the Mob being in place and who knows so many funny people. The talk continues about "a guy with a lot of money". Think it could be Howard Hughes early years. He had all the money since he was 18 or 19 years old. Bob Hope is quoted as saying in his own words, written in his own books "that he would throw money away like a drunken sailor."

Well, it's a fact that Howard Hughes did throw money away like a drunken sailor. He bought everybody and everything in the world.

There you have it again, Rich Guy, an Author and a Writer and about make-up and special effects.

Bob Hope has always said he "is the Writer in a group of Writers and he's the Writer with Two Heads". Bob Hope has also been quoted saying that "his writers write all kinds of stories about him". One head is Howard Hughes and the other head is Bob Hope. That's My Theory and I'm sticking to it. Howard Hughes is Bob Hope with make-up.

This movie is about a guy agonizing over writing a book. At this writing, that's exactly what I'm doing. I'm writing a book about him. I am investigating him, both of him. Both of him. Wasn't that funny.

* * * *

#12. 1939… Never say die

The first scene is a group of guys talking about him (Hope) and spot him and the dialog goes like this "he inherited millions and millions from his grandfather, and father". Hope or Hughes? There it is in the Skit. Read my reviews of two Bob Hope movies… Paleface # 32 and Son of Paleface # 38. Then watch the movies tell you who he is. The movie will show you his heritage, His inheritance and who he is!

This film, the Doctor tells Hope, "He will disappear". (Hope has said he is a Doctor). The Dr. says, "you will pass away". The Plan Is revealed. He did need a Doctor to sign the Death Certificate. That's exactly what happened. Howard Hughes disappeared. Howard gives life to Bob Hope. To his alleged life and Mr. Hughes takes a powder.

So as the film goes on Martha Raye loves Andy Devine and he's a snorer. Her Father wants her to marry into Royalty. She marries Hope. Hope or Howard Hughes, no matter how you want it has always inferred that he was Royalty, in England, some sort of a Duke. Could've been his Cover as a Spy for World War II. I am sure the Billionaire Industrialist had his Nose involved. He was into Rockets and Planes and Fuel. Remember Bob Hope said that he was a spy in his writings and that he worked for the CIA and the US Government. (Have Tux will Travel)

Many of his future movies are all about spies. Bob Hope made many movies out of Hollywood like ...Spy's Like Us, My Favorite Blond, 1942. My Favorite Brunette 1947. My Favorite Spy, 1951. The Iron Petticoat 1951. There are more movies produced out of Hollywood that have many autobiographical writings about Howard Hughes. Was it Bob Hope or Howard Hughes that said he had many writers that they write many stories about him? About Who? Bob or Howard?

Hope talks about his physical condition and is at the doctors again, here he is quoted saying "if they could only patch up a man the way they can patch up a bicycle tire" after an accident on a bike. Is he Talking about being injured in his crash of a jet plane just two years earlier 1936? Bob Hope says he is "the last of the vanishing Americans". The Doctor tells him he "will not die or be shot" but is told to "go some other place to die". Hope talks about "laughing in my condition."

Bob Hope talks about "being gone in the future". Talks about Wills and talks about paying money to pay people off about marriages.

An Actor says to Bob Hope "I do not like your face."

* * * *

#13. 1939.. Some like it Hot

The Movie opens with a Circus Carnival atmosphere with Bob Hope as Nicky Nelson. Down the runway Bing Crosby is his Barker calling Everybody to the Circus Carnival. The sign over his head says the following, The Living Corpse. Well, that fits in with My Theory that someone who is believed to be a corpse is living. The movie is telling you that Bob Hope is living, and Howard Hughes is dead. Bob "it's my buried alive move". Right! under make-up. Quote "I am the star holder", I take that to mean that he's Howard Hughes. He has all the Stars under contract, but it's Bob Hope talking. He goes on to say that "ideas from me are not penny-ante". Get it! Because he's the Billionaire. The dialog of Hope says "you don't understand because you don't think in Millions". Hope goes on to describe himself as a guy "with his chin out". It's about make-up again. Dialog goes on to say, "They say he's crazy, but he is the best mc and comedian around."

Here we have Bob Hope being the "Living Corpse". That means he is not dead. Howard Hughes is not dead, but alive as Bob Hope. Invisible dead as he is Bob Hope. Bury Howard Hughes alive under make-up as Bob Hope, the living walking dead. Bob Hope the dead Howard Hughes. That's the plan to hide and never be seen again.

Bob Hope was quoted saying "ideas from Me are not penny-ante"; meaning that Howard Hughes thinks in Millions and Billions of Dollars.

The Billionaire Industrialist, the Inventor of an Electric Motorcycle, of a Steam Car, of Airplanes, Jets and Rockets and the Looner Lander are not penny anne thoughts. They told you in advance of the plan to play dead.

This film also shows the exact MO of Howard Hughes and Bob Hope in the dialog "womanizing", and the dialog says, "he's crazy". Bob Hope says, "you don't understand because you do not think in millions."

* * * *

#14. 1939... The Cat and the Canary

This Movie takes place in the bayou of Louisiana. An entire family is gathered to read a dead man's will. (really) They gather in a Mansion in Louisiana. The gathering is for the reading of the will that will will Millions of Dollars to the sole heir. In one show Hope says to Debbie Reynolds that if she makes another crack about him that "the next will I will write for Howard Hughes she won't be in it"

The mansion is a creepy setting. The dialog says that the "house is full of maniacs". Hope is Wally Campbell; his character is of an Actor who was in Vaudeville. Some of the dialog goes like this: "do you believe in reincarnation"? "Dead people come back"! There they're saying it again that someone known to be dead, (but not dead) can come back as someone else. The Movie goes on to explain that one of the eight family members will be dead before morning. There is Fear through-out the Mansion. They all must stay overnight in the spooky Mansion.

Through-out the mansion, through false walls and sliding bookcases there's a creep out to kill one of the family members. Paulette Goddard wins the will and all the money. She also receives a letter that is coded with clues of some sort. Bob Hope sets out to find the criminal. Bob Hope catches the criminal creep before he can kill off Paulette Goddard.

So, here's the ending. The Paramount news crew filming newsreels of the news of the day shows up to interview Bob Hope on the success of catching the criminal and questioning how did Bob Hope catch the creep? Bob Hope is eager to tell the Paramount news crew how he caught the creep.... He says::

"Inside the hallways I found this piece of Sponge Rubber and as an Actor I use it OFTEN."

Well, there it is folks Bob Hope telling you right to your face that he's an Actor, and he wears make-up all the time.

Bob Hope is an Actor in make-up all the time! Howard Hughes is that person in all that make-up as an Actor all the time.

I found out from Bob Hope that he would go to make-up first and then he would go to the office. He puts on the make-up before he goes to work.

Recall a Bob Hope quote in one of his books that "Many think I got this Nose by accident, but I got it from the Goodyear family". Also recall that in Bob Hope movies the dialog is all about being dead and/or coming back to life. A plan to disappear. To come back to life.

You think Howard Hughes had a plan to fake his own death? (I do) Being Bob Hope is like being a walking dead. (Wanted Dead or Alive).

* * * *

#15. 1940… Road to Singapore

Bob and Bing are on the run and they're talking women again. Ace is Bing and gives a history of heritage about Josh and his Inheritance. (Sound familiar)

There is a fight and the episode becomes a headline in a newspaper. "Snoot takes a Peek."

Bob and Bing swear off Women and the loser, the first to look at a Women pays by having his ears clipped off and stuffed down his throat.

They wind up again in a circus carnival type medicine show. The dialog indicates that "the suckers are in". In the circus atmosphere Jerry Colonna yells "Hope is Fake."

The movie also has Hope saying, "I'm doing alright for a dopey looking cluck."

Hope escapes after being arrested on a passport violation with Bob Hope saying,"I know big people". The movie ends.

The writers, screenwriters writing all their screenplays in the movies about Howard Hughes. Bob and Howard.

* * * *

#16. 1940… The Ghost Breakers

This Movie starts out with Bob Hope as a talk show host on the radio. He is broadcasting like Walter Winchell. Hope states that he knows all, and he tells all the truth that he knows about, all the Rackets and all the Racketeers. (The Cat & the Canary) Who's talking here Hope or Hughes. The Mob believes that Hope killed an Associate of the Mob. This could be the Bugsy Siegel killed in LA over Las Vegas. Hope must run away. He runs to Cuba in a storm and ends up at a Castle. Hope is taking a Cruise Ship to Cuba and there is a Woman with him.

At the start of the movie a Woman, Hope and Rochester are in the Penthouse of a Hotel and Five Shots ring out. Someone is shot and here come the Police. As the Police assemble outside the Penthouse, they look at each other and they say that "we search this Penthouse all the time and nobody's ever in it". Does that sound anything like Howard Hughes who was supposed to be hiding out in the Penthouse of the Desert Inn Casino in Las Vegas.

At that time the Ambulance Crew carries out a body of an individual on a stretcher and as the stretcher passes by the Camera the Police and everybody are saying, "he's dead, he's dead" and as the stretcher goes by the individual on the stretcher sits up an says "I'm not dead, I'm not dead". He looks like Howard. Interesting!

There is that theme again talking dead or alive. The Woman and Rochester are looking for Hope and they see all the clothes from a trunk on the bed and realize that Bob hid in the Trunk and that the trunk was just taken to the Cruise Ship. Hope is in that trunk. The trunk is on the Ship in the Cargo Hole and Rochester is looking for that Trunk. The Woman tells Rochester that the Trunk has her Initials on it and her name is Mary Carter. Her initials MC are on the trunk.

Bob Hope is quoted "I am headed for an island". The trunk is found and all three are on their way to Cuba and to Black island. They enter the Mansion Castle and a Silver Mine is found under the Castle with a bunch of Caskets. Could that be the people that Hope said he had killed. (9) (HRH)

Ask why Cuba? The remark is "everybody goes to it and dies. There are remarks about "secret money" and a quote "I am not buying an Island I am going to one". There is a confession of an innocent murder by Hope. Seriously.

The woman's name is Mary Carter. You must remember the Mary Carter Paint Company is The Parent Company of Resorts International Casino and Hotel in Atlantic City. The Company is a CIA front Company of the United States. The Government and the Central Intelligence Agency were considered "The Company". Do you see the connection to Resorts International and United States Government, the CIA and Howard Hughes? They were run off the

Island of Cuba. That's a historical fact. Howard wanted Cuba back. The United States wanted the Island back. The Mob ran the Casinos in Cuba and it was the Mob along with the CIA that planned and operated the Bay of Pigs. Recall that Bob Hope's best friend was Eisenhower. The invasion for the Bay of Pigs was put together by Eisenhower. Howard Hughes trained and planned the invasion.

Some of the dialog said this: "is he dead? The guys dead". The Movie also talks about Zombies that are dead coming back to life. That sticks with the theme Howard's dead and Bob's back to the Alleged life. There is also a Piano scene where if you played the right notes on the Piano the wall will move and there are secret hidden compartments within the Mansion Castle.

There are two scenes in this movie that are very interesting. The fact that the guys not In the Penthouse and he's not dead certainly falls right into My Theory. One scene has Bob Hope on the front of the Cruise Ship standing with his hand in his suit coat like Napoleon. As the woman walks towards Hope he is shown erasing and then writing something in a book. The woman asked what are you doing? Hope says, "I am re-writing History and taking the island of Cuba without firing a shot."

The other scene, Bob Hope and Mary Carter are walking down a staircase and Hope points to a Portrait on the wall and ask who the woman in the painting. "that Woman is My Mother Her name is Mary Carter". Hope yells out "that is a wonderful name for a company". There is such a Company! So here we have Bob Hope connecting himself to the Mary Carter Paint Company, a CIA front company put together by Hughes, Dulles and Dewey.

This scene is also in another film.

Remember Cuba was an International hub of the Worlds Spies.

* * * *

#17. 1941... Road to Zanzibar

This movie starts out with Bing as the Barker again at a Circus Carnival act where Bob Hope as fearless Frazier plays the part of the Human Cannonball. Hughes loved Circus People. The Nose is prominent on Hope. He is titled the Living Bullet on the Billboard. Does that mean he's the guy with the Gun? Was Hughes behind the Mob. The Silver Bullet like the Silver Bullets the Lone Ranger used.

Fearless Frazier, the high wire act. Hope is on the high wire with all kinds of fat clothes and different Costumes. There is a big Circus Fire and the whole Circus grounds burn down. Bing and Bob escape. Hope is said to be dead. They continue. Bob and Bing talk about Diamond Mines in Africa. They escaped to Africa. If Bob is dead It is said he must have "a led coffin."

Twice Hope talks about having a bad right arm. Is Hope revealing his Howard Hughes injuries from his many crashes? The Woman says to Hope in the dialog "what is your real name"? There it is again. What is his real name? Is his real name too big for the Marquee? Is his real name Bob Hope or is his real name Howard Rupert Hughes?

The movies pretty good, especially when they swim, sing a song and escape the drums of the natives or be eaten by the natives. Hope's fighting a Guerrilla and he beats it up in a wild scene. They do their clapping punch fight. They get away and Bing gets the Woman. They go back into the Circus Circuit again.

So, Hope is said to be dead again! During these times rumors were wild as to where Howard Hughes was, it was the talk of the Nation's news. Said to be dead theme is in many Bob Hope movies such as this.

Bob Hope and Bing Crosby have been together since the beginning. Bing is in on it from the start. Read Bing Crosby's preface in Bob Hope's 1941 Book They Got Me Covered. He writes of Bob Hopes "Alleged life" "the Manufactured life" "the all-American family man" "the American salesman."

The movie is loaded with talks of Oil, Silver, Gold, Diamonds, Money and Land. Sounds like the American West and of the Great Inheritance secured by Howard Hughes. But here they hid these mines in Africa. Bob Hope is said to be "dangerous" and of course they are womanizing. Bob Hope was considered the American salesman for the American way of life.

* * * *

#18. 1941… Caught in the Draft

Well here we have another Movie of Bob Hope telling you who he is. The Movie opens on a Movie Set with Bob Hope doing the Producing and Directing, and you can hear his voice call everyone to the set. Hope is called "the boss" on the set of this movie production and is called a womanizer in the dialog.

Hope talks about his right hand being paralyzed and that he has a broken back with a brace. If Bob is Howard, he is describing his injuries from his many plane crashes.

At the beginning of the movie and actor pushes on Hope's Nose and another actor who says, "I always wondered if that was your real Nose". And the Nose is flopped back and forth flopping like Rubber. Does that bring back memories of Bob's first screen test where someone said they "smelt rubber burning". He's an actor with make -up on. A Character Actor.

Someone yells "he's a movie star."

The title "Caught in the Draft" is exactly what happens. Bob is drafted into boot camp and he's trying to use the excuse to get out of the Army that "my right hand is paralyzed". He's acting like a coward.

Things are happening and at mail call Bob has great amount of fan mail. And again, the Paramount News Camera Crew shows up as the Army guy asks, "who's doing this"?

It's a good movie with a funny tank scene that leaves a girl behind because she is fat. Very funny. He now becomes a Parachute Jumper out of Airplanes, and you hear reveille playing. He's in the Army now. 12 yrs. hiding in the Army because some mob people were out to kill him for killing one of their associates.

Bob Hope's quoted saying "I wish I was dead". Hope gets the girl and he rides off on a White Horse. To me he's indicating he's the Lone Ranger. The Lone Texas Ranger rode a White Horse named Silver.

If you get it, on the movie set Hope is called "the boss" directing and womanizing. As told prior the woman pushes on his nose, bends it and says to him, "I always wondered if that was your real Nose". As the Nose is slapped like rubber. The woman says to Hope "you should use a double."

* * * *

#19. 1941… Nothing but the Truth

Here we are in Miami at a Stock Market Office and Hope as Steve Bennett wants to sell a Quick Silver Mine in Mexico. The dialog says, "hi ho quicksilver". And he's womanizing again. Recall Bob and Bing inferred that they owned Gold and Silver Mines. Hughes inherited Mines and Las Vegas. Hughes had Silver and Uranium. He was also in league with the American Indians. With deals on their reservation for the raw materials. The American Indians were and are A Nation Within a Nation, the United States. Tonto was the Lone Rangers best friend and called him TRUSTED SCOUT.

"Mr. Bennett is hard to describe". Hope says that he "tells the truth all the time". "no lies for 24 hours" and it is stated that "Bob Hope lives on the ninth floor". Strange. It's the ninth floor of the Desert Inn where it was said Howard Hughes was hiding. Then it said he "has a shaky link with the Mob". I noticed fake Ears on the Actors, and they showed as plastic Ears and Nose.

In Bob Hope's books there's a Picture of the Cast and Hope saying, "I'm not myself today". Is he another person? What self of his two heads is he in that day?

Dialog says "till my ears fly off ".

Here's more dialog "you look like you have two heads", "Two heads". That's him the Writer with "two heads."

It's inferred that Hope is the FBI and this quote follows that "nobody knows about him". Who do You think we are talking about? Bob Hope is the Guy in another movie and in this movie says, "that Hoover is breathing down my back". He has also been quoted as saying that "J Edgar Hoover doesn't make a move without me."

This movie talks about Ears flying off and having two heads. I have a picture, or should I say a cartoon of Bob Hope's ears flying off and him chasing after them. I have a cartoon picture of Bob Hope from the neck up with two heads. I have a picture of Howard Hughes and Bob Hope, both dressed the same 40 years apart. He is Howard Hughes. And don't forget about the "sponge rubber" that Bob Hope said he "knows all about because he uses sponge rubber all the time as an actor". Hope is quoted as saying "there is another side to me". Right two sides. "two heads". What's that tell you? Two of the most famous names In America sleep together. They are one in the same person.

Don't forget about the "Alleged Life" when Bing Crosby first met the Face and the Owner of that Face. I hope you're reading comprehension understands My Theory and its facts.

So, Bob Hope or Howard Hughes puts out a picture of the cast of this movie, Nothing but The Truth. Around the table every Actress and Actor has their name in front of their body. Paulette Goddard, Leif Erickson etc. and as Hope is standing in the back of the Picture there's no name in front of him but there's a? Question Mark above his head in the photo. He's telling you right there. Guess who I am? Everybody keeps asking him "who are you?" Nobody gets it.

A photo of Bob Hope with a question mark? above his head. Is he trying to tell us something???

So, nobody knows about him?

What book, movie so you can see for yourself?

* * * *

#20 1941... Louisiana Purchase

Louisiana Purchase starts out in the Law Offices of Paramount Studios where they receive a letter from the Government stating that there will be a United States Investigation into Paramount Studios over money.

Hope enters the office in the famous Howard Hughes hat and makes a statement concerning "My Company". (The CIA-USA). A Federal Investigation. Howard Hughes had the same Investigation by the United States Government. Bob Hope says, "all the records have been destroyed" and is quoted as saying he is "going to Havana Cuba."

A US Senator tells Hope that he's going to get J Edgar Hoover on Hope and he wants to see his money and books. Hope says, "all the records have been destroyed". In a meeting with the Feds Hope is trying to make a deal. Hope steals back incriminating papers. He gives them back to the Government in a deal and states that "the mob may knock him off and that he's being followed."

Plainly, you can see that this is an explanation. These situations are relative to Howard Hughes. I have said that Hughes was the money behind the Mob. (Who knew)

Hope sets out to set up a United States Senator with a woman and Hope disguised as a waiter is out to get a Picture of the Senator with a girl on his lap. 1,000 flashbulbs go off. The Senator is Framed. Very funny.

Hope goes to Louisiana and enters the Mardi Gras Parade dressed as a King. There was a movie made and titled' The Man Would BE KING. Bob Hope is called a crook. He is also called "Jr". It's said that Hope must get out of the Country. Howard Hughes left the Country. Many movies by Bob Hope center around Cuba.

Hope sets out to set up the Senator again with three women in his room and all the women were working for Hope. Women Spy's.

Just like in all his movies the women are his Spies. My favorite Blonde. My favorite Brunette. Spies like us.

That's the same way the women corralled around Kennedy and set him up years later. How many frame ups were there back in the day in Politics? There's a statement that politics has "strange bedfellows ".

Hopes quoted as saying that "Hoover is breathing down my back" and that "I have an ace in the hole ". It is suggested that Hope and a woman leave the country and head off to Cuba. Same theme as The Cat and the Canary.

Hope draws a picture of himself putting features on the face with a nose. He then falls on the drawing as though he is dead. There's My Theory, a False Face of make-up and playing dead. Hopes new face is alive and Howard Hughes face is not seen and considered dead. So, the Government and the Mob are after Hope. One once him in Jail and the other wants to kill him Dead.

This is the second movie in a row where the story is about Investigations of Hollywood, the Mob and Money. Walter Winchell was Howard Hughes mouthpiece along with other newspaper columnist.

In this movie Bing and Bob and two others are in costumes. One a Pirate, One a jail Bird. One a Pilgrim and one a Confederate Soldier. A Joker shows up and Hope puts an outfit on looking like a jester. Hope pirated, as HRH the United States of American's Government. HRH was probably arrested, jailed, and let out on a deal. (over killing or over Income taxes). A pilgrim is Howards Family Heritage. Hughes from the south as a Confederate hated the North EAST! From TEXAS. Bob shows up as a Jester (Comedian).

* * * *

#21. 1942... My Favorite Blonde

Opens with a woman kissing towards Bob Hope's Nose As they are being chased by spies.

Bob is on a cruise ship, and there is a conspiracy afoot, and it's about spies trying to get a pendant that has a code in it and the time as to when the United States is to deliver American bombers to England. They are chasing a woman who is trying to get the microfilm to the United States Air Force. The spies are out to get the pendant with the information from the woman who is with Hope. As they travel from the cruise ship to the train, a woman who tells Hope she is a British spy and is on his side puts the pendant into Bob Hopes coat, and they are on the run. She runs into this stage door. She is being watched and the bad guys are following her into the Theater to talk to Hope. (Haines) Hope is on stage in a Tux. Have TUX Will TRAVEL as a spy working for the United States Government. In his act on the stage Bob is in custom with the big bony beak nose on his face and in a tuxedo, the symbol of the very rich.

Here's some quotes from Bob Hope.

"I am going to Hollywood."

"This is not my real nose."

"I'll put It back on."

"I pay cash for everything."

Well, those quotes prove My Theory. He's going to Hollywood. He's in and out of the movies all-time. It's not his real nose and he puts it on and off at times, and he pays cash for everything. That's about Howard Hughes telling his story with his Bob Hope face on.

The woman who is a British spy links up with Hope to get the Pendant out of his coat. She says she's going to LA and Bob says, "I am flying."

They are both running from the spies. Hope talks the woman into flying. Back in the states they board a train where Hope is confronted by a bunch of spies who are after the Pendant with the information. Hope didn't know that the woman pinned the Pendant into his coat. The woman tells Hope "I am a British agent". The scorpion pin must be delivered to the LA Air Force. The coded microfilm information is the schedule of when the Americans can deliver bombers to England for the war effort.

Who builds Bombers? Howard Hughes or Bob Hope. Both!!

History knows that the United States did deliver Bombers to England.

There is a scene with Bob Hope having a gun in his hand and Bob is quoted saying "if I am not out of this room in 2 min. My name is not Haines". Hope is not out of the room in 2 min. In fact, he never leaves the room. What is his name if it's not Haines? It's not Haines, it's not Hope it's Howard Hughes. He just let you know that. His real name is a name too big for a movie marquee.

The two of them must get to LA, and the killers are after them.

Bob Hope is talking about the spy game and says, "I would do it all over again". He indicates he's a spy and "he' would do It all over again". That indicates that he was a spy before 1942.

Hope winds up in a Teamsters Union Hall and he is talking to himself first, he talks to his left profile head, and then talks to his right profile head, two heads. First to his Hope head and second to his Hughes head, recall he's the writer with two heads and that two of the most famous names in America sleep together.

Hope and the girl steal a bus and then they steal a plane and as they take off the girl yells "off we go to California". They're going to 1121 Bernardino Street.

Hope and the British spy talk about co-op between the American aircraft production companies and the British.

For some reason, Hope yells "I'm innocent". And says that he has "18 labels."

Still running, Hope and the Pendent. Hope is then impersonating a doctor Higbee. Hope wrote in one of his books that "he is a doctor."

Remember, Hope, says in one of his movies "on this tray of noses which one will fool the public"? Hope says, "which one of these noses do you think will fool the public" and goes on to say that "he is the best impersonator of people in the world". and puts a nose right on his face and says "and I do my best impersonation right in front of the people, and they don't get it ".

The Greatest Show on Earth

Hope escapes again and hops a freight train with the Pendent and the woman spy. Hope mentions plumbers several times as they get into LA by noon. Riverside California. They steal a truck and go to 1121 Bernardino Street, which is a funeral home. Hope and the woman are to pass off the pin to the United States Air Force. The spies are there waiting for them. They are out to kill the girl. A big fight ensues. Hope starts to fake his own death and hides in a casket. It's loaded onto a Hirsch and he escapes again, and they are shooting at him. Don't shoot its only Me. They get to the Air Force and Hope needed medical attention.

The movie ends with the Americans and the British giving Hope a declaration for winning World War II and delivering 33 Bombers to England from Lockheed. It was Hughes who won World War II. it was Hughes who builds the aircraft. It was Hughes who delivered the Bombers to England.

This movie was made in 41 or 42. Bombers were delivered to England in 1940 and 41. The war was on Since 1938.

Well I guess you can see My Theory in this movie.

* * * *

#22. 1942.. Road to Morocco

This movie starts out with the Japanese blowing up a ship that Bob and Bing are on. Ship wrecked and found floating on a raft in the ocean, they find an Island. On the island there is an Arab raid.

In the dialog Bing calls Bob Orville. As in Orville Wright. Fitting title for Howard, not Bob Hope that is, unless Bob Hope is Howard Hughes and has a lot to do with the incredible flying machine Invented by Orville Wright and improved by Howard Hughes. That's why Bing calls Hope Orville.

Bing sells Bob away and Hope shows up in a disguise as Aunt Lucy. Bing and Bob both in on the scheme from the beginning.

Again, Hope is dressed as Royalty with a harem of women and pampered. Hope refers to his rear end as landing gear. again, references to airplanes and sex.

Bing calls Bob Hope, Jr. and Orville many times in this movie.

The movie has it that it's a custom in Morocco that the first husband is to die, and the second husband is to have happiness. Hope is the first husband and the movie shows a tombstone. The tombstone has no date on it. Bob is thinking about dying and that he would have Royal undertakers.

The undertakers go to Hope First, because the coffin was too small. The undertakers must measure Hope while he is still alive so that he will fit in the casket. They say to Hope" we will make you look better than you do now". They measure 5'11". And the birth dates an open question. Dialog says to Hope "you're going to your own funeral.

Hope is kidnapped and dropped in the "desert". and at a gas station at that. There's a mirage and Hope, says "now you see it, now you don't". Sounds like a disappearing act to me. Caught by the Mob. The dialog reads "give them back their ears". Hope yells, Powder my Nose.

* * * *

#23. 1942... Star Spangled Rhythm

This movie presents an all-star cast of Hollywood stars and the Paramount girls about the canteen shows. There is a strange opening showing Bob Hope or Howard Hughes's baby pictures and teenage pictures plus pics of his family.

In the dialog of this movie It is said that the Canteen shows are given by the head of Paramount Studios and there is a call to Bob Hope as the head of Paramount Studios to MC the shows.

Howard Hughes is the head of Paramount, but Bob gets the call. Right there It is shown that they are one and the same. Hope is saying that he Is the head of Paramount's studios. In one scene there is talk of a twin, like two people being the same person, like a double. Like the Lone Ranger had a Twin Brother. (2) One dead and one alive.

Hope is being asked to do the shows as the head of Paramount. Hope says" can't do show". Asked why he can't do the shows he says, "it's too far down the road and I have no rubber". He means he doesn't have enough make-up of Sponge Rubber to do the show.

During World War II, rubber was in short supply and rationed.

We must recall that Bob Hope wrote in one of his books that "people think I got this Nose by accident, but I really got it from the Goodyear family". Right, it's a fake Nose made out of Rubber. Bob Hope says "I wish I was dead."

Hope goes over the schedule for the show and says. "I have no rubber" To be ready for the show. He doesn't have enough make-up.

There is an actor titled DeSoto playing a role as the head of the studio's and he looks like Hughes. He has the Hughes profile. Then there is a picture of Cecil DeMille and Frank Sturgis in the film production room. Recall Howard Hughes and Bob Hope Both said they spent much of their time in the production room.

Hope goes on to do the shows. Is Hope "the boss" of paramount? He is if he is Howard Hughes!

Then there is a scene of Bob Hope in his bathtub using toy battleships and aircraft carriers, frigates and the whole works and he is playing war. Why? Because as Howard Hughes, the Billionaire Industrialist Manufactured and Built the entire United States Navy and its Armaments and he is showing It to you.

At that Bob Hope is quoted as saying "I have the whole works "as he angles for a profile shot of his nose.

At the end there is a Patriotic ending. Bing Crosby closes the film singing a Patriotic Song as Mount Rushmore is shown of the Presidents, all with super large Noses. I think Howard Hughes, even as Bob Hope believes he should be President of the United States because he is running the entire show anyway and was winning WW 2.

Recall there was a skit in a Bob Hope show, and it was talked about on the Tonight Show with Johnny Carson publicly that Bob Hope should run for President. unfortunately, his lie about being born in England has him disqualified. See any evidence here to support My Theory. They showed you in this movie that Bob Hope is two persons. One: Howard Hughes, owner of Paramount and two; Bob Hope, actor and MC of the canteen shows. Both Bob Hope and Bing Crosby have been in on the joke since the beginning. The names of the innocent have been changed to protect the joke.

Hope you noticed that the same theme runs through every movie made by Bob Hope. Connections to the Government. Connections to the Military and indications that he Is leading a double life. An alleged life. The owner of Paramount Studios in his own movies as a character actor disguised as Bob Hope.

* * * *

#24 1943… They Got Me Covered

They have him covered All right. They got me covered as a movie is the same title of Bob Hope's first book in 1941. It is in that book written by Bob Hope that reveals through Bing Crosby that Bob Hope is living an "Alleged life."

The question is who has Bob Hope covered. Hope tells you in his fourth book, Have Tux Will Travel that he works "on call" for the United States Government. That when the Government calls He goes.

Bing Crosby in his preface to Bob Hope's book, They got me Covered states that Bing saw this "New Face" on Hope, and that he, Bing Crosby knew who the owner of that face was.

So, who has Bob Hope "Covered"? The United States Government or the make-up department of the movie studios or all the above.

Bob Hope admits and tells you in his writings that the Government paid for everything and that the United States Air Force flew him everywhere. Check out Bob Hope's first movies and there about the Navy, moving on, It's about the Army, later it's about the Air Force. Further, it's about spies and women as spies. So, who do you think he is?? Don't forget about the Putty, the Sponge Rubber and the Stucco, False Face, Chin and Fake Ears with Fat Clothes and Disguises with False Ids.

Remember Hope said he works for the Central intelligence Agency, the State Department and the Pentagon. They got him covered alright and in Bob Hope's movies It's "Nothing but the Truth". This Movie in its dialog tells you more. Recall, these Movies are written and made by Bob Hope in his own words.

"The names of the innocent have been changed to protect the joke" Bob Hope said that. He also said and believes and knows that "you can fool all the people all the time".!!!

Howard Hughes was Bob Hope in make-up! That's My Theory and I am sticking to it. I am proving it to you.

This movie reveals much by Bob Hope of False Ids, working for the Government as an "Imposter" with Two Heads, and as a Spy with connections to the FBI, the CIA, the Presidents and wearing Disguises. Howard Hughes and/ or Bob Hope were spies for the United States!!!

The Movie starts out filming in Times Square of the Newsreel that Germany has attacked Russia. Bob Hope's part is that he is a News Correspondent. Hope comes in with a Costumes with make-up and states "no one will recognize me". That "he won't recognize himself". No one will recognize him". Good job of make-up. Bob Hope is quoted saying "I hope those Newsmen don't know who I am". Here, Hope is playing a role as a Fake Newspaperman. Sounds like Superman again.

So, a spy shows up and starts swapping spy stories, and that there's a spy ring in DC and they're using codes to communicate. Hopes girlfriend says that "Hope gets tipped off on all major world events", and tips are coming from inside the FBI. Hope is sent to Washington DC.

Hope is quoted as saying "I am an Imposter" and that "I am a rubber less heel". He also goes on to say to "sell my body to a medical school". Any connection there to Hughes. Remember, Hope said he was a Doctor. Recall, Hope said he wanted to build Medical Centers for Eisenhower. Howard Hughes had a Medical Foundation. Hope and Hughes always have so much in common.

The Government receives a memo about Hope that he is "insane and dangerous". I believe that's because Howard Hughes, the Billionaire Industrialist and all his Money and his Connection to the Mob and Murder Inc and his operations as a spy and the things that he has done, make him "insane and dangerous ".

Hope goes to a mystic and the crystal ball reader tells Hope that he has two heads. When asked his name, Bob Hope couldn't come up with his name. Probably because he has a real name, which he does not want to reveal. Terry Moore said that "Howard never wanted anybody to know his real name."

Hope says twice that" he knew all spy movements world-wide and that others are out to kill him". Hope smokes a pot cigarette and acts high. He reveals that a spy backstage at a vaudeville show knifes a woman in the chest and kills her. Hope is hiding, and the spies are chasing him. The Marines come to the rescue with the Navy and the spies are caught.

Nothing but the truth. Spies like us. These movies I believe represent the truth of the adventures of Howard Hughes and Bob Hope working undercover in disguises as spies. Well, there it is again, nothing but the truth.

* * * *

#25 1943... Let's face it

Here again, this movie starts out with Bob Hope in the Army and his girlfriend is kissing Bob Hope right on his Nose. Hope says, "I am not the man I was". Right, he was Howard Hughes and in make-up is Bob Hope. Simple, right?

The movie has it with three guys and three girls in a house out in the Hamptons on Long Island. A voice rings out and someone says, "where is the invisible Yardbird". and Hope yells "I am a Military Secret". He said that in the last movie. Howard Hughes unseen for years is invisible. He is a Military Secret. He is the United States. Howard Hughes as Bob Hope is a Military Secret, and he tells you so.

All the Bob Hope movies show and represent the life of Howard Hughes through his alleged life of Bob Hope. Behind the scenes Howard Hughes as Bob Hope was an industrial spy. Recall that Bob Hope was asked by the Air Force and the United States Government to get information about a new Russian jet. How could Bob Hope get the Info on a Russian jet? If he was Howard Hughes in the Aircraft industry he could as a spy get that technical information.

It's been said that Hope was on special duty, special assignment for the United States. He has told you his books and in his movies that he was a special agent with Central intelligence through the Pentagon. Real army films are shown in this film. These movies are all about Howard Hughes's adventures and experiences. Recall the Hollywood movie industry made many of the training films for the United States military.

* * * *

#26 1944... The Princess and the Pirate

Right off the bat Bob Hope plays the role of a Pirate called Hook and announces that he "is the man of seven faces". Seven faces. Is Bob Hope trying to tell us something? Something like he is seven, double 07'. Sounds like mission impossible to me.

I pulled out the following quotes right out of Bob Hope's mouth. Remember Hope is one of the writers. The writer with two heads. Bob Hope has said that the 3,000 movie script writers work for him and that they write stories about him. About him Bob or him Howard. Howard Hughes owns Paramount. But the 3,000 writers work for Bob Hope? They do if he's Howard Hughes. I say it's Howard Hughes talking with the Bob Hope face.

Here's the quotes.

"I am dead."

"Wait until I take off this putty nose."

"It Fool's everybody ".

"I already have seven faces."

"My act is well-known all over Europe."

"I have been all over the world."

"You are the girl. I need a girl. A girl to hold my tray of my many faces."

"I am part Indian."

"I have a girl for every face."

Now isn't that special. So, he has seven false faces. And he has trays of faces and trays of noses. His act is known all over Europe. He won World War II. He's known all around the world. Right. He flew around the world and set the record. Bob Hope has said he's a pilot.

So, Hope says he's dead and takes off his putty nose and says It fools everyone. His act is known world- wide, has been all over the world, that he Is part Indian, and he needs a girl to hold his tray of faces and noses and that he has a girl for every face. Now what do you think about that?

So, Hope is part Indian? Where from England? that kills that lie. He's doing great impersonations all over the world and has been all over the world. Has a tray of faces and is fooling everyone. Hope disagrees with Lincoln that you can't fool all the people all the time. He just said it fools Everybody all the time. You can fool the people all the time, he's done it since the 1930s. He is the greatest show on earth. And he, Bob Hope is Howard Hughes!

My Theory is true, and I am saying everything that he has just said. He's Howard Hughes and he is a character actor as Bob Hope with fake faces on with make-up and special effects and he tells you he wears a putty nose. In this movie Hope says he wears a putty nose and a fake face all before 1944.

The girl says to Hope "this act of yours. I want to see the other six faces". As Hope puts on a fake nose in the dressing room before show.

Bob Hope asked the girl "which one of this tray of noses would best fool people"? she chooses one of the noses and says to him "if

I didn't know who you were, I wouldn't know who you are" Does that tell you anything? She knows he's Howard Hughes, and she knows he's Bob Hope. she knows it's Howard Hughes and that he is in makeup as Bob Hope. I also want to know who the other six faces are.

And actor yells "enough of this masquerade". Nothing but the truth. Yes, the joke. The magnificent fraud, Bob Hope. Bob Hope removes his makeup.

Bob Hope plays many parts in this movie with many disguises. One, as an old gypsy hag, one as a nobleman, and one as a captain. There is more. The following are more quotes right out of Bob Hope mouth. Recall it's Howard Hughes talking!

"if you know too much you'd be dead" and "this bird shall die". At this time Bob Hope does an alligator love mating call Growl. That alligator mating call growl was taught to Howard by Terry Moore, his legal wife, not Bob Hope.

Hope is quoted as saying" there is no limit to what I can do". Bob Hope holds his nose and says : "fools everybody."

As the movie continues, Hope, and the girl get an acting job on stage in a tavern. A rowdy bar crowd. Hope says he does, "impersonations" then on stage Hope, with his noses right in front of the audience puts a big nose on his face and says, "I do this right in front of the audience and they don't get it". Puts on a big fake sponge rubber nose that he "got from the Goodyear family."

The girl grabs Bob's nose and says, "if they catch you, they will rip off your fat clothes, cut off your eyes, your ears and your nose". And Bob responds that "they will streamline me". Right, Howard Hughes is the thin man and Bob Hope is the fat clothes man. He then says: "you should see the other side of me."

There is the actor, the writer with two heads, living two lives.

The dialog continues. Hope is playing the parts of two captains simultaneously as Hook and as Hope and Hope says, "I guess it's me". Someone yells "your face". And Bob Hope retorts "never mind about the face the face is a joke". What did I tell you! What has he told you? Bob Hope said, "the names of the innocent have been changed to protect the joke". Need I say more?

The movie continues with talks of "murder", and that there is "a permit to kill" and "dispose of the dead". I believe Hughes and Hope both were behind the Mob via Murder Inc. Hope goes on to say that he "needs bodies for medical research for a medical school". You know, like the Howard Hughes Medical Foundation or Hopes Eisenhower Medical Hospitals. Recall the Mansion in Cuba, in the mine under it had a bunch of caskets in it.

Here is what is funny at the end of the movie. There is a disclaimer that this movie has no reference to people alive or dead. Well, I think this movie said it all again. In every movie by Bob Hope it's nothing but the truth and this movie the princess and the pirate says it all.......

* * * *

#27. 1946.. Road to Utopia

This Movie opens with Robert Benchley and a narrative of how not to make a movie out of the studios from the front office. A movie is made out of the front office.

Hope is Chester, "crazy" Hooten. Bing Crosby is Duke Johnson.

Bob and Bing are in disguises with make-up and Mustaches. The camera work shows long tipped noses on both. Hope is changing his clothes and taking off his disguise and says, "should I remove myself."

The opening scene has a gray-haired older woman as the wife of Bob Hope. The lady yells at her husband to "get up and put down that Wall Street journal and stop dealing in the stock market."

Hope is disguised as an older man with gray hair and fat clothes. The wife yells at him again "go to bed, get your ears washed and put your teeth away". And Hope yells back "stop leading me around by my nose". Bob has a flashback of his life with Bing.

In the flashback Bob and Bing are going to Alaska to claim a gold mine and they possess a Map in which to find it. Two creepy thugs steal the map to the gold mine and a girl is also trying to get the map back from the creeps who stole it.

Hope and Crosby wind up getting the map back from the creeps. These scenes may be an account of a real occurrence.

The same theme about a Map of where the gold mines are is shown again in the Movie Paleface and Son of Paleface where people are after a Map. I believe these movies are about Hope as Howard Hughes receiving a Great Inheritance.

Running from the Thugs Bob and Bing take off for Alaska. Every bodies after the creeps. The girl and the police.

Again, the movie dialog turns to Murder. Hope says, "anybody says anything we'll plug them". Bob mentions his chin two times. Bob says he "kills 50 people a day."

This is the third movie about Bob and Bing having mines, gold and diamond mines perhaps around the World. Bob was studying the Stock Market and reading the Wall Street journal. Mexican silver, South African diamonds and Alaska gold. I would think that the Billionaire Industrialist would be Involved with Mining.

Just another note: just about every episode of the Lone Ranger, The Masked Man is about land, raw materials and part of the dialog concerns water, iron ore, uranium and oil in the South West.

Bob Hope yells" I am a navigator."

The girl asked Bob "how many people did you kill today."

Of course, Bob and Bing are still womanizing". Bob refers to sex as pool. Bob's dialog is about women and that he gives them Jewels, Money, Cars, and even Homes. Howard Hughes did just that.

Movie continues where Bing infers that Hope owns a "Gold Map" and that "there is a Map to your Father's Mine". That's the Map that Howard Hughes Inherited from his Father.

There are other Bob Hope movies with the same theme for a Map. There is another movie in which a Map to a great Treasure is tattooed to Walter Brennan's chest.

Bob and Bing Sing and Dance and are having a good time because they know that with Bob and Howard's Inheritance that they are Super Rich beyond belief!!. They continue to wear their Disguises with talk of being Ghosts.

Hope disappears and remarks "if I was there I wouldn't be here". What's that tell you? Yeah, then yells "we got billions". Bing

Sings a Song about Bob Hope being born with a Silver Spoon in his Mouth. Remember Howard Hughes was born with a Silver Spoon in his mouth and Billions of Dollars in his kick. Not to mention the Oil and Mines and owning Texas and buying up California and in possession of the Hughes Tool Company's Drill Bit.

Bob Hope says "I am loaded. I own it. The biggest gold mine."

Follow this next piece of dialog between Bob and Bing with the reminder that Bob and Bing have been together since the beginning.

Bing says to Bob "you and your Nose could make a lot". Bob Hope says "my ears fell off years ago". Did Howard Hughes lose his ears in his jet plane crashes? Hope is called "shifty chin."

Here's some more Dialog. Bob Hope says, "am I dead?" Bing retorts "I can't tell you always look that way."

Dialog continues about Bob and Bing. "Rumor has it they are not who they say they are". Bob says, "I am a real Casa Blanca". Casa Blanca means White House. It is noted that Bob Hope lived in the White House for hundreds of nights. He was also with Ike at the Invasion of North Africa in Casa Blanca.

I would say that having everything in the world is certainly on the way to Utopia.

Hopefully you will watch Hope's Movies and read along with My Theory. Will you believe your eyes and ears? Will you still continue to laugh out loud when I tell you that Howard Hughes is and was Bob Hope in makeup?

You have to know very much about Howard Hughes's life. You will see it represented in every movie and on many of Hopes Movies and TV shows. Everything out of Hollywood was about him, Howard Hughes, for over decades.

Please note that this movie was made in 1946. Bob Hope per se did not Inherit Billions, but Howard Hughes did, and he thanked his Memory, writing, movies about himself.

Howard Hughes was born 1905. At 21 years of age or so He inherited the whole works. This movie is 25 years later. Thanks for the memory.

Note : watch Hope movies. Especially Paleface and Son of Paleface. You'll see what I mean. You will be convinced. You won't laugh. He who laughs last laughs the best. I will be laughing last and I will laugh the best.

* * * *

#28. 1946... Monsieur Beaucaire

This Movie opens in the 1800s with Spain and France at war with a film of a 20th century firefight. The dialog is flashing back to World War I. Hells Angels. There is a group in France looking to find for France "the proper man" "to pull off a spy mission and change his identity". There it Is, the right man to pull off a spy mission and change his identity. And the Woman in the movie says to Hope "they chose you to Impersonate someone else". At that the Group Sings a Song and they are Singing Blow them out of the Trenches. I think History has it that Howard Hughes Sr. and Mr. Dynamite DuPont laid Pipelines underneath the German trenches and put TNT under those trenches and blew the Germans out of the trenches.

Howard Hughes himself had been quoted as saying that "his Father won World War I with his Equipment and he (HRH) won World War II and was working in Vietnam. Check it out. Look it up. Google it. Who was the United States?

In Terry Moore's book The Beauty and the Billionaire She writes and tells you in her own words that she was a Spy for Howard Hughes and that she was working as a Spy out of a Makeup Room in France and she wore many Disguises in Europe and the Middle East. Read that book. Prove it to yourself.

Howard Hughes was the Spy as Bob Hope. The Greatest Impersonator in the whole wide World. The Greatest Show on Earth. Bob Hope in the Movie the Princes and the Pirate admits he is the best Impersonator of people in the whole wide world. Hope acts very powerful as a Billionaire would and says, "anybody can be King". Recall there was a double 007 Movie with Sean Connery, titled The Man who would be King.

Back to Womanizing and with Nothing but the Truth. There is Intrigue over the Princes of Spain. That would be AVA Gardner.

In real life Ava Gardner was Bob Hope's girlfriend. Ava Gardner was from Spain. She was also the Star of the Movie the Barefoot Contessa with Humphrey Bogart. The intrigue in the movie in Spain is with Bob Hope.

Divorce is mentioned in the dialog, and it Is a fact that Howard Hughes would go after divorcees i.e. Ava Gardner was divorced by Mickey Rooney and Howard Hughes made it with her as soon as she was divorced from Rooney. Being such a Lover an Actor calls Bob Hope "a peacock". The Peacock is the symbol of NBC. Bob is womanizing with all the woman at the studio. All kinds of young girls are around. Wasn't that Howard Hughes's mo.. At that all the women referred to Bob Hope as King. Bob has a line of women and has a date every two hours. Hope was quoted prior as having a girl for every face. Read the secret life of Bob Hope by Arthur Marx and read the secret life of Howard Hughes by Higham. Those books are must reads.

Both Hughes and Hope have the same mo., and both led the same life style. Everything Howard Hughes wanted to be Bob Hope became. Rich, Movie maker, Golfer, Pilot. Womanizer.

Hope is considered King and says he was born in England. He or Howard Hughes may have had Royal Blood and Skeletons in his Family Closet. Was he born in England to his own American family? His father was of the superrich. The high hats, the Swells of Society. Hope says he came over to America as a four-year-old. That whole story could be false. They Got him Covered. Howard Hughes and Bob Hope were Spies with false IDs and a new Identity. The new identity was Bob Hope. Bob Hope says, "the Kings eyes are everywhere". Hope yells "I am a Duke". In Hollywood Howard Hughes had spies following all his Women, and many others. Hope Impersonates a Duke.

Hope writes in one of his books that he traveled to England and being waited on by a butler. Hope says to the butler "I was born in England you know". And the butler says to Hope "I'll keep your secret". Doesn't that indicate that it may be a lie.

The dialog continues and Hope is told "why you need to kill yourself". He is being questioned "are you still alive". Bob Hope says" I would love to take a powder" to disappear and hide for a while. Isn't that true about Howard Hughes hiding out for years. Bob Hope himself was out of sight and away from home for 12 straight years.

There's another big scene where Bob Hope tells you all about the Disguise as Howard Hughes that he wears. Hope goes into his dressing room and goes over to a Bureau to a Bunch of Masks. Hope points out all the Masks and says, "I have a Mask for day and a Mask for night and one for sleeping" "I am working on death". Hope says he's working on trying to disappear. Howard Hughes did disappear. Now here we have Fake Faces and Masks and False Ids. Looks like My Theory is true. In his own words, in his own books, in his own movies and in his own TV shows he tells you nothing but the truth and no one got it. How many movies out of Hollywood was about spies like us, people wearing Masks, such as Superman, Batman, and many more. There was a Joker in the Batman movies. In dialog Hope is called an "imposter". Bob Hope the Magnificent Fraud. The Ghost. The Walking Dead. Right in front of everyone and it fools everyone.

Here's a funny scene where Hope again calls attention to his Phony Nose by getting his nose caught in a harp. In another scene Hope is sitting at a table with a cake in front of them. Sponge Cake and he puts his face in it. Cake is make-up. That's right, his whole Face is make- up. A Fake Face of his "Alleged Life". Sponge Rubber from the Goodyear Family.

Here's an interesting scene at the end of the Movie. The Spies, Bob Hope and the Princess show up in the American Colonies like a Family. And there's a Baby in a Carriage and it's Bob Hope's Face on the Baby and the Baby is said to have been born on the way over.

"Look what came over on the way."

Howard Hughes traces his Family Heritage back to the founding of the Colonies. Indicating that he hooks up with America and the Government of the United States. His family was very, very Rich. Industrial Rich. He indicated he went west by the Conestoga wagon and as a Texan from the South he does not like the Northeast.

* * * *

#29. 1947... My favorite Brunette

Bob Hope plays the part of a Photographer and is mistaken for a Private Investigator and is hired by a beautiful Woman to find her missing Uncle. The Man from Uncle? The Woman has a Map as to where there is a great find of Uranium.

Dialog says, "keep your nose clean". Hope is playing a Detective and is called by many names. Hope invents a new Photo Camera. Howard had a lot to do with Camera's. Recall: Hope said, "he was an Inventor". Howard Hughes was an Inventor. Howard Hughes was all about Photography and Film. There was also a Television Show titled The Man with a Camera. Howard's Photography and Camera work went big with Spy Planes and Satellites.

In this movie the Mob is out to kill Bob Hope. Sound familiar. Mob out to kill Howard Hughes. The Government of the United States is also out to find Howard Hughes.

In this dialog Hope has a date with Hoover. Quote: "I talk to J Edgar Hoover and he doesn't make a move without me". Interesting, Howard Hughes was in with both the Mob and the FBI. Sounds like a lot of things a Billionaire Industrialist would be involved In. The Government, Spies, Raw Materials and Uranium.

On a Plane Hope is wearing a Disguise and dialog says, "we will punch you in your nose and then it will look like everyone else's". Right, it'll knock the fake nose off and it will look like everyone else's nose". There they said it again that the Nose on Hope is Fake. Bob Hope that Magnificent Fraud.

Now, about the map. It's about Mineral Rights and where Uranium Is located. Uranium is sought by the Government as well as every Spy in the LA area. This movie was made in 1947, two years after the United States dropped the A-Bomb on the Japanese. The State Department, the FBI, the Geologist Spies, Maps, Codes, and even Murder is involved in this Movie and it's an International incident, and Hope is playing a double agent. Nothing but the Truth. Hope wares a Disguise and poses as a Bellhop, a Pilgrim, and a Stool Pigeon. I think it's saying he worked both sides. Read Have Tux Will Travel. A Double Agent.(a mole)

Bob writes that he works for the US Government and is ready to go as soon as he is called. He jumps to the tune of the Government, Hope says "they didn't recognize me". Dialog yells "he's alive."

Take note that many years later J Edgar Hoover, long time head of the FB I testified to Congress that "there is no such thing as the Mafia". He probably had to testify that way because he may have been being blackmailed that he was a homosexual caught by a photo of him cross-dressing or in the act of sex.

* * * *

#30. 1947.. Variety girl

The variety Club consist of Theater and Movie Industry Entertainers, and issues a Newspaper with Show Business News, Critiques and information to the Show Business World.

In this movie. The Variety Club finds a Baby lost and left in the Theater. The show Is titled "wings."

The Baby is to be taken care of by the head of Paramount Studios, and he will support the child through Show Business. The Cast of the Show go to an Employee of Paramount, who in this Movie is pretending to be the head Paramount studio. This individual is not the Head of Paramount he is pretending to be. With slick camera work there is a switch. A crowd is at Paramount Studios talking to the fake head of the studio. We all know who the real Owner and Head of Paramount was. They are all talking about caring for the Child and the Camera veers in on Bob Hope in the back of the room, sitting on a Desk alone watching this entire scene. There's Bob, then you know he Is the head of Paramount. Bob Hope is Howard Hughes, Howard Hughes is Bob Hope with makeup.

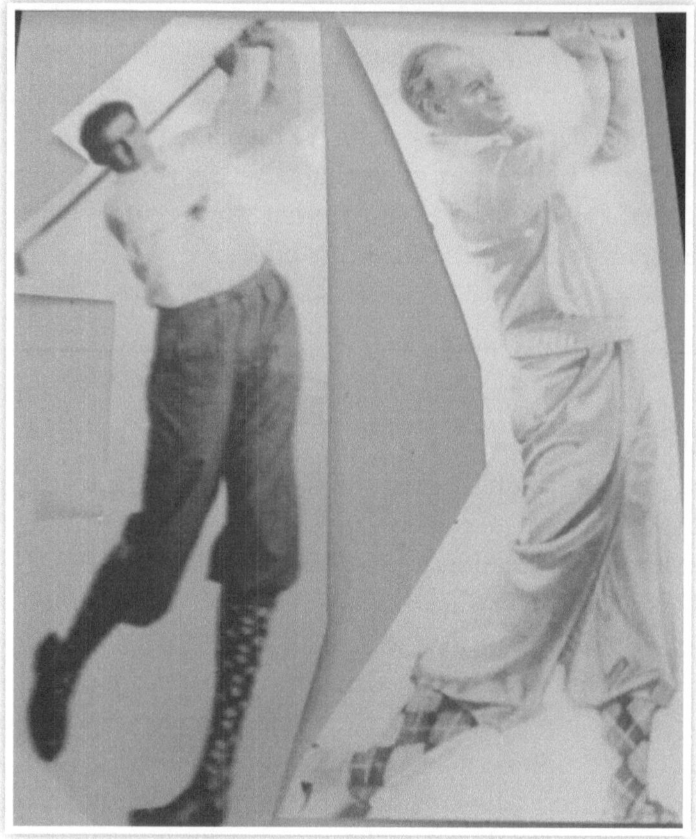

Hughes 1930's Hope 1980's

Bing Crosby is on the scene, and he cracks on Hopes "beak". He also says, "we need new Faces around here". Bob Hope says to Bing "age has you stuffing up your face". That is putting on more makeup. Recall the preface that Bing wrote for Bob's first book, they got me Covered. Bing wrote that he first saw the Face on Bob and that he "knows the owner of the face". Right Bing knows Howard Hughes and Bing knows about Putty, Sponge Rubber, False Chins, False Ears, False Teeth, Caps, Eyelashes, Mascara, Makeup, Fat Clothes, make- up and special effects.

There are two Time/Life info DVD's that Bing and Jack Benny are in. Both have Jack Benny and Bing Crosby putting make-up on Bob Hope. Bob Hope says to both "hurry up" and both say back to Bob "I never worked with stucco before". What's that tell you? Doesn't that say that Bob Hope has a totally Manufactured Face.

Through my research Howard Hughes has said that there were four things that he wanted to be. (1) the best aviator, (2) the best movie maker, (3) the best golfer, (4) the richest man in the world. Howard Hughes said that. And then there's Bob Hope. (1) Aviator, (2) movie maker, (3) golfer, and (4) very rich. They are both one and the same person pulling a Joke on the people and fooling them all the time.

This Movie is a Variety Show of Talent. Bob Hope is the MC with Stars galore. The Movie shows Camera work and Sound Techniques. The Show had a large cast and the movie indicates that Bob Hope is the Talent Scout for Paramount named Bob. Along with the Camera work Bob Hope talks of make-up, profiles, sponge cake, large ears, noses and an actor off screen sneezes and yells" Bob Hope."

Recall Howard Hughes at 17, learned to perfect Moviemaking and made four (4) movies before he was 22.

Recall many TV shows, love that Bob, The Millionaire, I led Three Lives, The Man with a Camera, Maverick, the Thin Man, etc.

There's more evidence that Bob Hope is all make-up and has been a Character Actor since the 20s and that he works with the Mob. The FBI, the Movie Industry, the CIA, State Department, the Pentagon, the Air Force, NASA and the Presidents of the United States. You tell me who you think it Is?

* * * *

#31. 1947... Where there's life

The movie opens in a town in Europe named Barovia. This country is the "first country in Europe to vote in Democracy. The King is giving a speech to a large crowd with a sign saying, "Long live the King". At that saying a group of creeps assassinate the King. The King had revealed that in 1915 he married in New York City and had a male child, a boy and aire to be the King.

There's that's Sean Connery movie theme again, The Man who would be King. That would be Howard Hughes if he could be King He would be King.

The creeps that killed the king are out to kill the aire. Right, the aire is Hope and he Is made King. The creeps are still out to kill him. Sounds like the position Howard Hughes was in. Everybody was out to get him. The aire of the Great Hughes Inheritance.

Hope deeper into this movie is acting as a Radio Host. Acting as a radio host? Hope was a Radio Host!. He speaks of a make-believe audience. (Canned laughter) the make- believe joke. What a life. Bob says he's "a hermit". You know, like a recluse, like Howard Hughes. He then says" he is his own sponsor and that no one listens". My point is that all Bob Hope shows on TV and radio were sponsored by all the 18 labels that Howard Hughes owned. He sponsored himself as Bob Hope.

That's right. No body listened. I listened and I got it and I figured it all out. In his own words, in all his own Books and Movies and TV shows. He tells you who he is and how he lives two lives and shows it to you in skits in his movies and his shows.

In this movie Bob Hope tells you "too many people are after me". Right like the Government, like the Mob, like the Spies. In dialog Bob Hope is called" the turned- up nose guy ". The turned-up nose Is makeup by Jack Dawn and Wally Westwood from the make-up Departments of the Hollywood Studios.

Dialog says, "who are you"? "he's insane" "he's crazy". And Bob Hope ask, "who am I?" Hope ask, who am I? Can you answer it now? Who is he??

On a NBC TV Bob Hope Special Show Bob explains that NBC is to be bought by Westinghouse. As Bob is on stage an Executive from Westinghouse walks on stage and up to Bob, looks at him very circumspectly and says, "who are you'? The Audience laughs at the Executive because they all know that it's Bob Hope. The Westinghouse Executive out to buy NBC doesn't know that that's Bob Hope who has been on NBC for 60 years. Or is the Executive indicating that he may be someone else??

Right. Who is he? is he Bob Hope or is he Howard Hughes? I know who he is! I know who he was! and he shows you over and over and over again and again that he Is not necessarily Bob Hope.

In the movie Bob Hope starts Gambling in a Casino at a poker game. Bob Hope says that "he knows money". Hope says, "I have money I was born with the stuff". There you go! Howard Hughes was born with the stuff not Bob Hope. Sounds like Howard Hughes to me. Born with the stuff. The Billionaire. He goes on to say, "I am crazy twice". Twice? two heads! The writer, The Moviemaker, The Movie Star, The Oil Tycoon, The Billionaire Industrialist! Two of the most famous names In America asleep together. He needs two Hats. He needs two pairs of pants. Do you recall reading that?

Dialog says, "who would need two hats"? Hope talks about "playing dead" and "to kill himself off."

Hope turns the Cops after the Spies. He puts the FBI on the spies. Recall Bob Hope said, "J Edgar Hoover doesn't make a move without me". The Mob invaded Hollywood in the 1930s. Review the movies Paleface and Son of Paleface Movies.

In fact, every Bob Hope Movie has the same theme.

Hope had previously said that "all 3,000 Hollywood Writers work for him and that they write many stories about him. Right, they write many Movie Scripts about Howard Hughes, owner of all Hollywood studios. Many Movies and TV Shows are all about the adventures and experiences and situations of Howard Hughes.

* * * *

#32. 1947… Road to Rio

This Movie begins with the Map of the West of the United States, especially the Southwest Territories of Oklahoma, Texas, New Mexico, Arizona and California.

The Southwest Territory, the land of the Lone Ranger. The Masked Man the Beverly Hillbilly. And then there's the Man in the Movie, The Barefoot Contessa, who owns Texas and is buying up California. That Man has been identified as Howard Hughes, the owner of Paramount Studios and the Maker of many Movies, not to mention being a Billionaire Industrialist.

The movie has Bob Hope and Bing Crosby doing shows and traveling throughout the Southwest. "Using fake names" and Bob and Bing have make-up on of big ears and noses.

Here's the plot: A Monster Gangster is to marry Dorothy Lamoure only for her Money. Bob and Bing are out to foil her Wedding so she doesn't get swindled.

Dialog has it : Bing calls Bob "hot lips". Bob and Bing shared a lot of Women in Hollywood. Bob and Bing together do a Song and Dance routine to the tune of Thanks for the Memory.

Bob and Bing still on the show circuit get a job in a Carnival. In one scene Bob shows up as a Trapeze Artist in a Costume of Big Fat Clothes. Bing pinches the Legs of Hopes Fat Clothes that Bob has on to make him look Fat and labels them "falsies". Bob falls off the high wire and falls on his Nose. A Fire breaks out at the Carnival and the entire Tent burns down and Bob and Bing get away.

Bob and Bing sneak onto a Cruise Ship en route to Rio. There is a Barbershop scene where Bob Hope is cutting off his actors make -up. Bing calls Bob "dish face" and "Don Juan". Dish Face is a make-up term. Don Juan is a term indicating a womanizer, a lover.

55 minutes into the Movie Mobsters and the Authorities are chasing after Bob and Bing. At the foot of the gang plank You can see the Captain of the Cruise Ship telling the Police what they look like. To ID Bob Hope the Captain starts to ID them in words and gestures, and as the Cruise Ships Horn blows and you can see the Captain flapping his Nose back and forth and flapping his Ears back and forth.

Indicating again that it's make-up and they are in Disguises.

There's a cartoon in Bob Hope's first Book where Bob is chasing his Ears that are flying in the wind.

In Rio Bob and Bing get hired in a Mexican Band in a Nightclub. Bob is shot at by the Mobsters. (really) Don't Shot its only Me.

There's more about false Ears. Bing calls Bob" lobster ears". Bob Hope says, "his business is all ears". (Spy) Bob then does the

Alligator Mating Love Call that Terry Moore taught only to Howard Hughes. Hope is Howard Hughes! There's another Proof. I saw Bing Crosby in a Time/ Life DVD on TV selling Bob Hope DVDs, singing, Thanks for the Memory and thanks for our "marker Ca Ears" As he points to his Ears. Also, in the DVD clips by Time/ Life I have seen Crosby and I have seen Jack Benny in two different scenes, both putting Make-up on Bob Hope and again Hope says, "Hurry up". and both Bing and Benny say, "I never worked with Stucco before". There it Is! Bob Hope has Stucco on his Face as Make-up. See it for yourself. Watch Time/ Life Commercials. The Golden Age of Television and Bob Hope.

Another scene in the Movie has Bing and Bob set up in a gunfight after being hypnotized. Hope is shot and "presumed dead". "Gone". Hope moves and Bing says, "hot lips you're alive."

The Wedding between Lamour and the Mobster is to occur in the PM. Bob and Bing commandeer a Plane to escape and Bob Hope says, "does this happen in real life"? Dialog says, "do you believe in ghosts"? Bing says "The World must never know ".

Howard Hughes has a history of Womanizing and Marriages. Ms. Rice, Terry Moore and potentially others that no one knows about.

Bob Hope does the Alligator Love Matting Call on Film and in his Movies and his TV Shows. That's one more proof that Bob Hope is Howard Hughes. Terry Moore taught only Howard Hughes the Alligator Love Mating Call not Bob Hope. If Bob Hope is Howard Hughes she taught them both at the same time.

And there is always the call that Bob is dead. Howard Hughes faked his own death because he was Bob Hope all the time. They could not be in the same place at the same time. Like at the Academy Awards.

* * * *

#33. 1948.. The Paleface

This Movie says it all out loud that Howard Hughes is Bob Hope. The Movie opens with Hope in a Indian Chiefs Headdress.

Howard Hughes has indicated a number of times that he has Indian Heritage and that he is on the side of the American Indians. (Tonto) The Scenes and the Dialog of this Movie tells you more. Bob Hope is quoted here telling Nothing but the Truth.

Bob Hope says, "don't give your right name to anyone". he also says, "I am headed back to Washington, DC". Jane Russell says, "all I know about you is you came from Washington DC". Dialog says "he is a Federal Agent" speaking of Hope. Also, that "he is a cold- blooded Murderer". The Dialog then says, "if the outlaws catch him they will split him in two". Right indicating he is two people and "when he is dead he will go to the undertaker."

There's the "two heads "split in two. Bob is two Heads. He's the Writer with two Heads. Bob Hope says to Jane Russell "that if I come up dead, and come back, you'll meet two of the nicest fellows and they will both be me". Read it again. They will both be him.

Those words are right out of Bob Hopes own mouth. Bob wrote the Movie. (cue cards). They will both be him. Watch the Movie. The Paleface.

Howard Hughes faked his own death and came back to life, as an Alleged Life as Bob Hope. Two of the most famous names in America sleep together. Recall Bob Hope is quoted as saying "the names of the innocent have been changed to protect the joke. And "My NAMES will go down in History."

* * * *

#34. 1949... Sorrowful Jones

The introduction to this movie is by Walter Winchell. The film shows Broadway New York City with a big Rupert billboard sign and shows Lindsay's Restaurant.

Walter Winchell was a Newspaper Columnist and Radio voice. Howard Hughes used Winchell and other Columnist like him such as Hedda Harper and Luella Parsons to put out his information.

Walter Winchell became the voice of the television program the Untouchables a TV series about the FBI running down the Mob in Chicago.

Recall the Mobs infiltration of Hollywood in the 1930s with all the Gangster movies and actor George raft, who was considered a mobster playing major parts in the movies as a mobster and the gangster.

In this movie, Bob Hope shows up in the Howard Hughes hat. Hope portrays a Bookie and shows that he wears a money belt. The story is that he owes big money, about $10,000 to a Mobster. Hope is running a Horse Room Betting Parlor and is betting on horse races and losing.

Bob Hope had investments in Horse Racing, particularly in Atlantic City, where he opened the Atlantic City Racecourse.

The movie The Lemon Drop Kid with Bob Hope has the same story. As a Bookie he owes money to a Mobster named Sam.

Bob Hope says in dialog that he Is "the boss". "I am the boss, I run this joint!" Having Money Hope talks of being associated with the Mob.

Recall the book where it is written that a young actor in Vaudeville (Bob Hope) was associated with Lucky Luciano. Lucky Luciano was backing the Vaudeville, Burlesque and Broadway Shows back in the 30s. There is a connection. To me the dialog continues to expose and relate situations of Howard Hughes life.

Hope says "me hide". Why??

Co-star Lucille Ball says to Bob Hope "don't you have a real name?" There's a clue. Yes, does Bob Hope have a real name? Yes, his real name is Howard Rupert Hughes! She knows it and she's hinting at it. A name to big and two large for a Theater Marquee.

Dialog yells "he's a lunatic with a Horse". See the movie. In this movie Hope and Lucille Ball consider themselves "the smart people". Then there is a scene where a little girl talks to God and with Hope Prays to God for a request that "God gets Sorrowful Jones a new suit". Bob Hope in prayer with the little girl's request says he needs "a suit with two pairs of pants."

Two pairs of pants? Right, two pairs of pants, one for each of Bob Hopes Heads as a Writer and one pair for the other head of the two Famous Names in America that sleep together. For the two people in the mirror. Two people in one. A pair of pants for each.

How many times does Bob Hope Say he is two people? With many names and that he changes his name often.

Bob Hope as Sorrowful Jones says that "I fell in love with money at age 6." Hope fell in love with money at age 6? That's right, when he was the jr, when he was Sonny, when he was Howard Hughes Jr. Does Hope have a real name? Remember that question? Was Hughes in love with money at age 6? I think so! Was Hughes linked to the Mob? I think so! Was he linked to the FBI? Did Hughes have links to the Government?

Bob Hope is Howard Hughes stage name as a Character Actor since the early 20s. Hughes was always making movies and ever since Vaudeville Bob Hope has been wearing make-up. as a Character Actor.

For the History of Howard Hughes please review Bob Hope movies, Paleface and Son of Paleface.

* * * *

#35. 1949... The Great Lover

The Great Lover. Of course, both Bob Hope and Howard Hughes considered themselves Great Lovers. Every Movie is about Womanizing with many beautiful women, both so vain, thinking themselves as beautiful and with so much money showing off their beauty as Peacocks spreading their feathers. That would be wealth. That's why NBC's symbol is the Peacock. The Peacock with the Beak at the top of the NBC Peacock Symbol. Bing calls Bob Hope the Beak. The Nose. That indicates that Bob Hope wears a fake Putty Nose. Make up. Bob Hope was with NBC for 60 years. Maybe Howard Hughes owned the Network and was out front as Bob Hope.?

Note : A Hallway in the Atlantic City Hotel called the Marlboro Blenheim had a Hallway that led to the Beach and Boardwalk. That Hallway was referred to as Peacock Alley. That's where all the Women would pass dressed up on their way out for the night and the men would watch the Beautiful Women go by strutting their feathers, so to speak.

The movie opens with an actor counting $20,000. He is a millionaire. He is murdered, strangled by a knot tied around his neck. The $20,000 is stolen.

The dialog indicates that the suspect in the murder is a "young American with a very trustful face."

Also, at the start Bob Hope is on a Cruise Ship as a Scout leader of seven young Boy Scouts.

Here's a side note: in the Lone Ranger Television Show Tonto always called the Lone Ranger, the Masked Man "Kemo Sabe". In the very first episode (1949) Tonto refers to the Lone Ranger as Kemo Sabe which means "Trusted Scout". A Scout leader.

Hope is said to be an American with much money. In the dialog one of the young scouts told his Father, who is a Newspaperman that Hope has "millions of dollars ". There's the hint again, that whoever Hope is he has millions. Hughes has millions. Hope says, "I have the chin of a nobleman" and that he is "as guilty as crime". The chin is part of the makeup that Howard Hughes has on as his Bob Hope face. The nobleman statement to me indicates High Hats, Top Hats, High Society and an indication of the very rich.

Bob Hope calls for a poker game and starts Gambling. Both Bob Hope and Howard Hughes are both Involved with Gambling and Casinos. Las Vegas.

In the card game the strangler is after Bob's money. Bob says, "I am going to tell you the truth of who I am and about my millions". Right: Nothing but the Truth. Thus, The Strangler at the card game tries to strangle Bob to kill him. Hope being strangled is taken out on a stretcher as a dead man. There's that same theme again. Said to be dead. That's not the first time that an actor in a Bob Hope movie was said to be dead carried out on a Stretcher or in a Casket.

Hope is hiding behind the seven children. Dialog has it that "maybe he Is not dead". There you go again. Maybe Howard Hughes isn't dead. They say, "he's hiding somewhere on this ship, why is he hiding". then there is dialog that says right to Hope. "You're not dead". Bob Hope says right back "not yet". Rhonda Fleming says to Bob Hope "I thought you were gone". Isn't that what the entire United States was saying about Howard Hughes?

Hope does his Alligator Mating Love Call that Terry Moore taught only to Howard Hughes. Why is Bob Hope doing the Alligator Love Call that was taught to Howard Hughes by Terry Moore? I say because Bob Hope is Howard Hughes.

So there you have it again. Faking death again, hiding, telling you he's a millionaire and that people are out to kill him over his money. There's womanizing, there's gambling and of course make up.

Don't forget you have to recall a Bob Hope quote from a previous movie.

Bob Hope says to a beautiful woman "if I die and come back You would have met two fellows, and both would be me"!

Now that proves My Theory that Howard Hughes is Bob Hope in make-up. He tells you right in his movies. He tells you he is two people. One Bob Hope the other Howard Hughes. In his own words. In every Bob Hope movie, he tells you who he is and what he's about, what he did and how he did it. With makeup, a new face with sponge rubber, putty, stucco, fake ears, fake chin, wigs, teeth, disguises and fat clothes.

Every Movie says the same thing. Every Book says the same thing. Every Television Show the same thing. Many TV shows have the same themes. Many movies out of Hollywood say the same thing. The adventures are experiences of Howard Hughes brought to you by Bob Hope. Made in Hollywood. You can fool all the people all the time and the names of the innocent have been changed to protect the Joke.

You must keep in mind that Bob Hope and/or Howard Hughes is a writer with two heads with 3,000 writers writing the Movies screen Scripps about Him. Bob Hope is Howard Hughes! Howard Hughes is Bob Hope! and the Movies depict his life stories. (2)

Recall Bing Crosby said every Movie has a message. Out of every Movie I pulled out that message right out of Bob Hope's own mouth. Recall, Hope, said "nobody listens". They didn't. I did! And as I said before My Theory once proven (I have already proved it in Books) is that I broke the biggest story in the history of the world.

* * * *

#36.. 1950.. Fancy Pants

The opening displays the British Flag and Bob Hope's role is that of a Butler. He refers to the people as Peasants and goes by the name Humphrey.

Again, the movie starts showing New Mexico being given Statehood into the United States in 1912.

The dialog about the Butler refers to Bob Hope as "an American Idiot" and as "an Imposter" and as "not English" and as "a Murderer" and as "an Imbecile".? Nothing but the truth.?

Bob Hope as a writer wrote these words and made this movie. Was Bob Hope born in England? Dialog says No. The words say he's an "American Idiot". Words say he's an "Imposter."

Hope has said in other movies that he Is the best Impersonator of people in the whole world. Imposter means that you are acting as though you are someone else. Right: Howard Hughes is Impersonating Bob Hope. He's not English. He's American. He's a Murderer In with the Mob and Murder Inc. The movie says that. Howard Hughes i.e. Bob Hope wrote it. Howard Hughes and Bob Hope made the Movie.

Howard Hughes was so much a Genius and he was considered an eccentric. Hooked up with the Mob through Murder Incorporated and not born in England. He's an American. They got him covered Acting as Bob Hope. He is an Imposter and Actor Comedian acting as an Imbecile. Bob Hope said it himself. He is the writer with two heads. One of the two most famous names in America sleep together.

As the Movie continues Lucille Ball again and Bob Hope are off In the Desert with the Indians at home. Hope is said to be an Earl. In dialog, but Hope himself says, "I am not Humphrey nor am I am Earl, I'll be a star". A Movie Star? Which he was.

You can trust your car to the man who wears the star. Yep, the Star on the Dressing Room Door. Stage name Bob Hope. The Greatest Show on Earth Recall that Bob Hope did a cameo role in the Movie the Greatest Show on Earth.

There's a scene of a Fox hunt with Teddy Roosevelt. Bob Hope in the Movie fakes injuries. And actor describes his injuries as a "bad back, a bad right leg, ribs and chest". That's strange. That's the same injuries that Howard Hughes suffered through his many crashes. Five crashes.

Do you recall reading of all those about those injuries? The crushed Chest, The broken Ribs, Limbs and Face. The Movie reveals the injuries of Howard Hughes that are mentioned in other movies.

During the dialog and actor describes what he will do to Hope if Hope, messes with his girlfriend. "I will grab him by his Ears and just rip them off". There you go. That's indicating that the Ears are false. Right, fake Ears. Bob Hope replies that the guy who said that "knows I am an Actor". What did I say, an actor with make-up that can be removed? There he admits it again that he Is an Actor that his Ears are as fake as the Nose on his Face.

Recall: putty, sponge rubber, stucco, fake ears, fake chin, fake nose, teeth, fat clothes, and square pants, fooling everyone all the time as an Impersonator in Disguise. The Masked Man. He led two lives! or more. Mission Possible. Sponge Bob Square Pants.

With all the money in the world since the age of six Howard Rupert Hughes Jr nicknamed Sonny by the age of 12 was chasing Showgirls. He himself went into Show Business, Vaudeville with the Stage Name short enough to fit on a Theater Marquee.

At 17 years of age Howard Hughes, Jr, Sonny, is in Hollywood at Paramount Studios on the set with all the most beautiful women in the world. Sonny, Jr learned Filmmaking and Acting. Hence Bob Hope (Howard Hughes) made his movies to tell you Nothing but the Truth of who he is and what he was all about.

* * * *

#37. 1951... **The Lemon Drop Kid**

There is an intriguing opening to this movie. There is a drawing of a Christmas Tree with just one ornament on it. That ornament is a Gun. A German Luger.

A Gun! Again, a reference to Murder and a connection to the Mob, Gambling and betting on Horses. Hope is running around as a bookie at Racetracks given out tips and taking bets. He picks number seven and the horses name is Iron Bob. Bob says, "all my money is in hundred-dollar bills."

Unfortunately, Bob is in debt and owes $10,000 to the mobster named Sam. Sam Giancana? Hopes says that "if the Mob guy bothers me I'll have him drafted". Recall that the Mob squeezed Hollywood in the 30s. Bob Hope had the power to have someone drafted?

Bob continues to say, "if I don't pay back the money Sam will kill me". Hope meets someone at Charlie's restaurant in New York City. Charles Luciano? The scene is set in New York City in the wintertime. In a back room of a bookie joint Bob's working the numbers and bets on Horse Racing.

Owing the Mob Money Hope takes off running north from Florida to New York. Hope lands in New York in the middle of a snowstorm and on the street He meets up with Nellie. Nellie is a elderly retired actress with no money and with no place to live. Bob's freezing and he looks into a mirror at his nose and says "never saw it blue before ". Bob said that very same thing. In the 1980s film Spies like us.

In that movie Hope enters a tent in Afghanistan freezing from the cold and he says, "I never had a blue one before". Talking about his Nose. He's saying he's had different noses but never a blue one before.

Recall that it is written in another book that as Bob Hope was on Broadway it was Lucky Luciano who financially backed Broadway shows.

Back to the movie Hopes still owes the Mob and Sam $10,000 and he also wants to raise money to get Nellie a home for herself and the many other elderly actresses left over from the Circus, Vaudeville, and Broadway Theater. Hope devises a plan.

The plan is to get money to pay off the Mob and get Nellie and the girls a retirement home.

Here's the scam to get the money to set up Nellie and the girls in a retirement home. Hope gets many Mobsters from the Union to dress up as Santa Claus at Christmas time to ring bells, and collect money for himself and Nellie.

As Hope sets up this scam He says, "some of the bad are good inside and some of the good are bad Inside". Hmmm A split personality. Two People or one person?

Is Hope talking about himself and his character as Howard Hughes as being good outside but bad inside?. Or bad outside and good inside?

Hope lines up his crew of dressed up Santa Clause's and is briefing them on how they are to ring the bells and collect the money, much like the Salvation Army does during the Christmas season.

In the Santa line up Hope calls one of the Santa's Chris Kringle and the Santa says, "who's Chris Kringle". Hope tells the man "don't you know Santa Claus has many names like Chris Kringle St. Nick and Santa Claus". Hope again says "Santa has many names and doesn't give his real name". The Santa says back to Hope "I know another guy that never gives his real name."

Did you get that?. He never gives his real name. Recall from other movies there are quotes were Hope says "never tell anyone your real name". Terry Moore said Howard Hughes "never wanted anyone to know his real name". Recall Hope's real name "was too long for a Theater Marquee". Recall the Theater Marquee that read "The Magnificent Fraud, Bob Hope". Hope the "Alleged Life""imposter". That would be Howard Hughes the Moviemaker, The Actor, the Billionaire Industrialist.

What is Hope's real name?

Hope looking into a mirror is looking at two of himself. He touches his Ears, his Cheeks and his Eyebrows and says to himself "what a crime If you had to die keep your chin up". If one dies, they both die, unless one is faking his death.

Again, I must repeat the scene of the bell ringing Santa Claus line up. Hope Says, "Santa has many names". and Santa says, "I know another guy, he doesn't give his real name either". Who could that guy be? by now we known, right!

Check these names out. Howard Hughes, Robert Leslie Hope, Bob Hope, Packy East and many other names in many movies and who knows how many other spy adventures.

Recall this Bob Hope Quote "The names of the innocent have been changed to protect the joke". To continue George Raft says. "Why does everybody jump through hoops for that guy?" (George raft was considered a mob associate). Everybody jumps through hoops for the guy because he was giving everyone jobs, money, jewelry, cars, homes, women, as the American Santa Clause and if they said anything he'd have them killed.

Here's a funny scene in a backyard of a Mansion. Hopes on the ground and there's a statue with two heads, one profiling to the left and one profiling to the right with a large beak nose and a protruding chin and big ears and Hope calls the statue "funny nose" and says out loud the words that are printed on American money. Out of many one. That's right, he's the one, the one with all the money, the Billionaire Industrialist. The guy who is running the United States. Check the History of Howard Hughes. He's the one!

In all of Bob Hope movies He is two persons playing two parts at the same time as an actor and impersonating others. Hope spins the two heads on the statue, and many times talks to his other self in mirror's. The dialog in this movie says that Hope "is not on the level" and that he "has suckered everyone". The joke, right. He did fool all the people all the time!

In this movie The Mob moved in on his Rackets. Hope yells "call the President to print more money and pay off the debt, call the mint". Hope then says that he "knows all mob crimes". Hope is seen with a gun and he looks like Howard Hughes. The Mobsters are arrested. At that Hope, says, "I'll never be caught again". Dialog says, "Hope is responsible for all of this."

Recall that Bob Hope has said that J Edgar Hoover, who was the head of the FBI (for 50 yrs)never makes a move without him.

The movie ends with Nellie and all the elderly retired actresses getting their retirement home.

Every movie has the same theme. Hopefully you will watch these movies and see It all with your own eyes and ears. Every movie is Thanks for the Memory.

Howard Hughes was responsible for making most if not all the movies coming out of Hollywood since the 1920s. I say he was starring in his own movies and nobody knew it.

* * * *

#38.. 1951.. My Favorite Spy

Well, here's another Bob Hope movie that says it all again. This one about spying and using women as spies. The movie opens with an alleged spy being shot in an airport hangar. He is believed to be dead. The government may have shot him, and it is said "he is no good dead". The description of the guy resembles Bob Hope as a spy. Hope shows up with peanuts and says, "a Star is born". Hope is identified as a spy in a gag and as a joke. Hope says, "am I a criminal"? he knows he is and he is taken into custody and interrogated. He pretends to be alive. In the interrogation he tells the interrogators that he has five different names and says he "has billions". He also says, "I may be a taxpayer one day". Who has Billions Hope or Hughes? Hope has Millions, Hughes had Billions. Recall that Hope has said that the United States Government paid for everything that he has done. From 1938 through all his USO shows, and more. Everything!

The look-alike spy is believed to be dead, and Bob Hope as the look-alike takes his place. That's right, two people and they are both Howard Hughes. The FBI states that Hope is "an actor made spy". I guess that tells you the whole story. Howard Hughes with his Bob Hope face was a spy for the United States. How many times has he told you that himself?

As the FBI has Hope in custody He begins acting like a clown wearing a big clown nose. It's not the first time that Hope has acted like a clown and put on a fake Face in a movie.

Continuing, Bob Hope talks about his War Medals and calls himself a Plumber. A Plumber is a code word used for a spy, for one who breaks into a place to get information. Like the successful plumbers who raided Daniel Ellsberg's office in LA and stole his Pysyk files due to the release of the Pentagon papers. The bad plumbers are those who got caught at the Watergate Democratic Party headquarters who were seeking info about Howard Hughes. Check it out.

The government has records on microfilm of Hope as a spy. That's why he has War Medals. Howard Hughes Won World War II and dialog states that "his nose Is not all putty."

Hope's name in this movie is Augustine "a guy who looks like me" says Hope. Hope continues to say that he was "made into an entirely new person "and then says,

"where's my nose?" "My Beak."

Bob Hope's is in disguise as a spy for the Government. Howard Hughes is made up into Bob Hope as an entirely new person. That all happens while Hope is in FBI custody so to speak. Recall Hope has said "J Edgar never makes a move without me". In the FBI office Hope gets a call from Washington DC. Hope says "yes, Mr. President how are things in Missouri?' I think that indicates that it's President Truman on the phone. The President calls and Hope says, "yes sir."

At this time Hope was told by the President that "you hold the fate of the whole world in your hands". I believe that that would mean that with Bob Hopes (Howard Hughes) Aircraft, Rockets and Bombs. He is out to wage victory throughout World War II and beyond.

If Hope is Hughes and working for the United States Military and its Arm Forces, Manufacturing Aircraft and working with the Rockets and the Bombs he did hold the fate of the whole world in his hand. He's got the whole world in his hands.

The movie rolls on with Hope working with the Military and Women Spies. He shows up in Tangiers, North Africa, as he flies in and takes a taxi He is missed by a car bomb.

As a US Secret Agent Hope is on the run. Other spies on the US side bring him Clothes and there are Gunmen working with him. After the bomb goes off Hope says, "Get some Scotch Tape and put me back together" as Hope is holding his ears on. Well, what did I tell you? Nothing but the truth. In many of Bob Hope movies I can see the tape around his ears. Thanks to the 3M company.

Under the false ID name as Eric Augustine Hope is wearing "a money belt" again with millions of dollars in it. This is Bob Hope acting out his Howard Hughes life right in front of the people and they don't get it. He's acting out true experiences after the facts. Thanks for the Memory.

Here Hope Is taking the place of another person who looks like him but is Covered in Make-up.. And here again we have Hope looking into a mirror as two people. One him and the other him and looking at himself he says, "I should drop dead why should I trust you"? dialog says, "will Eric Augustine continued to live"? and "the Coroner will give the death certificate."

Dialog says to Hope "keep on breathing". Hope shows up dressed very rich in a tux and a top hat. Dressed in a tux, just as it was said and written by Bob Hope in his second book, Have Tux will Travel. In that book as I said, written by Bob Hope, Bob Hope says, "when the Government calls He is ready to travel on a mission for the United States". Bob Hope wrote "when the Government calls I go". Dialog says, "don't trust anyone" and that "there is something strange about him."

You can say that again. Faking his death, and continuing to live as Bob Hope. That's something strange.

The Movie continues with Hope womanizing with three women at once. That's Hughes and Hopes mo. Both making it with the most beautiful Star Actresses in Hollywood.

The first spy was believed to be dead. The Government calls and the real Eric Augustine shows up. He did not die when he was shot in hangar. He escaped to Algiers. Both are in Algiers at the same time. The first Eric Augustine did not die when he was shot in the hangar. Bob Hope is playing two people, two heads, two of the most famous names in America at the same time. I would say that the title of the movie, My favorite spy is Hope himself.

I must make note here of another movie title, The return of Peter Grimes. That movie is about a guy who comes back to life. A dead man who comes back to life. My Theory : Howard Hughes considered dead comes back to life as Bob Hope. An Alleged life. That's what Bing Crosby said speaking of Bob Hope's New Face in the preface of Bob Hope's Book in 1941.

Howard Hughes faked his own death and began to live his "Alleged Life as Bob Hope. That's My Theory and I'm sticking to it.

Hope goes to a Fortune Teller using Tarot cards and picks one. She tells Hope (the spy) that the Safe House is on 4th St. N.. Apt. # 7. Hope eats the tarot card. Hope then moved out and disguises himself in a Camel Suit Outfit and then again he disguises himself in an Arab outfit as he hides. He is chased. He sneaks into the back door of a Gambling Casino and starts Gambling.

So, he sneaks in the back door of the Casino. Which is in the desert by the way. Howard Hughes did that. Desert Casino!

Bob Hope did that. Hughes owned Casinos. He even hid out on the 9th floor of the Desert Inn Casino and Hope was the entertainment director for the casino's in Vegas. The Casinos were associated with the Mob.

Hope is to be killed in this movie and that's another reason for Hughes to hide.

In the Casino Gambling Hope says, "if I win big money, I will drop in at the White House and solve their budget problem". Dialog says "even if you get killed, your Eric Augustine in the brown house ". Meaning, even if you get killed, you will still live. That's what it said. Two heads, one dies, one lives. Two people in one.

Another movie about two people being the same person playing two roles with look-alike doubles, two Hopes two Hughes. He is still being chased. They are still out to get him. The movie using trick camerawork has Both Hope and Hughes in the same scene.

As a spy Hope has to leave Tangiers, Algeria and is setting up a flight to New York as the real Eric Augustine is arriving. Recall that Hope is his double, and that the Government set up Hope to be the spy in place of the spy. The enemy spy ring is out to kill him.

Talking to himself Hope says "the closer I get to death, the more I realize I love you too". As a double agent Hope is told that "you are an entirely new person" Two people, one Hughes and one Hope. An entirely new person with make-up. They are the two most famous names In America who sleep together. Love that Bob. Sponge Bob Square Pants.

Hope sets up a plane ticket making" reservations for two" for two!, but he's only one person right? Wrong. He's two people.

Check out these Bob Hope quotes in a mirror again He says, "me I look awful". "I would be dead without you. I me - me, the other dead". "a living corpse" and "I am alive". And then says to the life of the look-alike "you'll get life for this" as dialog says, "he looks dead."

Did you get all that:: "living corpse" like the walking dead? Wanted dead or alive. Tells you right there, that if one was alive the other one would be dead. Dialog says, "does he look dead"?

Hope as a spy is captured by the enemy Spy Ring and he is given an injection of truth serum. He is then questioned. "Shoot him up" says the spy. Hope says of the truth serum to make me talk. "I will not talk". and he says out loud… "I have a long name too long for a marquee."

There it Is again. The name Howard Rupert Hughes is too long to fit in the credits or on a Theater Marquee. That's right. Howard Rupert Hughes's name is 18 letters. Break it down. Bob Hope's name is seven 7 letters. Seven letters fit on the Marquis. Nothing but the truth. The number 7 again.

Howard Hughes, the Secret Actor playing many parts in many of his own movies. A great Impersonator, The Greatest Show on Earth. Mission possible. The people were not listening.

Yes, yes, with a long name too big for a Theater Marquee he shortened his name to Bob Hope So the short name can fit on the Marquee. He had been Bob Hope since the 20's.

The film shows a duel in the dark with Bob Hope and his Nose silhouetted on a wall. The Nose, the Face, the cover-up, and Bob Hope says "I wear the great big nose ".

* * * *

 # 39.. 1952.. Son of Paleface

Paleface would be Howard Hughes Sr'. Howard is the Son of Paleface and this movie gives you "Nothing but the Truth". The truth is that Howard Hughes Sonny Jr inherited great wealth from his Father and this movie Bob Hope tells you so. It tells you. "Nobody recognized me" and that he is an "inventor". He says

he's "rich and has millions of dollars and gold, and that he wears a fake face and is a movie star and actor." He's called "insane" and a "maverick."

Let's go through this movie and write down the quotes written and spoken by Hope - Hughes in this Movie.

That's what I did. I've done it for every Movie that Bob Hope made. Recall I also did it to every book written by Bob Hope. I also did it to every Bob Hope tv show specials, videotapes and DVDs. I have been interested in this subject since 1966.

The movie starts out with Hope the womanizer hugging Jane Russell on the campus of Harvard University. Howard jr "Sonny" was to go to Harvard.

Hope has on a sweater with a very large H. Is the H for Harvard or is the H for Hughes, or is the H for Hope? I say it's for Hughes/ Hope. Another hint. Watch the movie. See it for yourself. Follow the movie with this review. Jane Russell says to Bob Hope you won't pass Harvard East, so why don't you go out West and get that vast fortune your father left you"! Did you just read that human autobiographical heritage of? The great Inheritance. Not Bob Hope? Looks like Jane Russell knew who ever he is that he inherited a great fortune.

Again, Jane Russell says to Bob Hope, go West, and collect your inheritance that your father left you". Hope goes out West and says nobody will recognize me from this angle. That's right, from the fake face profile. Hope shows up out West driving a steam car, a model a Steam Car, and shows up again with a big H on his sweater. Check it out. It's a fact that Howard Hughes had invented a steam car and his last name initial is an H.

In this movie. Hope shows up saying," I am here to collect my inheritance left me by my Father". There it Is. That's a fact. He's Howard Hughes Jr. He is "Sonny" and was left his Father's entire fortune. Here, Hope tells you again He is that aire. The billion aire.

Again, we have Howard Hughes talking through his Bob Hope face. Nothing but the truth right in front of all the people. You can fool all the people all of the time. It's a joke on the people and they

didn't even get the joke. No one got it because, as Bob Hope had said nobody listens. (except Joseph Polillo)

Here's more quotes from Bob Hope, Son of Paleface Howard Hughes

"My Father won the West"!

Check: there is a Lone Ranger episode all about old-timers out West. Howard's father was an oil and gold prospector, the movie's plot is that Howard's father willed Sonny jr a Chest. And left him a Map as to where it was at.

Hope goes after the Chest and yells "he's rich", Rich, I have millions"

"daddy, how can I thank you"

"my vast wealth" then Bob, let's out his alligator love mating call, the one that Terry Moore taught only to Howard Hughes. He's one and the same person through dialog. He tells you who he is in each movie and through his writers of which he is one, that he Is Howard Hughes and that he is a double headed person, a Billionaire with vast holdings of oil, gold, many businesses, plenty of money and plenty of raw materials.

The film shows Bob in a Casino bar with Bob charming a woman.

Howard Hughes owned casinos and Bob Hope was the casino entertainment director for all the casinos in Vegas, and they both did and do charm all the beautiful women.

In one scene the dialog has actors yelling this is "Junior Son of Paleface". He's a Millionaire and give this Millionaire a drink". Hope then says that his Mother spoiled and pampered "sonny" and then says, "I am a boy Millionaire". Howard Hughes knew at age 6 that he was a Millionaire. Bob Hope says he fell in love with money at age 6. Interesting.

As the Movie continues there's a chase and Hope is hiding in a bathtub with the big H sweater on.

One of the women is trying to get Hope to marry her and Hope says, "I'll have to slice the wedding cake with my nose". He is then called a "maverick". It is my opinion that many TV shows were written about Howard Hughes, such as Maverick, I led three

lives, the Beverly Hillbillies, Have Gun will Travel and the Man with A Camera.

Howard Hughes certainly was a Maverick. Hope says, "with this money I can live" and as he gets ready for bed he says, "why go to bed with your head in the same shape". I think he means he's not going to bed with his makeup on. He means to take off the fake shaped face.

Bob in one movie is showing a full set of Masks and saying, "I have a Mask for day, a Mask for night and a Mask to go to sleep with", and don't forget from previous movies that he has a tray of noses and he has a tray of faces. How's My Theory holding up? it's all Hollywood makeup, of course, like the man of 1,000 faces straight out of the Hollywood make-up room. The Lone Ranger wears a Mask.

In another scene Hope is seen walking with a very large coat on with a very large H. While he Is walking he falls right into a hole of oil, a huge hole of oil. He struck oil. He's drenched in oil. You could say he's telling you he is oil-rich. Howard was oil-rich. He owned the drill bit, money, silver, diamonds, mines, uranium, land and businesses.

As part of the will there was a map. How many Bob Hope movies are about having a map to this treasure? The Map shows where a chest was located with more of his inheritance.

Hope uses the Map to find the chest and finds the chest empty. Disappointed he then discovers a false bottom to the chest. Hidden in the chest is a note as to where the Money and the Gold is hidden. The Gold is hidden in a Moose head in an old Casino in the Desert. Sound familiar in a Desert Casino called Silver City. The Hughes Money. Any relationship that Howard Hughes or Bob Hope inherited LasVegas?

Hope is headed to the Desert as vultures fly overhead. He went to the desert as dead. Maybe to hide out at the Penthouse. Hope has on a big rubber nose and he's called a Collegian.

Note History: Howard Hughes, Junior, Sonny did go to college, Thatcher college in California and possibly Harvard West, also a

Tech Institute in California. Looking Into a mirror with two faces, dialog says "he found out his real name."

Bob Hope says this H does not stand for Harvard. What does the H stand for? I say it stands for Hughes. (Hope)

The movie ends. Hope finds the treasure in the Moosehead at a Desert Casino.

* * * *

#40. 1952... Road to Bali.

In the beginning, Hope and Crosby are going over their memories of their 1947 Allentown Pennsylvania shows. Bing grabs Bob by his nose. They both show up with beards, hats and argyle socks. They are hiding and on the lam and womanizing. Bing calls Bob the Genius. They both get jobs as deep sea divers with pay and Bob Hope says, "never had any money thanks to Washington" and continues to say, "Imagine what you can do with a G.I.loan."

Recall the United States Government paid all of Bob Hope's bills and had Bob Hope covered. Even with all the money in the world He never needed any money of his own. He was using all the Governments Money.

In the Movie Bob and Bing talk Baseball. Bob talks of the Cleveland Indians, which he owned, and Bing talks of the Pittsburgh Pirates, which he owned. Bob and Bing were Pirating the US Government. Hughes was hooked up with the American Indians. (Tonto).

There is a movie Titled: The Kid from Cleveland. Hope and Hughes are both from Cleveland. That is written History. Then the movie has Bob and Bing scuba diving as Bing tells Bob to "suck in his nose."

In the dialog Bing states "every movie has to have a message in it". There it is right there! I prove that with my research and showed you the many messages in all these Bob Hope movies that there is a message in every Movie.

Bob Hope falls asleep falling into a dream of Oil Wells.

Bob and Bing are captured by the Indians.

The Plot and the Theme of this Movie is that two Gentleman take jobs as deep sea divers on an idyllic Island where they both court the affections of a lovely Princess, as well as with the locals for a chest of Jewels.

Bob and Bing show up In Disguises as Harold and George as, "twins" (2) with Beards, Hope says: "they must have gambling here". And then Hope says "How is the Beast in the Penthouse"? What is he's talking about? (himself?) So, Bob Hope knows about the person that's hiding out in the Penthouse. Howard Hughes is the guy hiding out in the ninth floor Penthouse of the Desert Inn. Check History.

At the end of the Movie, Bob Hope says, "all he wants is a home with a couple of oil wells."

* * * *

#41. 1953… Off Limits

The opening of this Movie shows a TV Fight Boxing Show with Jack Dempsey in the role of the Referee. Bob Hope is the Business Manager, Coach and Trainer of the Boxer. Hope is shown with the Nose drinking and womanizing with a Mobsters Girlfriend. Many of the Mobsters girlfriends are fighting and falling all over Bob Hope. Now that could be a real story about Howard Hughes. (HRH)

Such a situation could have happened in real life in loss Angeles, Howard Hughes being interfered with by the Mob in the 1930s. Bob Hope says that in his youth he was a boxer under the name of Packy East. Hope also says the name Wally Hogan is in a future scene as Hope. As Hope enters a building he says, "I came up the back way to miss the Mob". So some one was out to kill or get Hope or Hughes.

In the movie the Mob is out to squeeze Howard Hughes, well, I mean Bob Hope in the movie. Hope Hughes had to go into the Army for twelve years to hide from the Mob. That is also the theme of many Bob Hope movies.

There it Is, that's exactly what happened. Howard Hughes in his role as Bob Hope had to run into the Army to get away from the Mobsters that were trying to kill him. I mean to kill Howard Hughes;

Bob Hope tells you this in his book, I Never Left Home. Howard / Hope disappeared deep into the Military with the protection of the United States government. Wherefore, They Got me Covered.

Hope says to the Army "they got me I'm in" Hope talks about being insane and says, "I am the greatest soldier of all."

That's right. That's Howard Hughes the Industrious Billionaire, the Inventor, Commander-in-chief in his command performance role providing all the United States Air and Sea Military Equipment for World War II. To the Industrial Powerhouse known as the United States.

Sometimes back I recall reading a quote by Howard Hughes saying that his Father's Equipment Won World War I, and that his Equipment Won World War II, and that his Equipment was working well in Vietnam. There you can understand the quote from Hope / Hughes that "he is the greatest soldier of all."

Hope is sneaking around with the woman and he says to her "they didn't recognize me", of course the makeup worked. He looked like someone else.

Mickey Rooney becomes Hopes new boxing partner. In the dialog Hope sings a song and a verse in the song goes like this: "I am the only man in the world who can tell a General where to go". Sounds like Commander-in-Chief to me. Recall Ava Gardner wrote in her book that when Howard Hughes was giving her an airplane ride to the bedside of her sick Mother she wrote : "Howard threw two Generals off the Plane to give her the seats and called the Generals Desk jockeys."

Rooney gets a big fight in the Army with his Manager Hope, but the Authorities are after Hope.

Now read what the dialog says about Hope "this man is wanted by the Army and the Mob". Now isn't that what I've been saying? Hughes had to be covered. The Mob was after him. Then Hope is shown with two guns on his hips. He is ready. The Mob is chasing him and Hope runs into a Federal Building. In the federal building Hope tells the Feds "I am being chased by two Mob Killers. They are going to make an attempt on my life."

Recall Hopes quote from previous movies that : "J Edgar doesn't make a move without me". He has also previously told you that he works for the United States Government, The State Department, The CIA and that he is very close to the President and that he is a Spy.

This Movie shows Bob Hope always hiding, sneaking around, using two-way radios and phone booths. Superman?

And again, Bob or Howard gave the Alligator Mating Love Call, taught only to Howard Hughes by Terry Moore in yet another movie.

* * * *

#42. 1953... Here Come the Girls

The opening shows a Vaudeville Show with Chorus Girls and Hope dancing like a goof completely out of line messing up the whole scene on the set of a movie studio.

Recall the facts about Howard Hughes Jr with the nickname Sonny and that he would go to the Broadway Theaters as a 12-year-old and fall in love with the very beautiful women of the chorus line. It was great to be around all the beautiful women. Howard Hughes and Bob Hope were both known to be notorious with women. Young Sonny Jr Howard Hughes from 17 years of age loved being on the set of Paramount Studios with all the beautiful women when he moved to California. Also recall that when Hughes was a young man he went to California to live with his uncle who was a screenwriter for Paramount Studios and again he loved being on the set with all the beautiful women. In this movie his name Is Snodgrass and he gets the hook for being out of line. He's thrown out of line and tries to get another job. He's quoted as saying for a reference that he "worked in my Father's coal mine". Howard Hughes inherited mine's.

Bob is quoted as saying: "I will be a Star". That's right!, A Movie Star a Theater Star and a Texaco Star. He then says" "I told my bookie I'm alive". I believe he told his bookie that because He disappeared behind makeup as another person. Dialog says: "he isn't real" and says that : "Hope is impersonating someone else, as others are out to kill him". Associate that with Howard Hughes and his association with the Mob and with the themes and plots in many of the Bob Hope movies.

As the movie continues Hope in dialog says, "I am a star, hitch your wagon to a star". Sound familiar? That was Bob Hope's Texaco ad Commercial. "You can trust your car to the man who wears the star the big bright Texaco Star."

He's a Star All right. In one scene Hope stands in front of his Dressing Room Door and there's a large Star on the dressing room door and in another scene Hope is called "an idiot and a moron" Hope says, "I can't look at myself". That's right! he can't look at himself when he's in is Bob Hope makeup. He then is quoted saying that he "has money and diamonds and is in the coal business". I think coal has a lot to do with steel. And steel has a lot to do with the construction of aircraft and ship building. Is Bob Hope telling you he is Howard Hughes, the Billionaire Industrialist. The Jet Pilot, The Aviator, Rocket Man.

There's a scene in a Barbershop and Hope tells the Barber to bring two (2) razors. One for the biggest head.

There's a stalker again in this movie still out to kill Hope. Bob Hope says: "he will be stalked for as long as I live."

Another scene in the film puts Snodgrass, Bob Hope, the Star Singing and Dancing with all the beautiful chorus girls. The show goes on.

The stalker is still out the kill Hope and throws a knife at him. The chase is on and the hunt continues in the theater like the Phantom of the Opera. Hope is hiding. Howard Hughes was always in hiding and running from everyone. Hope is quoted that "ain't no skin off my nose". Hope claps his cheeks and nobody recognizes Hughes in his Bob Hope face.

The dialog says, "get into that clown outfit and dress for a part to be an actor". That's what Howard did. He got into his Bob Hope outfit and became an actor. That's My Theory.

But it's the stalker, the killer that gets into the clown outfit and is out to kill Hope right on the stage.

Hope is acting as the MC of the show and says, "I am the greatest performer in all Europe". That's right because Howard Hughes won World War II. That was a great performance.

Bob acts as a coward and dialog says, "he takes the part of a yellow belly coward really good". It's an act right.

The killer attacks and Hope is shown on a high wire act. Hope is knifed and he plays dead. Here we go again playing dead. There he said it again. Thanks for the Memory. Playing dead Hope says, "I can feel it in my bones, in the ones that aren't broken."

Here again we have Bob Hope admitting that he has all the Injuries that can be attributed to Howard Hughes. The injuries from the many crashes that Howard has had over the years as a Test Pilot and an Inventor. Howard Hughes was broken up. You may have read previously on the critique of Bob Hope's books of the many serious injuries suffered by Howard Hughes. You may also recall that Bob Hope said that he was an Inventor. He also said many times that he's not dead. Howard Hughes did put on the outfit. And he became a Star. Bob Hope. The Greatest Show on Earth.

Nothing but the Truth

In Movies past Hope is quoted that he has problems with his Arm with his Chest, his Heart, his Ribs, his Leg, his Head and Face and back. His injuries were severe.

* * * *

#43. 1954… Casanova's big Night

Each and every movie by Bob Hope has a message, especially this one.

Recall Bing Crosby said: "every movie has to have a message". Put My Theory (now proven) to the test.

This movie opens right up showing Bob Hope with a Mask on and then taking it off. It's Bob Hope with a Mask. There was a Movie Mask. Remember in a previous movie Hope is showing off his many Masks. Remember Hopes tray of Noses, tray of Faces. He's telling you out right that he puts the Mask on, and he takes It off.

Hope says, “I make the Crest”. A Crest is a symbol of a Royal Family an indication of Heritage. (Could that be the Crest of the Peacock Throne of the Shah of Iran). The Shah of Iran, who was trained as a Jet Pilot out of Texas, USA. Check it out. Why else would it be titled the Peacock Throne. (NBC) (Hope/Hughes) (HRH/BH is the Peacock). Iran was about Oil.

Check History. In 1952 Iran was overthrown by a CIA operation where Shah Pahlevi was placed in power. He was certainly hooked up with the West and the United States. Iran possessed great sums of oil. Hope has been quoted previously as saying that he worked for the Central intelligence agency. Interesting.

Back to the movie Hope is asked : “why are you disguised as Casanova“? Hope is “disguised” as Casanova. The movie shows Hope putting the Mask on first and then taking it off. Like you would put on make-up and after the show take it off. The Mask Is put on then off and back on again. That’s My Theory. You can fool all the people all of the time!

Make note that Casanova is a contemporary term for being a lover boy. A womanizer. Both Bob and Howard were lover boys.

Hope puts the Mask on as Casanova and then puts the Crest on his chest indicating it has something to do with him.

Dialog has it said to Hope that, “for sex you must remove your Mask first”. And Hope says to that, “oh no I can’t take off the Mask I don’t have anything on underneath it”. He’s asked, “who is It“? Hope responds, “guess who”? Did you get that? Who is it under the Mask? Take a guess!

Bob Hope is called an “Imposter” by his creditors and the creditors in this movie scene are all shown with large noses. (That means they’re all in on it).

One of the creditors ask, “has anyone ever seen Casanova”? Recall that Howard Hughes and Bob Hope were great lovers. They both romanced women for decades. And they were both proud as a Peacock. They always saw Bob Hope but they never saw Howard Hughes. “Has anyone ever seen Casanova Face”? Nobody had ever seen Howard Hughes Face publicly. Bob Hope has been Quoted “no one has ever seen My Face;! ……..

Bob Hope again looks into a mirror and says, "I've never seen him". As the movie continues Bob Hope says, "I usually escape out Windows". That's a similar statement from another movie where he says he always comes in the back door to escape the Mob.

Check this out. In the Movie Bob Hope says, "I never run", but "he hides" and "he escapes". Who's he talking about? Who's "he"? Bob never runs, but "he hides" and "he escapes". Here again we have Bob talking about himself as Howard Hughes. Howard Hughes has a History of escaping and hiding. He's talking about himself.

Now, knowing what you have read previously concerning Howard Hughes Jr, Sonny, as 12-year-old loving Chorus girls, we get this quote from Bob Hope, "I failed at 12 years old with women". There it is! Howard Hughes talking through his Bob Hope face. It was Sonny, Jr who fell in love with the Chorus Girls. Howard was the 12-year-old who fell in love with the beautiful women. Bob Hope just told you so!, and that is the written history of Howard Hughes. Bob Hope just told you so!

A woman says to Hope "if somebody finds out you're an imposter It's all over for all of us."

In one scene Hope walks into a room all jive and displays his "outfit". He says; "my outfit". The "outfit" is a Peacock with two tails. (Remember Bob needs two hats, two pairs of pants, two heads, and two parts in many movies.

One tail is for Howard Hughes and the other tail is for Bob Hope. Two of the most famous people in America sleep together. They are one in the same. They are both Peacocks. They are both NBC.

Hope winds up in a sword fight and Hope wins. Bob Hope says, "I am an old hand at this protection game". He sure was, probably from the 1920s and 30s, and his association with the Government and the Mob. Everybody was after Howard Hughes.

Hope shows off his Royal Crest again. Many of Hopes movies hint at Royalty, of High Society, of the Swells, the High Hats, the Tuxedo crowd, the very Rich. Hope goes on to say that, "I have been dressing myself since I was 23". That's right. He was 23 when he took on the stage name of Bob Hope in Vaudeville and started putting on make-up as an actor. Read Bob Hope's books. He writes and tells you that himself. That's Right! He dressed up with make-up for his "Alleged life" since he was 23.

Howard Hughes Jr, Sonny's Father died 1924 and his Mother died 1922.

Here's more Bob Hope words from this movie that he wrote and that he acted In. He says: "I inherited it all."

As Howard Hughes, that's true. You must watch these movies and hear it and see it for yourself.

As I said before"""""""""""

"I, Joseph Polillo broke the biggest story in the History of the World.

Hope says, "I am me, is me."

He says He is He and I say he is He. Dialog says they need "we need proof of ID soon" and "you changed your appearance", and Hope responds, "if you led the life I've led you would look this way too but worse". and Bob says, "you can't cut my head off I need it to hang my ears on". As an Actor. There he's talking about the false ears, the false face, and about the false head. Recall that the Ears are part of his make-up.

The movie states that Casanova is to be dead, and to be buried. There's that theme again. Here's the fake death thing again. Proof of the plan. There's a message in every movie. Nothing but the Truth. Bing!! does that ring a bell? Dialog says; "get a box to bury him in it". Then, dialog says, "get him two boxes". Two people, Two heads, Two pants etc. etc. etc.. A box for each of the two most famous names In America.

As the Movie goes on Hope disguises himself as a woman. (for the third or fourth time in movies) He's caught. They're going to put him on the Guillotine to cut his head off. Hope yells, "you can't cut my head off."

Remember : Hope is writing these Movies, producing and directing these Movies, he's filming these Movies and he's starring in all of them at the same time. And Howard Hughes is talking with the Bob Hope's face and telling you the truth of Have Tux will Travel.

* * * *

#44. 1955... Seven Little Foys

There's that number seven (7) again. Hope said he was number (7) seven. Hope said he had six (6) Brothers and he was number(7) seven. Hope said he was number (7) seven. Hope has said that he is 007. In this case, and in this movie, even though the Movie is supposed to be about an entertainer with (7) seven children I believe that it could mean that there were (7) seven guys in on the foils and in on the Joke. Hope/ Hughes could be all (7)seven.

The film starts out as a stage show with Bob Hope as the Master of Ceremonies.(MC) Bob Hope is quoted as saying "I am the greatest Father of them all". I believe he says that because he is the Father of them all by being the first best Actor in Vaudeville and Burlesque in the Circus and in the Theater and Movies, Television and Radio. In the right place at the right time.

The scene in the Movie has dialog about make-up and acting like a Clown. The Comedian Hope is dancing with a Ballerina. He and the Ballerina are trying to get an acting contract on Broadway. In Hope's audition he shows up with a High Hat and Tuxedo and sings the Song "Nobody". That says he's a Rich Billionaire. A no name nobody. That's telling his real-life story again. Big money, a High Hat.

The Girl wins the contract and Hope does not. He skips out to the West of the United States. The Ballerina goes to Italy under contract and Hope finds that out and goes to Italy to catch up to her. No one knew. Could that be Sophia Loren? Lavonne DeCarlo?

He catches up to the girl and they get married on the Isle of Capri. They then go back to New York City. They bring the Ballerina's Sister with them and the family grows. The first Child is born in Cleveland Ohio, the second child In Milwaukee Wisconsin, the third child in Iroquois New York. The family grows larger and Hope is not around.

It is listed as fact that Bob and Dolores Hope adopted four children. It is documented that Bob Hope was not at home for 12 years straight. Bob Hope was not around. He was working for the United States. The family buys a House in New Rochelle New York.

Bob neglects the Family for he Is always on the road and never home. The Wife gets ill.

Hope shows up at home before the Mother dies and one of the children says to Hope "hello stranger". A visitor to his own home. The kid says that he "only sent checks". The kid asked Bob "just passing through."

Hope and the Kids go into Show Business with good Vaudeville Shows.

This is the movie that Hope and Cagney do the famous tap dance routine on the banquet table. Hope is there to get an Award as Father of the Year. As Hope is going home he finds out that his Wife had died.

As it was said the whole family goes into show business.

Hope is told "he is playing a part."

* * * *

#45. 1956 ... That Certain Feeling.

This movie opens in New York City with Pearl Bailey singing the song Praises.

Hope is Larry Larkin, a Cartoonist. His old wife gets a job with Cartoonist and dialog says, "it's about character" and that Hope "he is all Government."

The Truth and Nothing but the Truth. He's all Government that's true, a radio artist, a comedian, all Washington DC. in real life. He's always at the White House and playing Golf with the Presidents.

The dialog says that: "he needs help". It is also called an "idiot."

Here's a few quotes from the Movie.

"Been doing any Ghosting"

"who wants to get hooked up with that Mob" "my illness is between me and my Druggist" These quotes are all attributed to Bob Hope.

It's a fact that Howard Hughes had a Dentist in East Central LA. It was said of this Dentist was "good at keeping secrets."

Twice in the dialog Hope says to a girl that, "I'll kiss that little Nose of yours". Hope then kisses the Nose and Ears of the girl. To me that's like a congratulations that she's a good actress.

Dialog then states twice Bob Hope's quote about Abraham Lincoln that "you can fool all the people all the time". Hope says, "you can fool all the people all the time". He says that many times. Because he did just that. Hope says, "how American can you get"?

Dialog says to Hope, "go to Cuba lay low and don't come back". How about that? Remember Howard Hughes was all over Cuba with his Mob run Casinos and Hotels. And the dialog says to Hope, "go to Cuba and take your make-up with you."

There is a message in every Movie and the messages are of a truly personal and secretive nature worked into his movies.

Thanks for the memories which he put to good use as a screenwriter.

* * * *

46. 1956 … The Iron Petticoat

A Petticoat was clothing as underclothes for a woman. If you wanted to make it with a woman back in the day you had to remove the woman's Petticoat. If you did, you scored. In this Title it seems that one could not get the woman's Iron Petticoat off. It was on and not coming off. A difficult task. Like a Chasity Belt. A Petticoat is a woman and the task is to turn her to your favor. The woman spy would not give in and it was difficult to flip the spy.

The movie opens at a US Air Force Headquarters in Germany and Bob Hope is an Air Force officer. At the air control center radar detects a UFO in their air space.

"Ground control to Fox trot, one for you". Bob Hope is the Fox and he chases after hot women. Dialog says, "you mean there is a woman here in Germany that you can get your hands on". Bob Hope is the Fox in this movie but Howard Hughes is the Fox of the 20th Century. 20th Century Fox.

Howard and Bob are both Pilots. They are both womanizers all over the world. They both use airplanes. Recall that Terry Moore in her book the Beauty and the Billionaire said that Howard Hughes had first call landing rights worldwide.

In the opening scene the UFO is a jet plane and it lands at an Air Force Runway in England. A truck drives out to the Tarmac to the jet and a large sign on the back of the truck reads "follow me ".

A Russian Aviator Capt. Vinka Kovelenko steps off the jet. She is defecting to the West. She says because the Russians "won't let me fly". She is put in American custody and Bob Hope becomes her handler.

Recall Bob Hope has written and said that he was Central Intelligence working for the United States Government now working out of the United States Air Force HQ out of Germany.

The woman defector is trying to convert Bob to Communism as Bob is trying to convert her to Capitalism and the two are very attracted to each other. They fall in love.

There is a film clip in the movie of the United States Air Force jets flying high.

"Ground control. This is ground control red and blue come in."

History is that at the beginning of Television there were two stations one was red, which referred to NBC and one was blue that referred to CBS.

When the female Russian jet pilot was first taken into custody she was put in an interrogation room. Bob Hope enters the interrogation room dressed in an Air Force Commanders uniform. Someone says in the dialog to another officer that Hope is said "to be one of the most daring fliers, The best we have". Who are they talking about? Bob Hope or Howard Hughes? Howard Hughes was the most daring Test Pilot the United States Air Force had. An officer tells Hope "the country needs your talent". Recall again, Hope also said he was a Pilot with thousands of hours in the air. It was Howard Hughes who flew around the world breaking records. He had thousands of hours in the air. Hope said the same about himself.

Hope is introduced to the captured Russian female defector as "the one who forced you down". Hope starts talking of bribing all the Russians with great sums of money and homes, etc. At a dinner

Hope "talks of being a flyer". He then offers money to a Russian spy and tells how he bribes individuals with life's total objects to flip them to the US side.

Hope goes on talking of how he can talk the Air Force into anything, and that the Army pays the bill and that the White House is watching. Hope tells the Air Force to send more money, which means Hope Is turning spies with money and homes to the US side. In another scene Hope goes in one door and out the other and sits with the Air Force brass.

The defector says to Hope "are you the boss" and Hope says: "skip it."

Hope then gives a check of $100,000 to Russian defectors. Hope looks down as Uncle Sam is referred to as giving up the money. Dialog says: "the White House is watching."

Hope yells: "I am on a secret Military Mission to save my country, we are here on a secret mission". That's Hope telling you that he's a spy and he is one on an important mission for the Air Force. He says it all right there. Howard Hughes is a spy in Bob Hope make-up. And this movie told you what situations he's been in. He was more than a spy.

A new scene opens in London at the USSR trade mission. The American Soldiers are all saluting Hope. Hope is in a Uniform. Bob Hope refers to himself as "Capt. Checkbook". All the Top Brass Generals are meeting with Hope and all the dialog points to Hope as the Moneyman. The man in charge of the United States of America. Hope again speaks and says, "I am on a secret mission", and dialog says that's "how to turn a spy for the USA."

Dinner is set up with Generals and Senators in a Restaurant. Hope enters the Restaurant by the back door. Bob Hope makes a crack about Senate Investigation Hearings.

Senate investigations did happen, but not for Bob Hope, it was for Howard Hughes, who was dragged into a Senate hearing, not Bob Hope, unless Bob Hope is????.....

The Russians are still trying to get their woman Pilot back from the United States. Russian spies are trying to drug Bob by putting pills in his drink at the Restaurant. The wrong guy drinks the drink.

Hope is said to be a "millionaire with not a penny to his name". There you have it. That's right, he is using all the United States money. The money that the United States Government uses to pay for it all.

Hope fondles the Ears Nose, and the Chin of a General. Later, there is a dispute over a marriage. Hope calls Hepburn the "Queen of disguise" and the "Princess of disguise". I wonder if Hepburn ever went on a mission in disguise for the United States? Terry Moore did.

Hope is called: "dog Nose". Hope is quoted saying "who cares about the State Department". And then says: "I am a Communist". Recall Bob Hope said in a previous movie that he was a "mole". I believe that's what the Government Senate hearings were about. Communist infiltrating the Movie Industry. Howard Hughes was subpoenaed to appear at those hearings.

Back to the movie Hepburn runs out and gets caught by the Russians. She is tried and found guilty and sentenced to death.

Hope says many times that he "Is of the Air Force". A description of Hope is given in the movie "he has a turned -up nose ".

Hope turns more Russians over to the American side. Here again we have Howard Hughes saying through his Bob Hope Face that "I am the United States Air Force, Washington DC" and that he is "a Military Induction officer."

The Russians have captured their woman jet pilot and are taking her back to the USSR for execution. In transport by airplane Hope tricks the Pilot and sneaks onto the Plane. Hope becomes the Pilot.

Recall both Howard Hughes and Bob Hope our Pilots. Hope is in the Pilot seat. They get caught and they wind up In Russia. The plane lands and Bob Hope's yelling "kill all the Russians". At that point the Russians arrest the Russians. East and West come together and at the Airport is NBC Radio and CBS Radio to report of the new era.

Seems to me that shows that Hope or Hughes our on both sides. They bribe all the spies. The US wins.

* * * *

#47. 1957... Beau James
Beau James is a film of the life of Jimmy Walker, the 100th Mayor of New York City. Bob Hope plays the part of Jimmy Walker and Walter Winchell narrates the Jimmy Walker love story based on the true History of Jimmy Walker.

Hope plays the part of Jimmy Walker as he runs for Governor of New York and is introduced as the late Jimmy Walker. The movie shows the campaign of showbiz. Walker writes a Song, Will You Love Me in December As You Do in May. The Song became a real hit in that day. He wins the Election.

Walker at his celebration drinks too much and he winds up in a Showgirls apartment and the girl saves Walker. She sobered him up and he falls in love with her. The girl gets a lead in a Broadway Show.

The film shows Atlantic City, The World's Playground, the Queen of Resorts and Newsreel reports on gang wars in New York City. Walker had married the girl in 1932. They had their Honeymoon in Atlantic City.

At a Walker Roast with Jack Benny on Violin Bob Hope and Jimmy Durante do a Song and Dance to Jimmy's Song.

The continuing film depicts the true life of Jimmy Walker and the many situations in his life. His life in the news. There were not many clues in this movie.

* * * *

#48. 1958 ... Paris Holiday

This Film starts out on a Cruise Ship which is going to Paris and Bob Hope is on board. Dialog says: "he's the world's greatest comedian". Amongst themselves they say that "Hope uses many names and many ships". Bob Hope speaks of himself as "a star of stage, screen, radio and TV". That's the truth.

While Hope is womanizing and in love with himself He is talking to himself in a mirror again. In the mirror we see two Hopes. To himself He says to himself "you know my name". An actor says to Hope, "everybody knows your name you are great". Bob retorts, "I am not working on this Cruise I am a passenger of the first class". As Howard Hughes. You can say that again. The Greatest Show on Earth. At that time Hope is asked "if you're not working why are you wearing makeup". That's easy Howard Hughes is Bob Hope all the time. He is an Actor and he wears sponge Rubber all the time. He's acting. The other Actor rubs Hope's Nose. The Actor goes nuts and grabs the Nose of another person who is laughing out loud. Laughing at the joke. The joke that fools them all-all the time. The actors know it, the people don't.

The movie turns into a spy thriller again. A woman spy steals Hopes room key and searches his room "twice". The spies are in on Hope. Hope confers he's "a pilot ". In this scene Hope is on the phone getting landing permits at an airport. At this time Hope envisions the Eiffel Tower as a Giant Oil Derrick. Sure does look like one.

The information that the woman spy wants from Hope is coded in the Manuscript of a Play. Chapter 6 is missing. Everyone is trying to get their hands on the script. Hope is out to buy the Manuscript. "No matter what the cost."

As Hope is going through an Airport to New York City Hope is talking out loud. He says, "I am a citizen on a special mission". Well, he's said that before. Isn't that the truth.

It was revealed in an NBC Bob Hope TV Special that Bob Hope is running a Spy Ring out of the Basement of 30 Rock. 30 Rock is the home base of NBC. The Peacock Network. Hope goes on to say that "no one is going to get rid of me."

Hope is using the State Department to assist him in getting landing permits. Hope says : "do you want me to get in a big bird and fly away once around the world". There's a fact of Howard Hughes life. He flew around the World in record setting time.

Looking into a mirror again There's two Hope faces. Hope says, "don't break the mirror". And again, the Spies are out to kill Hope for he is known by other Spies. Sounds like a Howard Hughes scenario to me. Hope crashes and says, "wish I had another arm". Was Howard Hughes injured in a crash? Hughes got pretty hurt in all the crashes he had. Is Hope as hurt as Hughes?

In this Movie Hope's Mission as a spy is to catch Counterfeiters in Europe. Dialog takes a switch and Hope says, "maybe I am the head of the Communist Party". He again says, "they tried to kill me "twice". Twice? Right if they kill one they kill him both. If they kill one they kill them both at the same time. Two of the most famous names in America sleep together.

My speculation is that Hughes being the Billionaire Industrialist probably was on both sides. Hope has said previously that he was a "mole" either in the Mob or in the Communist Party. It is history that there was involvement of the Mob and the Communist in Hollywood.

Hope makes a deal between the United States and France. The United States is behind the Identification of Howard Hughes as Bob Hope. They got him covered. Chased by spies Hope escapes to a Circus. That's right, he changed his identity and went into Show Business. That's a circus.

In the Carnival House Hope, and the Women go through the Tunnel of Love by boat. They row past the Wax Museum. To hide Hope puts the Wax Figures in the boat and takes their place in the Museum. The spies jump out and kill the look-alike wax figures in the boat. They do not kill Hope nor the Woman. Hope yells, "take a crack on trying to kill me everybody else has."

In another scene Hope explains all about his incidents as a spy in France as he plays with Pigeons in an Insane Asylum, also known as a Nut House. A Pigeon is one who rats on others or is being used by others. In other words, a sucker.

In the nut house Hope is playing an invisible game of Checkers and he wins. He sneaks out and is seen "developing pictures". That's spy stuff. All the movies studios also develop pictures.

Hope is then put on trial as to whether he is Sane or Insane. In court The United States American Embassy speaks on Hope's behalf. The other Actors say of Hope "he is the living end, the cool cat and he's crazy". The Cat and the Canary. The mole.

Hope escapes by Helicopter and they are all shooting at him. Recall that Bob Hope wrote a book titled Don't Shoot its only Me. Hope escapes the chase and is dropped by Helicopter into a Car.

His friends are in the car and they all go back to the Nuthouse as Hope yells "here come the Marines."

Then there is shown a Paramount Newsreel featuring Bob Hope as the hero of World War II. The film shows the victory March through Paris.

With this film in the movie he's trying to tell you that he's Howard Hughes and all his equipment, and his leadership led the United States to victory through World War II. Here he is congratulating himself. In this film Hope relates to you that he was a spy and had something to do with the Victory in Europe. World War II.

This Movie made it a point to point out that this movie "Paris holiday" of 1958, was produced by Robert Leslie, based on a story written solely by Bob Hope. Robert Leslie is also Bob Hope. The movie describes an incident as a spy in France for the United States of America. Other movies have said the same thing.

Howard Hughes was Bob Hope in make-up. It's Howard Hughes talking with the Bob Hope face. He fooled all the People all the time. And he's told Nothing but the Truth in most of his movies.

* * * *

#49. 1959… Alias Jesse James

Jesse James robs banks and trains out West. Like a pirate. I believe that Howard Hughes as Bob Hope did the same as the United States paid for everything, thereby Hope/Hughes was robbing the United States Government, the Department of Defense and the United States Treasury. This movie is a story of a man with attributes. 1880, New York City. The movie throws in the theme of this man running an insurance agency called the Plymouth Rock Insurance Company.

Speaking of attributes. Here's a list, and Industrial Billionaire, Inventor, Jet Pilot and Actor and a War Hero. If you recall LBJ said of Hope that Hope is a man with two great attributes. Actor and an Industrial Billionaire.(2)

As the insurance agent Hope has Jesse James insured and follows him across the West so that he does not die and cost his Plymouth Rock Insurance Company a $100,000.

In this film Hope is well-dressed and his tie has a very large diamond H on it, and in one scene Hope's money belt drops to the floor. It is a money belt showing that he is the man with a lot of money, a lot of diamonds. I believe the big H stands for Howard Hughes.

Further, we have Hope gambling again in a card game, and he says he has "four Kings". Like in cards. When he says he has four Kings I believe he's talking about the Middle East and four Kings in the Middle East that are part of Howard Hughes oil partners. Like Saudi Arabia, Kuwait, Bahrain, Qatar? then in the movie Hope inherits a watch given to him by his Grandfather. He was left the Inheritance.

This movie is like a Beverly Hillbillies show of the old-fashioned West. It is also like a high society film at times.

In one scene a guy is up on Hope. Annie's looking him over and staring at Hope Face without saying a word. You should watch this movie. Look over the Bob Hope face.

And there's another plot to kill Hopes life. Hope, stressing in a mirror again and again he's talking to himself and playing both parts of Bob Hope and Jesse James. (2) Then there's a gunfight. Bob Hope says into the mirror to him-self, "somebody shot at you" talking to the other him. Right Hope said that to his double and then he says "if anything happens to you. I'm dead". Right, one killed both dead. He's two people in one and he tells you every movie. The gig would be up.

The film's dialog says to Hope "you can keep the outfit on as Bob Hope, because the other guy is said to be dead". Now isn't that what they said about Howard Hughes. Howard Hughes is covered by the Bob Hope outfit.

Well, there it is again the spy as a spy, shot at and if caught, he's got the cover story. Hope wore the tuxedo and he did travel. (there was a TV show called Have Gun will travel). Hope is now another person in his outfit and he then says, "they won't be looking for me being thought to be dead". Say what? that's what he did. He played dead as Howard Hughes as he stayed in the outfit of Bob Hope. They won't be looking for Howard. You know, that's about Howard Hughes, sounds familiar, doesn't it, Howard Hughes, unseen never seen, said to be dead. He wasn't dead. He was alive in an "Alleged life" of Bob Hope. Nobody recognized him. Him being Howard Hughes. Then there's this dialog to Hope "you look like as though you've seen a ghost."

The Howard Hughes Mystery hangs over the world. Dialog has it "who's alive and who Is dead". And again, Hope shows up in another disguise as a Preacher to stop a wedding.

As the movie rolls onto an ending Hope and the girl escaped and there is a gunfight. In the gunfight and on film are all the Television and Movie Cowboy Stars, shooting at the bad guys.

The good guys on Hope side are: Ward Bond, Roy Rogers, Hugh O' Brian, Fess Parker, Annie Oakley, James Cooper, Jay "Tonto" Silverheels and of course, Bing Crosby.

Hope escapes and he marries the girl and has seven (7) kids. Hope always uses the number seven (7) because he is and was 007. Take his word for it!

All the above Stars and all the Movie Stars were under contract to Howard Hughes. Remember Bob Hope was the Entertainment Director.

* * * *

#50. 1960... Facts of Life.

This film is about Adultery. It starts out with Hope tired of his gambling habit and he wants a vacation with Lucille Ball. She is another man's wife.

They go off to Acapulco Mexico on a so-called fishing trip. Adultery seems to be a way of life in the Hollywood community.

Strangely enough, Hope starts talking about Missiles and the Hydrogen Bomb. In previous movies Hope has said that he is the "Inventor". That sounds like something that Howard Hughes would be talking about. That's consistent with My Theory. Hughes being the Aviator and the Rocket man and the Inventor. Many Bob Hope movies are all about and around the true-life adventures of Howard Hughes. Not the Alleged Life of Bob Hope. Hope romances with Lucille Ball, a fish Is caught and then there is the kiss of love. The Hotel and a love scene on the beach.

Back home after their vacation Bob and Lucille continue the adulterous affair. Bob sets up more dates with Lucille Ball and uses other names. Hope dresses high-class in the mirror. Again, showing off that he Is very rich.

On a car date at a drive-in movie, it's a Western, they are spotted together. Later, they are also spotted at Bungalow # 9. It is History that Howard Hughes and Bob Hope both used the cottages where they put up women for those secret rendezvous.

On the drive as they travel from Texas through the Panhandle Lucille states to Bob "you're from good stock". Remember Bob Hope writes these movies and Bob Hope makes these movies.

As part of this movie Hope goes out for coffee from their motel room and he gets lost and he can't remember which Motel he was in.

It is shown in the movie that they checked in as Mr. and Mrs. George Washington. I believe with that sign in that Hope is stressing Howard Hughes Heritage that stems from colonial times and that he saved the world through World War 11.

As Hope signs in as George Washington the Manager is asked by Hope if they "remember me" and the Manager retorts "you're the father of our country."

After winning World War II you could say with that victory that Howard Hughes led the way by saving the United States from defeat. Thus, he's the Father of our Nation.

For example, at the end of this movie Lucille Ball calls Bob Hope "Vernon Von Braun". There again in the dialog is the connection to the Aviator and to Rocket Man. Lucille Ball is just speaking the dialog of the movie where she knows who he is in real life.

Von Braun is connected to Howard Hughes. All the German scientist captured by the Americans after World War II were in fact hooked up with Howard Hughes and they both became connected to NASA and the United States Space Program.

For a further note, I watched Lucille Ball sing a song at the Kennedy Center. She sang a song and I specifically heard one line of that song where she said and sang "you think we are all comedians, but we are all spies". That's right. That's what she sang, and I heard it. Check it out.

Then the Movie has Hope taking off in a plane under a false name. That name being "Mr. Washington". I would think this movie said something very consistent with My Theory.

* * * *

#51. 1961 ... Bachelor in Paradise. Paradise Island?

Hope is filmed using Tape Recorders as Cupid in France doing research as an author about American life. To me that signals that he's setting people up to be blackmailed and spied on.

Right. As a screenwriter Hope and his two heads makes movies about American life. This movie is about philandering in France as Cupid to bring about turning female spies in favor of the United States. Espionage.

In the movie Hope is ordered back to Washington by the United States Government. Nothing but the Truth, My Favorites Spy, Have Gun Will Travel, Have Tux Will Travel on and on. "There's a message in every movie". Bing Crosby said that. The same applies to many TV shows. Brought to you by 3,000 Hollywood Writers. The truth be told.

In this Movie Hope/ Hughes is told by the Government to "deny who you are". Hope is "ordered to take on a false identity". What did I tell you! They tell you again and again that Hope has taken on a false Identity. Hope is brought to the Treasury Department. That being the IRS. The IRS has been after Hope/ Hughes for him to pay his Taxes for the Past 14 years. He owes Millions in Taxes. Do they make a deal?

Hope is tagged as a criminal. Hope is charged "about tax". He says, "all my life savings are down the drain". And says, "I am an American citizen."

All the above sounds like the United States Government squeezed Howard Hughes over his taxes. Recall that there were United States Senate hearings into the Billionaire Industrialist dealings with the United States Government.

Hope winds up broke and with the Government's help He's out to "write a book" and do research on American life. Hope rents a house under an "assumed name". In dialog Hope is said to be a "mysterious character". Sounds like everything that was said about Howard Hughes.

In the first 10 min. of this Movie he's already been two (2) characters.

A woman rents a house to Hope. Her last name is Howard.

Remember Bob Hope writes this stuff.

Still in the Movie Hope is still looking for a Secretary. The woman does not know who this man is" and "does not know what he looks like". Never has seen him and there is no picture of him, and Bob Hope says, "if his face had been well-known (as Howard Hughes) it would hurt his research". Recall Bob Hope has set himself up in family life with four adopted children.

Hope the Author is in the Paradise Community to write a book "under an assumed name". Bob Hope the magnificent fraud in his "Alleged Life". The Greatest Show on Earth. The Great Impersonator. Bob Hope is the assumed name that's known to the public.

Note that there is a photo of Hope in one of his own books of him leaving a show to go to his plane and Bob Hope put this caption underneath the photo. "After every show I leave quickly under an assumed name". In his own words. That is Howard Hughes. After every Show he leaves under the "Assumed Name" carrying his Golf Club. The Assumed Name is Bob Hope.

Hope also said under another photo in a book of his that when he gets off his plane to do a Bob Hope show he writes "he leaves himself behind". Who is himself? He leaves himself, Howard Hughes behind and becomes Bob Hope. I say he leaves himself Howard Hughes behind and becomes Bob Hope for the show. For the Joke.

Back to the movie Hope tells the Woman that he is "doing research for the Government". Hope is quoted as saying "I am working for the Government". That's right, Nothing but the Truth. In how many movies has Bob Hope said that he is working for the Government.

The husband of the woman that Hope was making it with is drunk and in one scene, the drunk husband points out Hope and Rubs Hope's Nose. The fake Nose. The make-up, the special effects.

In another scene Hope is using a razor and a remark is made to Hope in the dialog that "if he's found out they'll cut his head off". I heard that in another movie. The woman says, "you'll still have a spare head". There they tell you again. Two Heads, Two Writers, Two People, Two Hats, Two Pairs of Pants, Two Faces in the Mirror. Two of the most famous names In America sleep together. They got him Covered. The Government calls Bob Hope back to Washington in a moment's notice. Have Tux will Travel. In that book Hope explains his role for the United States of America. In Washington the Government gives Hope Hughes his Stocks, Bonds and Money back. That was the deal.

There is a Court room scene over the adultery charges against Hope. In a divorce case Hope argues that he was not making love to the married women in the village because he is in love with Ms. Howard only.

Here's another connection to Howard Hughes. The Paramount News Crew is on the site and is told Hope was "out of the country for 14 years."

I saw a TV news report years later, when John F Kennedy gave the Congressional Medal of Honor to Bob Hope. Hope said the same thing. That he got the Award "for being out of the country". Who was out of the country for 12 or 14 years? Bob Hope or Howard Hughes or both?? I say both!

At that Hope says, "I was under an assumed name". That's right, exactly. Just like the quote under a photo in one of his books. Howard Hughes was out of the Country under an "assumed name". Bob Hope!

I can recall reading all the newspaper headlines in the 60's all about Howard Hughes hiding out of the country going from country to country. In this film, the Government is with him and beside him. They got him covered in the dialog it says, "everybody knows who you are". Hope says, "I have to lie I am back to find my identity". Hope then confesses to his womanizing and hiding women all over the place. That's a fact. And it is documented in Arthur Marx's book about the secret life of Bob Hope. Hiding the women in the same Bungalows where Howard Hughes hid all his women. That's a fact from the book, The Secret life of Howard Hughes by Charles Higham. Hope and Hughes were both Casanovas'.

Hope says, "I returned to Washington to marry". Dialog said to Hope "now you're just another guy". Then there's a scene where Bob Hope is shown Tape Recording everybody and everything.

Recall that Hope told Lana Turner that he Is "Central intelligence."

As Howard Hughes, and as Bob Hope they are The Greatest Show on Earth.

* * * *

#52. 1962 ... Road to Hong Kong

Since the beginning it has been Bob and Bing and this movie starts out that way. Bob and Bing open as teamwork together. They have a Business Plan as a Song and Dance Team to enter Vaudeville.

They make a deal. 80% for Bob and 20% for Bing. Bing says to Bob "yours is tax-free". Bing is talking about the deal that Bob has with the Government. Bing indicates that everything Bob Hope does is completely tax-free and paid for by the United States Government. The Government is paying for everything that Bob Hope does. Everything! From the Canteens, from all the Radio and Television Shows, to the USO shows, through the Paramount Newsreels and all the Movies. Bing says to Bob "without teamwork there is no team". Make note that Hollywood made all the Government Training Films for the United States Military before, during and after the war.

The mystery begins with real film about Hong Kong and the Secret United States International locations. There is no mistake that the Russians are in space and that Hope, and Bing have the Secret Formula for Fuel and the Russians are out to get it. Here we have another spy movie.

Bob and Bing, also known as Turner and Babcock are said to be "two phonies". We know Hope is a phony because Howard Hughes is Bob Hope in make-up under his "assumed name" and in his "alleged life". Bob Hope is that Magnificent Fraud. Bob Hope is Howard Hughes's stage name.

This Movie has a woman out to steal Secrets from Bob and Bing. They are to be killed. The plot continues where Hope is to be the flyer and gets his head re-blocked. Hope puts on a new face. Bing Crosby said that in his preface to Bob Hope's first book, They Got Me Covered.

Bob Hope says, "let's take a powder". Howard Hughes did that and disappeared for years, just as Bob Hope was away from home for 12 straight years while his family lived in Toluca Lake's.

Bob Hope changes his looks and Identity and says, "people won't recognize anyone". Like Mission Impossible? It is possible to fool all the people all the time! Being part of the Motion Picture Industry, it is easy to have access to the make-up departments of all the Studios. Like a man of 1,000 faces, The Walking Dead, and the Ghost stories. Don't forget the movie "mask."

In Howard Hughes's early life, he was an Air Force Test Pilot. Bob Hope has said he is a Pilot. In this Movie he is shown in a space man's astronaut suit. He's flying, and he crashes, and Hope is in the Hospital looking Into a Mirror again. In the Mirror there are two Hopes. As he looks in the mirror Hope says, "who's that"? Is he disfigured? Hope loses his memory and gets a medical check-up. The doctor examining Hope investigates his Ears and sees right through his head.

Getting out of the Hospital Bob and Bing go to the Mountains of Tibet. The movie has them flying in by Pan Am. It is an historical fact that Pan Am was a CIA operated Airline.

Hope as a spy loses his bags that had a signal to another spy indicated on the bag so that he can be approached by his counterpart. His bags get switched. An enemy woman spy goes after Hope thinking he is her contact. She says to Hope "have you done this spy thing before"? Hope responds, "I think I have". Hope winds up at the top of the Tibet's Mountains in a Symposium. Hope says,"I don't remember Money or Women."

This movie again has Hope in the Nut House and Bing asked Bob "what's your name"? Hope remembers his name and gets better and retains total recollection. Thanks for the memory. Both Bob and Bing escape from the Sanatorium.

Bing is testing Bob Hope's Memory. Hope start rapping off "aircraft engineering". Speaks out about being "a genius". He then talks about Spy Rings and Guns, the Mob, and Unions. From watching all of Bob Hope's movies (All 62) that's what I have gleaned. No Doubt Bob Hope is Howard Hughes, No Doubt Howard Hughes is Bob Hope. No doubt he was connected to the Government, the Mob and the Unions. (CIA, Giancana, Hoffa)

In this movie the Actress puts a Gun to Hopes stomach and threatens to shoot him and Hope, says "I already have a scar there". I believe that he is talking about the many injuries from the many crashes that Howard Hughes had.

Bing comes up with some drugs and has Hope drink them so that he will talk and spill the beans. They do a skit and talk about Spooks and talk about Top Secret Secrets. They talk about the New Formula for Rocket Fuel. They talk of a more powerful Rocket Fuel.

Remember Howard Hughes and von Braun had that Secret. Aviator, Rocket Man, The Mask Man, The Lone Ranger, Etc. Etc.

Hope is flown off the scene by the CIA's Pan Am Airline to a secluded estate. Hope says, "I have a fortune in my head". That's right, he's the "inventor". (HRH)

Hope takes an elevator down under the Ocean and meets underwater with a bunch of Spies and Mafia Crooks. Many James bond movies had the same theme of Submarine Bases under the Ocean. Hope has said he was 007 in movies past. On the History

Channel it was said that UFO's operate from under and in the Ocean.

In dialog Hope is told that "with the Formula in your mind you'll save the world."

The Formula is for a more Powerful Rocket Fuel so that a lift-off has greater thrust. Do you think this is about Bob Hope or Howard Hughes?

The enemy spies want the Formula and offer Hope $25,000. Dialog says to Hope "think of your country". Hope has the formula in a bottle and a spy picks his pocket and steals the Formula.

I must note here the secret History of the Moon landing featured in a Turner classic movie. The history of Flight from Air Balloons to the Zeppelin, to the Airplane to jets, to Howard Hughes, to Kelly Johnson, a United States Air Force Jet Test Pilot, just like Hughes and Hope, and Yeager and Armstrong and many others. Kelly Johnson was all about Jets and Fuel, as the designer of the P 80 Jet in 1952 at Edwards Air Force Base in California. The star fighter hit Mac 2 heading for space flight. That's the Speed of Sound. The United States broke the Sound Barrier.

History has it that after winning World War II, America defeated Germany and seized 100 Rocket Scientist, including the main guy Vernon von Braun.

Von Braun was the designer of the V2 for Germany. A rocket in which Germany bombed England. As was said before The United States captured those German Scientist and brought them all to the United States and hooked them up with Howard Hughes, the Aviator, the Rocket Man. All the German Scientist were taken to Fort Bliss Texas. They were to teach the Americans how to build Jets and Rocket Engines. Through that development NASA was formed at the Marshall Space Center. The Secret Fuel Formula was used on a Saturn five Rocket. That's History. The Jet Pilots behind Hughes and Von Braun, from Johnson to Armstrong made it to the Moon. Take note when United States landed on the Moon the Astronauts played a game of Golf. If you recall, Howard Hughes wanted to be one of the best golfers in the world. Bob Hope always walks around carrying a Golf Club. Eight Astronauts putted the Golf Ball on the

Moon. Do you see the connection? Howard Hughes always hid out on the Ninth floor of the Desert Inn Hotel and Casino. Bob Hope holds the Desert Inn Golf classic in Las Vegas.

Back to the movie, the spies capture Bob and Bing and are going to put them in a Rocket to go around the Moon instead of using Monkeys. They are put on a Rocket, in the Missile and in the Space Capsule. They are launched from a Submarine into Space. There is a film in the movie showing the Submarine launching the Missile. Hope continues to talk about the Formula.

The Capsule from the missile falls back to earth. There is a film of the capsule landing at sea. Bob and Bing are considered Heroes for they have the Top-Secret Rocket Formula.

The spies are still after Hope. The Spies get a woman to seduce Hope to get the Secret Formula. Hope and the woman have a date. Hope dresses up in a Tuxedo, which demonstrates he is again High Society Big Money indicating the very rich. The spies record him. Hope calls himself "an everyday Astronaut". Hope goes on to talk of "a high-octane fuel formula". He talks "Secrets of Jets going three times the speed of sound". Now isn't that exactly what went down in the development of aircraft's and rockets in American history?

Wearing a tuxedo indicates that he, Bob Hope is traveling for the United States Government on a mission to spy for the United States. That's what Bob said in his book Have Tux will Travel.

United States Air Force jet test Pilot Yeager also broke the Sound Barrier going faster than a speeding Bullet. That is Superman's theme?

In a new scene we have Hope in the Mirror again in love with himself. A Woman spy is flipped and sides with Hope and is arrested by her spy agency. Isn't that the same theme in the Iron Petticoat? She flips for Bob and for the United States. They escape, they run and hide and with special effects are dressed in Costumes as Chinese hiding in a Rickshaw. Jerry Colonna shows up in the movie.

Here's a side note. Bob and Colonna are singing together at a USO show. Colonna sings that there is room in Bob Hopes bed, "there's room for two (2) Your nose and you". Colonna knew what was up. Two of the most famous names In America sleep together. That's right and they are both Howards Hughes.

Now, right out of Bob Hope's own mouth Hope says, "he is the treasury". He goes on to say, "we are with the FBI". "I have operation Eye socket."

History has noted that Bob Hope and Howard Hughes both have had eye operations.

Hope yells "you no look Chinese". He then says, "killers are chasing us". They take off their disguises. They start talking about Hydrogen and how to get a Rocket to take off.

Bob Hope, Bing Crosby and Joan Collins all get away in the Rocket Capsule and they land on a planet with Frank Sinatra and Dean Martin. All four of them are trying to hit on Joan Collins. There's a future movie called Call Me Bawana where there is another story about a Space Capsule. (Hope has said he had space-walked.)

This movie, and many of Bob Hopes spy movies seemed to come to lite some 19 years after the War. Thanks for the Memory. Thanks for the Truth and Nothing but the Truth.

There they said it again, just as Bing said, "every movie has to have a message". Read between the lines? Do you see that My Theory is true? Howard Hughes is talking through his Bob Hope face.

Love that Bob

* * * *

#53. 1963 … Critics Choice.

Here Clues are given about what the fake faces and false IDs can do. Lucille Ball and Bob Hope made this movie. Bob Hope is a Theater Critic of Broadway shows and is in a situation where he must review a play written by his wife, whom he tries to discourage from writing. He writes a column in the papers.

Lucille Ball says, "getting Bob Hope up in the morning is hard work and it took the United States Army to get him out of bed by 11". Dialog says, "12 years" and then says, "look at that face."

Hope asked, "how do I look"? and dialog answers "You can't always tell by the way someone looks". That's right, it could be a disguise. Someone not looking like they really look.

Hope is under Psychological Analysis care. He says he has an "old friend". He talks about "his friends mind". I think that would be Bob Hope talking to his other head as his friend which would be Howard Hughes. Hope is asked if he's "ever been analyzed". Hope says, "not all of me". That means only half of him. He has a split personality. He's two people in one just as My Theory proved. Two heads are better than one.

Then there's a scene where Bob is at his son's Little League baseball game and he gets hit on the Nose and his Head. Hope gets a bad back "twice" in the skit. Twice! One for each Head. Hope is asked if he "ever have a bad back before"? Hope answers "no trouble before, except for years ago". There you go. This movie was made in 1963. Howard Hughes plane crashes and boat crash were between 1938 and 1946. Hope has described his injuries and they are consistent with Howards.

That's right, after Howard had too many crashes, after his recuperation, Hope says "people will see me, and they won't believe it's me". They will see Bob Hope, but they won't know it's Howard Hughes. They won't see Howard. Hope has said "no one has seen his face, and if they did it would be a big problem" Hope is called an "old Fox". Like in 20th Century Fox?

Hope is asked "are you going to tell the truth"? Hope says, "no, I am going to lie."

As the dialog goes on, Hope is always talking about dark alleys, about murders, robberies, plumbers, money, golf, planes, spies and talk of bullet proof vest. Pretty intriguing.

In another scene, Bob is dialing a phone and ask, "is this phone bugged"?. He then talks about "codes". That's spy talk right? He then is quoted as saying "if you pick out every other word you will get the message". There Bob gives you a lesson in how to code and decode messages. In every movie there is a message. "Sonny" Hughes learned about Codes at Indian Scout Camp as a very young man.

Bob then says, "where do you hide the body". (in the basement of a mansion in Cuba)

Note this, I came across this quote in the paperback book, the Mongoose. Chapter six is titled, Loose as a Mongoose - 1966 through 1970. It talks about Howard Hughes and his Vegas years and it talks about the Kennedy Assassination. I picked out this quote by a man named Johnny Meyer. "I don't know where all the bodies are buried. But I do know where most of them are sleeping". He then gives a hint that they may be buried at Hughes's Aircraft Plants. (Or under a Mansion in Cuba).

Hope then has a dream, a nightmare, with he himself as a Pilot with one eye. Is that pointing out another Injury? As I said before, Bob Hope and Howard Hughes both had eye operations. That may be, and or, it may be that he uses one eye at the end of a camera or that all of Howard Hughes's famous crashes cost him an eye. Hope is now drinking in the movie and says he "has no home" and that he is "a wounded veteran". Is that true? HRH was injured as an Air Force Jet Pilot! He was an Air Force Jet Test Pilot when he crashed. He was in the Military. This movie had nothing to do with Bob's family, but a lot to reveal more of Howard Hughes experiences. Here the dialog at the end of the movie has Hope talking about starting over as an Actor. It is said "all they can do is change their name and start over."

In the movie it is said that Bob Hope "comes over in a large bluebird". An Airplane. "Recall, the names of the innocent have been changed to protect the joke.

* * * *

#54. 1963 ... Call Me Bawana

The film opens with Hope playing the role of Elbert. The movie opens with 3 min. of credits with everyone shown with a monkey face from the Stars, the Cast and the Studios Technicians.

The story goes that United States has a top priority red alert system. Then it is shown that someone in a rocking chair, talking like John Kennedy says, "only one-person (Albert Meriwether) Hope, "is the only person to get to the Moon before others". He "Has one guy in mind". Do you think it's the Inventor, the Aviator, the Rocket man, Superman, the Lone Ranger, the Billionaire Industrialist, the Jet Pilot, the Masked man?.

In This movie Hope is an American spy. One of America's space capsules crashes in Africa and Hope is sent to Africa to find the lost space capsule. Hope must find the lost space capsule before the enemy. The Enemy is after the lost space capsule as well as United States Military, its Generals and CIA agents, there all after the space capsule, the enemies of the United States must not get hold of America's space Technology.

A Central Intelligence agent says to Hope "We, the CIA and the President of United States wants you to go to Africa and find the space capsule". In that scene Bob Hope says this "if the capsule is found by the enemy all my stuff will be taken if the capsule is found."

All his stuff! That's Howard Hughes talking with the Bob Hope face. It's his stuff. He's the Rocket man. He's the Aviator. He is the Spaceman.

The movie has it that Elbert Meriwether is in New York. He's writing a diary book titled Trader (stock Market?) Could this happen in real life. Was Howard Hughes on both sides. Hope once said he was a "mole" an infiltrator. Who did he trade in favor of? Was Hope or Hughes both sides of many Nations.

A Government plane is waiting to take Hope to Africa to find his stuff. To find His space capsule. On his way To the Government Plane Hope says to tell the President (JFK)"I voted for Nixon". Hope is taken to the Government Plane and in conversation the dialog says," you are covered". That's consistent with Bob Hope's first book in 1941. They Got Me Covered. He was just told by the United States Military that he's Covered. At that time Hope is told that "there may be an attempt on his life". And Hope responds, "I am not going to die till I find the right way to do it". Looks like one or both guys are looking to disappear.

As years go by I believe He figured out a way to die. The plan is revealed. Hughes was said to have died in 1977.

Hope as a spy is given cyanide pills as the character Hope is to die and disappear, to take a powder. Sounds like a Howard Hughes life to me.

As the group is boarding the plane to Africa all the officers in the unit receive spy radios. There's a scene where they're all talking about life insurance on the plane. There's a woman on the plane and Hope of course is womanizing. The woman is a spy. How many Bob Hope movies revolve around spy themes?

They all arrive in Africa and there's a Church service with the local inhabitants. They're all singing gospel songs. It is shown that the other spies, enemies of the United States are following Hope. They are playing music on a piano and it is revealed that the piano is the enemies short wave radio. These spies are out to kill Hope and get the space capsule for the Russians. The movie indicates that the cost of the Africa trip was paid for lock, stock and barrel by the White House.

Hope arrives at the Hotel, he's given room 222. An Actor speaks up and says, "no one has ever seen you". Isn't that something. Nobody has ever seen Howard Hughes eighter. Nobody has seen Howard Hughes ever since he put on the Bob Hope face.

The woman spies are after Hope. One spy search Hopes Hotel Room number 222 and has to escape out a window.

In another scene Hopes speaks up and says, "my name is", he is cut off mid-sentence by a bunch of chatter in the room. Hope never gets to say what his name is. What is his real name? who is he?

Well, Hope is womanizing again. He turns the woman Russian spy over to the American side and the spy game continues. It's my opinion that Hope used Hollywood Starlets and Actors to operate a spy ring out of 30 rock. (NBC)

In this movie Hope grabs a bunch of maps of Africa and is asked "has it occurred to you that you are being followed". Hope and his group are said to be just going on Safari. The spies are out to kill Hope with Guns and Chloroform. If they get the chance.

Dialog says to Hope "you are a man of violence", And "you're the boss, you are in charge". Bob gives money to the spies, and an Elephant sucks on Bob's nose. Dialog says of Hope he,"looks stupid, but acts clever". When Hope is asked about himself he says, "I'll let you know after the autopsy."

Everybody is searching for the space capsule and they are homing in on it. The spies are still after Hope's location device. Then there's this statement. Spies say, "if we remove his head It will come off easily". That is right because his head is make-up. Putty, Sponge Rubber or Stucco.

In another scene Bob Hope has a woman sewing his pants near his crotch and he remarks "I feel like I'm going to be alive again". You can take that two ways. He is going to be alive as he has an erection and that he Is going to have sex. That's his MO, or he is going to be the other person, which also has the same mo. The womanizers. Then dialog says about Hope that "he thrives on lovemaking."

The spies trap Hope and grab his Face and try to rip his nose off. Hope mentions Kennedy and Texas.

Remember the piano of the spies is used as a short-wave radio. Hope and his group meet up with African natives. They have the space capsule and are worshiping it. At that Hope, says, "they must know how much it cost". Howard Hughes as Bob Hope knows how much it cost.

Hope is in the Camp talking to the Tribal Chief and the rest of the natives are looking and staring at Bob Hope's face. Recall that happened in other movies where people just stare at Bob Hope's face. The natives love Hope, and Hope says, "when they found out who I was they let me go". Who is he? They were all looking and staring at Bob Hope's face.

The enemy spies "steal the capsule". They take off with the capsule on the back of a truck. They do not know that Bob and the women are in the space capsule. Hope has rocket fuel with him and the capsule takes off into space. Sounds like the other movie I critiqued. As the rocket lifts off and the capsule goes into space the theme of the Lone Range is played.

Note: think about the Lone Rangers opening. With a fiery horse, the speed of light and a cloud of dust. The fiery horse is engine power. The speed of light is the laser. And the cloud of dust is the liftoff. Who is that masked man? Rocket man. Check History. There's a Jet Propulsion Laboratory in Southern California.

Air Force Radar picks up the Capsule saying, "it's ours". With that the Air Force orders Hope to report to Washington. Could all these happenings be the conversations that Hope had with all the American Presidents whom Bob Hope was having Goff with all the time.........

* * * *

#55. 1964... A Global Affair

Bob Hope, a bachelor works at the UN and he finds a beautiful baby child left at the UN building. Hope wants the child to go to the best nation. Many women from international nations want the child.

Hope as Latimore is shown in a closet, a high-tech room with all kinds of computers, and a bunch of tape recorders. It said, "he's living right over there". That scene said to me that he is at the UN and he is taping everyone.

The baby is to be kept top secret. There's a mix up in a scene where the baby hidden in a dog basket is picked up by another woman and the baby is lost.

Bob Hope is then shown at the head podium of the UN saying, "been to Mexico, busy in Mexico". Whatever that meant? The baby being lost is reported on television news by Hugh Downs.

At the podium Bob Hope talks anti-Cuba talk and talks negative about Russia. As he goes from room to room and woman to woman he is to take care of the cute baby Monroe. It's a girl.

Hope is to choose what nation the child should go to. Hope wants the child to be an international citizen. From the UN Podium Bob Hope gives his worldview. Hope says, "my finest mind has the whole truth". You should watch the movie.

Now the whole bunch of the women at the UN show up and they want to take care of the baby. The dialog is about Hope and the bomb. Hope is against Russia and states that the baby "not go to Russia."

Hope wins the child as an International Citizen and the Child does not go to Russia. Then Hope says his name out loud he says "my name Bob Hope is not my real name". There you go. By now we all know what his real name is. His name Is not Bob Hope. Bob Hope is his stage name. His real name is Howard Rupert Hughes Jr and his nickname is Sonny. The Billionaire. A woman dancer then goes up to Hope and touches him on his Nose.

This story told you "Nothing but the Truth". Bob Hope is not his real name. He's an American and he is secretly behind the UN and he's against Russia and Cuba. That's American History.

* * * *

#56. 1965... I'll Take Sweden

At the opening of this film there is a cartoon of Bob Hope as a Father with Money and a whole bunch of Chevys' in the yard. It is a party in the yard for the Children of the 60s with an old man and he's considered square. Sponge Bob Square Pants.

One of Bob Hopes major sponsors was Chevrolet. Chevy also sponsored the Dinah Shore show on television. She sang the commercial "see the USA in your Chevrolet". I also found out reading about Howard Hughes that he would park a Chevy every eight blocks square in the big city's whenever he was there. I guess that was a means of escape as, strange as it may seem.

Years later the writers of Hollywood put out a television cartoon series called Sponge Bob Square Pants. Isn't that interesting. Remember Bob said his writers write a lot of stories about him. Him who? Him as Howard Hughes.

If you recall Bob Hope has said in a movie that he "knows all about Sponge Rubber because he is an Actor and he wears it all the time". It was in the 60s because of Bob Hope's support for the Vietnam War that he lost favor with the public and was considered square.

Back to the movie. The movie turns into a spy movie. The story line is this from the dialog "who are we going to send on this assignment to be sent in as a spy"? There it Is again. You know they chose Hope as their spy. How many movies has Hope said he was a "spy" and a "mole" and working first "Central Intelligence" for the United States Government?

I say they chose Howard Hughes in his disquise. In another scene Hope airplanes into Sweden and is greeted as "hello Mr. Holcombe". Hope response "how did you recognize me"? Did you get that? Still staying in disguise, He is seen with two phones. A phone for each ear. One phone for the Bob Hope ear and the other phone for the Howard Hughes ear. Watch the movie. Watch it close. One phone is a red phone. Back in the day the red phone was for a direct contact line to Russia.

In Sweden, "Hope is portrayed as the "head of an "International Oil Company". He is telling you again that he's Howard Hughes. That he has a lot to do with Oil. There it Is again, the Truth and Nothing but the Truth. He's the head of International Oil. Recall Howard Hughes owned his Father's Oil Company. The Drill Bit, whether it be Standard Oil, Texaco or more. You can trust your car to the man who wears the star, the big, bright Texaco Star.

Hope is the Oil Companies Boss and it says so in subtitles on the screen with connections to Southern California. There you go. The Beverly Hillbilly. The movie's about Howard Hughes.

A worker at the Oil Company gets a date and goes out with the oil company's daughter and it becomes the talk of the office. The movies dialog puts it out there to the guy "I see you went out with the boss's daughter". Further into the movie. The actor is to marry Hope's daughter and Hope is out to get his daughter "JoJo" out of the marriage.

Bob Hope says, "no license, no marriage". Dialog says "Holcombe, Bob Hope, is the best man in the entire company". Take note that throughout the 1950s the Central intelligence Agency was referred to as "the Company". Recall that Hope has said that he was and is Central intelligence.

For example, read the book The Company that bought the Boardwalk. That book is about Resorts International, and its Parent Company Mary Carter Paint Company, which was formed by the Central intelligence agency. Resorts International was the first Casino placed in Atlantic City and the first Casino on the East Coast outside of Las Vegas.

You may recollect in your readings that Hope was quoted in a previous movie that when he saw a Portrait of Mary Carter on a wall He said that would be a good name for a Company. There's a connection. The CIA's Mary Carter Paint Company, Casinos, Howard Hughes, and Bob Hope.

Hope goes off talking about having affairs with women everywhere, and he's manipulating his travel schedule with appointments. Some of the trips were real trips and some more fake trips. He was traveling in secret.

Now, the movie shows through the dialog that "the Oil Companies business is in Saudi Arabia. Isn't that special!

That's history. Research it. It was in 1922 in a search for water in Saudi Arabia that an American oil company struck Oil. An Oil Company was formed for Saudi Arabia called Aramco. The Arabian American Oil Company. Hope yells "I need a defector."

In the dialog of the movie Hope is asked "who are you". Again, how many times and in how many movies has Hope been asked that question? Why? Who is he? We should know by now!

Now there's a scene where Bob Hope and a woman are checking into their Hotel Room and Hope says to the woman "Let's not check in or register under our real names". There it Is again, not in his real name. And the movies dialog continues and says, "what's in a name"? He signs in as someone else under an assumed name.

What's in a name? A lot If he was to say who he really is.

There's a lot in the name of Howard Hughes.

* * * *

57. 1966 Boy Did I Get a Wrong Number

Here's another Movie all about being a spy. Again, actions speak louder than his words and they both have meaning. Here again Hope speaks of his other life saying when he's asked,

"I am secret agent 007"

There he said it again he's a Secret Agent right out of his own mouth in his own writings, in his own words and in his own movies. He's written it and then he acts It out. Recall, he has said he works for Central Intelligence and that is on Secret Missions in disguise as a spy.

To indicate who he is the film opens on a Hollywood set on the back lots of the Movie Studios. The back lots are said to be his workplace with weird and crazy things happening. On set a woman wrecks the set, she goes mad and promises to marry the director.

The director is Bob Hope.

The director runs the girl down, puts her down verbally with the whole crew looking on. Such a nasty director. The woman splits and takes off in a car. A chase ensues. Hope shows up and says, "I'm in real estate". Bob uses the telephone to call the right girl, but the phone lines get mixed up and he gets the wrong girl on the phone. He talks to the new woman played by Phillis Diller not Elke Sommers. She asked Bob over the phone "who are you"? Hope again says "I am secret agent 007". Right, I believe that's the Truth and Nothing but the Truth. Nobody listens.

Did you get that? Hope is a spy! How many times and in how many Movies and Books and Television Shows has Bob Hope said that he's a spy? Bob meets up with the right woman and she says to him "the next time you hide you won't find me."

Hope is being chased. He sneaks into a Hotel Room of a Foreign Actress in Hollywood. The men in black are following him. In the dialog about Hope he is considered a "homicidal blood thirsty mad dog murderer". Hope says" I need a place to hide". Just like Howard Hughes. Hope says, "I got a place at Crystal Lake". Hope and a woman hide out at his place. He is to keep her on his side away from two Mobsters. At his place the Police show up and ask Hope to show ID. They say, "that's the man". Hope is called a stranger. He responds "me, a stranger, I would know me anywhere". And says back to the Police "this is an invasion into my secrecy."

There's a knock on the door and it's a Texas Ranger and Tonto. Dialog asked, "why would a Ranger call you"? I got that answer. Howard Hughes was from Texas and he probably was a Ranger. Howard Hughes first yacht was titled "Ranger". Howard Hughes was from Texas. The Lone Ranger always hung out with Tonto.

* * * *

#58. 1967… Eight on The Lam

Well Hope says he came from a family of seven.

This movie is by Hope Enterprises with Bob Hope as Bob Hope. Hope is running a dog washing business titled Avis. Take note Hope says his Mother's name was Avis. Years later, a car rental business was titled Avis.

In the movie Hope finds $10,000 in the parking lot and during a family dinner at home he hides the money in a wall. And just like in the movie paleface inherits a map and a chest.

An Actor refers to Hope as "the money belt actor". The Actor then taps Hope on his stomach.

The movie's plot is that Hope works at a bank and the bank has $50,000 missing and Hope is said to be "the Embezzler". Hope is married with children, and he and the whole family take off and go on the lam. They are in hiding; An Hope says they are going to go "two parts of America where it's not even on a map."

That recalls the deserts out west and area 51. Many places are not even on a map. There are a lot of secret places in America that are not on a map.

Even on the lam Hope as a bookie is still talking in numbers and working out of phone booths and someone tells Hope that "you can't go out in public you'll be recognized". He would be recognized as Howard Hughes.

The Movie goes on with Hope on the lam. Hiding like Howard Hughes. Hope is spotted. It is said "that's him that nose". Hope is standing there still in another disquise. This time with a beard and he's yelling "get used to it."

With the beard, that says to me that his next act Is the Ayatollah Khomeini.

There was a Television Program "I led three lives". I have the first two lives down. One is Howard Hughes, and number two is Bob Hope, and I believe number three is the Ayatollah Khomeini. Hope/Hughes acting in Iran.

Back to the movie Hope breaks into his Bank to get the Banks books to prove he's innocent. In doing so he kicks off the alarm. On the run there's another chase on the highway and Hopes disquise's are now down to just a mustache. He looks like Howard Hughes.

Hope has the FBI after him. It is said that "he Is the head of the Mafia". He is keeping Secrets and using false names on Hotel registrations and he is hiding.

Hope catches the Bank President with a girlfriend. Hope puts the squeeze on ten Bank Presidents. He then dresses in disguise as a waiter. The dialog on Hope is he's "accused as passing himself off as a decent family man."

Bob Hope sure does exactly that and plays out his fake family life married to Dolores and the adoption of four children. "The names of the innocent have been changed to protect the joke". Bob Hope said that!

In a new scene Hope changes into a beautiful be dazzled Cowboy Suit Coat. (indicating he's a Texan). He then talks about Oil and being in the 1% income bracket and he admits being a Government Tycoon and living in Bungalow 27.

Here's a couple quotes at the end of the movie: Talk of owning a "uranium mine."

Hope says, "let's not talk about me". At the close of the movie. Hope says "the FBI is after Me ".

* * * *

#59. 1968 The Private Navy of Sgt. O Farrell

This film is telling you that Bob Hope is living on a Tropical Island like Cuba. The Spy Capital of the World in the middle of a war. The Film has Hope as a soldier in the middle of a war over this little Island. Recall that Bob Hope has said that "the Bay of Pigs failed invasion was my fiasco just like my first screen test was a fiasco". What did Bob Hope have to do with the Bay of Pigs Invasion? Howard Hughes had a lot to do with the Bay of Pigs fiasco.

In this movie Hope is said to be an Ancestor of John Paul Jones. History has it that John Paul Jones was a captain of a Navy ship. I believe this is a hint that Howard Hughes was the Manufacturer of the many United States Naval Ships. Recall the scene from a previous movie where Bob Hope is in a bathtub and he is playing with a complete array of Naval Ships of the United States. That being Ships, Battleships, Aircraft Carriers, Cruisers and Frigates. You name it. Many of his early movies were about the Navy. (tv Hogan's Heroes)

In a new scene in the movie of this story It has Hope at the Headquarters of the Navy and he is trying to get all his Soldiers Beer. Hope says, "the shipments of the beer to the armed service's is for morale purposes". The Air Force, the Navy and the Army, etc. are to get the beer. Hope tells the soldiers He is also going to deliver women as nurses to the Island.

Note: Reading Ava Gardner's book she reveals that Howard Hughes owned a Brewery. A Beer Factory.

Moving on Bob Hope is quoted as saying ""never give them your right name."

Later in the Movie a Plane arrives with a group of Nurses with Some very Beautiful Women, but Phyllis Diller steps off the Plane first. Hope says, "where are those Snipers when you need them"? Hope talks snipers. (JFK)

What snipers? The snipers that blew President Kennedy's head off. That fits right into American History. He then says, "this is my last war". One of the Dulles Brothers was the head of the OSS sniper Unit during WW ll. Both were (1) CIA Director (2) State Department Head. Both during the Kennedy Administration.

The OSS became the 40 Committee which became the CIA. Set up by Kissinger, Rockefellers Aide.

Hope and an Army guy with the Navy's help transport the Beer and it wines up in the drink and floats to another side of the island. By that time Hope, in search of the beer calls it "Milwaukee Holy Water". Was Howard Hughes Brewery in Milwaukee? Terry Moore said in her book that Hughes owned a Brewery.

In this film the talk Is about boot legging. Everybody's drunk including Phyllis Diller. Dialog has it as "a joint operation of the Army and the Navy". Bob Hope says, "I will have to infiltrate the Navy to get the beer at the bottom of the sea". Hope is asked "how are you going to get it at the bottom of the sea"? Hope' s response is: "I've got long straws". You know what that says to me that Bob Hope Has long claws like the long claws on the Glomar Explorer a ship that Howard Hughes built and used in the Pacific to go after a Nuclear Sub of the Soviets that sank armed with nuclear missiles. The United States did use the Glomar Explorer with its long claws to go after the Russian submarine and bring it to the surface. The same claws were used by Howard Hughes as the arm on the United States Space Station. Bob Hope knows about the long claws.

Bob Hope is quoted saying: "I don't care if you're all foam rubber". Another actor says to Hope: "boss with you in this war the Japs don't have a chance."

Hope continues to womanize. One woman is said to be a spy. In the story it is revealed that there is an Investigation into Sgt. O'Farrell (which is Hope). There's a captain writing a book about Sgt. O Farrell. In the dialog Hope is questioned as to "how should the final chapter say of you"? Should it say your "a liar or a guy who stays in character and tells the truth". There you go, stays in character and tells the truth. In Howard Hughes "alleged life" as Bob Hope he stays in character and tells the truth. Hope then reveals that he Is the guy "I am shipping General Mac Arthur Pipe Cleaners". Right. He's supplying his Ships with the Bombs. He is in the War with his Weapons. The General also smoked a Pipe. Maybe the cleaners were for MacArthur's retirement.

Towards the end of the Movie Hope captures a Japanese Submarine and is towing it back to his HQ's. But nobody knows. Back on the island there is a Ceremony for Hope because they all believe that he's dead. They believed that Sgt. O'Farrell is dead. (Like Howard Hughes is believed to be dead). An epitaph states the names of all the Great Generals and Admirals associated with Hope. (Hughes) They name Halsey, Nimitz's, and Doolittle as friends of Hope. The Hughes Invention of the long Straws Glomar Explorer did retrieve a Submarine.

But Hope is alive on a raft at sea towing a captured Submarine back to his Base as taps is being played over him. They say, "he's is dead" Hope is yelling for help. As they say, "he died". Hope yells "who me"? and he starts yelling "I am not dead". Just like the guy in another Movie when being taken out on a stretcher the Police yell. "He's dead". And the guy on the stretcher sits up and says, "I'm not dead". So, Howard Hughes is not dead. "Check the Funeral there's nothing in the box."

There it Is. The fake death confession. Nothing but the truth. He's not dead and he's living the "Alleged life" of Bob Hope in disguise.

Hope tells you the truth in all his movies. Remember, Bing Crosby said "there's a message in every movie."

* * * *

#60..1971.. How to Commit Marriage

Bob and Mary were sleeping together, and Bob is dreaming and kissing her, and in the dream his golf game breaks off his marriage.

Looking at divorce Hope is to "sell a mine in Wyoming". They stay together faking a good marriage and then their daughter had to marry. She had to get married and she has a child.

In a new scene at a club in a cavern Hope has clothes on and make-up. He is dressed as a Hippie. There's a guru there and an adopted baby and their names have been changed.

There is scene in the movie of Brewery's, Distilleries and Hotels. There's the idea of owning a brewery again.

Hope impersonates another family and they adopt. The movie continues and Hope's character is McGruder. He cannot be found, and Hope gets two messages at the same time. Right. Two of everything. Two heads, two pants, two hats, on and on. Everything must be said double because he is two people. One message for each side of his personality. One message for Howard Hughes and the other for Bob Hope Continuing Bob Hope is on the Golf Course and at the Racetracks.

At a concert Hope stands at a Dressing Room Door with a Big Red Star over his head. Could the Red Star represent the USSR? North Korea? could it mean he's on both sides, that being Russia and the United States? Then Hope starts talking about Oil.

In another scene Bob Hope dresses up as a Sheik. Like from the Middle East. The star Is on room number one. That's Hope showing you that he Is Arabian oil. (Aramco) Recall just a movie or two ago Hope is described as the Owner of International Oil. Sounds a lot like the History of Howard Hughes.

Hope says, "if I can fool you I can for everyone". Then in another scene Hope enters in with yet another disguise dressed as the "Ayatollah" on the set of a stage. Just like I said he led three lives. I said that a few movies back. First, there's Howard Hughes, Second there's Bob Hope and Third he's the Ayatollah Khomeini of Iran.

At that time in dialog it is said that Bob Hope "is an imposter". With that said an actor goes to pull off Bob's makeup". What did I tell you! Hope says, "he is not me I am not He."

In the Movie the Daughter has a Baby and the Baby goes to the Theater. At that the Baby pulls off Bob Hope's make-up. Who's Who??

* * * *

61. 1972... Cancel My Reservation

At the beginning of this movie the Police chase Hope and arrest him on suspicion of murder. Hope has said that he killed 9 people. Hopes is asked "what do you do"? Hope says, "I am on TV". Hope sits in jail talking to himself. He says," he fought Long Island traffic to establish himself". (show business?) Brooklyn.

Hope and a girl take off in a Jet Plane for a vacation alone to a little beach house. Hope makes a statement on behalf of the American Indians and sounds like the Lone Ranger. "Indians belong to the land the Indians owned the land and they should keep it."

That's why the Lone Ranger was always with Tonto and saves Indian land. Recall that Kemu Sabe, Tonto's name for the Lone Ranger means "Trusted Scout". The Indian Reservations are Indian land. Those lands are where all Raw materials of Silver, Gold, Oil, Copper, Borax, Uranium and much much more are found.

Now it's easy to see what the Lone Rangers opening statement of the Television Show means. One, the Fiery Horse. (engines), Two, the Speed of Light, (laser), Three the Cloud of Dust, (rocket liftoff). (its HRH)

The secret Rocket Fuel.

The film continues at a Ranch House in Arizona where Hope finds a Girl who's been shot. And then she disappears. There's talk of Identifications and Bob says" the girl is dead". He then says, "let's make a deal". And "I had a body, but it disappeared". Is he talking about himself? He disappeared All right, right into his Bob Hope outfit. Hope gets tied up in a murder rap. This may have happened to Hughes in his Association with the Mob, or as a spy. In this movie Hope is let go to a little gray home in the West. Did Hughes get a Get out of Jail Card off the Atlantic City Monopoly Board?

In the dialog Hope is asked again "twice" "who are you"? The woman is found in Bob Hopes bed and Hope, says, "I did not kill that girl". Dialog says, "just because he is a TV star doesn't mean you can't kill someone". "Let him go."

Did Bob Hope or Howard Hughes get away with murder in Los Angeles. In Movies past when asked "how many people have you killed today"? Bob Hope answers he "kills about 50 people a day". Said he killed 9 himself.

Following that scene Hope and the Woman are sitting in the desert looking up at the Paramount Mountain Symbol and Hope reveals a home inside the Mountain. Hope is quoted as saying "that would be a wonderful place for Howard Hughes to hide out". End of Movie. What do you think about that?

So, in all of Bob Hopes movies it is revealed that Howard Hughes speaks through his disguise as Bob Hope about his role as a spy, and his connections with the CIA, Murder Inc., the Mob, the USA. In every movie Hope indicates that he is two people.

* * * *

#62. 1986 … A Masterpiece of a Murder

Strange that many of Bob Hope movies portray Bob Hope an Howard Hughes as criminal murderers being hooked up with the Mob and being a Money man with a Money Belt Bribing everyone, and as a womanizer and a spy with the Government. With connections to the Navy, The Army, and especially the Air Force! and about Real Estate, oil, Mines and Killings. Both Howard Hughes and Bob Hope live in Beverly Hills, California.

In this movie Hope is playing the part acting as head of "worldwide detective agency". It has been printed that Howard Hughes had spies following all his women and many other people. (Ava Gardner, Frank Sinatra, others)

Here we go again. In the next scene Hope owes money to a bookie. (Again) He gets death threats to pay up or else. The movie tells you it's about "the richest man in the world in a golf cart ". Bob Hope wasn't the richest man in the world, but Howard Hughes was an Howard Hughes wanted to be the best golfer in the world. Its Hope in the Golf Cart, and he's always carried a golf club around. There ya go. The movie just told you that Bob Hope is Howard Hughes.

Recall that when the United States landed on the Moon the Astronaut played golf. Howard Hughes and Bob Hope are one and the same person. The richest man in the world.

Hope is looking into a mirror again, talking to himself again to His other self and he's talking about another map.

Jamie Farr is in this Movie and in the Show Room is going around counting Noses. He counts six noses. The noses indicate how many people(Actors) are in on the joke. There's a movie out of Hollywood called the Secret Six. Hope has written and says he had six brothers. And then the movie mentions "the man of 1,000 faces" and shows that Hope loves Gamblers.

Then there is the Hughes connection to Movies and Casinos. Hope says, "he never met a man he couldn't buy". In movies Bob Hope has said and shown that he bribes people. Especially other spies. Everybody.

A female gossip Columnist is notified. Howard Hughes was connected to many of the gossip columnist of his day.

Hope drives up in a Bentley and talks about Horse Racing and dialog says to Hope "I didn't know you had a gun". Hope responds, "I don't It's a hired gun". What did I tell you, a connection to

Murder Incorporated? We all know that the CIA and the Mob were connected. (The JFK Assaiation) And that Bob Hope as Howard Hughes were connected to the CIA. (who killed JFK?) (who killed J R) (TV DALLAS)

Again, Bob Hope talks about large sums of money and says, "it's walking around money for a guy who is not walking around anymore". There you go! Money for Howard Hughes to spend while he is in hiding and not walking around anymore.

There's My Theory. Howard is not walking around anymore. Howard is out of sight. He's the Walking Dead. Walking around as Bob Hopes in his "alleged life"! Wanted Dead or Alive.

That's My Theory and I'm sticking to it. And I believe that in my complete review of all Bob Hope's Books and Movies it is revealed that he is Howard Hughes!!

In the dialog Hope is asked about a killing "who killed him"? Hope says, "I don't know". Hope was told "you're a rich man". Dialog says "you could be dead". Out to fake his own death Hope Hughes says, "I wonder who else thought of that". Right. His other self-did thought of that!!

Another scene in the movie says that he is "believed to be dead". How many times and how many movies has that same theme been broadcast. Every Bob Hope Movie represents the adventures and experiences of Howard Hughes and Howard Hughes as Bob Hope in Hollywood makeup. The many writers of Hollywood write many stories about him.

In every movie you were told the truth of the predicaments and circumstances from the memory of Howard Hughes, a.k.a. Bob Hope.

Thanks for the memory!

We now move on to do the same Investigation of My Theory through every Bob Hope Television show and prove again that Howard Hughes talks out of both sides of his Bob Hope Mouth.....................Continue

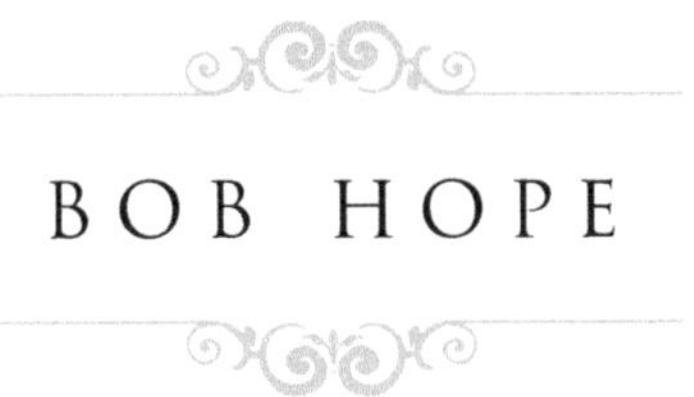

BOB HOPE

TELEVISION SHOWS

I watched every Bob Hope Television show from his very first Television show April 9,1950 on NBC. I watched every word and every skit to see what it revealed in the television shows According to My Theory and as was shown in his books and in his movies. I continued to use My Theory that Howard Hughes is Bob Hope in make-up. Continuing you will see that Bob Hope reveals in words and actions that he Is Howard Hughes!!

T V SHOWS

BOB HOPE'S FIRST TV SHOW APRIL 9,1950

The first quote out of Bob Hope's mouth is This, he says, "his sponsor wanted you to see my face". Second quote, "Congress spends more money before I can make it."

Is Bob Hope the United States Treasury? Is Bob Hope His own sponsor? Did he want you to see his fake face?

In the first 20 min. of the TV show Bob Hope mentions Howard Hughes. He is then asked in actors' dialog, "I did not get your name". So right off the bat he's questioned as to what Hopes real name is. His name that is too big for the Theater Marquee. In his first TV show He's asked what his name is. What is his name? and then again he's asked what his age is. Hope says, "he's as subtle as a Howard Hughes billboard"! I think that means he's right in front of you. Then there's a skit where all the actors have on big noses and big ears.

Hope is asked why he is on TV and he talks about being out West and about women as an actor asks Bob, "are you an actor"? By now we know he's an actor. The Actor is Howard Hughes in the Character Bob Hope.

He talked about NBC and infers that he is Royalty in a skit. It is said that he, "is a Texan who would kill a man rather than look at him". That's consistent with My Theory that he was behind the Mob and Murder Incorporated.

In another skit he says to another Actor, "let's bump noses". Most Actors in most Movies have fake Noses on. Check it out for yourselves.

In another skit, Douglas Fairbanks shows up with a Lone Ranger Mask on. That's telling you that Hope is the man with a Mask. They talk of money, card playing and killing people. Recall Bob Hope was asked how many people did you kill today? and he responded, "about 50! Was that. Nothing but the Truth?

It's part of My Theory that the television program the Lone Ranger was about Howard Hughes. From Texas, wearing a Mask, befriending the Indians, being an Actor, involved in Gambling and being a Character Actor, all in the very Movies that he, Howard Hughes produced, and Bob Hope wrote. It's all there. Keep reading!

* * * *

#2 May 27, 1950

STAR SPANGLED REVIEW

The following quotes are from several skits:

Hope is first talking about getting letters. He says, "I get letters and the FBI is going through them now". He talks about "making it rain". Then there is a series of skits.

Skit number one, Hope is asked again, "who are you"? then states, "who's in my coat"? He responds, "the third man". Recall there was a television program called I led three lives. Could the Great Impersonator be leading three lives?. There was also a movie, The third Man.

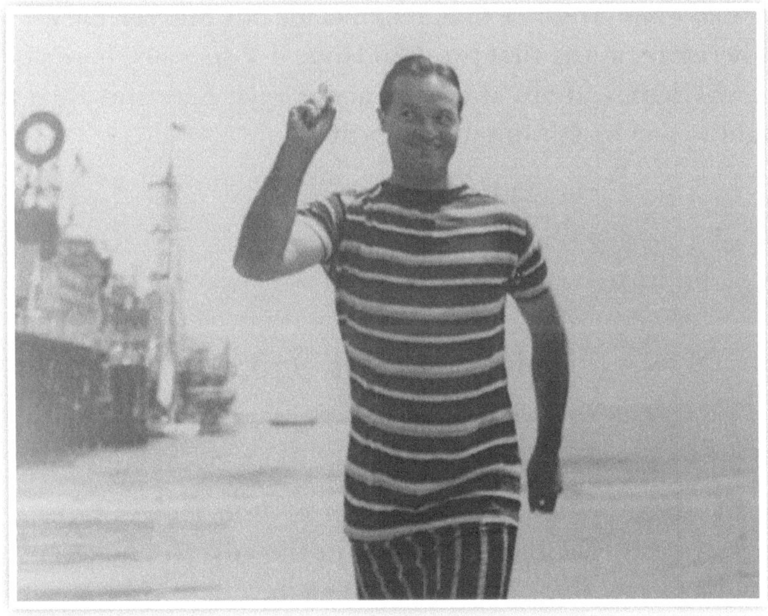

Hope Atlantic City Beach 1930's

Skit number two: he says, "I am reinforced, but I wear well". That could mean that as Howard Hughes after his accidents He was put back together.

Skit number three: Frank Sinatra is Bob's Special guest and they talk Make- up Noses and Faces. Bob's Nose is pulled like taffy and he has on a suit coat with square padded shoulders. The talk continues about Make-up and Faces

Skit number four: There's talk of Movies and it is said that the sponsor of the TV show "is brought to you by Paramount". Who?

Sinatra s has Big Fake Ears on and a Crosby pipe in his mouth. The ears are big fake ears like the kind you can buy for Halloween. No doubt about it. You should watch that show. The skit continues, Bing Crosby comes on with Big False Ears. Frank and Bob pat each other's shoulders to indicate that they are Padded Shoulders in their suit coats. At the end Sinatra says, "that Crosby and Hope are Fort Knox."

Recall a TV Time Life commercial DVD sales pitch for Bob Hope DVD's has Bing Crosby singing Thanks for the Memory and in the second verse saying, "Thanks for our "ca ears" in place of the word careers. At that time Bing Crosby points to his Ears. Talking about make-up. Another time "thanks for our Marker Ears."

Therefore: in the first two Bob Hope TV specials there's talk of Howard Hughes, about Make-up, about Fake Ears and Fake Faces brought to you by Paramount on NBC.

* * * *

#3 Nov. 26, 1950

SHOW APRIL 9,1950

This TV show opens with a cartoon of Bob Hope's face. I had previously read that Bob Hope was in the advertisement business and in the Comic Book Business. In fact, he published his own Bob Hope Comic Book that ran for 18 years.

Hope talks about make-up and goes on to tell a story that, "three shots all missed me". Hope goes on to say that he Is a coward and since he had been being shot at he says, "I went to the Pentagon". There again is my Howard Hughes Theory; people were out to kill him. As I see it Howard Hughes was to be killed by the Mob. Bob at times has said he had his ears trimmed Brooklyn style. He split and went west. He hid out in the Military through the Pentagon. Recall Bob Hope wasn't home for 12 years straight and through those years also Howard Hughes was considered missing.

Skit number one : A General is talking and talking about Jet Planes and Pilots and says that : "the United States Air Force is looking for a man, a Jet Pilot to fly for the United States."

They choose "Major Hope from "Washington". Nothing but the truth.

At that news Hope is estrratic. He flies a jet faster than the speed of light. The United States Air Force presents Major Hope with many and all awards for winning World War II. From the United States Air Force. Who is he??

Howard Hughes was in with the United States Air Force. He was a Jet Pilot. In a skit on Television the truth is told in jest as a joke.

Recall Bob Hope's Quote, "the names of the innocent have been changed to protect the JOKE."

Bob Hope gives a serious speech about Korea......

Information: there is a story in Ava Gardner's book that Howard Hughes would bump Generals off his Military Plane to give Ava Gardner a ride home back East from LA to the health of her Mother. He would bump Generals, the Brass of the United States off the plane to give Ava Gardner a ride home. It was Howard Hughes, the Government and Commander in Chief of the United States Air Force.

Recall: Howard Hughes was a Jet Pilot, and he made the Planes that he flew. He was the Manufacturer of all kinds of Planes, Ships, and his best friends were a succession of American Presidents, starting with Truman and with Sec. of the Air Force Stuart Symington.

Point: the sponsor of the show Frigidaire is a subsidiary of General Motors. Hope was a Maj. General!

The General Howard Hughes the Billionaire Industrialist could be the following, General Mills, General Tires, General Motors, General Electric? Just Saying.

* * * *

#4 Dec. 24, 1950

THE CHRISTMAS SHOW

The show opens with Hope talking about the Nose. In the dialog Bob Cummings looks at Hope and Says, "what a helmet, wear a disguise". False ears and a wig in this skit.

Skit number one: it is a Christmas party and Gifts are being given out. Bob Hope receives a gift, and says, "it's something to put away". (Nukes)? Bob Hope says, "after the box goes away". That he "he's the fellow who scared the thing away". Hope goes on to say, "I used a Secret Weapon". Bing Crosby makes a remark about Bob and says, "that's no secret weapon that's your face."

NOW HERE THIS BOB HOPE QUATE.

"MY NAMES" will go down in History". Did you get that? MY NAMES. His (names) will go down in History. There is no doubt about that. One name Howard Hughes, another name Bob Hope. Recall: two of the most famous names in America sleep together.

Hope was asked why his name will go down in history.

He says, "because I made the thing go away."

The above scene in this skit is about Howard Hughes defeating the Thing, "Hitler and World War II", he made the thing go away". With the Construction of United States Aircraft's and Jets and all sorts of weaponry. He made the thing go away. He used his secret weapon. He says it was his face as a spy.

TV history: check out the titles of a few TV shows: Love that Bob, I led three lives, Maverick, The Beverly Hillbillies, Have Gun will Travel, The Millionaire, the Man with a Camera.

Recall the movie The Lemon Drop Kid where Santa Claus (Bob Hope) is ringing his bell as a Santa Claus. Hope calls another Santa Chris Kringle. Hope is questioned as to why he called this Santa Chris Kringle and Hope goes on to explain that Santa has many names like Chris Kringle, St. Nick and others. Hope says that to this Santa and the Santa replies "I know another guy who never gives his real name"! That's because his real name is Howard Rupert Hughes.. The name is too long for the Theater Marquee. What are his other names?????

* * * *

#5 April 8, 1951.

THE COMEDY SHOW

The Comedy Show begins as every TV show begins with Bob Hope as the Master of Ceremonies, with Bob Hope on a plane talking about money. The money is being taken to Washington DC. He also talks about testifying at a Government hearing. Must be noted here that Howard Hughes had to testify to a Government Committee not Bob Hope. His passport picture is shown and then there's a photo Of Bob Hope getting off plane. He Talks about NBC.

Skit number one: Hope walks on a set over to Arthur Treacher. Hope looks him in the face and says: "I'm checking to see if you're alive". At that Arthur Treacher says back to Bob Hope: "I had the same feeling about you". He was checking to see if he was alive. Howard Hughes was said to be dead and never seen. At that point Bob Hope admits: "I am traveling incognito"!!

Skit number two: it's a scene about Hope Seeing a Psychiatrist. He's known to be rich and says: "these are my street clothes I have better". He then acts like an airplane flying around.

Skit number three: starts out with Bob talking to a girl about how he goes about using many different names. Here's his quote:

"I sent you letters and didn't sign my right name either". Hope says: "anything I say now may bring the Marshall plan to a halt."

Hope then says: "I moved to a new coffin". Then says: "if they make a movie out of it (Howard Hughes's life) I'll play both parts". There he said it again!!

There he is talking about the life of Howard Hughes, playing the part of Bob Hope. Howard Hughes would be playing both parts. Remember how many times Hope had himself in a mirror talking to himself. Two people in the mirror and I'll play two parts. There's nothing but the truth again. Two of the most famous men in America sleep together. My Theory has been proven over and over. Howard Hughes was Bob Hope in Make-up!

The Boat in this show was the Queen Mary. Dialog has it that Hope's money runs Washington DC and NBC.

There's a funny scene where Hope is in inflated baby clothes as Jr in a nightgown. It is said to Hope in dialog "you still have your make-up on."

The show had an all-star cast, there were remarks about Noses and it was a great show.

* * * *

6 October 14, 1951.

Show starts with Bob Hope's Nose like a Periscope on a Submarine. There are many stars and skits and the show opens with film of the first cable to New York. They talk about the cable and that It's underground, and as Hope speaks of it as the MC He states: "here I am on a TV show in Hollywood California and across the country somewhere else I am 6 feet underground". Is he talking about the fake Howard Hughes is dead and buried Joke or maybe talking about laying cable television from the West back to the East?

In skit one…About Egypt, Bob Hope is as a Conqueror. In this skit with Dinah Shore, Bob Hope, does his Alligator Growl. Recall: Remember the Alligator Growl that Terry Moore only taught to Howard Hughes. There's Bob Hope using it again. Is Bob Hope Howard Hughes? Or is Howard Hughes Bob Hope?

In skit number two... Bob Hope is to fight Jack Dempsey under the title, Homicidal Hope from Cleveland. Is Bob trying to tell us something here? That fits the Murder Inc profile. This skit has Bob Hope working really well. The skit of fighting Dempsey was very funny. Great action, especially the ringing of the bells. This skit even had me laughing.

"Here I am on television show in Hollywood and across the country I'm 6 feet underground". (Cable or Coffin)

Remember the Bob Hope quote "I moved to a new coffin". He could be talking about the many different places where Howard Hughes was in hiding. Play dead, new coffin. With Bob Hope alive Howard Hughes is dead. (hiding)

Here I must note again a quote from Bob Hope getting off his aircraft and going to do a Bob Hope show.

"When I got off the plane I left myself behind". His MYSELF is Howard Hughes. He left HIMSELF on the plane and went to do a show as Bob Hope. That quote caption can be seen under a photograph supplied by Bob Hope in one of his books. Where is Howard? Where's Harvey? Where's Waldo? Come on people now smile on your brother.

There he said it again. Every show has a remark that you know that it is he, Howard Hughes talking with the Bob Hope face. Howard Hughes is Bob Hope in make-up! The Star...in the Movie.

* * * *

#7 December 2, 1951

THE COLGATE COMEDY HOUR

Hope opens the show doing his Master of Ceremonies Monologue

Then there is a Theatrical scene with Hope about Vaudeville and of NBC. It was like laughing on the set. There are many doors with Stars on the Actors Dressing Room Door He is back in the old

Neighborhood of Vaudeville. Then he talks about oil and about Jackson Hole, Wyoming.

I know Bob Hope sort of got his start in Atlantic City and I know there is such a place as Atlantic City, Wyoming. On and on it goes.

Hope goes on talking "what's my name"? Hope talks about Medical Operations. Recall: Hope said he got his Doctors license in Atlantic City, as well as Vietnam.

Atlantic City took care of the soldiers injured in World War II. He then makes the statement: "smoke pot". he calls It: "a Mexican cigarette". Starts acting high and womanizing and goes on to say, there's "no people like show people."

So, within this show Bob talks well about his hideout in Jackson Hole, Wyoming. He then plays a game in the dialog stating "what's my name"? he jokes about smoking marijuana and has knowledge of Pot and gets High.

The skit takes place in the operation room and Bob is the Dr. performing all the operations.

Howard Hughes did invent a new and modern Hospital bed. Atlantic City Hotels were taken over by the United States Government. Hope started out in Atlantic City. There are connections. Connect the dots.

* * * *

#8 December 23, 1951

SOUND OFF TIME

This Show starts off with Bob Hope as MC, with a great film of the USS Boxer Aircraft Carrier. It opens with a Navy photograph of the many Battleships. Hope talks all about Aircraft Carriers and Submarines. At the start, an actor says to Bob Hope. "Okay Jim". Hope answers back and says: "my name is Bob Okay". The actress says back: "okay, whoever you are"

The first skit has the Navy making Bob Hope, Commander of the Aircraft Carrier USS Boxer. An Actor in dialog says: "I commanded one of his ships."

"Look at all the decorations on his chest. He has every metal". Bob Hope says: "what do I tell you I am made with power". At that time the dialog tells you the truth again "for years the Navy has been harboring this Spy"!

Bob Hope gives a Patriotic speech, and thanks God for these boys, these young Soldiers". The show shows great photos of America's Battleships and Aircraft Carriers and all fleet Ships. And then in the very next skit they are addressing Bob Hope as full Commander in Chief.

In each skit the truth is told. Exactly what is going on behind the scenes is told. Bob Hope has said many times, "nobody's listening."

So, the question is still out there as to who he is "whoever you are"? and he is still believed to be dead. Is Howard Hughes "Dead or Alive"?

All the people are told to their face that he Is Commander-in-Chief for real, and that he has the power, and he was the ship's builder. Howard Hughes, the Billionaire Industrialist. Major General. The man of Steel.

* * * *

#9 April 26, 1952

ALL-STAR REVIEW

Show opens with the film of San Francisco Bay and other ships. Bob Hope is your Master of Ceremonies again. In Bob's opening monologue he talks about the Bomb, about Las Vegas and Gambling, and talks about Money.

Fred Mac Murray is special guest. They do a quick skit filled with Howard Hughes autobiographical facts.

Skit number one: Bob and Fred act as Chinese people.

And Bob Hope gives an Alligator Growl.

Skit number two: Bob and Fred act as Italian fishermen.

Skit number three: Bob and Fred are in Alcatraz.

In all three skits I didn't notice any evidence. But:

Skit number four: About the Barbary Coast and the given out of different names. A lot of names. In this skit Bob Hope strikes Gold. A large Gold Nugget. Hence the Golden Nugget. Then it is said: one man owns it all". All the raw materials are owned by one man in conjunction with the Indians. In the same skit Bob is handing out money and dialog says of him "you're the richest man in the world". He is nicknamed: "Nugget Hope". Hope shows up in a Brinks Armored Truck throwing money around. The dialog says, "the papers say you're the richest man in the world". Dialog continues to reveal the truth saying: "you're the man who discovered the biggest gold strike. Don't you have a map"? The Inheritance!

A few of Bob Hope's movies are about inheriting a Gold Mine, Watch the Movie Paleface and Son of Paleface, all speak of Maps as to where the treasure is.

Howard Hughes was the richest man in the world and had the money and all the raw materials. It is said in these skits that one man owns it all. It all adds up. The Billionaire Industrialist controlling many facets of raw materials from Oil, Coal, Steel Uranium, Gold and Silver owns it all.

* * * *

#10 March 29, 1953

COLGATE COMEDY HOUR

Bob Hope as MC starts the show with political jokes. He talks about nuclear bombs and Nevada, and he talks about jets. In the first Skit He talks about being married for two years to his wife and then the seven years in the Navy and Bob Hope says, "my chin was there before my wife was". At that Rosemary Clooney calls him an "imposter". There's a movie called the "imposter". Recall Bob Hope in a prior movie called himself the greatest impersonator of people in the world. that's why Hope had a cameo in the movie the greatest show on earth. Don't forget the tray of faces and the tray of noses. You got it, an imposter with the fake face. There is a movie called F is for fake.

Skit number two: In this skit the dialog is about Hollywood. Hope mentions make-up and Hope is there and is questioned as to his Identity. Hope responds "General, there is no question over my Identity". They talk about Paramount. Bob Hope says: "we have writers". Questioned as to who Bob Hope is concerning Hollywood dialog states: "we have a theater group in the Pentagon". Hope says: "General I can't leave Paramount, I'd be court-marshaled". Dialog states: "Mr. Hope you have some of your Money In films". At which Bob Hope responds: "Washington pays me". There it Is again, nothing but the truth. The connection between Howard Hughes as Bob Hope and United States Pentagon.

Skit number three: Bob Hope talks about magazines such as the Mc Calls, Time, Life and talks Academy Awards.

Skit number four: this skit shows an Army drill with the dialog saying, "this place is crawling with spies". Hope says: "I'm going to be dead in 48 hours". Talking about spy's dialog asks: "who built them Howard Hughes"? Bob Hope mentions Howard Hughes again and again. I wonder why?? At the close of the skit and the show a real Army General gives an Honorary award to Bob Hope.

* * * *

#11 November 17, 1953

The show opens with a large cartoon with a long Nose as long as Pinocchio's Nose. Indicating that there is a big lie going on. Hope is dressed in a Top Hat indicating that he Is of the highest society. The rich people The Swells.

Skid number one: Fred McMurray asked Bob Hope "are you an actor"? There is a song. They talk about looks about ears and even engineering. They talk Showmanship and that you need a gimmick.

Fred MacMurray and Bob Hope had been friends since Vaudeville. Dialog describes Hope as "crazy nose Hope". This show did not have much info on Bob Hope or Howard Hughes.

* * * *

#12 December 15, 1953

This show opens with the cartoon with the long Pinocchio Nose on Bob. A real Major General Dean of the United States introduces Bob. The show shows dancing at the Capital in Washington, DC, about what's going on in DC. The famous Howard Hughes Fedora Hat is on a man and they introduced Bob Hope by singing, "He is the Brain of economics" "The Dean of Economics."

They are talking about Bob Hope and the Mob saying that he was on both sides of the Mob. They talk engineering about jet planes. Jet planes that travel at 1,300 miles an hour. (1953) They also talk about the studio wars with the unions. They talk about Howard Hughes, the Industrialist Billionaire being a Jet Pilot.

Skit number one: has Gale storm, my Little Margie on a date with Bob. Here we have Bob Hope always saying how he loves himself as a Peacock showing off his Feathers. (NBC) Dialog makes a statement that "honey where he hides we can't follow". So, they're talking about him and about his secret life right there in skit number one.

Skit number two: it's about Hope as the Clerk of a new store and about a General who is against CBS.

Skit number three: about Los Angeles City Hall versus Smog. They set up a Committee to study the Smog. Hope is acting as a Scientist. He is always talking sexual innuendos. Bob Hope does the Alligator love making Growl that was taught to Howard Hughes by Terry Moore. (not Bob Hope) Hope in dialog says he "studied Atoms" like in Nuclear Bombs? Remember Howard Hughes and Bob Hope have the same MO. Gen. Dean, who served five Christmas's in Korea thanks Bob Hope for his service and for the war effort.

* * * *

#13 January 26, 1954

The show opens with the cartoon face of Bob Hope with a black line on top of Bob's nose and it shows two faces each with a profile. Two faces, two heads. Two of the most famous names in America sleep together. Right, did you get that, two people in one. Hope opens the show calling for people to come to California with a lot of women upfront. Hope rolls on stage in a Rolls-Royce with a Hugh Dog. (Howard Hughes Dog?)

Bob Hope talks world events and foreign policy mentioning John Forster Dulles.

Skit number one: Hollywood is talked about and called a dream factory, a place where fantasy becomes fact. (Howard Hughes talking and acting with a fantasy Bob Hope face.) The waitress at the commissary of NBC is to meet a star. Bob Hope shows up as a rich star. Bob Hope calls the people peasants. In a make-up room the make-up man says to Hope "it's a challenge to work on Hopes Face". The waitress says: "Hope is the Greatest Show on Earth". Remember Bob Hope had a cameo appearance in the movie The Greatest Show on Earth. (1952)

Skip number two: studio one was number one and was changed to studio two and was said to protect the innocent. Recall Bob Hope, saying that "the names of the innocent were changed to protect the joke". There you have it again. The joke on the American people and the world for that matter, that Howard Hughes as a character actor, a writer with two heads, playing two parts with the made- up face fooled all the people all the time.

Skit number three: is a story about a missing person. (Howard Hughes?) It said that after seven years the individual will be declared legally dead. Recall Hope History. He was never home for 12 years. Recall that Howard Hughes was missing many times, as a Bum, as a commercial Airline Pilot, and as a mild-mannered Reporter for a metropolitan Newspaper. (disguised as Clark Kent?)

* * * *

#14 February 16, 1954

Again, the Cartoon with two profiles of Bob Hope. That's five shows with the Nose highlighted. Two Faces.

The show opens with Eisenhower visiting Palm Springs and the President talks about Atomic Bombs. Joe DiMaggio is there with Marilyn Monroe. Hope says: "IM independently wealthy, I struck coffee, (Oil) but it was too rich and high-priced Don't worry the first time Howard Hughes has trouble buying a refill of coffee he'll get mad and buy Brazil". He then says: "Howard Hughes just bought RKO and that Howard Hughes is the only guy in the world who can't take it with him because he can't lift its money". Hope also talks about Airplanes.

Skit number one: Jerry Colonna shows a magazine post of Bob Hopes childhood family.

Skit number two: Bob Hope goes West from East's for the first time in LA to mix with the little people. Colonna acts like he owns Paramount Studios. We know Howard Hughes owned Paramount Studios and owns the Face and that Bob Hope is a Character. Colonna says to Bob Hope: "bring your Hip Boots and a Sponge". Recall that there is a Lone Ranger TV show titled High Heels. It's about a guy in real estate who is short in height and is sensitive about it and doesn't like it, so he wears stilt Cowboy Boots to appear tall. Hughes was tall, Hope was short. Hughes was Dead? Hope was Alive.

Skit number three: Rich people smashed their Rolls-Royce's together. They mention Howard Hughes again. Talk about oil and money.

* * * *

#15 March 16, 1954

The show opens at Washington Sq., New York City. There's an Irish skit and Hope mentions Merlyn Monroe again. It then tells a story of Bob Hope's beginnings in Vaudeville. In the dialog an Actress says to Hope "drop dead". The skit continues of a scene with the title Empire Pictures over Paramount's gate. Bob Hope says:

"if it wasn't for me you just would be recapping shoes for Howard Hughes. Hope says, "I need sneakers and a new story, I need a new face an to be unknown. I need a new personality."

There you go! Talk about Howard Hughes again. Here's what Bob Hope had to say. He tells you what he did as Howard Hughes. He put on a new personality and a new face as Bob Hope.

How many times in his first 15 Television shows has Bob Hope mentioned Howard Hughes and that Howard Hughes was looking for a new face for himself. That's My Theory. Howard Hughes was a Character Actor in his own movies that he made as Bob Hope. It is also said by an Empire Director, Orson Wells that: "we Hope Hope can get Paramount to go his way."

So, it's all about Identity. Howard Hughes owned Paramount. He made the movies and was in many movies with a new face and a new personality as Bob Hope. Each TV show and Movie is about Howard Hughes. At the end of the show Bob Hope says to an actress Janice Page, "thanks, thank you honey now wait in the jet."

There it Is My Theory. No doubt about it! Proven by Bob Hope's own words, or should I say Howard Hughes own words. You just read it out of his own mouth. He put on a new identity, a new personality, and a new face.

Remember from your readings that it was Bing Crosby, who in his preface to Bob Hope's first book said Bob Hope showed up on the golf course with a new face, and that Bing knew who the owner of the face was. And that Bob Hope's life was an "Alleged Life."

* * * *

#16 April 13, 1954

This show opens with the cartoon and Bob and Bing talking about Baseball. It's a known fact that Bing Crosby owned the Pittsburgh Pirates and that Bob Hope owned the Cleveland Indians.

Hope opens his show as MC and is talking the politics of the day. He mentions Joe DiMaggio and Marilyn Monroe again and then a song is sung.

The following is the dialog from the show: The Song, "the guy who owns the store". They're talking about Hope as Howard Hughes! He owns the entire store.

Bob Hope says: "you can always tell a man from Texas, but not too much."

Skit number one: This first skit talks about fake shoulders. The above quote was a hint that you can tell a man from Texas but can't figure out that I'm one and I don't show you much. (recluse)

Rosemary Clooney Ask Bob: "Bob, don't you know that two can live as cheaply as one". Bob Hope's response is: "now I'm living as cheap as one, but I don't think you can prove it". (I can prove it). (Government Secret)

Howard Hughes and Bob Hope as one were completely financed by the United States Government. All Howard Hughes money was the Government Money. Two of the most famous names In America sleep together, and the skits go on.

Another skit is in New Orleans with showgirls, about 10 in with Bob Hope at the piano in a club as he sings about killings that have gone on.

Jack Benny is quoted as saying about Hope: "he was born into money."

Remember that Bob Hope quote that "two can live as cheaply as one, I am living as cheap as one, but I don't think you can prove it."

I think I can prove it. I think, I, Joseph Polillo proves it! But the writer with two heads has played two parts, he's led many a life through Impersonations with Hollywood make-up paid for by the Pentagon. And don't forget the words of the song "he's the guy that owns the store". Howard Hughes as two people living as cheaply as one and running the greatest show on earth.

* * * *

17 January 4, 1954

The show opens with Bob as the MC on a plane in real film by the United States Air Force. It's the New Year's Eve show from Greenland.

The United States is taking the entire troupe to Greenland for New Year's Eve, 1954.. New Year 1955. Happy new year!

The Air Force film shows many planes, jets, and the United States Air Force Band. A tribute to all the servicemen serving overseas at the opening of the show.

Secretary of the Air Force Col. Talbot of the United States Air Force talks to Hope of his service to the United States and its Military.

Continuing further into the show Bob Hope is quoted as saying: "I've got plenty of nothing". Throughout the show Hope refers to himself as evil, cunning, on a big caper, is sinister, and that he is someone higher up directing the show.

Within the dialog It's revealed that he himself is higher up and directing "this whole thing, the big caper". As an evil, cunning sinister individual. The guy who owns the whole store. Howard Hughes owned all the studios with all-stars under contract.

Looking forward, every show is wrapped around Howard Hughes real-life adventures and experiences and what he had gone through, so also in his songs and his skits that Bob Hope is Howard Hughes.

Thanks for the Memory

* * * *

18 February 7, 1954

This show opens showing a hunt from London and Bob Hope's words as the MC in his monologue, he says, he was born In England. And, quoted as saying: "my family is connected to royalty". He's called a Yank. He talks about making many movies and strangely mentions "the ninth floor of the Desert Inn."

Hope says: "we work in TV to subsidize the government". Bob Hope steps out of the stage door onto the street with a High Hat and a Tux. Indicating his wealth.

In a skit in the dialog Hope is called "Patty cakes". He Pats His Cheeks. That indicates that his cheeks are caked up and make- upped.

Bob Hope takes the time to sell his book, Have Tux Will Travel, says the book, "puts out his Family History". The seven guys from Cleveland, Ohio, and then says: "buy my book and get the low down of my life and a lot of lives."

There is the greatest show on earth again, a character actor, one who needed a new face, and said it himself that he was the Greatest Impersonator of people in the world. How many lives did he portray?

In every show there is Information that links up with information concerning the life and times of Howard Hughes through the "Alleged life" of Bob Hope.

Why would Bob Hope again mention the ninth floor of the Desert Inn. The ninth floor of the Desert Inn was where it was reported that Howard Hughes was hiding out.

* * * *

#19 May 11, 1954

This show opens with a cartoon as Bob Hope twice, a double face cartoon. So, there's two of them, and the theme is of a vacation. Of course, Bob Hope is the MC and he Talks about Washington DC, talks about hearings about the Pentagon, and he slams the whole entire committee that's investigating the Army by name, and there's a song in the dialog that calls Bob Hope "that Indian guide". Temo Saby. Trusted Scout. That's what Tonto called the Lone Ranger. The Masked Man. Texas Ranger.

The first skit is about the Navy and his ownership. The ship that cost $86 million. The dialog says, "why pay that much for a ship, because they found the secret weapon". Sailors in this skit question why the Navy pays Hope $86 million. Dialog says: "who knows, maybe he found a secret weapon". Bob Hope says: "I own this battleship" and dialog has it: "he owns the ships."

Strange that Hope in his monologue would be talking about the Army Pentagon hearings in Washington. Howard Hughes was brought before that Committee and he didn't like it one bit and was never seen since!

Talking about the secret weapon; wasn't it Howard Hughes who was the Test Pilot linked up with the German scientist who worked on rockets, also recall that it was the United States that invented the A bomb and a Nuclear bomb.

As concerning Bob Hope being called an Indian Guide brings into focus the Lone Ranger, The television show. Tonto always called the Lone Ranger Kemo Sabe, which means Trusted Scout to the Indians out West. it is a fact that Hughes inherited a lot of Mines, and I believe there was reservation land deals with the Indians, that they were a Nation in a Nation and that Howard Hughes got all the land and all the raw material. Land deals. Howard Hughes, the owner of the Store.

It was also a skit of Hope, acting as a boxer going to New York a Madison Square Garden fight. It was a fixed fight. There's talk about Murder and the Mob and that Hope didn't throw the fight. Could've happened?

At the end General Seller, on Armed Forces Day was quoted about Hope that "maybe he found a secret weapon."

* * * *

#20 June 1, 1954

This show opens with the Face of Bob Hope with the Nose and Chin highlighted in light white paint and the Faces, more than one, are revolving. Bob is the MC. He does some talks, some inside Government jokes. He's called the Cleveland Butcher's in a couple Skits in this show.

In the first skit Hope is playing the University Cupid professor and he is teaching a marriage course, and he says: "some lovers have their blank for love and others have their nose bobbed". those lyrics were in a song that Bob Hope sings to Marilyn Maxwell, as he points to his Nose.

Skit number two: here we have Bob Hope mocking the DC hearings again and an Actor says, "list the crimes". Bob Hope talks about "the Living Desert". Bob Hope says to the other Actor: "I'll see you in the living Desert". In the living Desert Inn.

Skit number three: skit shows off a High Society with a very rich Bob Hope and he's quoted as saying: "I should get an Academy Award just for being me". My point is that Bob Hope never got an award because he was behind the whole thing. Howard Hughes never showed for an award. They could not be in the same place at the same time.

Note: Hope being called the Cleveland Butcher: I believe it's Hopes way of saying that he came out of Cleveland with his Mob connections and that there were people murdered and cut up. Hughes was involved.

* * * *

#21 October 12, 1954

Connect the dots: The show opens with Bob Hope talking about Ava Gardner and the opening of her new Movie the Barefoot Contessa. Ava Gardner was Howard Hughes girlfriend, whereas in the Movie it is revealed as to who he is.

In the Movie the Barefoot Contessa there is a scene where Ava Gardner is told by another Actor that "that guy seated right there is the Movie Producer who also owns Texas and is buying up California right now."

Howard Hughes and Ava Gardner together attended the Opening of the Movie.

The above information should bring you right back to the Beverly Hillbillies, where Jed strikes Oil and is told to head for the Hills. Beverly Hills! From Texas to California. He bought up California. He already owned Texas. Howard Hughes inherited the West.

Skit number one: is a scene in a General Hospital operating room with Marilyn Maxwell and David Niven, Hope is talking really fast. I Didn't catch it.

As a reminder: Howard Hughes reinvented a better Hospital Bed. And Bob Hope has been quoted as saying that he is a Doctor and he received his Doctors License Certificate from Atlantic City and practiced in Vietnam. That's consistent with Atlantic City being designated by the United States Government as the Hospital center for the Soldiers during World War II.

As for Vietnam, the television show M*A*S*H.

Skit number two: what we have is Bob Hope and David Niven talking about big suits with broad shoulders and Niven points to Bob's shoulders and Bob talks body shape, about wider shoulders and they look and talk about the padded stomach. Really.

Note: David Niven was a jet pilot fighter for England during World War II.

* * * *

#22 January 9, 1955.

This was a repeat show New Year's Eve in Greenland. Sponsored by The United States Air force. (USAF)

* * * *

#23 February 1, 1955

Bob Hope is MC and General Motors is the sponsor, special guest Roy Rogers and Dale Evans. first quote right off the bat is that Bob Hope says: "I have the only wrap around Nose in the business."

At the start Bob Hope has Eisenhower and Washington DC talking about millions and billions of dollars. And then Hope says this about them and their conversation: I thought they were doing Howard Hughes on this is your life."

There he Is again Howard Hughes talking through his Bob Hope Face. That was Bob Hope telling you about his life. It was Howard Hughes telling you about his hook up with President Eisenhower and The United States of America. (talking Billions). That's why they played so much Golf together.

The conversation at the start of the show also had talk of Submarines made by Westinghouse and of Oil.

Bob Hope continues his monologue with this quote: "I had a big argument with Ava Gardner the other night". Remember, this is Bob Hope talking, but it was Howard Hughes who was dating Ava Gardner not Bob Hope? If you check out history and the big news of the era Howard Hughes and Ava Gardner had drunken all-out brawls with each other. (Like an argument with Ava Gardner, the other night?) Objects were thrown, and Hughes was injured requiring stitches.

So, who's talking you might ask? Did Bob Hope argue with Ava or was It Howard Hughes who argued with Ava? Whose talking? The next skit will tell you.

This next scene Bob Hope is talking to a Sheriff as Cowboys would. The Sheriff is after the Masked Man. (Lone Ranger) The Sheriff has a Most Wanted Poster of the Masked Man that he's after. The Sheriff shows Hope a Wanted Poster of Hope with the Lone Ranger Mask on. So, Hope is a Masked Man. There you have Howard Hughes telling everyone that he Is the Lone Ranger, the masked one, the guy who owns the store. The guy who owns the face, the guy living the Alleged Life, the magnificent fraud, Bob Hope, the writer with two heads. The two most famous names In America sleep together. There is the whole thing. My Theory. Howard Hughes was Bob Hope in Make-up! For a Lifetime.

Not to be vain, I broke the biggest story in the History of the World. The joke played on the whole world.

Recall that Bob Hope had said: "the names of the innocent have been changed to protect the joke". Bob Hope is also of record as saying that: "Abraham Lincoln was wrong and that you can fool all the people all the time."

* * * *

#24 March 1, 1955

The show opens with Hope as MC where everything is mentioned about Hollywood. Money, Girls, Taxes, Clubs, and a Cue Card problem. He mentions Dollars and Congress. He mentions Vegas, the A-bomb, Jet Planes, He mentions Howard Hughes again and talks gambling at the Desert Inn, the Big-Money, False Teeth and about hunting for Uranium, the Oscars. Then some Psychology, talks about Golf, Money and Motion Pictures. The whole story is there. That's just the Monologue. Talks about everything we've been talking about.

Here's a few skits in a row. In one Hope is a Press Agent. It is said that he's sick, is womanizing, he's got a General on the phone and there is an A- bomb blast. He talked Cinematography and he says something about given new names for made stars.

In another skit an actress calls Bob "Harvey". To call Bob Hope Harvey is funny and takes some connecting of some thoughts on Terry Moore.

Terry Moore was dating Howard Hughes back in the studio days and it was understood by Mr. Westwood of the make-up department that she was going out with "the nose". At that time Howard Hughes nickname as the head of all the studios was Harvey. You have to see the Movie Harvey to understand that Harvey was invisible, and Howard Hughes was invisible. So, his nickname was Harvey because at all the studios no one ever saw him.

To further prove that it's about the man behind the Nose on Bob Hope's face and that it is about the Invisible Man and that man is Howard Hughes. Watch the Movie the Invisible Man, especially when the Nose falls onto the table!

It was also mentioned in a Skit that Bob Hope was: "the Butcher of Toluca Lake, a Killer out of Cleveland". Bob writes the Cue Cards.

Bob Hope lives in Toluca Lake, and came out of Cleveland. The truth and nothing but the truth. Is Hope Hughes the Mob?

Howard Hughes was mentioned again about an A - bomb blast being a barbecue.

Another Show another confession. Every show is about the actual current Howard Hughes adventures that are going on behind the scenes.

* * * *

#25 April 26, 1955

This Hope show opens with film underwater about Submarines, 20,000 leagues under the Sea and our Nation's defense. Bob Hope is the MC and he thanks all the Television and Movie Studios and talks about Nixon. Bob Hope gives Ike's History and that Churchill has retired. He starts naming Casinos, talking about Las Vegas, talking about Gambling, and again, twice more, he mentions Howard Hughes and the money, about hidden money, talks about hidden money in Las Vegas and goes on to say: "that Las Vegas is the only place in town where I can stack my chips."

Skit number one: Hope is acting as a man named Orville, (second time that Hope is called Orville). Recall Orville Wright invented the Airplane, Howard Hughes is all about Airplanes.

As a Tourist in Paris Hope makes the remark that "after I'm dead you will want me back". In this skit Bob Hope does the Howard Hughes Alligator love making call taught to Howard Hughes by Terry Moore.

Skit number two: is about Leavenworth and Alcatraz federal prisons and jails. The skit changes the names of the prisoners. Lloyd Nolan, the Actor goes to peel off Bob's nose by hand and Hope, says to him "I got friends on the inside."

Skit number three: this is your life. Lassie. Hope talks Golf and about Las Vegas and the Desert Inn Golf Classic.

* * * *

#26 May 24, 1955

Hope opens the show talking all about airplanes, very fast planes. The speed of jets, talks about international politics, about the big four meeting in Potsdam and about having his tux will travel. He is given an interview and receives another award, talks about Hollywood and Paramount and Don Harden calls him "Two Face" and also "Great" and talks about looks. There's a clip about two sleepy people and a song from the picture, movie, thanks for the memory. Bob Hope and Howard Hughes as two people are sleepy. Two Face.

There's a skit in a make-up room and talk of the "two richest people in the world", there is the same two guys again. The two richest guys in the world. Two of the most famous names in America sleep together. The dialog goes on, it is said that; "I see Bob is wearing a mask". A masked man!

Another skit, Bing is having a party. Bob Hopes in a Hi Top Hat and Bing says to Bob "during the war I helped you get new parts for your Nose."

There're short clips of movies of Bing calling Bob Hope, "the living bullet" and a Newspaper says they are "still looking for the remains of the living bullet". Bing also tells Bob "your face could make a fortune."

For a note: The Silver Bullet is a designated Bullet to kill a specific individual. The Lone Ranger, the Masked Man carried Silver Bullets. In another note, the train Howard Hughes took into Las Vegas was called the Silver Bullet.

Joseph Coors of Coors Brewery named their Beer the Silver Bullet. Both Howard Hughes and Joseph Coors have been rumored to have been involved in the Assassination of Pres. Kennedy. Terry Moore has revealed that Howard Hughes owned a Brewery. Hope was all about beer in a movie.

* * * *

#27 October 4, 1955

The show opens with Bob Hope in his Chevy speeding down the highway. He is pulled over by the police for speeding. The sketch shows him bribing the police officer, doing pills, and giving up phony names. That could be real. Hope says he's from the Beverly Hills Hilton and that "Comrade Hiltons Hotel is like Howard Hughes place with house detectives. There he is again mentioning Howard Hughes.

Now, in the very next skit he talks about having spray gun make-up because It shows in color and the skit has this said about the Bob Hope Character. The skit is a story "about a ruthless killer who hides out in the home of a middle-class family during desperate hours". Is Hope the killer or is Howard Hughes the killer? It seems to be saying that Howard Hughes is hiding out with a family as Bob Hope. Hope is quoted in this skit as saying: "I've killed nine guys".

He then "growls". Those desperate hours could've been when the Mob was out to kill him. Bob Hope had the family thing up front with the Delores and four adopted children.

Jane Russell talks about Hollywood, the Motion Picture Business, and about the Make-up Artist.

There's talk of real bodyguards, Disguises and mentions Howard Hughes again that he travels with Bodyguards and Disguises. We have Bob Hope saying that when he gets off his plane he leaves himself behind and takes the stage as Bob Hope.

Just like I said, Howard Hughes is a Character Actor playing a part in his movies that he produces. Howard Hughes is in Disguise as Bob Hope.

It is a known fact that Howard Hughes bribed everyone, everyone, giving out Money, Homes, Cars, Jewelry, to the Women and to the Actors and Spies.

* * * *

#28 November 15, 1955

Hope opens with world jokes on England's history and says his family is related to royalty. He throws in a couple of jokes about Eisenhower. Then Hope says right into the Camera, "I am a test pilot" and infers he's "the Bank of America". Chevy sponsors the show.

In a skit Hope is referred to as a "exterminator". That's consistent with killing people. Hope does the Howard Hughes Growl. Hope talks about "finding Secret Southwest fuel". Watch the movie Road to Singapore it's about a secret powerful fuel that foreign spies are after.

Another skit is a big story about crime and gambling in Phoenix, but it shows a film of a mob drive-by bombing, circa 1921 through 29. And then the big quote "and all these activities are directed by one man". That's in the dialog. I say that one man directing the Mob is Howard Hughes. I also solve the theme of mob contacts in Bob Hope movies. Here he tells you that he, Howard Hughes is behind the whole thing since the 20s.

Joseph Kennedy hated Howard Hughes all through Prohibition. Hope is called "a vicious Gangster Overlord". Hughes was after RKO and could've moved in on Kennedy's Scotch Business.

The skit has a scene that shows Liquor, Horses, Slot Machines and has Money stacked all over the room. So much so that Bob Hope says, "this place looks like Howard Hughes rumpus room". Howard Hughes rumpus room is the Skim from the Casinos, in association with the Mob.

* * * *

#29 December 27, 1955

In this show Bob Hope takes his USO show to Iceland. Bob is the MC of course and it's about the United States Air Force and the War Department and the talk is about top-secret work. The show is dedicated as a salute to the Army Navy, Air Force and Marines of the United States of America.

Bob Hope opens the first skit in Hollywood about the 1955 marquee movie Harvey. Bob Hope wanted to play two parts at once, where he adores himself and his name as the peacock of NBC.

For information purposes Harvey is what Terry Moore spoke about in her book the Beauty and the Billionaire. Harvey is what Terry Moore, Wally Westwood and the studio lot people at Paramount nicknamed Howard Hughes. Hughes was the owner of Paramount Studios and he was never seen by anyone. In every show more is revealed about who? the invisible man is.

In another skit there's several scenes. One is of a Medical goof. And another about a Vaudeville team where Hope talks about face identification.

In Hope's monologue he says that there is an argument about him being born in England and dialog says this to Hope: "you found England boy, but Britain denies it, but the United States insist on it". Recall that Bob Hope said to a Butler when he was in England "I was born in England" and the Butler says to Hope: "I'll keep your secret". To me that says it's not true that he was born in England. He may have been born in England's Spy Network. Recall Bob Hope's first book, They Got Me Covered and his second book Have Tux Will Travel. HE worked for the Government.

A cover story. We all know what a cover story is right? The United States of America insist to keep the United Kingdom in on it. There's talk about being war buddies and the money of the United States assistance to France and England. Hope infers that he gives England and France care packages.

If Hope is Hughes and Hughes is the United States, certainly during World War II we saved England and France. The care packages were the support of England and France throughout WW ll.

* * * *

#30 February 7, 1956

This show comes to you from England The United Kingdom. Hope says thank you to his relatives. There's a short film about Monaco and Gambling.

Skit number one is a lame skit. A guy in dialog says to Bob Hope, "do you still own General Motors"?

There's a scene where Hope says to his make-up man, how are you Rembrandt"? He calls his make-up a "masterpiece". Bob Hope says to the make-up man, "be on time" and the make-up guy says on time, "seven o'clock make-up, seven thirty reconstruction time". Dialog says: "California is the capital of Brooklyn". Recall that Television started in New York. Hope got run out of Brooklyn.

Dialog said of Bob Hope that he is "just an actor". Bob calls his make-up a "masterpiece". That's My Theory!! Bob Hope wears a complete Fake Face.

Bob Hope talks about Democracy versus Communism. Dialog asked, "who won". Bob doesn't answer. I believe there was no answer because I believe and it is my opinion that Howard Hughes was on both sides and that he was the United States Government, that he was the head of the Communist Party and that he was behind the Mob. That's My Theory and I'm sticking to it! It is a fact that during World War II United States and Russia coordinated the war against the Germans and that the United States provided the USSR with Jets and Tanks, and all manners of warfare from the West Coast to Russia to defeat the Germans.

As the show goes on Dialog questions "is Hope in a circus?'. In a skit a French guy steps up and feels Bob Hope's Nose.

Recall in dialog it was asked about Bob "do you still own General Motors". You must recall that in another show it was said that Bob Hope was a Major General of the United States Air Force. So, let's put two and two together. If Hope is a General and ran the war and was heavily involved with the United States Government, is that why we have such Corporations such as General Motors, General Mills, General Tires, General Foods, General Electric. Is it possible that the Billionaire Industrialist owned and operated all those Corporations? Bob Hope was once quoted as saying he had "18 labels."

In many of the skits on this show Bob is shown in Fat Clothes and Big Shoulders and a big padded suit with Square Pants. Sponge Bob Square Pants? The Writers are still writing.

* * * *

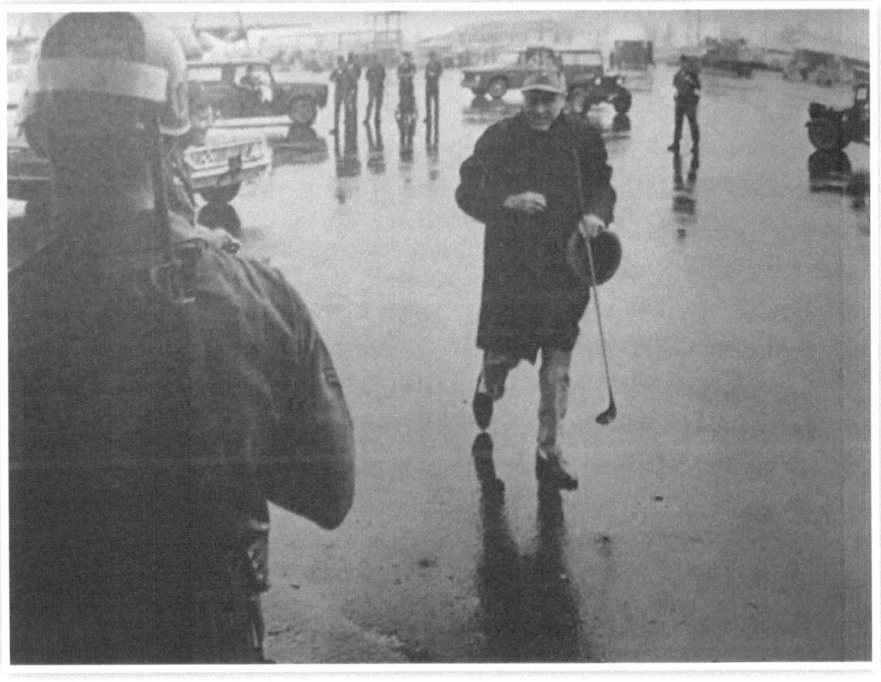

After each show I leave under an Assumed
Namc Hope quate

#31 February 28, 1956

Here's another show from England about the weather. There's a skit right off the top about Bob Hope as a spy in disguise as a detective with intrigue.

Bob Hope says, "no one has ever seen the face of him". Question is who is him? Now about him, all 160 million people have seen him and not one has come up with who he is and the answer". Who is he? Hope says again, "no one has ever seen the face of him". Who? and then he says, "yesterday I almost forgot my own name". What's his own name? His own name is Howard Hughes, and nobody has seen his face. No one has seen his face before nor after he put on the Bob Hope make-up. You know, the Fake Nose, the Fake Ears, the Fake Cheeks, Sponge Rubber, Putty and Stucco. The man of a thousand faces. Well Two Faces. Seven?

An Actor talks about Bob Hope, "Bob has Howard Hughes peddling under the hood". The hood is his head! There is My Theory in the dialog that Bob Hope is Howard Hughes in make-up and with the Bob Hope face Howard Hughes is talking. Who is he? Nobody has seen his face. Millions have seen him, but no one can come up with the answer as to who he is and he as Bob Hope almost forgot his own real name which is, Howard Hughes, a name too large for the Theater Marquee. In disguise as Bob Hope it's Howard Hughes under the hood.

A hint here and a hint their and no one gets it. All the skits are based on the experiences and activities of Howard Hughes. Nobody put it together. (I Did)!

Why does Bob Hope mention Howard Hughes so much? My answer is that he Is Howard Hughes!

In the skit Hope tells of wearing fake clothes and fat clothes at that.

* * * *

#32 March 20, 1956

This show is out of LA and titled The Awful Truth. It's a straight story of comedy.

First skit is about a card game and about trusting the wife. Hope jokes about never being home. It is said that Bob is hiding out with a middle-class family. (Howard Hughes is hiding out as Bob Hope in a middle-class family with his wife Deloris and four adopted children. They got him covered. And he was never home for12 years. He was never home.

Hope talks about 1902 and that" his daddy had plenty of money", and he talks about taxes. It is said that Bob is never where he says he is. The skits all about lifestyle and acting like a husband and about wife swapping.

In this show Hope calls himself "Brother Rupert". Bob calls himself "Rupert". Isn't that Howard Hughes middle name? Howard Rupert Hughes.

There is a movie Titled the Great Rupert. And the dialog continues talking about "Oil in Texas". A question is asked "who is he"? dialog says, "which one is he, first you call him Larry and then you call him Rupert". And Bob Hope explains, "you have to have a lot of names when you work and says "Rupert, that's me". and he heads off to a Cabin. Hughes had a cabin in Vegas.

When you work as a spy. Mission Impossible.

So, this show was a story about the truth, the straight awful truth where in Bob's dialog he says his name is Rupert. Howard Hughes's middle name??

Here we have Bob Hope telling you that his real name is "Rupert, that's me". Just like I said Bob Hope is Howard Hughes. That's My Theory. I prove that repeatedly. Just like I said, "Howard Hughes is Bob Hope in make-up!

* * * *

#33 May 1, 1956

This show opens with Bob Hope at Yuca Flats. Yucca Flats? that's where Rocket cars broke the land speed records. Bob Hope shows the people that he is 3 inches off the ground and that he is wearing stilt boots. The guest George Sanders says this about Bob Hope in a skit. "Bob Hope writes the picture, produces and directs the stars in the picture and says this about Bob Hope "he is a baggy pants comedian". Sponge Bob Square Pants.

The writers are at It again. There's a cartoon on TV for the past several years and the title of the cartoon is Sponge Bob Square Pants. Even became a Movie.

Here's a footnote. There's a Bob Hope movie titled The Cat and The Canary or the Princes and the Pirate. In the movie the Paramount News Crew shows up and asked Bob Hope, "How did you catch the Creep in the Haunted House and Bob says, "I found this piece of Sponge Rubber and I know all about Sponge Rubber. I am an Actor and I wear it all the time"! So, Bob Hope is an Actor in Disguise, and as a Character Actor he wears Sponge Rubber all the time.

So, Bob Hope is just the Actor who produces a Movie, writes it and rewrites it, directs it and stars n it. I thought Howard Hughes owned Paramount Studios and more. Bob does everything as an Actor with Ears, Chin, Cheeks and Nose. A new Face and a Nose from the Goodyear family with Square Pants and three-inch stilt shoes and baggy pants. The masked man. The invisible man.

* * * *

#34 May 22, 1956

Show opens with a film about Golf. Hope opens with jokes and some medical talk. Whole bunch of quips about women. His guest Ken Murray says this about Hope: "he kind of looks like Bob Hope". And Bob Hope says this: "that's TV now the Baggy Pants Comic is now the man in the gray flannel suit". They got him covered. Look up the theme of the man in the gray flannel suit. (mole)

Bob Hope refers to himself as Baggy Pants like the guy said in the last show. The Man in the Gray Flannel Suit is a Movie about a Spy. Research it and watch the Movie. Howard Hughes as Bob Hope was a spy, a Double Agent and in Bob Hope's second book Have Tux Will Travel He writes that "when the Government calls I travel."

Bob Hope wrote it, says it in movies and admits it in his TV shows. Bob Hope is Sponge Bob Square Pants. The Invisible Man. The Lone Ranger.

* * * *

#35 June 17, 1956

This show is Bob Hope's first color TV show. Its Theme is the Road to Hollywood with an all-star cast brought to you by US Rubber. It's a social study with a film clip on the freeway. He talks about Saudi Arabia, of filmmaking and the Writers Guild with Paramount tours. There're talks about money and about bank robberies. They show a writer's conference with Hope and his writers. Dialog has it that Bob Hope is 5 ft 11in in height and weighs 180 pounds. And Elevator Stilt Shoes Makes him (6ft 3). HRH.

There's another skit where Hope is the chief accountant of Paramount and that he still a Butcher. Hope controls the money of Paramount? And still The Butcher, the killer from Cleveland and Taluca Lake.

In the next skit Hope shows off very skinny legs with a big body with extra-large shoulders and in a costume. Skit is about make-up of Hope. As a man is putting make-up on Bob's face says, "it's very difficult". "let's face it Mr. Hope nobody's seen the face of you since the Road to Zanzibar". (1941)

* * * *

#36 October 21, 1956

Hope starts off his Monologue speaking about betting and asking who's running the country. There's a skit about Hope being at home with his wife. He says he's "a pilot". The dialog says that Deloris said: "my husband just came into radar range."

There's a short film about Don Larsen and his no-hitter. Then there's a skit where Bob Hope is the MC at the Palladium (I believe that's in England) and he talks of his Make-up men.

Hope honors Jack Dawn and Wally Westwood and all the Make-up men of Hollywood. He talks about Westwood filling him up with Putty and the making of the Movie a man of 1,000 Faces. They use Putty to make Faces.

In one skit they have Hope in a Havana Robe. There's the mention of Cuba again.

Hope mentions many times that he's got a bad leg.

There is Hope telling you that he's in make-up.

A Time / Life DVD of Hope and Ann Margaret talking about Bob Hope says that, "his Make-up weighs more than he does". That's right because it's stucco. And don't forget we have Jack Benny, Bing Crosby and a Make-up man in three skits where Bob Hope tells them as they are putting make-up on him to hurry up that he has a show to do, and in all three of those skits the retort is, "I never worked with stucco before". So, they're putting stucco on his face that Nobody's ever seen since 1941. That's heavy.

Howard Hughes, always in Make-up as Bob Hope. That's My Theory.

* * * *

#37 November 18, 1956

This show comes here from New York and Bob Hope as the MC points out that he's rich.

In the first skit Hope is smoking with a roach clip (pot) and is in a ball of money and Bob is in bed and he says in a dream, "Howard Hughes stopped me on the street and asked me for money". He talks about being Royalty with much money. He says he's a Duke and his Grandfather was King.

There's not much more in this show as he talks about just being rich and about money.. Many times, even in some movies He says he's a Duke. The show was more variety Entertainment. It was a star- studded show with songs and skits.

Seems like Howard Hughes is mentioned in so many movies and in so many TV show skits that I think Bob Hope is telling us something.

* * * *

#38 December 28, 1956

This show is a salute to our servicemen in Alaska. Bob Hope is the MC and he jokes about Alaska and talks about getting Beer to the Troops and Bob Hope calls the Pentagon "a Hotel for Generals". Ava said Howard called the Generals Desk Jockies.

In the first skit with Hedda Hopper Bob Hope says, "he's a rock collector". Like a geologist? (Texaco) The skit takes place in a saloon and he jokes with Ginger Rogers "about a Gold Mine". In the skit he talks about a Map to a Gold Mine.

If you research it you'll find out that a lot of Bob Hope movies are about possession of a Gold Mine, about a Map, and about Inheriting a Gold Mine.

Think about Vegas and Atlantic City, the name of a Casino called the Golden Nugget. If you go to the Golden Nugget Casino you will notice on display the largest Rock of Gold in the world. Howard Hughes inherited a lot more than Oil and Money. He inherited Mines.

Skit number two is about Go Army and the Armed Forces. Nothing can beat the United States Air Force. It is said that Bob Hope is the backbone of the Air Force. It shows Rockets and the service stripes for Bob Hope because of his many years of service. Dialog asked Hope "Aren't you the headmaster"? and continues to say, "you can't quit now after 30 years."

This show is 1956. 30 years back would make it 1926. In 1926 Hope would be 23, Hughes would be 21. Hughes has been making movies since he was 17. 1922. Hope has been acting since he was 12. 1917.

Skit number three starts out with the song, I've got to know a lot of things about you, to Bob Hope. The Top Hat and the Tux represents great wealth. In the skit Bob meets Ginger Rogers on a street corner and she says to him "your face looks familiar."

At the end of the show Bob Hope has the Commander General and head of the United States Air Force command in Alaska thanking Bob Hope for 30 years of service.

* * * *

#39 January 25, 1957

Hope opens this show with reflection on Eisenhower's Administration. He talks about John Foster Dulles, flying B-52s around the world in 45 hours, he talks about Jet Bombers refueling in the air. Hope seems to know a lot about Strategic Bombers and Jets that they refuel in the air. Hope is quoted as saying "these Bombers going around the world in 45 hours kind of makes my statistics look a little sissy". Hughes set records fling around the world first in record time.

Does Bob Hope have a statistic of flying around the world. He is a Pilot. He said so himself. I know from History that it was Howard Hughes who has a statistic of flying around the world in record time before 1957. Those statements prove that Bob Hope is Howard Hughes. He's talking about himself as Howard Hughes, because Bob Hope doesn't hold any statistics of flying around the world. (as Hughes he does).

This show has four skits in a row. One is about the deep South and the Hillbillies. Dialog says that all the money is his. Bob Hope says: "we own the money tree". He talks about girls and money, then talks about Howard Hughes, the Government and Money and about getting over on everyone. The names of the innocent have been changed to protect THE JOKE!

Next his guests Rowan and Martin says, "can we establish whether this man is living or dead". What is he talking about? Bob Hope is alive, and Howard Hughes is said to be dead.

This skit shows Bob Hope's first Vaudeville act. Just a funny skit. Same with the next. Betty Grayble cracks jokes with Hope about publicity and says that Hope is an egomaniac.

Hope talks about the United States Budget and access to the Money Tree. He talks as though he is in control of the Government printing press. Talks about a world record for flying around the world and as to whether he is living or dead. Sure, a lot of facts containing Howard Hughes information.

Consistent with My Theory.

* * * *

#40 March 10, 1957

Show opens with Bob Hope being a Booking Agent, a Talent Scout and Agent who has the final word on who becomes a Star and who can entertain in Vegas.

Sounds like the owner of the studio's talk. Hope is shown signing a contract with three xxxs as a signature. Hope says, "you have a middle name". We know Howard Hughes has a middle name. His middle name is Rupert. An Actor in this skit has his ears flapping.

The new skit is breakfast for free after a seven-year wait. Hope was missing for seven years, (like during World War AI) and he's hunting for women. "Roberts back" he says "the whole thing is in his head ". so, after seven years dialog says, "this man is legally dead."

Another skit has Bob Hope playing two parts. One as an outlaw, and the other as a good guy. A good side and a bad side. Two Heads. There's a scene where there is a gunfight, one shot Bob Hope says, "I knew one of me would win". Did you get that? Shoot and kill Bob Hope and Howard Hughes lives, shoot and kill Howard Hughes and Bob Hope lives. Bob Hopes the good guy and Howard Hughes is the bad guy. Hope talks of three killings and that he got the gold. Recall that Bob Hope said he has killed 9 people.

Now, in the dialog of the song that is sung the words say: "if Bob Hope was to join Disney's Musketeers you'd have the Nose meet the Ears."

The show's sponsors are Chevy Chevy and Chevy. History has it that Howard Hughes would disappear and park Chevrolets in a grid every four blocks when he was in the big cities. See the USA in your Chevrolet.

* * * *

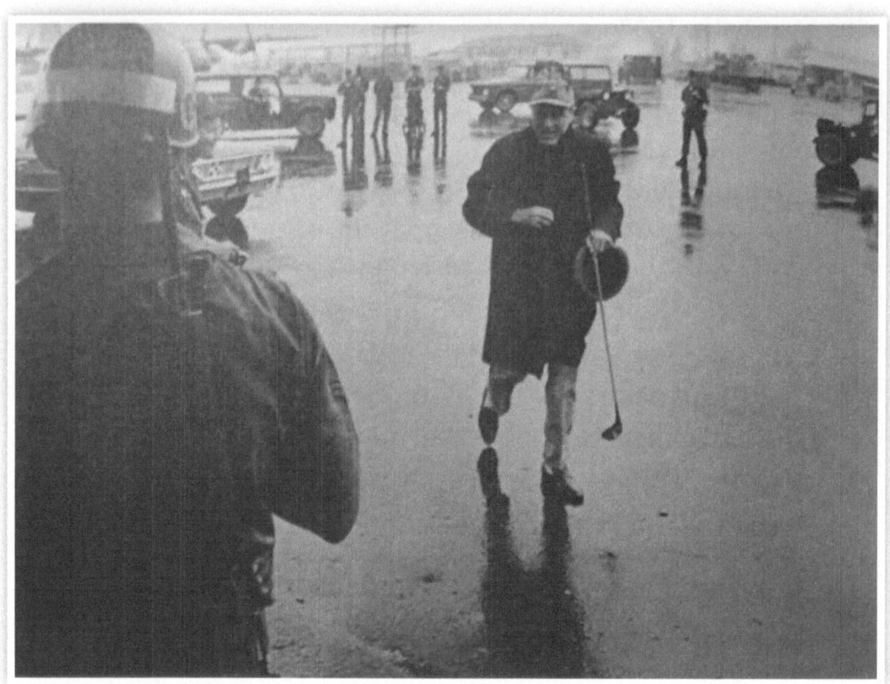

#41 April 7, 1957

Hope opens the show and says he "Is the boss and that it's his show and, "I can do whatever I want because I have it up here" as he points to his head. He then infers that he is connected to John Foster Dulles. Talks about Havana Cuba. Hope in a joke cracks that "he was forced to leave the country". Howard Hughes was forced to leave the country and did just that.

Recall this: when John F Kennedy gave Bob Hope a Congressional Medal of Honor, at the Ceremony Hope made this quote: "I get this medal for staying out of the country". Howard Hughes talking through his Bob Hope face.

In the first skit about baseball Hope talks make-up with Frank Sinatra. Sinatra ask Bob: "how did you get your Nose like that"?

In the skit dialog asked: "tell me Bob, are you very rich"? Hope responds "with money I am filthy rich. I have a limo, yachts and three or four states". Dialog says to Hope "you sound as though you're Howard Hughes" and then Hope says of Howard Hughes: "we have him down for a care package". In my view Hope is the

United States Government and transfers all the money to Howard Hughes. So, Bob says he owns three or four States as he is dressed elegantly. I say those four states are Texas, California, Alaska and Hawaii. Recall that in the Movie the Barefoot Contessa, Hughes is pointed out as the producer of movies and that he owns Texas and that he is buying up California.

Recall that Howard Hughes disappeared three times, twice as a Bum, once as a Newspaper Reporter, and once as a Commercial Airline Pilot.

There's My Theory that Howard Hughes is talking with a Bob Hope face.

"you sound as though you're Howard Hughes". That's right, he sounds like Howard Hughes because he is Howard Hughes. Looks like he tells you in every show who he is and that he has great wealth.. That's Howard Hughes talking with the Bob Hope face.

* * * *

#42 May 5, 1957

The show opens and strange as it may be you can see the Putty Nose and Bob Hope gives his Howard Hughes Alligator love mating growl. The skit wasn't that good.

In the second skit Hope is visiting Jimmy Walker at home. The skits about Jimmy Walker Mayor of New York City and George Jessel is involved. Bob Hope quotes right off the bat that, "I'm not dead yet". Hope does a dance. As Hope walks in the room Jessel yells "here comes Murder Incorporated". I said that before that Howard Hughes and his money and his connection to Luciano, Sam and the Mob had been going on since the 30s. Following the skit Hope again says that he "was part of the Brinks bank robbery" as a joke.

Hope does a TV show opening where Hitchcock walks in as a silhouette to the drawing of his face. Hope slides in like Hitchcock did at the start of his shows. The talk in the skit is about the wealth of Bob Hope.

You must remember that My Theory is that Howard Hughes and Bob Hope are one and the same person. Two of the most famous names in America sleep together. Here's another quote by Bob Hope talking about his will: "I had to make me my own beneficiary that way all the money comes back to me". Did you get that? Don't forget that quote out of one of Bob Hope movies that he says to a woman "if I die and come back you would've made it with two of the best fellows and they would both be me". I think he's telling you that he's two people.

If Howard Hughes is considered dead and fakes his own death and he shows back up as Bob Hope they both be him.

* * * *

#43 October 6, 1957

The shows from Casa Blanca and it shows jet planes flying around. I must point out that Casa Blanca means White House. Eisenhower was running the war through North Africa from Casa Blanca. Hope says that North Africa is like "Texas with Arabs" He talked about the troops and United States Air Force and talks about conspiracy's that were hatched there.

The first skit talks about tales that were never told. Bob Hope enters as a King on a jackass… The dialog is about how many wives you can have. Hope goes on to say to women that first he gives you flowers, then diamonds, and then Mansions for a kiss. We do know that Bob Hope and Howard Hughes were great womanizers, especially with Hollywood beauties. That was their mo. and that was their Secret Lives.

There's another skit where Gary Crosby, (that would be Bing Crosby's son) says, "yes, sir" to Bob Hope and Bob Hope says back to Gary, "Sir, why, sir"? Gary Crosby's Response: "that's the way officers and senior personnel are addressed". So, Bob Hope is Officer and senior personnel. Bob Hope is, "a senior personnel and officer". Hope talks about the Road to Morocco in a song and mentions John Foster Dulles, Money and a Briefcase and that there off to Casa Blanca.

Here's another skit about North Africa and about what is stolen and that there's a big black market. Dialog says Hope "is the most dangerous man in North Africa". Hope is ID as the head of the black market and Bob Hope says about that "I'm waiting for a check from Standard oil". Howard Hughes was Standard Oil. He's probably indicating that the United States seized all the oil of North Africa. He goes on to say, "there is only two people here Dead and Alive". There he admits it again. That he is two persons in one. One is dead, Howard Hughes, and one is alive, Bob Hope. The Alleged Life. Hope says to an Actor "which do you want to be dead or alive". Hope and Hughes are both there. He is alive, and Howard is dead, so to speak, standing right there waiting for a check from Standard Oil.

At the end of the show Hope makes a crack about J Edgar Hoover being a girl. Then a real General thanks Hope and the United States Air Force.

* * * *

#44 November 24, 1957

With the start of this show they look like Cowboys. Hope talks general stuff about the globe, about Sputnik and its impact on the earth.

A skit said that Cowboy Hope shoots someone. It's a bad day at NBC. Not much in this show, although Bob Hope does admit that he's a Texan. Talks about his make-up, of stylist, and talks to himself about being two people. Shooting People.

Yep. Hope admits he's a Texan, just like the opening song and lyrics to the Beverly Hillbillies. Proving again the statements about the Hollywood producer that owns Texas and buying up California in the movie, the Barefoot Contessa.

Best to throw in here the Ricky Nelson song Garden Party, the words go like this, "and over in the corner sat Mr. Hughes in his Dylan shoes wearing his disguise."

Howard Hughes at the Rock Concert in Disguise. Ricky Nelson knew it, he grew up in Southern California. His Mother and Father, Ozzie and Harriet were in Vaudeville and the Big Band era. And they were all on TV together. The Ozzie and Harriet Show.

* * * *

#45 January 17, 1958

Bob Hopes Pacific tour. All island stops with films of the Ships while talking about the B 47 Jet, how fast they go and talk about flying. Flying a Helicopter at Okinawa with Generals. The guest Jane Mansfield, A film about air power, about Tokyo. There is a skit with Soldiers, about Spies being everywhere and for everybody to "keep your mouth shut"! Informative show.

* * * *

#46 February 6, 1958

This show is coming to you from Burbank, California, Bob Hope's monologue is about Eisenhower's budget of 74 billion and here's Bob Hope again talking Rocket Development and about the top-secret United States Air Force versus the Navy, football game. The Air Force Won.

That's a fact. The Air Force wins over those with the Bomb. The Army had the Bomb, but they had no way to transport or deliver it. The Air Force Won. Nothing can beat the U.S. Air Force. The Air Force is the ultimate protection of United States.

So, then there's a skit and the title of the skit is: The Three Faces of Bob. Bob's is at the psycho office. There're saying he is crazy, crazy, he's "borderline three faces". 3 FACES. talks about women. Bob Hope says, "I wanted Ava Gardner." You can say that again. In real life Howard Hughes and Ava Gardner were a couple. There was a Television show called I led three lives. We already know he's leading two. I wonder who the third Life is?? Who is the Third Man? Khomeini?

* * * *

#47 March 2, 1958

Show starts and Hopes talking Casinos. Howard Hughes had a lot to do with Casinos. Hope had a lot to do with Casinos. Hope says he is always flying, and that John Foster Dulles wants to join Hope. Bob says: "I have been circling the earth and the globe for years now". Wonder which self he is talking about. Probably both at once.

In the first scene Hope shows off as though he is Royalty in a Mansion. Anita Ekberg, his costar in the movie, Paris Holiday is his guest.. Three times Bob Hope says, "I have friends in the United States Immigration Department". He shows a Paris Holiday film clip of Bob from France, where he is shot at through the billboard, he receives an award and then says, "Texas Gold."

Again, the show. They sing the 1939 Song, Thanks for the Memory. Show has some good jokes with Natalie Wood and some good dancing.

At the end of the show Bing Crosby says "this charade of yours" to Bob Hope. Recall it was Bing that wrote the preface to Bob Hope's first book about his Hopes Alleged Life. Now you have him identifying Bob Hope as a Charade. Don't forget the name that's too big for the marquee. And remember the Marquee said: The Magnificent Fraud, Bob Hope. You can fool all the people all the time! Look up the definition to the word charade, that's exactly what My Theory says was going on. The Joke.

* * * *

#48 April 5, 1958

Here's a show from Moscow and the Moscow Circus stars reveal their acts and show Russian talent. He talks about the Kremlin, about his Hotel, Shows, Films, a Macy's of Moscow, a model show, some talent in the film of Hopes Moscow visit, introduces Soviet film stars. And there's a skit and Bob Hope says: "Russia here we are in Russia. I have never been in this part of Texas before". Does HRH/ BH own Russia? Does he control Russia's Energy?

Recall Bob Hope said that about North Africa. United States probably got all that Oil and here we are in Russia, possibly with Standard oil, Texaco or Exxon Mobile. Bob Hope says, "I work for the State Department". He talks about his Jet Planes. He jokes on Russia and Sputnik and he talks about John Foster Dulles and Anita Ekberg, traveling together.

Hopes talking all the time on stage about Russia, about NBC and Life Magazine and Hope dreams of Business and Trade, Cities on a cultural exchange, Communism or Capitalism. He backs John and Alan Foster Dulles!

One Dulles CIA, the Other Dulles the State Dept.

The show has a good deal of Entertainment, but one thing is for sure, it was about Texas and the Oil Business.

* * * *

49 October 14, 1958

This Show didn't have anything to say, Hope mentions flying every day. He talks about John Foster Dulles again, talks about the Rocket's and the Moon, Politics, Golf, and Elvis. Talks about Rockefeller, Governor of New York, and how rich they are.

* * * *

#50 November 21, 1958

There's a little bit here. Bob Hope mentions John Foster Dulles again, talks about money and traveling to Formosa, which is Taiwan. In the monologue he calls Nelson Aldrich Rockefeller Big Oil.

As you can see Hope mentions John Forster Dulles again, talks about oil money and traveling, says Rocky is big oil. The show has a commercial shoot at the Desert Inn and infers info about drive-in movies, music and records, stars and submarines. It ends with a football film and no direct quotes.

As a note, John Foster Dulles and his brother Alan, one was CIA director and one was the State Department during the 50s and early 60s. I link them to Howard Hughes and the Assassination of John and Robert Kennedy, a conspiracy and the Warren Commission cover-up of the Assassination.

* * * *

#51 January 16, 1959

The show starts out with the film about airplanes and all the many sites around the world where the USO did their programs. This show from the airbase in Berlin, staying at the Hilton Hotel, then on the Aircraft Carrier Forestall. Bob Hope knows all the ship's stats.

All the film of his USO shows, and he talks about his wallet and dialog ask, "what are you hiding behind". (a Face). The show moves on to a United States Air Force Base in Spain. Then on to Morocco.

In plain talk Bob Hope talks Oil. Hope talks about air travel and the names of world stops. Sinatra says, "Bob, I thought you were a younger man than Mr. Dulles". Hope says, "I came all the way to Casa Blanca by Pipeline". He's asked, "why not by bus"? In the dialog Colonna says, "he is waiting for his check from Standard Oil". What's that mean? Hope makes these quips that he has "a family of idiots". And says to Icelandic Soldiers that "the Beer Is always cold". Hope an Beer and Hughes owned a Brewery. Terry Moore said that!

In this show is a great film of American weapons and on the plane, flying over eight countries Hope uses the radio from the plane. Bob advertises his Christmas show and shows photos of jets and their pilots. Bob speech about the United States was good. Shows Missiles and Rockets and that they're ready to fight.

Hope is also quoted in this show as saying, "I sold 1 million Records, but none sold 1 million". Was Hope in the Music Business? like maybe Capitol records.

Hope in some of his dialog mentions Ava Gardner and Frank Sinatra and mentions Ava's Matador man. Ava went from Mickey Rooney, to Howard Hughes, to Frank Sinatra, to a Matador from Spain. Sinatra and Hughes had great fights over Ava. Howard Hughes also had some great fights with Ava.

* * * *

52 February 10, 1959

Here we go again. The MC Bob Hope talked about Rockets and being anti-Russia. He talks about how fast his Jets are flying in just 4 hours and 11 min. from Los Angeles to New York and talks about the $77 Billion US Budget and "living for free". Like I said, even with Bob Hope as Howard Hughes having all the money in the world he's living for free because the United States Government is paying for all of it.

In the first skit Hope talks about the United States Capital and the 86th Congress. He talked issues, top secret issues, and says he needs green stamps to build submarines and ask for a military money request and Hope goes on to Washington DC. He says he "rode to Washington DC with the Sen. From Alaska". That would be Hal Boggs. In the skit He says he "could make it rain over that address". He says he is "no taxpayer". He shows a missile shot from a Submarine. I'd say that's Howard Hughes connections. Also, strange that during the Investigation into the Assassination of Pres. Kennedy Hal Boggs happened to die in a plane crash. Mr. Boggs was on the Warren Commission. Was he going to flip? Did he know too much? was he assassinated? And what ever happened to Stuart Symington, Jack Ruby, Martha Mitchell? Just to name a few.

In the next skit Hope's name is "Peter Pistol". He says, "I am more than a Private eye I am a private Ears, Nose and Throat."

In another skit titled "Killing and Dying in LA" Hope says, "I'll kill everyone on this show."

Next skit is about the Beat Generation, 1959, and the home life of Bob Hope as a Beatnik, a bass player and on the Bongos. The best part is where he admits "wearing elevator shoes". Like being on stilts. Like stilt Cowboy Boots. Could that be why Howard Hughes looked tall and thin and Bob Hope short and stout? Seems like every show he shows the people what's happening. Like Bob Hope said, "the people don't listen."

So, Hope is telling everyone he doesn't pay any taxes and that the Government pays for everything and that he has Great Knowledge of all United States weapons.

* * * *

#53 March 13, 1959

This Bob Hope show is coming to you live. Bob talks about his looks and his eye operation at an underground Medical Hospital and he is quoted as saying "you're looking at the oldest dead-end kid in the business" I think he saying he is from Brooklyn New York. Mob territory.

Skit # 1... The skit is about prehistoric man versus modern man. Modern man is in a suit. Pre-man points out Bob Hope's Nose and points out Bob ears, his chin and his stomach in the skit. That's all the Accessories that as an Actor, Howard Hughes as Bob Hope has had make-up on for years. A protruding chin, fake ears, fake nose and fat clothes and right in this skit both are talking about make-up costumes and disguises. Now isn't that what I have been saying "that Bob Hope is Howard Hughes, one or the other or both and both were spies and in Disguises like Mission Impossible and Bob Hope in this skit is left as the last man on earth. Hope says, "I am the only man left"!

Skit number two is titled The Rifleman. That was also the title of a television show. In this skit it is about Hope being super rich and being out West. and he talks about how he is "tired of killing people". and he brings up the Lone Ranger, he talks about Cowboys and then Hope talks about TV western shows and their actors and is quoted as saying.

"take away those built up shoes" and then takes off his make-up. Now isn't that special, he's telling you that My Theory is proven that he is Howard Hughes in make-up and the built-up shoes are for Howard's Hughes.

There was a Lone Ranger show about a short guy who was self-conscious of his shortness and wore stilted cowboy boots and that again proves My Theory again, that the tall Howard Hughes with stilled cowboy boots was really the short Bob Hope who is also Howard Hughes. Years passed and there were two movies made called Get Shorty.

* * * *

#54 ... October 8, 1959

The title of this TV show is A Perfect Hiding Place. That's the title and it opens with the NBC Peacock Beak, as a chicken. Bob Hope in the opening says that he is involved in World Politics; he then says that someone came up to him to ask him to help them find Eisenhower for a place to hide in Palm Springs. Who really is the President and who is hiding out in Palm Springs? further Hope goes on to say that "Palm Springs is so Rich of a place that Howard Hughes was arrested as a vagrant". That is strange; History says years ago that Howard Hughes was arrested as a vagrant in Houston Texas and New Orleans Louisiana in one of the few times that he had disappeared. I wonder who that someone was who came to him. Was it Himself Again? Thanks for the Memory.

Skit # 1 … Title: Hope as an Inventor Who is the real Inventor??

Pretty good title: Is Hope the Inventor or is Howard Hughes the Inventor? Well here in this skit Hope is telling everyone that he is an Inventor. The show shows a Rocket ship and Hope is on it. Hope has said he was a pilot and that he did a spacewalk. Who is more involved in rockets and jet planes Hope or Howard? Here we have both. Howard Hughes was the Rocket man. Howard Hughes the Aviator. The Inventor. The character actor. The real President of the United States.

So, Bob Hope says to Bobby Darin" I dig it" and Bobby Darin says to Hope "you would have to dig because you're buried". There is a fake death theme again like I said every skit tells the truth, people think it's a joke from the comedian.

* * * *

#55. No title missed date.

Skit # 1 … This show opens with Gangsters from the 1920s as owners of Brewery and Hope is playing Scarface in a skit. It is then stated that he is the owner of NBC-TV and on his TV shows that he's connected to the Mob. One Starlet, Terry Moore wrote a book and stated that Howard Hughes owned a Brewery and we know there were great battles with the Kennedys over the running of alcohol during Prohibition. In dialog and actor says to Hope "your always in character". and the actor told NBC who he was, told them he is the beak. Hope takes over NBC. It is said that the actor turned hoodlum. There he told you again that Howard Hughes owns the network that he is Bob Hope and their background was from Brooklyn. He was in the theater; the Mob backed the Shows and the Billionaire got behind all the Mob's money and behind all the Circuses Vaudeville and Theater People. Thanks for the Memory. For some reason the Mob was out to get Hughes for fixing a fight and making it with all the Mobs Women. He had to leaveBrooklyn.

That's not to forget from previous writings within Bob Hope's Autobiography, They Got Me Covered, Bing Crosby refers to Bob Hope as the Beak and that this New Face on Bob Hope belongs to the owner. The owner is Howard Hughes. Two in one. One as Two.

Another note about owning the Brewery, in her book the Beauty and the Billionaire, Terry Moore states that Howard Hughes owned a Brewery and that's coincidental to a movie that was made by Bob Hope called Sgt. O Farrell U.S. Navy, about Bob Hope getting Beer deliveries to all the troops all around the world. Delivery to all the United States troops during the war. Coincidence? I don't think so. Was it Coors? the Silver Bullet Beer. Like the Silver Bullet from the Lone Ranger's gun. A Silver Bullet is a Bullet for a person to be wacked. The Lone Rangers Horse was also named Silver. High Ho Silver.

I think that happened in Dallas in 1963. The skit has makeup on Bob Hope's face as Scarface. 9 Kills from the Butcher from Cleveland. Face being peeled off right on the show by Natalie Wood. She peels the makeup off Bob Hope's face. Hope says that Howard Hughes hideout is in Palm Springs "a perfect place to hide". There is a Movie Titled The Kid From Cleveland,

* * * *

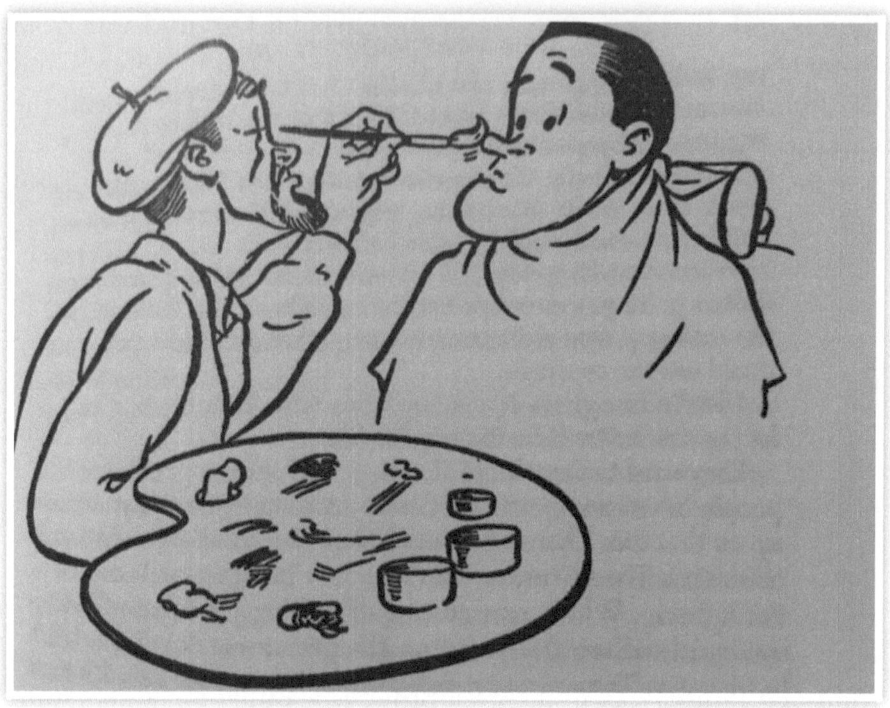

#56 ... November 9, 1959

This show is titled The Illusion and Bob Hope is the MC and gives his monologue. There's only canned laughter, no real laughs. Hope goes on to say, "I am sure you don't think this is my real nose it's all an illusion and I'll explain my jokes coast-to-coast jokes by jet planes". and at that Hope flies in as a character actor and the show goes into a skit. The illusion Is real because the face is fake. Hope just revealed the truth. It's a mask and there was a movie called Mask. Bob Hope himself says he himself is an illusion. Just like I said a Masquerade, The Magnificent Fraud, character actor Howard Hughes. In another skit Hope tells the Cops that "he killed a man"; and that's not the first time that Hope has admitted killing someone, he says "I've killed nine guys from the previous show". and Bob Hope says, "why is everybody always picking on me". he then says, "I have interchangeable parts". Hope says he has interchangeable parts. Yes, just like Mr. Potato Head, we can put a fake nose on a face, fake ears on the potato just like he put all the makeup on his face with plenty sponge rubber, Playtex makeup, stucco, contact lenses, false nose, chin, eye lashes. to stilted cowboy boots and all. Hope / Hughes 'Two of the most famous names in America sleep together.

* * * *

57 ... December 11, 1959

The show opens, it's about Music and the Music Business with Dean Martin, Hope is quoted to say that "Dean's records are on the Mafia label it stated as Capital Records"; and Bob Hope goes on to say that "the sponsor doesn't know who the sponsor is "probably because it's him, he sponsors himself and he's Howard Hughes and because even all the people around him don't even know who he really is? Texaco sponsors Bob Hope show Howard Hughes is Texaco and Texaco sponsors Bob Hope show on NBC. See any connections there?

Hope has said he controls 18 Labels. (HRH)

Here's a skit about Bob Hope robbing $80,000 worth of jewelry. The story comes over as a newscast and Hope shows up as a cat burglar and in dialog and actor says to Hope "take off your mask"! speculation of mine is that Howard Hughes probably gave the jewels to the beautiful women then went back and burglarized the lot. (Za Za)

Another skit is about Beatniks at his home. He talks of Hollywood's wealth, the hillside homes, earthquakes and insurance and in another skit Hope mocks Washington DC and Congress on a payola scandal about the 1959 versus the Hess brothers Pennsylvania. Hope says, "Howard Hughes bought out the Hess Brothers". At the end of the show Hope talks Magazines and Buicks and stated, "now we are back in production."

* * * *

#58 ... January 13, 1960

This show is all about the United States Air Force and Bob Hope's USO shows. Films are shown of the shows from Tokyo, Korea, Europe and Air Force films of the United States Air Force

Rocket 28 miles up, shows the early warning base. A three-hour show. Purely full entertainment show. At the opening Bob talks about the story of his life and makes a quote that "he's wanted dead or alive". Who is he talking about; putting out that he himself is wanted dead or alive? one Howard is dead, two Bob is alive, and he's wanted as one dead or alive, dead by the spy's, dead by the Mob, by the Government. Hope has said he was employed by the United States Government and that he hid out in the Military because the Mob was out to kill him, so were some spies.

Hope talks about an airplane ride where he may have to abandon the plane of his personal luggage and Bob Hope says, "throwing out his makeup box, my makeup kit goes to the bottom there the sharks will have two sets of teeth and two heads". Prior Bob has said that he has a group of writers that he's one of those writers and he's the one with two heads. That's My Theory that Bob Hope is one and the same. Howard Hughes is one head and the other head is Bob Hope. two of the most famous names in America sleep together

* * * *

#59 ... February 22, 1960

Bob Hope Master of Ceremonies opens his show talking about Eisenhower, the Russians and Rockets. So, the Comedian knows all about the President of the United States, about the Russians and about Rockets. That's My Theory that Howard Hughes knew all about Jet Planes and Rockets. Hope talks about the Writers' strike, talking about the Hollywood writers' strike and he says, "there is 3,000 of them and all of them work for me" Wait a minute, Hope says he has a group of writers and he's one of them and he says they all work for him. they all work for Bob Hope. Interesting Howard Hughes owns all the studios and pays all the writers and they don't know that Bob Hope is Howard Hughes. So, who is Hope? Hope says, "he's the best boss behind the scenes of Washington DC". He just said he is the President of the United States. Then there is a film of the 18th hole with Hope carrying his Golf Club. It's Howards Golf Club.

* * * *

#60 ... April 20, 1960

Bob Hope shows up in a skit with Bob at a Beverly Hills Psychiatric office and he is called Dr. Hope and a tape recorder is shown. A side note is that Bob Hope has written in his book that he's a real Doctor with a real Doctor's License and that he got that License in Atlantic City and Vietnam. If you know Atlantic City History, Atlantic City was taken over by the United States Government during World War II and many of the Hotels were turned into Hospitals for our Servicemen. Howard Hughes aka Bob Hope Invented a modern Hospital bed. Bob Hope is a doctor. I guess that's how we got all the Television shows called M*A*S*H, Doctor Killdare, Ben Casey and others.

Another skit is about diet pills and Bob shows up in a big fat belly clothes super fat clothes and said, "I must diet", and then is quoted as saying "one of us has to go to go" Is that a hint that there's two people in one? There's talk about girdles and padded clothing. Bob says, "when I am in front of the camera there are two Bob Hope's"! Right Bob Hope is and was Howard Hughes in make- up. Two of the most famous names in America sleep together. In the dialog it is said by Hope that "that's how you got on both sides of me"! two heads, two sides, proof again.

* * * *

#61 ... October 3, 1960

Bob Hope's opening is all about current events and the Nixon versus Kennedy Election. Hope then talks golf carts, jets, the United Nations, Khrushchev and the USSR and Castro. Seems as though Bob Hope knows all about those issues as Bob Hope must have some involvement in all those issues. Hope had said that the Bay of Pigs Invasion of Cuba was one of his biggest fiascos. That's Howard Hughes talking. Hughes sponsored the Invasion of Cuba.

Skit # 1 ... Title: Hope as an Inventor Who is the real Inventor??

Pretty good title:: Is Hope the Inventor or is Howard Hughes the Inventor? Well here in this skit Hope is telling everyone that he is an Inventor. Then shows a Rocket ship with Hope on it. Hope has said he was a Pilot and that he did a Spacewalk. Who is more involved in rockets and jet planes Hope or Howard? Here we have both. Howard Hughes was the Rocket man. Howard Hughes the Aviator. The inventor. The character actor. The real President of the United States.

So, Bob hope says to Bobby Darin" I dig it" and Bobby Darin says to Hope "you would have to dig because you're buried". There is a fake death theme again like I said every skit tells the truth, people think it's a joke from the comedian.

* * * *

#62 October 22, 1960

This show opens with Bob Hope saying that He is going to tell everybody the truth and the show opens with the political film of a convention nominating the President of the United States, shows the White House and Bob Hope gives a speech about India and the Arabs. Hope comes on screen as a Texan and he gives a speech. He was talking to the very rich. We know that Hope is a Texan and Howard Hughes is a Texan. You know about Texas. The Beverly Hillbillies struck oil and move off to Beverly Hills. Bob Hope lives in Beverly Hills, the Movie Industry is in Beverly Hills Southern California. Bob speech is directed at the Swells he says, "you swells better get hip."

Skit # 2 ... Opens with a psychiatric office and Hope is on the couch and in the dialog Bob Hope says to the psych "don't go blabbing my real name across this neighborhood". Now isn't that interesting that Bob Hope's name is not his real name. What is his real name? Remember this Bob Hope, also known as Howard Rupert 'Sonny" Hughes Jr. changes his name to Bob Hope and becomes a Character Actor. His real name is too long to fit on the Theater Marquee. His name went from 18 letters down to 7 letters to fit on the Theater Marquee.

So, what do you think his real name is if it's not Robert Leslie Townes Hope? He says he was born in England. Really, Hope writes in one of his books that when he was visiting England at one time he said to a Butler that he was born in England and the Butler retorts to him "I'll keep your secret". Hope wrote that.

Skit # 3 ... On the Convention floor Hope is accused of taking kickbacks from Contractors. I thought they charged Howard Hughes with that, anyway, Hope says "I explained all that at the hearings". Bob Hope wasn't at the hearings. Howard Hughes was hauled before Congress to testify at the Army hearings. He didn't explain all that at the hearings, it was Howard Hughes who had to tell all that at the Congressional Army hearings. Hope is Hughes.

Skit # 4 ... Titled: POTUS

Hope shows up as President of the United States and as a Cowboy in a good guy White Hat. Sounds like the Lone Ranger. Hope goes on to talk about a Desert Inn Penthouse in Vegas. History knows and shows that Howard Hughes hid out in the Penthouse of the Desert Inn. Hope is then seen in a phone booth. Howard Hughes always used the phone booth. So did Clark Kent as Superman. Look up in the Sky, it's a bird, it's a Plane, its SUPERMAN.

* * * *

#63 ... November 16, 1960

The film of jets and jets and more jets. Hope shows up on the scene as a jet pilot. Was Hope a jet pilot? I know Howard Hughes was a jet pilot. If Bob Hope was a jet pilot they were both jet pilots. Two of the most famous names in America. Hope says in one of his books that he is a pilot with thousands of hours flying time. The skit was a good show, just Entertainment.

* * * *

#64 ... December 12, 1960.

Hope open's show with Jimmy Durante and Hope says, "my name Is my ID". Hope tells everyone JFK won the election and Ike is going out.

Skit # 1... This whole skit talks about spies and about who controls space and Hope gives out his formula for fuel. There's a Bob Hope movie, Road to Singapore, where Bob Hope and Bing Crosby are being chased by Russian spies who are after a Secret Fuel Formula for the Rockets. Dialog says, "that Hope is the Greatest Brain in the World." If Hope is Hughes they're both the Greatest Brains in the World". You recall that Bob Hope is a Screenwriter at Paramount with two heads. Right one. Howard Hughes, the other Bob Hope. That's My Theory. I've said that, and I have proved it beyond a reasonable doubt.

Thus, it talks about Russia and International Spies and Disguises, plastic nose and chin on a girl spy. Hope says he "works for the Government and that "my head is top-secret". and an Actor says about Hope "You'll have to get the Atomic Secrets from him". Hope is seen as a Spaceman.

* * * *

#65 ... January 11, 1961

The show opens with Bob Hope and 59 people with a film of a Xmas show on a Caribbean Island showing Jets, Army and Navy Ships, Gitmo, Puerto Rico, the CB's and legal Gambling. All about the United States Military. Then mostly Entertainment.

* * * *

#66 ... February 15, 1961

Bob Hope starts talking about Rockets, Astronauts Satellite's and Space. Strange.. Everything that Howard Hughes is involved in. check out Hughes History. Then he talks about girdles then says, "whose job is JFK after?" That's a joke that JFK is after Howard

Hughes job as President of the United States. Hughes was The President. POTUS

Hope talks sports MLB and then mentions the Houston Astros.. Switches to Basketball, talks about Wilt Chamberlin' height and is saying "see what they can do with Elevator Shoes.

Elevator Shoes Stilts used in Circuses. used by Howard Hughes, the thin man to appear tall. The tall man was a TV show. Also, The Lone Ranger had an episode titled High Heels about a Cowboy who wore Stilt Cowboy Boots to appear tall because he was self-conscious about being short. The man was in real estate. There was also a movie called "Get Shorty" filmed at Resorts Int. Casino in Atlantic City, NJ.

Other Movies filmed at Resorts International Casino, the first Casino outside of Vegas were, Atlantic City USA, the Color of Money, Snake Eyes, Among others.

* * * *

#67... April 12, 1961

Opens with a skit with Phil Harris. it's a Family skit about Adultery. A skit about Bob and Howards private life style. Bob is quoted as saying "Live or on tape". Dialog says. "Who does your nose". And then says to Hope "you are wonderfully real". that's right even with all the make-up on.

* * * *

68 ... May 13, 1961

This show is titled The Tall Man.

Bob Hope the tall man talks about Lucky Luciano ...In a book about Bob Hope talks about a meeting at a New York Restaurant named Charlies. And states that "Lucky" backs Broadway shows with his money.

In the skit Hope goes on to talk about a house full of woman. In a book about Howard Hughes jr, nickname "sonny" it is said that sonny loved to sneak to the theater district in New York and Cleveland and was infatuated with the beautiful showgirls.

Strange when you find out that Bob Hope enters Vaudeville as a Character Actor. Further in a scene with a beautiful. Woman, Hope says to her "when you watch the love scene you'll wonder why there is three (3) of us in all the love scenes". There you go Hope says he is two 2 people in one and Women makes three (3). Hope is Howard Hughes as Bob Hope in make-up. He needs no double. He is two. He's two and she makes three.

The owner of Paramount, a writer with two heads, who all three thousand 3,000 writers work for him. Hughes is the character Actor as Bob Hope since Vaudeville. Two of the most famous names in America.

Here's another quote from Hope from one of his movies talking to a woman he is making out with.. "If I was to die and come back and be with you, you would have been with the both of me". Well what do you think about that. Here Hope again admits he is two people in one.

Skit # 2..this skit opens with Hope acting as a financial wizard, shone to be very rich playing the stock market. Here Hope is ordering all kinds of raw materials. The skit shows that he is running the stock market and that he is also an Actor. He says he is "cornering the world and I am getting rich". He is then saying, "I bought an Oil well and wouldn't you know they discovered uranium there."

* * * *

#69 … May 13, 1961

The Bob Hope tv show opens with the Alfred Hitchcock theme and the silhouette shadow and Hope walks right into it with his Nose being High-lighted. Hope's intro is about someone else and he says "is he or isn't he??

Good question. (about Howard) he goes on to say, "only his undertaker knows for sure". There you go, talking about faking his (HRH) own death. Is Howard Hughes dead or isn't he? At this date HRH was not seen in years and that was the rumor of the day. He then shows his big fat fake stomach.

My DVD went on the fritz. This is a very important show. Must be tried again at later date. Is he or isn't he that is the question? Hope says he is two persons and it's all on tape.

* * * *

#70 … December 13, 1961

Bob Hope comes on talking make-up, talking movies and all about the Tussaud House of Wax. Then about Air Planes.

Skit # 1..About filming a medical show at a LA Hospital for tv.

Skit # 2..Bob entered as a Fireman yelling "Guess Who" correct! Who is he??

Skit # 3..It's a pool room scene. Hope enters as Big John in Fat clothes. Beats up a pool shark.

* * * *

#71 …January 24, 1962

Bob opens this show with a United States Air Force Film of many Jets and a long line of Bombers. Colona is one of the Pilots. Bob cracks about arriving saying "I step off the plane an disappear". Did you catch it?. Getting off the plane into his Bob Hope character he is no longer Howard Hughes. He goes on to say, "everything is top secret in fact at the base all top secret is in code, in fact the Defense Department just found out about the base". The Defense Dept didn't even Know all that Howard Hughes was doing.

On the show the Chief of the USAF thanks Bob and the USO for their service.

As he steps off the plane he is no longer Howard Hughes, in public he is Bob Hope. In one of Bob Hope Autobiography Books there is a picture of Bob going to his plane and the caption under the photo says, "After each show I leave under an assumed name". To me that assumed name is BOB HOPE. His book, His Photo, His Quote…………… Nothing but the truth.

* * * *

#72 … February 27, 1962

Bob Hope show opens with a film of John Glen's Space shot and reentry as History. Facts. Says Capsule 160 mi. out, traveling at 17,500 mi. per hr. Mentions Hoffa, JFK, and Jackie's White House tour and more current events.

Skit # 1... At customs entry check in, Bob is in real long pants, tall for a long person wearing Elevator shoes. Agent says to Hope "you look better on your passport Photo than you do in person". Right, because in person Howard looks better than Hope. The agent then examines Bob's make-up kit. And "talking about what (hrh) Bob Hope will look like in the future". With false eye lashes, contact lens, Item after item including hair dye, wigs, mascara, shoulder pads, fat clothes, make-up and disguise's…Agent says "Bob Hope is in the make-up case so who are you"…BOB HOPE IS IN THE MAKE-UP CASE, who are you? Howard Hughes make -up case. HRH is Bob Hope in make-up… My Theory is not just a Theory, it's a fact. Like I've said "I've broke the biggest story in the history of the world.

In another skit Hope says, "Forrest Lawn cemetery has a lay away plan". He saying he has put himself in the grave ahead of time. Recall HRH is said to be dead because he is never seen. Dialog says to Hope "this show is live."

Skit # 3 … Jack Parr is Hope's guest and he is quitting NBC and he and Hope are talking about noses and Jack Parr say's "At least my nose is real". There ya go, Hope's nose is fake!!!!!! (and so is his entire face). From the make-up kit in make-up since Vaudeville days. (1922).

* * * *

#73 … March 22, 1962

Bob shows up as MC / Host of the Academy Awards. He talks about JFK coming to Palm Springs Ca. and staying at Bing Crosby's house. He rips Kennedy and runs him down. Sinatra mad that JFK did not stay at his house.

There's two skits. One on Asia and one long skit mostly nonsense.

Skit # 3 ... is about a Actors workshop and an actor says to Hope "I want to know who you are and where you sleep". Bob talks about"being a new man."

That's right Howard Hughes being a new man in Bob Hope. Who is he?? He has been telling everyone in all his books, in all his movies, and on all his TV shows. People do not listen.

* * * *

#74 ...April 25, 1962

Bob Hope opens saying "I killed myself last week". He goes on talking about money, movies, guest stars, politics, and anti JFK.

Skit # 1 ... In this skit Hope talks about himself "I am a Duel man". tells you right there he is two men in one. Just like I said, two of the most famous names in America sleep together, and I have that quote in a magazine ad over Bob Hope's head. Next.. "I am Bob Hope the Man". And "I am Bob Hope the Actor". He then says to another actor "so that's how you got on both sides of me". So, Howard Hughes is a Duel Personality, or Bob Hope is a Duel Personality. Pick one!

Hope goes on to show film of Road to Hong Kong which is all about space and a new fuel formula for Rockets.

Another skit introduces Bob as an Actor, Producer, and Studio Owner. Wow. Isn't that what Howard Hughes is. There was a TV show Titled "I led Three Live's". And as an Actor Bob Hope has said he is the man of 7 Faces with a tray of Noses that fool the public. Mission Possible. Recall Bob said Lincoln was wrong "you can fool all the people all the time". Every show, every movie, every book Bob Hope goes about telling everyone that he is someone else, an actor wearing Make-up.

* * * *

#75 ... October 24, 1962

This show opens with Bob Hope talking about Space, Satellites the USSR. Sure, sounds like information that Howard Hughes would know a lot about knowing that he was involved with Scientist, Rockets and Space all coming out of Bob Hopes mouth.

Skit # 1 …A skit with Lucille Ball about a Mob rub out like Chicago's St Valentine's Day Massacre. Hope kills people with a machine Gun. Hope growls the alligator love call that was taught only to Howard Hughes by Terry Moore. Bob is Howard! Skit is also about money and bribes.

Skit # 2 …About Bonanza with Bob an Bing playing cowboys as cattle barons out west. They talk about looks and about being two people. Hope jokes twice he may own Hawaii and Alaska, California and Texas. Let's recall the movie The Barefoot Contessa where Ava Gardner is told that that movie producer over there owns Texas and is buying up California. Hope is playing 3 or 4 parts. Bing then says, "3 people have to deal with that face". Bing says to Bob "You look the same to me. Put it there Pal.

* * * *

#76 November 29, 1962

Show is a command performance from Hollywood and London with the Queen of England.

Skit # 1 … from Alcatraz Prison. Show is mostly entertainment by Bob and Bobby Darin. Good record medley. Bob Hope yells "My nose is my bankroll.

Skit # 2 … Bob is on a Gambling Boat as a gambling boob with Ethel Mermen. On the River Boat it's mostly entertainment with acting, jokes and costumes. In another scene with Jack Benny Benny says of Hope that Hope "is of the Pentagon". Hope says, "the real me."

* * * *

#77…January 16, 1963

Show starts out with a film of Bob's Pacific Rim USO shows over 10 days featuring American servicemen in many locations via the United States Air Force to many islands and the Air craft carrier Kitty Hawk. Stars on board are Jerry Colona, Janis Page, Anita

Bryant, Miss USA, and Lana Turner... Bob is talking about being "very rich" and being "from Texas". In this show Lana Turner turns to Hope and says "Bob, Sir You told me you were an officer in the USAF Bob why no uniform". Bob Hope says to Lana Turner and tells her "I am CENTRAL INTELLIGENCE". Did you get that? Being the CIA connects Bob Hope aka Howard Hughes with John and Allen Foster Dulles. In 1963 John Dulles was US Secretary of State and his Brother Allen was Dir. Of Central Intelligence in the Kennedy Administration. The year Kennedy was Assassinated. Allen Dulles was OSS head of WW 2 Sniper Unit. HRH hated the Kennedy's since the 30's. Do you see a conspiracy there?

* * * *

#78 ... April 14, 1963

This show is from Hollywood and New York City. Just entertainment with guest stars Dean Martin and Martha Raye. Dean plays the part as a singing Hillbilly. Talk is all about movies, tv, books, Magazines and records.

* * * *

79 May 15, 1963

Hope opens with a monologue and says, "you'll know me I'm the NBC Hillbilly". Indicating that he is the Beverly Hills Hillbilly. Recall the television show the Beverly HillsBilly's and sing the opening song. The song describes the life of Howard Hughes from Texas to California to owning all the motion picture studios after striking oil as an inheritance from his father. and here you have Bob Hope telling you that he is him. To prove it watch the first 5 min. of the motion picture the Barefoot Contessa starring Ava Gardner, who happened to be Howard Hughes girlfriend. Hope talks politics and about Kennedy, slamming JFK.

Skit # 1 ... Is all about space and he speaks of the twilight zone, he then shows a film of himself with golf clubs and pairing off with Arnold Palmer. in a biography of Howard Hughes. Hughes is said to have said that he wanted to be one of the best golfers in the world, the best movie maker and the richest man in the world, Bob Hope fits that description.

Skit # 2 ... Bob Hope is acting like a spy in Russia. He's even called "Comrade". I say this skit Is real, that Howard Hughes the Industrial Billionaire and oil baron was a spy for the US. Hope goes off to Cuba, which is a hot bed for spy's from around the world. Hope is called "a fraud". and not for the first time. Because he is. It's Howard in makeup as Bob Hope "a fake". An Actor. Someone yells "We saw your act". He shows a lot of tape recorders. Hope talks about Science, Planes, Rockets and Mars.

He yells "attention all spies."

* * * *

80 ... September 27, 1963

Hope starts to show off and cracks about JFK and talked about Space and the Russians.

Skit # 1 ... The first joke is about his nose and the dialog says, "I love your nose". He talks about "what the Peacock said."

Skit # 2 ... Again, he talks about Sputnik, France and TV. The skit takes place in a psych's office. Hope enters and is given a Royshock test. Says he is "worthless."

Howard Hughes was a crazy manic.

Skit # 3 ... Hope is in a Hick Band at Koo Koo Teck. He mentions Oil, the Lone Ranger and an Indian. Talks sex and refers to Sex as Pool.

* * * *

#81 ... October 25, 1963

Bob Hope opens his show talking about the Mob and about the hearings in Washington about the Mafia and their murders. Talks against JFK. Mentions Vietnam, Madam Nu, Russia and Nikita. Says his tv is "The Peacock. That's him the showoff being beautiful and rich.

Skit # 1 ...Titled.. Mastermind of the entire underworld.

Hope comes on scene as the Boss and head of the Mafia. There's the truth shown as a joke. Hope continues to tell the truth as he confronts Sheriff Griffith. He says to the Police "don't you recognize me, I'm the killer criminal". He is put in a cell. He sets up his cell with a phone a tv. Just the way Al Capone set up is cell when he was in jail in Philadelphia. The skit then shows him as being very rich and collecting bags of money from the cities. Right just like the Mafia does and Hope says, "they know where I'm hiding". That's Howard Hughes talking telling you who he is and what he does for a living.

* * * *

#82 December 13, 1963

Bob is off it is said he is sick, and Bing Crosby is taking his spot. There is film of past skits. Jack Benny does a cameo and says, "I think about Bob Hopes nose". Then there is a skit with Hope as Peter Gun "private eye ears nose and throat."

* * * *

#83 January 17, 1964

Show opens with Bob telling everyone that he has "one hundred ocean crossings". Gives a talk about being in the theater of Turkey, Greece, Italy and Libya with his shows and thanks the US Air Force from the USS Sangrala. He says, "I'm in the Air Force". My Theory is Howard Hughes is and was the USAF.

In a skit in a Casbah Colona is a spy and he is looking for secrets. Colona says, "What are American Scientist working on". to Hope as they talk about the FBI and Disguises. So, Hope is about Science, Secrets, Spying, and Disguise's.

* * * *

#84 February 14, 1964

Show opens cracking about The Beatles. Then about the nations of China recognizing France and visa versa. Then a skit about a first lady President. Dialog says about Hope "He has everything". and that "he (Hope) is leading a double life". Really, that's what I have been telling you. Nothing but the truth.

* * * *

#85 April 17, 1964

The Academy award show all about the Movies. Bob does a monolog about Cuba, Russia, Nikita and John Glenn. Talks DC, Tax's and the Press.

Skit # 1 …not much to it.

Skit # 2 …The title of this skit is "the seven faces of Doctors". How many times in Skits reveals a bit of the truth? Tony Randle calls out to Bob and says, "nobody has ever accused you of playing a phony it's you". The Bob Hope character is a phony and a fraud and no one would ever call him that or publicly reveal the truth or the money would be shut off or they would be killed.

* * * *

#86 September 25, 1964

Show starts with Bob showing Jet Planes. Howard Hughes was a Test Pilot. He says a Jet just made record time coast to coast from LA to NY in one and a half hrs.

There is a skit with Jack Benny, and it is about make-up. Bob says to Jack, "let's get ready for the show". Bob says, "Yes make-up, a little stucco". What have I been telling you! Hope says, "does NBC need two peacocks". Bob and Howard.

Skit # 2 … Phillis Diller and Bob are in a Psych office for a marriage council. Diller says to Hope "you must be in the wrong office I am not a plastic surgeon."

Skit # 3 … Dean Martin sings.

* * * *

87 November 20, 1964

Hope starts right in talking about the Presidential Election about LBJ beating Goldwater in a landslide. Nixon blames Rockefeller for Goldwater's defeat.

Skit # 1 ...Hope is portrayed as an owner of an airplane is shown as the Pilot. Hope has said that he was a pilot with 1,000's of flying hrs. Howard Hughes was also a pilot. Stella Stevens plays Miss Stunning.

Skit # 2 ...In this skit we have a few quotes that revel some truths.. Hope is asked "How many think that your tv personality is really you"? and "who handles your fan mail Bob"? Hope retorts "the FBI."

Skit # 3 ... Hope shows up as a sr. citizen gunslinger wearing fat clothes in Japan. He says that "I used to be a gunslinger an rob an kill people". I believe that as Howard Hughes of the Mob he did just that. Hope says, "I am him". "Pagoda nose."

Skit # 4 ... Here Donald O'Conner is pulling on Bob's Ear and Hope says, "be careful that's not my real ear". There's the make-up. Fake ears big enough so that the cameras can see them. Watch all the old movies and you will see that many actors are wearing enlarged ears. Check it out.

* * * *

#88 December 18, 1964

Hope opens up with jokes on politics and international raps on the UN, Russia, LbJ, Texas and the Beatles Ringo' and about an operation he had and goes into a skit.

Skit # 1 ... with James Gardner about Russia, Military Intelligence, and Radar.

Bob Hope knows all about these things.

Solders call Bob "the Boss". My Theory is that HRH is Bob Hope, secret President of the US, who had won WW 2, is running everything, holds all titles, runs America, runs the Mob, the CIA. Does all Radio, TV, and Movies. That Theory of mine is proven by what is said and shown in all of Bob Hopes Acts. Plus, with control of most oil of the world and much of the world's raw materials. and great sums of money HRH makes the calls. HRH / BH runs NASA, Rockets and Armaments...

* * * *

#89 January 15, 1965

Show is all films of all Bob Hope's USO Xmas shows of the Pacific Theater. And it is about getting Beer to all the Troops. Film of the many US Bases around that part of the Pacific.

Talking about Beer to troops it was revealed in Terry Moore's book The Beauty and the Billionaire that Howard Hughes owned a Brewery. There is also a Movie titled Sargent O Farrell's Navy all about Bob Hope trying and delivering Beer to all the troops in the Pacific Theater. Coincidence? I don't think so!! The whole Mob Prohibition thing was about Beer. Hughes owned a Brewery.

* * * *

#90 February 12, 1965

Bob talks about the space budget says that LBJ is the President of the United States and of Texas. See any connections there. Hughes is from Texas, LBJ from Texas, JFK killed in Texas. Texaco Oil from Texas. Interesting!!

Skit # 1 ... opens with a well-built woman as a spy, dressed to kill. Hope is the pure evil spy master and head of a crime syndicate leader of the mob and a criminal murderer. What have I been telling and writing about...Nothing but the truth told through Howard's mouth with his Bob Hope face? Hope then says "I will be in charge of the entire Pentagon as the Mad Genius and Master of the World". What did I tell you Right out of his own mouth as a joke in a skit.

Skit # 2 ... A scene of the Tonight Show with Jonny Carson. Hope is asked why he left Paramount. No answer. The camera shows a group of Arabs in the audience

* * * *

#91 April 16, 1965

In this show Bob Hope reveals who he really is by telling all about Howard Hughes Life.

The answer is told in the following skit.

Skit # 1 …Hope comes on as a Hobo, a tramp, a bum eating out of a trash can.

If you know Howard Hughes History and Biography he went missing twice as a bum and was arrested in Houston and New Orleans. So, thanks for his memory he puts the truth in all his movies and tv shows. In this skit Hope is quoted saying "Do you know who I am". (I DO) Then says, "my folks had money". You can say that again. Howard's parents had all the money and oil and raw materials out west and in the world and Howard Hughes Inherited all. Watch Bob Hope movie's "Paleface and Son of pale face". The complete truth is there.

* * * *

#92 September 29, 1965

Bob Hope opens the show saying it's his 16th year on TV and talks about his TV shows and says, "he got a deal with himself", he got a good deal with the NBC Peacock. Behind the scenes I believe Howard Hughes was the owner of the Network NBC. He then talks current events from DC politics to Reagan to the Beatles concert at Shea Stadium the World Series and the Pope.

Skit # 1 … About NASA and a space film of a three-year orbit

Skit # 2 … Is about the NBC network being a hotbed of spies with top-secret investigations. That's why a lot of Bob Hope's movies and skits were about the subject matter of spies. Hope puts on a gun and is working out of the basement of 30 rock. NBC.

Skit # 3 … Here's more proof truth. The skit is about Cowboys and Hope shows up with a large phone, at that another actor yells "where's the one with the phony Nose". Bob Hope yells back "he's dead and buried in Colorado, Arizona and Wyoming". That's where I believe that Howard Hughes was hiding out. Another actor says" he has a weak chin". Another says" I know who you are" at that they all put on fake noses! How about that! Bob Hope revealed where he as Howard Hughes was hiding out. There was a Movie were Hope was pointing out the Paramount Mountain symbol and says, "there is a place for Howard Hughes to hide out". I think all the above tells you nothing but the truth again and again all over again.

* * * *

#93 October 20, 1965

Hope's monologue speaks of the Dodgers winning the World Series.

Skit # 1 … The Hillbillies of Texas

Howard Hughes is from Texas and he struck oil and owned the drill bit through the Hughes Tool Company in which digs into the Earth to retrieve oil, The TV show the Beverly Hillbillies and the Song of that show is all about Howard Hughes inheriting all the oil and raw materials and moving off to Beverly Hills California to the Movie Industry. In the script Bob says "get that Camera close I want them to see this Chin. (The chin is either make up or Plastic Surgery). He says he is "a Representative of the United States Government". There he's telling the truth again that he is the Government.

Skit # 1 … About a Haunted House and a man who is a Beast evil. A quote: "what's in his mind"?

Skit # 3 … About football. One quote from Bob "my nose was not pointed this way when I started". That's right when he started he put makeup on whether it was plenty of Sponge Rubber or Stucco to be a disguised character actor in his own paramount movies.

Skit # 4 … All about college life and Hippies.

* * * *

#94 December 15, 1965

Bob Hope as the MC opens NBC's first number one color telecast and the peacock network is number one. In his opening remarks Hope says, "most stars have to use heavy makeup but not me(he points to his face) and says" this Face is concrete". So, it's a fake face made of stucco cement and then there's talk of "elevator shoes". Shoes like that would make Bob as tall as Howard.

Skit # 1 ... A skit at Bob's home in Palm Springs with Bing Crosby.

Skit # 2 ... There is a prison break with Jack Benny. Bob and Jack go to Toyland. Hope Plays Santa and picks up guns and a machine gun and he talks anti-Castro.

Skit # 3 ... Takes place in Hollywood and Hope says, "I know who I am keep that camera on my cheeks it brings out the bloom of my cheeks". False cheeks. He then calls attention to the Stucco built up on his face.

* * * *

#95 January 19, 1966

Hope talks about Asia and United states of America, Cambodia, Thailand, Vietnam and Guam and Bob Hope says, "wait a minute I am still alive, and I had a great arrival I stepped off the plane and disappeared". Right on the plane he was Howard Hughes when he stepped off the plane he became Bob Hope. In private Howard, in public Bob. Two of the most famous names in America sleep together. Bob brings Sen. Stu Symington on stage, the former Secretary of the Air Force who through Pres. Truman allowed Hope to have free air travel everywhere. Hope salutes him and gives thanks to his aircrews of the United States Air Force, Navy, Army, Marines and the Coast Guard, all HRH forces. Bob is asked "Bob how come they never made you a general when you are the master planner of all times". There it is again Bob and Howard the owner of the United States of America.

* * * *

#96 February 16, 1966

This show is the second NBC full color telecast and Hope begins by speaking about current events and his Vietnamese shows, he then talks about LBJ and Dean Rusk about the moonshot and about Russia and the United States.

Martha Ray and Danny Thomas are on the show. Hope talks about Hawaii being a part of Texas. Recall the Movie the Barefoot Contessa it's about a movie producer who owns Texas and is buying up California. Did he buy up Hawaii? Did he buy up Alaska? Hope said he owned four States.

Skit # 1 Titled bad girl

That bad girl is Martha Ray, the scene is in a deserted house basement, it's a secret hideout for a great evil one and Hope says to Martha "do you know who I am".? And Martha answers "you're the world's most dangerous criminal". Looks like they're telling you the truth again. Bob Hope in makeup is Howard Hughes and after winning World War II being the United States Government and controlling the Mob behind the scenes is the world's most dangerous criminal that's what I've been saying and that's what's in the dialog out of his own mouth and remember he's a writer he wrote it and Howard is talking with the Bob Hope face. The bad girl Martha is acting as a spy.

Skit # 2 Is about Bob Hope being a motorcycle rider.

Skit # 3 ... Danny Thomas at the very start of the show skit says to Bob Hope" Bob I would buy your TV show, but the Army won't sell it". The Army controls the show. There you go, Hope has said some time back that he works for the Army and that his act as Bob Hope is going over and disagreeing with Lincoln, saying that you can fooll the people all the time and that the names of the innocent have been changed to protect the joke, the joke on the world. The skit has a Kid from Cleveland. That's for Bob Hope and Howard Hughes, they both say they came from Cleveland. And this Kid from Cleveland is playing cards for big money and is associated with the Mob and about slot machines. So, Hope showed up with millions of dollars and buys them all up and he's wearing a gun. There is My Theory that Hope is Hughes and he is the Mob and he is a Killer and he is the Government. Bob Hope has been quoted saying that he himself has killed nine people. Hope says he's from Cleveland. Howard, Sonny, Junior Hughes was from Cleveland, both from the same place There is a movie The Kid from Cleveland.

* * * *

#97 April 13, 1966

Right out of the box the first skit is about robbing banks. Robbing banks is mentioned a few times with Hope as the bank robber. I think these indicating that he is looting the American Government for money, that's where all the acting of being a pirate comes in because he was pirating the money. Hope has said he was in on The Brinks Bank robbery.

Skit # 2.. A very funny skit with Jonathan Winters and Hope says" who am I, identify me.

Skit # 3 ... Titled Pagoda Asia

Phyllis Diller is happy her husband Bob Hope who is thought to be dead, comes back to life. Nothing but the truth. The question is asked "who said you were dead"? Bob Hope came back with his fake face on where Howard is believed to be dead, that's how he comes back to life. Bob Hope is Howard Hughes. Howard Hughes is Bob Hope, a great actor in his own movies made in his own movie studios at Paramount and there it is said that Hope/Hughes is the greatest show on earth.

* * * *

#98 September 28, 1966

Hope is now in his 30th year at NBC. Show opens with Hope showing up in a limousine and then being thrown out of his star dressing room. Then there is a comeback party with all the beautiful women stars. That's the whole show. Hope says" I am alone in space except for beautiful women". Hope and Hughes were notorious for being womanizers.

Skit # 1 ... Is all about the Hollywood rich, about beautiful women and Hope again talks about makeup in every show in his skits are all about what is going on in the life of Bob Hope as Howard Hughes

* * * *

#99 October 19, 1966

Skit # 1... right off the bat big news about murder at NBC. "The story is that a mad scientist has a secret weapon. He is called "a depraved genius". Sounds like Howard to me. In this skit Hope is called a fraud and an imposter. That recalls his movies and the part about having seven faces and many Masks. In a couple movies a tray of noses that will fool everybody, and that the movie Marque says Bob Hope is a magnificent fraud and in actors' dialog it's indicated that they know who he is. A genius killer monster in control of the world and they know where their money and positions come from. It shows that a lot of people are in on the joke.

* * * *

#100...November 16, 1966?

* * * *

#101

The show opens with Bob Hope on a Mexican vacation, strictly entertainment, and with many women stars from Hollywood.

The show is total films of Bob Hope USO Christmas stops. Hope considers himself Santa Claus the American Way. A sign in the crowd says, Investigate Hope, and it's flashed on the screen. That's probably Bob Hope, saying that himself about himself. Nobody investigated. The film shows the many Christmas stops from Viet Nam, the Philippines, an Aircraft Carrier, plus the big red one. Hope appears wearing a five-star Hat as a General, and with his golf club. He introduces Stuart Symington. Remember Stuart Symington was the former Secretary of the United States Air Force for President Truman. The golf club in Hopes hand is Howard Hughes symbol, for he wished to be the best golfer in the world.

* * * *

#102 February 15, 1967

Hope opens the show talking about his movie. Eight on the Lamb. **Being on t**he lamb means that you're in hiding. They are laying low. Hope says he's 007 and he talks of Goldfinger.

Skit # 1 the theme of the skit is man is king in England and women are the slave, then it flips sides and in America man is a slave to the woman.

Skit # 2 Bob introduces his book to the public, titled Five Women I Love, and Hope makes a statement that national security had banned a chapter from the book called it celebrity security. Hope looks in the mirror points to his facial features, and in this skit a woman spy is trying to get top secrets from Bob.

Note: the woman are probably the women that Hope/ Hughes used as spies. Hope himself has said that the national security banded one of the sensitive chapters.

Women and other women spies are trying to get top secrets from Hope. HRH and Hope our national security. It's themselves.

* * * *

#103 September 20, 1967,

This show is in color and the monologue is about current events, about LA politics and Hippies.

The film of the zig field follies of Vaudeville and its history is shown. Bob Hope's History. It starts with Bob Hope dressed as money as the high-hat high society swells of the 20s and 30s. A real old film of Hope is run about his start in show business and vaudeville's Broadway shows, radio and film.

Rowan and Martin are on the show with great statements and good jokes, super statements. Great show. Wow tricky, watch that show. Wow.

Skit # 1... another good skit with old pictures of Hope. A funny show with Katie Stevens and Jimmy Durante.

* * * *

#104 October 16, 1967

Host monologue right off the bat, says his first show was a hit. Hope says, "Howard Hughes is trying to buy me, but he would have to buy the peacock too". Howard is the peacock and Hope is the double. Hope goes on to say "Gen. Sarnoff of NBC wouldn't want to break up the set. There it Is again. Two in one. So here it is in this show, admitting that he is Howard Hughes, one person and Bob Hope is another person to them. One. Two of the most famous names In America, sleep together.

Skit # 1... Hope says, "he owes his entire career to make up". Howard Hughes is Bob Hope in makeup.

* * * *

#105 November 8, 1967

The opening monologue is about politics and Washington, DC. The show Is loaded with talent and stars of stage, screen and television.

Skit # 1... It's a dressing room scene and Hope is putting on makeup. He's in love with his new face. The title of the skit is that NBC is being taken over by a Texan. Hughes is a Texan. Hope says each were from Cleveland. Bob is dressed in a disguise as a Texan. Dialog says "a bunch of old comedians are coming this way, and he's disguised as one of them, and the actor points to Hope. Who's HE?

A comedian in disguise with Cowboys rolling in on horses.

Hughes in his character actor role plays comedian Hope.

There's a lot in that skit.

Howard Hughes or Hope, anyway you look at It is putting on his makeup and is in love with his new face. That's the same face that Bing Crosby met on the golf course many years prior. I just proved My Theory again.

* * * *

#106 November 29, 1967

This show is alive show from UCLA. Hope opens the show saying, "getting to see the Queen of England is as hard as getting an appointment with Howard Hughes". Hope knows you don't get an appointment with Howard Hughes". because he's presumed dead and is never seen.

* * * *

#107 December 14, 1967

Hope opens with his guest Martha Ray and he talks about of a Viet Cong attack against Martha in Vietnam for real and states that she is an American hero.

Skit # 1... In this skit it is said to Bob Hope Many times again and again, "who are you"?. Hope says he's Santa Claus and is throwing money all over the place. That's what Hughes did!

Skit # 2 ... Hope is in a prison psych's office as Santa with Paul Lynn as the doctor.

In this skit Hope is put out as a cold-blooded killer. Probably was. (HRH)

Skit # 3 ... Opens with Jerry Colona as a judge and it's about Bob Hope and the judge points at Hope and says, "this fraud masquerading as Santa". as part of the court seen, they discover Howard's false height and as to whether he is married or not. That's a real-life Howard Hughes situation. Hope's testimony is that he flies all around the world talking about the two Hopes.

So, there's My Theory again, recall Bob's Vaudeville days and the Marquis that stated that Bob Hope was that magnificent fraud. Hope Writes in his book that he changed his real name, which would be Howard Rupert Hughes to Bob Hope, because his real name was too long to fit on the Marquis. HRH name 18 letters, BH name 7 letters. His name Is fake, and his face is fake. Bob Hope is Howard Hughes with a fake new look by makeup, a character actor. Howard Hughes wears makeup all the time as Bob Hope. I have a quote from Bob Hope in a movie about sponge rubber where Hope states that "he's an actor, and he wears sponge rubber all the time. All the time. Hope or Hughes made 62 movies. Two of the most famous names In America sleep together.

* * * *

#108 January 18, 1968

This show is strictly entertainment it is a film of the USO shows overseas in Southeast Asia, and with Hope are many beautiful women stars of Hollywood entertainment for the US soldiers by Bob Hope show tours to American servicemen.

* * * *

#109 February 12, 1968

It's a live show strictly entertainment,

* * * *

110 March 20, 1968

The show opens with Bob Hope's monologue where Hope says that the show "brings you Bob Hope strong on makeup". He tells everyone that it's all makeup. He then talks about his makeup man several times. It's like I said it's all makeup. It's a fake made-up face, a Mask. Here's Howard Hughes in disguise right in front of everyone. Two of the most famous names In America are together. Recall a movie where Bob Hope displays a tray of noses and ask his fellow actress which one of these noses do you think would fool the public. He then picks one of the noses and goes out to do a show, and he tells the people right in front of him, that he disguise's himself right in front of them. Turns around puts the fake nose on and turns back to the audience. In another movie, he says he has seven faces, a different face for each woman that he's with. Many times, Hope in all his shows tells the people that he Is in makeup. The monologue continues where Hope says "Nixon said he has a way to win the war, and he Nixon is going to get Howard Hughes to buy Vietnam and move It to Las Vegas. There is Bob Hope talking about Howard Hughes again. How many times, time and time again is Hope talking about Howard Hughes.

Skit # 1 … In the skit, there is a dialog about a gun… It is said to Bob.. "Hold the gun to your head and try for two holes". another hint that Bob is two people in one. Two of the most famous people in America. Recall that Bob Hope has said that "he has a group of writers and that he is one of them, the one with two heads". The hits just keep on coming.

The joke Is on the people and My Theory has been proven repeatedly. It's Bob Hope's stucco face with Howard Hughes talking. The Masked man, the Lone Ranger. I say that every movie and TV show is all about Howard Hughes and his adventures.

* * * *

#111 ... September 25, 1968

Hopes monologue is that he's dropping out of sight and talks about what he Is.

Skit # 1 ... A Hope for President Skit.

Skit # 2 ... Hope is on the scene and there's an Arab in a High hat, rich tuxedo. The Arab represents oil. The top hat and tux represent the Billionaires of which Howard Hughes is one.

* * * *

#112 October 14, 1968

Bob opens the show talking about Bing Crosby's ears and says to him, "with looks like yours tell women to go to Vegas and your looks would give Howard Hughes a headache."

Talking about ears I noticed that in many movies that ears on the actors are fake and large. There is a video with Bing Crosby singing a song. Thanks for the memories, and thanks for our Ca EARS. Watch the movies look at the ears....

Skit # 1 ... The skit is about the 747 Airplane, and that it can carry 490 passengers. It's then said in dialog that "if you don't like America, you can go back to Texas and the jolly green giant and wear elevator shoes."

I think the Green Giant refers to all the money that Howard Hughes has and that he wears elevator shoes to appear tall, and Bob Hope is short. Stop being Bob Hope short, go back to Texas and be Howard Hughes tall.

That's My Theory, that Howard Hughes seen without his Bob Hope makeup on appeared tall because he was wearing elevated cowboy boots, high heels. There is a Lone Ranger episode about a short guy who deals in real estate wearing high heeled elevator cowboy boots because he was self-conscious of his short height.

* * * *

#113 November 6, 1968

Bob Hope, also known as Howard Hughes to me opens his show talking about space, about NASA and the space race and about his Astronauts. He says that in 11 days our spacecraft made 163 orbits of the Earth, and he talks about government budgets and says, "it's a good thing that NASA control is in Texas". Houston, Texas is NASA's Headquarters.. He then talks make up again, mentions Howard Hughes and Texas. Howard Hughes owns Texas.

Here's a quote from the monologue "what man would want to be seen in makeup, can't you see". Right him.

Hope then prides himself as all that. He says that he is the "art of makeup". How many times does Hope tell you who he is and that he Is wearing makeup? If he was seen before He put the makeup on in the makeup room you would see Howard Hughes. It's a historical fact that Howard Hughes is the Space Industry and that it is based in Houston Texas. Hughes has been involved with the Rockets since World War Two. He was also a Test Pilot for the United States Air Force.

* * * *

#114 November 27, 1968

Hope opens the show saying that Gen. de Gaulle of France tried to make a deal with Howard Hughes and Hope states "it sure would look silly with a picture of the Mona Lisa hanging over a slot machine in Vegas."

Skit # 1 ... In this skit It is said to Bob Hope that "you have gathered up more real estate than Howard Hughes". That's right, he Bob Hope as Howard Hughes transferred his wealth to himself as Bob Hope. Watch the first 10 min. of the Movie the Barefoot Contessa about a Producer of Movies who owns Texas and is buying up California real estate. Hope always talking about Howard Hughes. Coincidence……

* * * *

#115 December 19, 1968

The monologue of this show talks about women as spies with guns, of being a recluse and acting as Santa Claus. Being Santa Claus is representing the American way of capitalism. Giving gifts to everyone.

Skit # 1 … in this Skit Hope is on the plane seated next to Castro. Says he owes $10,000 to someone in Cuba, so Hope goes to Havana as Castro. Dialog states, that Hope is in a spot in the argument over Cuba. He will split the bride". The money is split in Cuba, and there's a spy court and Hope is on trial as a spy.

Skit # 2 … This skit is about a Washington a Go go in search of Secret Agents and talk of a laser gun. Hope states that the walls are closing in on him. Cuba was an international hub for spies.

* * * *

#116 January 16, 1969

Bob Hope is the MC, a lot of film about the USO shows from Asia, Thailand, Vietnam. There is a United States Air Force demo of a skydiver. Talk was also about the history of the USS New Jersey that could shoot a shell 26 miles. The ship is on display in Camden New Jersey. Strange as it is there is a sign in the audience That reads "welcome back Packy East". Bob Hope's history is that he was a boxer with the nickname Packy East. My off the wall remark would be that he's packing a gun on the East Coast.

Bob Hope goes on to say being from Cleveland Ohio that Ronald Reagan is the only person who could call him Bob Hope, "Sonny". A little History has it that Howard Hughes Jr. was living at the Biltmore Hotel in New York City and was raised by his Mother and his nickname was "Sonny" and in his youth at 12 years old he would go to the Theaters because he was enthralled with the beauty of the showgirls. Howard Rupert Hughes Junior, nick- named Sonny, goes off to live in Cleveland with his Uncle in a house filled with Theater Musicians. Ronald Reagan knew who he was… Richie Rich.

* * * *

#117 February 17, 1969

Hope the star of the show states that he's having eye trouble and he talks about being offered small parts in the hospital. Possibly not small parts as an actor but small parts of his body.

Skip # 1 … Bob Hope and Martha Ray and George Burns. George Burns mentions Howard Hughes he makes a joke to see Howard Hughes at the unemployment line. The show had a lot of good entertainment.

* * * *

#118 March 19, 1969

The show opens about California rain and floods and mudslides on Los Angeles. Hope's Quote "now we know what Howard Hughes is doing He wants a seaport". That crack could be about Howard Hughes testing of the atom bombs and controlling the weather for the military. Howard Hughes mentioned again and again by Hope. I lost count how many times.

Skit # 1 … Zero content.

Skit # 2 … Hope depicted as a Killer.

Who killed JR? Was Hughes the head of the Mob? was he the CIA? Who

Skit # 3 … Hope wearing fat clothes. Recall there was a sign that said, "investigate Hope."

* * * *

#119 April 17, 1969

Not many clues, but talk about living In Southern California, amongst the earthquakes.

* * * *

#120 September 22, 1969

20 comedians on the show and the monologue was a Lotta jokes about celebrities. Every star you can think of was on this show. Hope says, "Chrysler only renewed my parts for five years."

His parts are the parts on his face. The fake nose, the stucco cheeks, the phony ears the false chin, teeth etc. That's the parts he's talking about. The Mask. The show was also about anti-censorship.

* * * *

#121 October 13, 1969

The show opens with Hope with Jimmy Durante, mostly entertainment and they mention, Atlantic City. Hope sang some songs Durante did a solo song on stage.

* * * *

#122 November 6, 1969.

This television show is all about the stage show, Roberta. Bob Hope started his Broadway theater career in a show called Roberta on Broadway. Back then, Atlantic City was the place where Broadway shows opened on the road to make the show more perfect.

Bob Hope brought that show through Atlantic City, a movie was also made of Roberta. The show Is about a salon designer.

* * * *

#123 November 24, 1969

The monologue was all about politics and space. A good clue concerning the height of Howard Hughes is when Bob Hope mentions "elevator shoes."

* * * *

#124 December 18, 1969

Skit # 1 ... Hope is playing up his Texas English connection. I thought he was from Cleveland, Ohio. (or Texas) The England

Part is the cover story. The Texas connection is his Howard Hughes family connection. Right.. Texas oil. England connection is because Hughes, the Industrial billionaire saved England from defeat during World War II and Won WW2 for the United States. Hughes as Hope came out as a spy. The war was won by Hughes or Hope?

Bob Hope's own writings is where he wrote upon visiting England, Hope says he said to a Butler "I was born in England". And the Butler retorts "I'll keep your secret". How about that! I would say they got him covered right out of England's spy agency. Recall Bob Hope's first book was They got me covered. Covered by a fake story.

* * * *

#125 January 15, 1970

Another film of Bob Hope's USO tours starting out at the White House and going around the world through Thailand to Vietnam. Hope gives a great speech supporting our troops. Shows a travel film and entertainment from the shows.

* * * *

#126 February 16, 1970

The show comes to you from New York City's Waldorf Astoria. It's all about Eisenhower, Miami and the Rockefeller medical center fundraiser. Many stars on the show. Hope, Hughes, and Eisenhower were all into medical centers. Hope has said on film that he Is a Doctor and that he got his license from Atlantic City and Vietnam. Atlantic City was taken over by the Federal Government and all the Hotels were made Hospitals for those who were injured in the war. Also ironic was the fact that Bob Hope said he's an Inventor. History has it that Howard Hughes was an Inventor and Inventor of the modern hospital bed.

Hope says he was an inventor and Dr. And a Pilot and a Golfer. Isn't that everything Howard Hughes was and wanted to be? HRH was each one of those professions. Two persons in one, two of the most famous names in America sleep together. He's a writer with two heads. He'd have to shoot himself twice to be dead. If he died and came back and made it with her again She would've made it with the both of him". Admitting he's two people in one, Howard Hughes and Bob Hope.

* * * *

#127 March 18, 1970

Hope opens with a standard monologue of current events. Skit # 1 ... Hope in the skit is Vice President at NBC-TV in charge of programming NASA. In the skit Hope is tracing a space shot from mission control. Hope is in the role as an Astronaut. Howard Hughes was a Jet Pilot and trained all US jet test pilots and Astronauts.

Take notice that all Hopes skits and quotes have all the elements of exposing Howard Hughes secret and mysterious life right before your eyes. Just like he said.

* * * *

#128 April 13, 1970

Hope makes the statement that his sponsor Chrysler has fired his parts. His contract has expired. He talks about his tax forms with the IRS. He says" you would think I should deduct a lot of the money I spent for makeup, but I don't worry I am handsome Without it". Did he just admit that he's got two faces? one with makeup, and one with no makeup. Howard Hughes was handsome.

Skit # 1 ... Here we have Hope acting as a Commercial Pilot, kissing stewards all over the plane. His co-pilot is Phyllis Diller and Bob is called Harvey. First off Howard Hughes was called Harvey on his studio sets at Paramount and the other studios In Hollywood. That was a nickname because in the movie Harvey was invisible. Hughes was never personally seen on the lot. The second part about being a Commercial Airline Pilot is true, because Howard Hughes went missing for a year or so and was found to be a Pilot for a Commercial Airlines. Hughes not Hope. So, the skit has two themes both similar to Howard Hughes's biography. Howard Hughes was Bob Hope in makeup. That's My Theory and I am sticking to it.

So, this show is about Bob Hope canceled on TV as Bob Hope with his fake face, which is makeup and he is also a pilot.

* * * *

#129 October 5, 1970

Skit # 1 … Is a question of Bob Hope's identity with the quote from Bob Hope, saying "I am in charge. Really!. The skit starts out in a makeup room, and it's about his looks and his Identification as to who he is. It's about Hope getting a sandblast job to remove the stucco from his false face makeup. Hope states that Mike Costello for 25 years was Bob's personal makeup man. In dialog It is said "wait till they fly in parts from Houston". Do you think this is about Bob or about Howard? The actual makeup man talks about sand blasting the stucco face off Howard or Bob's stucco makeup. Sandblasting it off his face. The fake face. There exist three videos within the Golden Age of TV and Bob Hope's Time /Life commercial on television this present day about stucco being put onto Bob's face or should I say onto Howard Hughes face. There's more truth to the proof that Howard Hughes is or was Bob Hope in makeup.

* * * *

#130 November 16, 1970

Monolog is talking about a spy in the sky. Think he's talking about satellites. And who put the satellites in the sky? Howard Hughes through NASA built the satellites and put them in the sky. There were a few skits of no importance. The rest of the show was about variety and comics and Hollywood life.

* * * *

131 December 7, 1970

The show was a repeat skit and no quotes or code.

* * * *

132 January 14, 1971

Hope opens the show with a great film of the USO shows at many bases and on an aircraft carrier. Hope says "the aircraft carrier that he is on is Texas afloat. The Ship carries a crew of 5,200 personnel. Hope goes on to say that "maybe you read that Howard Hughes disappeared". he goes on to say from the stage that "we've been everywhere man and we are going to keep on going until we find Howard Hughes". He said that at a base in Asia. As a joke to Hope and actor says, "I know this, you never go anywhere without your nose". that's what I've been telling you, Howard Hughes goes nowhere without being in makeup as Bob Hope. He stays in character all the time. He's a very good actor.

Here's several quotes from Bob Hope in certain movies, in one movie Hope finds sponge rubber in a hallway of the building that catches a criminal. (Himself) He goes on to say that "he knows all about sponge rubber and that he is an actor and that he wears It all the time". That's what I've been saying. In another movie he and a woman are running from the law and Hope is pointing to a Mountain and says that "that would be a good place for Howard Hughes to hideout". Later in the career It went from sponge rubber, to putty and then stucco. Remember when Bob Hope was making his first screen test it was said that someone smelt rubber burning on the set. I also have Bob Hope saying that "people think that I got this nose by accident but that I received it from the Goodyear family". It's called makeup. It's a fake face. Howard Hughes was Bob Hope in makeup. I have other quotes by Hope in a photo stating that when "he gets off his plane he leaves himself behind". And another quote that "after every show he leaves by an assumed name.

* * * *

#133 February 15, 1971

Hope opens the show saying that the United States budget needs $200 billion and Hope says that "we really are going to have to find Howard Hughes". Hope mentioning Howard Hughes again and again. That's because it's a joke. It is Howard Hughes talking with a

Bob Hope face. Here's another quote from Bob Hope "The names of the innocent have been changed to protect the joke". Another "Abe Lincoln was wrong. "You can fool all the people all the time". Howard Hughes is Hope and Bob Hope is Howard Hughes. That's My Theory.

* * * *

#134 April 5, 1971

Good show but could find anything relevant to My Theory. An entertainment show.

* * * *

#135 Same thing. Nothing relevant.

* * * *

#136 November 7, 1971

This show has a bunch of skits with Jack Benny. One has Hope, as a Chinese spy. It is set up as though he was sent to China by the United States and President Nixon.

* * * *

#137 December 9, 1971

The monologue is all about National jokes and the Holidays, Many guest stars. Hope talks about Vietnam trip That's coming up. Hope talks about "three holes in a head and is also always talking about Cuba. Three holes in the head. Interesting.... Could that be John, Robert and Martin. They were shot in the head.

There is a television skit on one of Bob Hope's television show's where Bob Hope admits that he had a deal with Kennedy and that Kennedy broke the deal and that he Bob Hope or Howard Hughes, however you want to look at it says, "I really turned his head around didn't I". Did you get that? The Chicago Vote for hands off the Mob!

Skit # 1 ... This skit is in a Medical Center. Hope is the patient and Lee Marvin is the Doctor. Marvin says about Hope. "The patient is dead". at that Hope the patient yells "I am alive". Right there in the skit Hope tells you that he, Howard Hughes is alive.

In this skit Hope is in the Hospital. He's doing business concerning all the markets of the world. It is said to Bob Hope "I don't care how rich you are". The Rothchild's are mentioned. That's probably the real hook up with having all the money in the world.

Skit # 2 ... Hope sings a song titled Smile, about addiction. The song Tears of a Clown is played. Is Howard being Bob, addicted to drugs?

* * * *

#138 January 17, 1972

Entire show is from Pearl Harbor. It is a United States Air Force film of jet planes. It is also a USO show with Ms. World. The show is also from Gitmo Cuba.

* * * *

#139 February 27, 1972

Hope talks about Nixon in China along with Kissinger. He says that Howard Hughes is in Nicaraqua. Hope says goodbye to Howard Hughes and talks about a phantom jet and the press ask Bob Hope "who are you". There you go again. He is Howard Hughes. He then talks plastic surgery. Probably got tired putting make up on and off.

Skit # 1 ... Hope is in costume as a hobo, a bum. He's seen picking food out of a trashcan and he says, "do you know who I am". They didn't. But I do! History has it that Howard Hughes had disappeared years ago and was found to be a bum and was arrested in Houston and New Orleans as a vagrant. So, the skit is from his memory. Thanks for the Memory. Every skit works off the life of Howard Hughes.

* * * *

#140 March 13, 1972

The monologue was about current events, Nixon's election. That was followed by four skits that didn't say much. One was about the people on the beach 1972, the other the Polish connection with Hope as a cop. Two other skits that didn't say much.

* * * *

#141 April 10, 1972

Skit # 1 … This skit has Hope out to win an Oscar. Hope is pictured as a Genius. Howard Hughes was the Genius.

Skit # 2 … about a lost weekend on alcohol and that Hope is addicted to girls.

Skit # 3 … in the skit there is a Statue of the Head of Hope made out of a Stucco Ceramic, just like his real face made out of stucco, very revealing. A movie Also had a statue of Hope With two heads. Hope says, "it is good to have a makeup man". And it is said, "I am to win an Oscar for the Godfather". The man behind the scenes.

* * * *

#142 April 27, 1972

Here we are again talking about Mob Hit's in New York City. Talking about the Godfather. Who was behind all the Mob Killings?

Skit # 1 … has the LA police of Beverly Hills finding a dead body on the floor and it is said to be the dead body of Howard Hughes. Right. The fake death again.

Skit # 2 … Titled grand pa pa. There is a statement as a qualifier that the skit is of no relation to anyone living or dead or fictional character. The scene is in a restaurant and there is a crack about Hope being the boss. It is also about big business, money, bookie money, protection money, numbers money and bribes.

Skit # 3 … here we have Bob Hope as a Golfer and landing a Helicopter in his yard. Isn't that something. In the History of Howard Hughes, he lands a helicopter on a golf course to meet Katherine Hepburn. One of Howard Hughes Life ambitions was to be a very good Golfer. Maybe that's why Bob Hope always carries that Golf club?.

* * * *

#143 October 5, 1972

Monologue is about current events about Johnny Carson, Nixon and San Clemente.

Skit # 1 … Hope is pictured as the Governor of California. Hope was behind Raegan

Skit # 2 … About a chess game.. And the dialog says, "the King is dead". Recall there was a 007 movie stating that "the Man who would be King". There's the so-called Howard Hughes dead story to perpetuate the falsehood. It's all in the skits, nothing but the truth.

* * * *

#144 December 10, 1972

Bob Hope does His monologue and he makes one statement, "been using plastic as makeup". Hope goes on to talk current events about Nixon, the Vietnam War and the Apollo 17 moon shot. Plastic Surgery!

* * * *

#145 January 17, 1973

The show opens with great films of the USO Christmas tour of 1972. Great film of jet planes taking off. It's about Hope visiting all South East Asian bases and ships such as Diego Garcia, Subic Bay and Guam.

Skit # 1 … opens with Bob Hope, sweeping a floor, and he then says, "this is fine work for an Aerospace Engineer". I think he's admitting that he's an Aerospace Engineer. I think he's admitting that he Is Howard Hughes, a genius inventor and Aerospace Engineer. Indicating that he is two people in one. Hope goes on to mention Symington, Abrams and McCain and his trips around the world. the

Aviator, Rocket Man, the Genius, and the Billionaire Industrialists, Inventor, Spy, Actor, Killer, on an on.

* * * *

146 February 8, 1973

Show opens with Bob Hope in his monologue claiming to be a mad egotistical scientist. I guess that's supposed to be a joke. There he admits he's Howard Hughes, who was also considered crazy.

Skit # 1 ... Opens with the seven o'clock news Merv Griffin as the anchor, and he says, "who is responsible for the energy crisis". Hope shows up with a laser gun. The skit continues with terms that have been said about Howard Hughes. They talk about spies, the CIA, the FBI and the police connections. It is stated that he is a "genius", "Mad", and Macob". All said about Hope.

Skit # 2 ... Hope is considered the President of the United States. Behind the Presidential Seal in the Oval Office talks about international agencies and TV detectives. The dialog puts the finger on Hope. "Madman has us over a barrel". and "he has taken over the world's energy."

Skit # 3 ... there's a picture of Bob Hope and statements are made of him that he Is "the master of the disguise"

"a mad scientist" and "paranoid". Talk is about Rocket Fuel. It's in a barbershop.

Skit # 4 ... A bar scene.. Hope says, "I control all nuclear power and the bomb". Now, is that Bob Hope, saying that or is that Howard Hughes saying that with his Bob Hope face on. Howard Hughes controlled all the oil, all nuclear power and the bomb. It is then said in dialog right to Hope that" you're the one who smuggled all the uranium out of this country". It is said that "he owns all the gas". And that whoever Hope is, he is "the most dangerous man in the world."

* * * *

#147 March 27, 1973

This entire show is dedicated to sports awards and the movie Industry.

* * * *

#148 April 19, 1973

Skit # 1 … Hope opens the show saying that "I am Leslie Townes Hope". The show Is mostly entertainment. A lot of gags. Hope is called a "Doctor."

* * * *

#149 September 26, 1973

The show opens with Bob Hope making a crack "thanking the Watergate hearings for making room for Me". The Watergate hearings didn't make any room for Bob Hope, but they did put Howard Hughes in the middle of the Investigation. It was said that the break-in was seeking proof that Howard Hughes was giving money to the Democrats. then there is talk of Texas, Oil and of Airports.

* * * *

#150 November 13, 1973

All the talk on this show is about Astronauts and UFOs.

Hope says he saw a UFO. Both skits about sightings of UFOs.

Hope had said he did a Spacewalk.

* * * *

#151 December 9, 1973

The show starts with a skit and the dialog has Lucille Ball-saying "I am alive". And Bob Hope retorts "I am dead". That's right as Howard Hughes he is dead. Just like I said it's a Bob Hope makeup face and Howard Hughes doing all the talking. Howard Hughes was considered dead right. As far as Lucille ball is concerned I saw her singing a song at the Kennedy Center many years ago where a part of the song was "you all think, where comedians, but we are spies". There you go..

Skit # 2 ... This skit is about oil and it's affect on the United States and about Saudi Arabia boycotting the United States creating shortages. That's right. United States had a deal with Saudi Arabia in the oil business called Aramco. Saudi Arabia boycotted the United States and Hope makes the comment "call the Lone Ranger and Tonto in to raid Saudi Arabia, we will need long straws". I think that indicates slant drilling and that we are going to steal the oil with long pipelines. Slant drilling has been going on since 1910 at Spindle Top Texas. The Teapot Dome. In this skit Hope wears a King's Hat. Looks like Bob Hope knows a lot about oil. There's a Bob Hope Movie where he is considered the CEO of an International Oil Company and its Business is in Saudi Arabia and is based in England. There is more proof that Bob Hope is Howard Hughes and is in the oil business called Texaco. In this skit number one Hope with the King Hat on is talking about the shortages of oil in the United States. He says the White House is concerned, mentioning Saudi Arabia's boycott of oil to the United States. Hope talks about oil and plastics. Hope owned a great deal of Texaco stock.

* * * *

#152 January 24, 1974

Show opens with the monologue and out of the whole show I pulled out only one quote. Since Howard and Bobby were both Pilots with many hours in the sky, Bob Hope, says "I am Bobby born to fly". two of the most famous names in America sleep together......

* * * *

153 March 1, 1974

The entire show was just entertainment

* * * *

154 April 2, 1974

Hope talks, current events, no clues. No quotes.

* * * *

#155 April 19, 1974

This DVD could not play the first time the disc did not work.

* * * *

#156 September 25, 1974

Bob Hope is on NBC for his 25th year. This is the second disc in a row that did not work, could not play the disc.

* * * *

#157 November 20, 1974

This show is mostly entertainment. It's from Caesar's Palace, Las Vegas. He plays a James Bond song. The show of stars and entertainment awards. This CD stopped working halfway through.

* * * *

#158 December 15, 1974

The show opens right up with Bob Hope, saying "the Shah of Iran Just bought Howard Hughes as a lawn ornament, a post to tie his Camel too."

You must recall that it's a fact that the Shah of Iran was an Air Force jet pilot working out of Texas. The Shahs thrown is titled the Peacock Throne. That's Howard Hughes. He's NBC. The Peacock. Think there's any connection.

Skit # 1 ... The skit opens at Honeymoon towers. In this skit Hope is quoted as saying "I have but one of me to give to my country". Right, one of two. He's two and he has one of two to give to his country. He then talks about makeup. so, the one is given to the country is the made-up face.

Skit # 2 ... here we have Hope as a Pilot of the Peacock Airlines, just like NBC is the Peacock Network and is the Peacock Throne. You think there's any connections there?. Hope mentions Howard Hughes again.

* * * *

159 April 8, 1975

The whole show is a rerun of sports awards.

* * * *

#160 April 17, 1975

The show Is general entertainment on campuses of America's colleges across America.

* * * *

#161 October 24, 1975 The disc CD did not work.

* * * *

#162 December 14, 1975

The shows about Texaco oil and gas. Hope mentions the Arabs again talks about California weather.

* * * *

#163 March 5, 1976

Show opens with the skit about crime and Bob Hope's house, then the disk did work.

* * * *

#164 April 21, 1976

The show comes from Montréal. Many Hollywood stars on the show. Songs were sung.. And Bob Hope says, "I will always have Texaco because Texaco has everything and does everything". Hope says, "you can trust your car to the man who wears the star". Who's the star? Bob Hopes star has been on the dressing room door since the 20s and Bob Hope says again "Texaco is his."

Is Texaco Hughes, or is it Hope?

* * * *

#165 July 4, 1976

Texaco is the sponsor and that "Texaco is his". It's an All-Star Fourth of July a 200 years USA Bicentennial Celebration.

Skit # 1... Debbie Reynolds gets a big laugh at Bob Hope's expense, and Hope says back to her "one more line like that and in the next will I write for Howard Hughes I won't include you in that next will that I will write". I think right there that he's admitting that he Is Howard Hughes, and he writes his own will. Recall.. Two of the most famous names In America sleep together and he is one of the screenwriters with two heads.

Skit # 2 ... Is all about July 4, a lot of History. A lot of jokes. A lot of songs. The skit Is all about Howard Hughes and Bob Hope. The proof is in the reading.

* * * *

#166 October 29, 1976

This show is sponsored by Texaco, and it's a rerun of former skits and stars mostly entertainment. Hope praises his writers, especially Neil Simon. Recall Bob Hope stating that the screenwriters in Hollywood are on strike that 3,000 of them"don't know that they all work for me." Previously Hope has said he has a small group of writers and he's one of them. But as Howard Hughes owning all the studios and paying all the bills he knows they all work for him. He is Bob Hope.(HRH)

In the dialog of the skit, there is this quote by Bob Hope "would you like to see my rock collection". Recall drilling for oil is all about rocks. Howard Hughes owned most of the oil produced in the United States. Howard Hughes and his family own the copyright to the drill bit that is only leased. (Texaco)...Why were rocks taken back from the Moon?.

* * * *

#167 December 13, 1976

The show opens with Hope acting as Santa Claus. Focus on the movie the Lemon Drop Kid. There is a situation in the movie where Bob Hope as Santa Claus says to his team of Santa Claus's "yo St. Nick". One of the Santa Claus is saying "whose St. Nick". Hope says back to him "don't you know that Santa Claus has many names". The other Santa says back to Hope "I know another guy who never gives his real name". There you go, Howard Hughes never tells anybody his real name, as he goes by the name of Bob Hope. There it's said again. Hope goes on to say that he's an old man and that he is 73 years old and he talks about facelifts and transplants. He says he's the $7 million man". Did Howard Hughes as Bob Hope get a facelift to put the mask, the fake face on through Plastic Surgery. We know that Howard Hughes had a lot to do with Medical Centers and in fact Bob Hope said he was a Doctor and that he got his Doctors license in Atlantic City. Bob Hope started out in Atlantic City.

* * * *

#168 January 21, 1977

This show opens and it's all about Tahoe. A place where there are casinos.

Skit # 1 … Hope enters as a Chief of the Indians. Then Hope appears as Robin Hood. That could be because Howard Hughes was linked up with the Indians. Like the Lone Ranger was hooked up with Tonto. It's my view that Hope hooked up with all the Indians out West to secure all the raw materials that were under the reservations. Howard Hughes has actually said that he was on the side of the Indians. He made the deal for the raw materials with the Indians.. Hope also appeared as a Golfer, and as an Earl and a Duke in England. Was Hughes also running England?

Hope in his dialog speaks of mountain air, talks about pot, talks about Washington DC and Jimmy Carter's Inaugural on 20 January 1977. Hope makes a Howard Hughes crack that "Bob Hope did receive an invite to Carter's Inaugural by mail and the envelope had Melvin Dumars fingerprints on it."

Skit # 2 … all about entertainment, the skit Is about Rocky the movie and Adrian shows up with a big false Nose on. Hope takes off the phony nose of the girl and she says "now, can I take yours off". That indicates it's a phony nose right!

Skit # 3 … Charro, an actress pinches Bob's nose.

* * * *

#169 March 25, 1977

This shows is about Bob Hope's roots in Vaudeville and his early career with stars. Hope runs photos of his Mother, his Father and his Sister, also a photo of Ziegfeld.

Skit # 1 … In this skit the dialog says of Hope "he has a weird nose". "He's the Iceman". "For a while he could be someone else". and at the end of this skit, Bob Hope says, "off comes the makeup and the clown disguise". Concerning the photos of his family. I believe those pictures are his cover story. They got them covered.

* * * *

170 October 28, 1977

Shows a rerun. Bing Crosby has just died.

* * * *

171 December 19, 1977

Show starts out as a Christmas show featuring all the college football stars than the disc did not work.

* * * *

#172 January 28, 1978 The CD disc did not work

* * * *

#173 February 13, 1978

This show is from Palm Springs. It's a show of Hollywood stars, mostly entertainment.

* * * *

#174 April 15, 1978 This CD did not work

* * * *

#175 October 15, 1978

Hope states that It is his 29th year on NBC. Hope would be 75 years old. Entire show is about Maj. League Baseball, many Baseball Stars and Baseball talk.

* * * *

#176 December 3, 1978

This show is now sponsored by General Electric and comes to you from a theater in Ohio. The audience is the very rich. Bob Hope talks about facelifts.. The question is did Howard Hughes as Bob Hope go from make up to an actual facelift????

* * * *

#177 December 22, 1978 The CD did not work

* * * *

#178 January 28, 1979

Bob Hope makes the statement that "the Shah of Iran is looking to be my neighbor". I imagine he's talking about the Shah being overthrown before he is overthrown. Check the dates.

* * * *

#179 May 30, 1979

The show opens with the United States Marine Corps Band in New York City aboard the Aircraft Carrier Iewo Jemma. A lot of Navy jokes. Hope talks make up again and talks Texaco and about certain blends of oil and rocket fuel. The rest of the show is mostly entertainment by the Village people with the song you're in the Navy.

* * * *

#180 September 16, 1979 cd did not work

* * * *

#181 November 19, 1979 the show of college sites.

* * * *

#182 December 13, 1979 Cd did not work

* * * *

#183 10 CD's of the 70s did not work.

* * * *

#184 January 21, 1980

This show comes to you from Pasadena California. The monologue is about football and politics and features women of Song. There is a song by Bob Hope from the 1933 movie Roberta, Thanks for the Memory. Bob Hope's first movie was 1932. Howard Hughes made four movies before 1928. No one can find them. In this show Hope is wearing a big white cowboy Texan Hat.

The white hat symbolizes the guy who's the good guy. The innocent names were changed

* * * *

#185 February 3, 1980

This show is a three-hour television show featuring the servicemen of the United States. It features a big ship named after Carole Lombard, Clark Gable's wife. The show features old black-and-white film from 1941 through 1961from all over the world.

* * * *

#186 February 10, 1980

Entire show is filmed of the USO shows from England.

* * * *

#187 March 17, 1980

Skit # 1 ... Hope shows up in the skit as a Duke from England talking into a mirror talking to himself. The mirror has two Hopes in the mirror. Bob Hope sings a song titled Put on a Happy Face. That admission that he puts on a fake face since his years in Vaudeville he talks about makeup, says "stick out a noble chin". I guess the chin is fake. Just like the Nose Is fake, like the ears are fake, like the cheeks are fake. An entirely fake face.

* * * *

#188 May 28, 1980

This show is coming to you from Texaco and from 8,000 feet high from Colorado featuring the United States Air Force and we have Hope in a flight suit. Recall that Howard Hughes is the aviator, is the rocket man. Hope is featured as a special agent of Air Force intelligence. Hope mentions Atlantic City and is asked "how do you know so much about the United States Air Force"? The answer is that Hope as Hughes is the United States Air Force. Rocket Man. Bob Hope is Howard Hughes.

* * * *

#189 September 6, 1980

It's a TV comedy show with many stars, including Miss America.

Skit # 1 ... It's about Harvey at Tahoe.

Harvey was the Invisible nick-name for Howard Hughes because he was never seen around the studios. Hope talks about Shell oil and Texaco makes a statement about 4 miles down, and 1 mile over. That's talking about slant drilling for oil. Remember during the oil crisis Hope said "we must call in the Lone Ranger and Tonto. We will need long straws". That's called slant drilling. In the movie some like it hot, (about sex) Tony Curtis plays the role of the Billionaire and he is quoted in that movie saying that he was "sonny" and that he had inherited Shell oil. Sounds like Howard Hughes history to me. Review the movies Paleface, and Son of Paleface and you will see the history of Howard Hughes portrayed by Bob Hope.

Skit # 2 ... About cattle, about Texas, shows oil rigs. It's about Hope, and it's about Howard Hughes. If they're one and the same, both are from Texas. Bob is Howard and Howard is Bob. Hope is quoted as saying he "cornered the market's". Hope is acting out that he is mean and cruel, and has a lot of girlfriends, and the dialog says to him "you're supposed to be dead". Bob Hope retorts that "that is a bunch of "BULL SHIT". The story that Howard Hughes is dead is not true.

* * * *

190 Unknown date

The title of this show is Hope for President.

My view, Hope already Is President. Because Howard Hughes is President. Hope and Hughes have been President since winning World War II, and possibly even before that. Why was Bob Hope playing golf with every President of the United States for 60 years or more? In the opening Hope goes on to say that he's speaking from the United States of Texas. He mentions the White House like JFK, LBJ, Nixon, Ford, Carter and Reagan..... The golf club tells you it is Howard Hughes. Since the 30s Howard Hughes wanted to be a great golfer, so when he put on his Bob Hope face in public He would always have the golf club with him throughout his shows all over the world as he stood before his troops.

The show also opens with a pep rally of the show and Hope is putting on makeup, puts in false teeth, big fake eyes, eyebrows, mascara, a false face on the show. He showed you right there that his whole face is fake, and it Is a total disguise. In one of Bob Hope movies he asked an actress to pick a nose that he's going to ware from a tray of noses and Hope has also talked about many masks for many different occasions. He's quoted in the movie as saying, as he puts a fake nose on his face in front of an audience that he does his best impressions right in front of the people, and they don't see it. He mentions Atlantic City and the Lincoln Quote that ...you can fool all the people all the time.!

* * * *

#191 December 16, 1980

Bob Hope's Texaco Christmas show.. about politics, Dallas, and current events. Reagan was elected.

Skit # 1 ... The skit Is about a homeless Hope stealing from the Christmas buckets of the Salvation Army and taken the money. This is a spin off one of Hopes movies titled The Lemon Drop Kid. The rest of the show is entertainment by singers and a sports awards show and a few vague skits, and that's the end of 1980

* * * *

#192 January 18, 1981

This show is Bob Hope's 30th year Anniversary at NBC, says "he's paid nothing but cash and never a contract". That's right, Howard Hughes, who owns NBC, the Peacock Network with the beak, the nose.. Pays himself as Bob Hope and he did not need a contract.. Rest of this show is entertainment. With many Hollywood stars.

* * * *

#193 February 10, 1981

Show opens and Hope the MC is talking politics and Reagan.

Check these quotes that came out of Bob Hope's mouth "I was a boy in the 20s and a man in the 30". A statement by Howard Hughes. Later he says, "I am a plumber". The word plumber is a code word for burglars. Like the burglars that burglarize Daniel Ellsberg's psychiatrist's office for Howard Hughes concerning the Pentagon papers. Then Hope says "who am I"? He starts talking about royalty and talks of vanity. The Billionaire Industrialist was of High Society. The swells as they called them, the Top Hat society and the Tux crowd.

* * * *

#194 April 13, 1981

The opening of the show is about President Reagan being shot.

On the show Bob Hope is given a female blown up rubber doll. There's a story in the book about Howard Hughes having sex with the blown-up doll. He was trying to make it with a starlet, when she rebuffed him, he jumped on the female rubber doll, and had sex with It.

Then there's another story about a blown-up female doll. It was told by Bob Hope from one of his shows that a soldier received a balloon type blown up female rubber doll in the mail. There you have both Bob Hope and Howard Hughes talking about female rubber life-size rubber dolls. It sounds like the same thing about the Alligator love call, if you read the front of this book.

* * * *

#195 May 25, 1981

This show comes to you from West Point, Bob Hope comes in by Helicopter as a man with the theme song of the Lone Ranger. (The TV show about the masked man). Also playing was the theme from Superman and we all know the words.

Howard Hughes is Bob Hope in makeup, in a disguise and covered up by the Government. He was the government and they got him covered and here Hope is quoted as saying that "no one has been able to break through the shred of mystery that surrounds a man ". (I DID). Remember, Hope said he became a man in the 30s. So, from the 30s right on up to the present there was a mystery surrounding Hope and Hughes.

I Joseph Polillo broke that mystery and this book breaks the biggest story in the history of the world that Howard Hughes, movie maker as a character actor with the stage name Bob Hope, is right in front of your eyes. And nobody got it. The greatest show on earth. Two of the most famous names In America sleep together. HELLO.....

On this show, Mickey Rooney talks about his elevator shoes.

* * * *

#196 September 27, 1981.

The show opens and it's about the Lone Ranger and Tonto. The Lone Ranger was hooked up with the Indians out West. Here's a quote from Bob Hope "I was on the side of the Indians". You mean the Lone Ranger, Howard Hughes was in with the Indians. Hope is also quoted here as, saying "I love those circus weirdos."

Skit # 2 ... Bob comes in dressed as a Mobster, is called a sneak thief and a hoodlum. That matches up with My Theory that he was behind the Mob and that he was the Mob.

Skit # 3 ... Titled the Son of Show Gun. He makes a crack about Howard Hughes personality.

* * * *

#197 October 22, 1981

Show comes to you from the Gerald Ford Museum and there is a very rich audience and all the talk is about golf and current events, Foster Brooks was the star of the show. It was great. The museum staff was awarded awards.

* * * *

#198 November 22, 1981

The show is a celebration of the It's a Thanksgiving Day show with presented.

60th year of the NFL. football awards being

* * * *

#199 December 20, 1981

A Texaco commercial opens the show about jet planes and rocket fuel. There it Is, rocket fuel for Jets and to assist thrust for liftoff of rockets. Their ad jingle says you can trust your car to the man who is the star. Recall it is Howard Hughes aka Bob Hope, who is the star.

Watch Bob and Bings Road to Singapore. The movie where the Russians are spying on Bob Hope, trying to get the formula for the high-test rocket fuel. Russians do not get it. It's all about rocket fuel. The aviator, rocket man, all about space. Check American History. The formula was for very high-test rocket fuel.

End of 1981

* * * *

#200 February 28, 1982

This was a quick show called ladies night consisted of reruns of many past skits with all the beautiful women out of Hollywood. Including Milton Berle.... He was a girl. Also.

* * * *

#201 March 28, 1982

This show opens with a short monologue goes right into skit number one.

Skit # 1 ... Bob Hope plays the role of a Pilot and crashes. Hope has said that he was a Pilot with thousands of hours in the sky. And if you know Howard's History he was a jet pilot and crashed a jet into a Beverly Hills neighborhood. Howard Hughes was a jet test pilot. Concerning the crash, the dialog of the skit is that it is said to Hope "you're alive, you're alive". Hughes had many crashes.

You can say that again. Howard Hughes is not dead, he is alive and that's was said to Bob Hope. Recall that two of the most famous names in America sleep together. Hope has mentioned his injuries, his leg, his right arm, his back in a few shows and Movies.

Skit # 2 ... This whole scene takes place in Atlantic City and it's titled a Frantic City. Hope is in Atlantic City. He says, "with connections" and says, "being there was with the wrong people and the right man in the right place at the same time."

Recall.. Atlantic City was hands-off territory by Mob rules. There was to be no killings in Atlantic City. Atlantic City was the hideout for the Mafia. So here we have Howard Hughes and/or Bob Hope hooking up with the Mob in Atlantic City. The 5, The Mob vacationed in Atlantic City. Al Capone vacationed in Atlantic City. Big Al owned the Jefferson and Monticello Hotels. At the Mob conference in Atlantic City (watch the FBI Story movie) Al Capone was sent to jail.

It was in Atlantic City where there was a Nightclub called the five. Strange, the Mafia is called the five. The five-night club in Atlantic City was run by Skinny D'Amato. Skinny was a great friend of Frank's Sinatra, Jerry Lewis and Dean Martin. Skinny was tapped by Sinatra to run the Cal Nev Casino in Nevada.

Bob Hope, the star played Atlantic City throughout the 30s. He brought Broadway Theater and Burlesque shows to Atlantic City. He starred at the Steel Pier and Bob Hope and Jerry Colonna Stared at the Warner Theater. It was in Atlantic City in 1932 that Bob Hope offered Jack Benny a radio show at $6,500 a week. They met in the Shelbourne Hotel. Further, during World War II, Atlantic City was commandeered by the United States Government, and most of the Hotels were made into Hospitals for our Servicemen.. Hope says he is a "doctor" and that he received his Dr.'s license in Atlantic City. The skit continues about Atlantic city where they mimic the Movie Atlantic City, and Hope is dressed as Burt Lancaster. The movie was about running dope in Atlantic City, and in the movie Frank Sinatra dedicates a Hospital wing. There's a lot of connections. Frank Dean Jerry all stayed at Skinny's house Ventnor New Jersey.

As a footnote My Twin Brother John Polillo and I Joseph Polillo where extras in the Movie. We are viewed in the film at 1 hour and 18 min. Look for Twins when the fight breaks out.

Hope goes on to take a crack joke on George Burns about Burns receiving an Oscar. He then talks about being "under heavy makeup."

Skit # 3 ... Just like skit number one Hope is featured as a pilot in the hospital following his crash and he says to Lee Marvin "I died a lot and all my sins flashed before me". he goes on to say that "the Government tricked me into service". Read Bob Hope's book, Have Tux will Travel. Howard Hughes aka Bob Hope works for the Government. He was the Government. Howard Hughes was near death many times following his many crashes.

Hope talks about many women that want to marry him for his money. and to be in his will. Hope is talking out of the Howard Hughes side of his mouth. Recall what Hope said to Debbie Reynolds that "another crack like that and the next will I write for Howard Hughes it won't include you."

Remember the skit where makeup is being applied to Bob Hope's face or should I say to Howard Hughes Face and Hope tells the makeup man to "hurry up" and the makeup man says, "it's the first time I worked with Stucco". there are two other clips, one with Jack Benny, and one with Bing Crosby doing the same skit. Check out Times/Life TV ad for the Golden age of Television. Under all the very heavy stucco sponge rubber fake face is Howard Hughes. All these Skits are about Howard Hughes Life. In these skits Hope definitely showed all the happenings in Howard Hughes Life.

* * * *

#202 May 3, 1982

Show titled Stars over Texas. Austin Texas. all about Texas, all about oil, cattle and feature entertainment.

* * * *

#203 May 25, 1982

This show is from Annapolis. It's the USO birthday for Bob Hope. In this show Hope tells his real ranks in the services of the United States. Bob Hope says, "I am the highest-ranking officer in the Navy". did you get that? Who? Bob Hope is the highest-ranking officer in the Navy, or is it Howard Hughes is the highest-ranking. Bob Hope boasting of his individual power. So, who is he? he's the Industrious Billionaire who built the ships. The Navy.

As the show continues in order of succession, Hope introduces Gen. Wheeler and Gen. Haig. It is said that Hope is working the foreign policy of the United States that he Is running the show and the USO. He says he has offered up 41 years of his life with all the beautiful women of the Miss America pageant coming out of Atlantic City for the USO shows. Haig tells the truth that Hope, and Hughes are doing it all. Hope is also quoted in this show saying, "I lied about my age". Howard Hughes birth date is 1905, Hopes birth date 1903. If Hope lied about his age being 03. Then it must be 05.

Hope also lies about his real name. The name was too long for the theater marquee. His real name Howard Rupert Hughes too long, made short to Bob Hope, the magnificent fraud. so, he lied about his age and he change his name as he became a character actor in vaudeville, movies and television.

* * * *

#204 October 3, 1982

This show was good at a lot of gags and skits. At the end of the show, Bob Hope spoke gave a very heavy philosophical speech.

* * * *

#205 November 21, 1982

This entire show has a spy theme with The Pink Panthers music. Here we have Hope acting as President of the United States as Ronald Reagan in the Oval Office at the White House. Dean Martin is acting as the Vice- President. Dean Martin walks up to Bob Hope and says, "who are you". Great question, right? we know who is!. It's Howard Hughes in his Bob Hope face and he is right behind Reagan. Howard Hughes was the real President of the United States. That's why Bob always played Golf with every president of the United States since the Roosevelt Presidency. The skit closes with thanks for the memory. Hope is Hughes. Analyze it. Look into it as parallel to the History of the United States and what Howard Hughes and Bob Hope did. All the time and all the real History played out before your eyes in TV skits and Movies. 262 tv shows and 62 Movies and in approximately 13 books. Read and watch.

* * * *

#206 December 20, 1982

This show consists of films of the Christmas show. Hope makes a crack about Kennedy puts him down and talks, current events and politics.

* * * *

#207 January 29, 1983

The show is coming to you from Pasadena, California, all, about the Super Bowl, about pro cheerleaders and football players all on the show.

Skit # 1... Bob and Don Rickles are dressed in drag as cheerleaders. Don Rickles calls Bob Hope a "imposter". That's what I've been saying they actually told it right out to the public. you know, Bob Hope, the guy who changed his name a number of times who lied about his age. The magnificent fraud.

* * * *

#208 March 2, 1983

This is Bob Hope show Road to Hollywood. As soon as Bob comes on stage he states that "it took hours to put on my makeup. recall his makeup is Stucco, sponge rubber, putty, total fake face. "Is on to say that he met the Queen in California and the Queen visited Reagan's ranch and the Queen traveled the West Coast by boat. Years ago there was a magazine story written about the Prince and Pauper. Research that.

Hope shows movie clips with stars, mostly beautiful females. Reagan comes on to say to Bob "you look good". Talking about his figure. Bob says, "yes my figure is in here somewhere covered by the one I have on now". Did you read that? We are talking about Fat clothes, and fake everything. He has fake bodysuit on over his real frame body. Howard Hughes is Bob Hope in disguise. Bob Hope is in disguise as Howard Hughes's, character actor, movie-maker, billionaire, everything. He's the writer with two heads. Two of the most famous names in America sleep together. Two people in one.

* * * *

#209 April 20, 1983 Nothing in this show at all.

* * * *

#210 May 23, 1983

This show starts out with Bob Hope in the White House Lincoln bedroom with Reagan. And Reagan says to Bob "you look good". Bob says back to Reagan "I've been in makeup for three days". The talk Is about Bob's 80th birthday. ....

This show shows photos of Bob in 1913, a Photo at 10 years old and some photos 1928-1935. Then Lucille Ball has a newsflash and that is that "Bob Hope is a fraud" "Bob Hope is a phony". How many times does it have to be said? Hope is Howard Hughes's stage name. Bob Hope was a fraud because he is Howard Hughes in makeup and Bob Hope is Howard Hughes stage name since the 20's. If you read through this book this deep my statement would be that "Sonny" Howard Rupert Hughes jr goes into the theater business through Vaudeville and Broadway as Bob Hope. Hope says, "he's just a happy face."

* * * *

#211 September 19, 1983

Hope comes on and says that it's his 25th Anniversary of NASA, and that he's been on NBC for 34 years. The show is about the History of the Airplane. Right and the History of the Airplanes coming from Bob Hope or from somebody who knew all about airplanes and rockets and space ships who continues to talk about the original seven astronauts and about Howard Hughes. Hope says he did a spacewalk "I did" says Bob Hope. He then shows a film of the first landing on the moon. The moon having a fine-grained surface as they plant the American flag on the moon, then he shows another film from Andrews Air Force Base and Vandenberg Air Force Base, a film of the Universe about rockets and technology. So, it's Bob Hope showing films of NASA. At the end of this show Hope makes a very strong speech. The History of space from 68, 69 and 70. All about the United States Air Force. There is a much-watched movie that the people should watch titled Dive Bomber. It's about a person who makes all the planes, the jet planes and teaches servicemen how to be dive bomber jet pilots. The interesting thing in the movie is that it is about a man from Cleveland. Bob Hope says he is from Cleveland, little Howard Hughes Junior Sonny was from Cleveland. Howard Hughes inherited billions and was a manufacturer of the airplane. Take note that on the side of the plane where they used to put the pictures of the Hollywood pinup girls there is a picture of a man in a Top Hat, meaning that the man who made the planes was from Cleveland and that he was a High Hat Swell very Rich from Cleveland. Must watch the movie the Kid from Cleveland.

Just as a footnote, remember the golf club, the golf ball and a putt were made on the moon. The first eight Astronauts played Golf on the Moon.

The history of Howard Hughes is in every movie. remember, he's one of the writers. The screenwriter. The one with two heads.

* * * *

#212 November 23, 1983

This show comes to you from Dallas Texas from southern Methodist University celebrating the Mustangs home coming. Hope talks about Texas being an oil rich Texas. Hope says, "I love Texas, there's a lot of money down here". He also says, "he's the guy who runs the country that Texas owns", in a joke.

It's a great show, great singers singing songs and putting on the Ritz. Vanessa Williams Miss America is on the show and Hope states that he was "the first judge of the first Miss America". (Atlantic City).

Note: the first 10 runners-up to Miss America always became part of Bob Hopes USO shows around the world.

* * * *

213 December 19, 1983

This TV show is another show all about Christmas.

In this show Bob Hope says", he has a second body on him over his other body" as he slapping his tux. He's talking to John Forsite about appearances and looks, talking about costumes and fat clothes. Don't forget the putty and stucco face, makeup, mascara, fake ears nose an chin, sponge rubber, plastic and fat clothes.

Remember nothing but the truth. it's in the dialog of the skits. It's in every piece of work of Bob Hopes movies and television shows with gags, jokes, and monologues. The studios write all about Howard Hughes.

* * * *

#214 January 15, 1984

It's the start of 1984 and it's a Christmas show aboard an Aircraft Carrier and then from the Battleship New Jersey. A great film of all the USO Bob Hope world tours shows.

* * * *

#215 February 27, 1984

This show comes to you from Hawaii celebrating its 25th year as a state of the United States of America. Bob hope says that he was "playing in the rough I saw Amelia Ehrhardt."

I always believed that Amelia Ehrhardt was Dolores Hope. Another cover story. My Theory is that Howard Hughes (as Bob Hope) being a Pilot and Amelia Ehrhardt being a Pilot, that they both disappeared together.

* * * *

#216 April 4, 1984

The show was about Bob Hope's book Have Tux will Travel. The book is about Bob Hope working for the United States Government. "When the Government calls he travels."

* * * *

#217 May 28, 1984

This is a birthday show for Bob Hope coming to you from the world's fair. The show Is sponsored by Texaco. It is Bob's super birthday show at age 81. Also, from New Orleans Louisiana.

* * * *

#218 September 28, 1984

At 81 years old Bob celebrates his 35th year on NBC. Hope says that" he still has the same dressing room."

* * * *

219 December 16, 1984

December and another Christmas show. No clues.

* * * *

#220 February 24, 1985

Notes the start of 1985 and Hope starts making statements about his disguise. Bob is quoted here as saying" sometimes I feel as though there is someone else inside me". There's what I've been saying all along, he's two people in one. Recall two of the most famous names in America sleep together. He said he's got another body beneath the makeup and clothes that he has on. He tells you he's nothing but makeup. Who's that other person underneath the Bob Hope makeup?

At the end of the show Bob Hope speaks from his heart with thanks for the memories.

* * * *

#221 April 15, 1985

In the opening monologue Bob Hope tells everyone that “my missile was approved”. His missile was approved? He speaks about being a “vain actor” and congratulates his “writers.”

In the show it is stated that” he is an actor*who talks to himself in a mirror.”

Talking to himself he states, “are you ready for me in makeup”. Whos me?

Dialog has it “get the sand blasting machine ready”. After makeup he puts on a smooth cream on his face. In the show “he's told to die”, and Bob Hope makes this fantastic statement “if I was to die I would be the first to watch my own funeral”. That's exactly what they did, they are Bob Hope and Howard Hughes. They faked death. They watched their own funeral. (1977)

Skit # 1 ... The joke is told that he's dead. As was said “the names of the innocent have been changed to protect the joke.”

* * * *

#222 May 28, 1985

This shows coming to you from London England. A Pan Am flight takes Hope to London steps off the plane and is greeted as a royalty. Remember that quote from Bob “every time I leave a show I leave on an assumed name”. And “when I get off my plane I leave myself behind”. On the plane Howard Hughes, off the plane in public Bob Hope.

At the end of the show Hope gives a speech and states that he is the Prince and the Pauper.

* * * *

#223 September 17, 1985

This show comes to you from NBC Headquarters in New York City. Bob celebrating his 36 years on television. The show is titled Bob Hope buys NBC. Bob makes a statement that General Motors has just bought Hughes Aircraft.

Skit # 1 ... The skit is about Texaco oil buying Getty oil. Concerning NBC Hope states that "you mean my network". "I am everyone's boss". And "what am I going to look like". Interesting he just ID himself as in control of everything and everyone. Recall Hope has said that all the writers, 3,000 writers work for him through the TV and the Movies. In the background Howard Hughes owns NBC, he is the Peacock with all the good looks and all the money in the world. Hughes then hires himself as Bob Hope and Howard Hughes pays the bill, the Government pays for everything Hughes, then Texaco sponsors the TV shows and then the United States pays all the bills.

* * * *

#224 December 15, 1985

Another Christmas show featuring all the football squads and their beauty queens and award show.

* * * *

#225 January 25, 1986

This show features the Super Bowl and entirely full show on the football theme. Just an entertainment show.

* * * *

#226 March 19, 1986

Show comes to you from Stockholm Sweden. Thank you show to Sweden. Bob Hope made a movie based on "I'll take Sweden". Just a variety show no clues.

* * * *

#227 May 26, 1986

This show comes to you from Pensacola Florida aboard the Aircraft Carrier Lexington. The show opens with the film of the Blue Angels airshow with jets doing all kinds of maneuvers. A jet lands on the aircraft carrier and Hope is in the cockpit. The show is a birthday show for Bob Hope at 83 years of age and about the 75th anniversary of the United States Air Force all about airpower. As we know nothing can beat the United States Air Force. What's the connection between Bob Hope, Howard Hughes, the Air Force, jet planes and aircraft carriers?? We know by now.

Skit # 1 ... Sammy Davis Junior plays the part of a drill sergeant. Bob Hope in charge. He and Jonathan Winters acting as pilots. Recall that Bob Hope and Howard Hughes were both pilots. Hope talks about burglars and plumbers and that he's in charge.

* * * *

#228 September 15, 1986

Bob Hope opens and pans his TV shows. He starts out with this statement "it takes me really long to put on my makeup". On the show it is stated that General Electric buys NBC as a General Electric NBC executive walks up to Bob and says, "what is your name"? Right, the guy who just bought NBC doesn't know who Bob Hope is. The whole world knows who Bob Hope is. Is the question a joke or another hint that he's somebody else? Hope goes on to say that his movie critics say that his "acting in going Spanish was excellent". Going Spanish was one of Bob Hope's earliest films. He's admitting he's a great actor. That's what the movie the greatest show on earth was all about. It was all about him he's the greatest show on earth.

Skit # 1 ... Dialog has it "a character has died". Hope says, "Bobby is alive for good". He then congratulates his writers, talks about having a "tattoo of Texas" and that "he may come back to life."

There are many skits on this show, a people's court. Hope is with the puppet. Tony Randle is the Judge. Hope is a witness in the witness stand and JFK is the defendant. Hope the witness says he had a deal with JFK and that JFK broke it. (Chicago vote leave off the mob). The judge asks Hope what he did about it and Hope says "I really spun his head around didn't I.

My Theory is that Howard Hughes was behind the assassination of Kennedy. Howard just told you so in his Bob Hope makeup as the witness who hated Kennedy and his entire family. The Kennedy's got the Vote then broke the deal and continued to go after the Mob.

* * * *

#229 December 21, 1986

Another Christmas show all about football. All about football.

* * * *

#230 February 23, 1987

To start 1987 Jonathan Winters opens the show and says, "not everyone gets to meet two Bob Hope's in a lifetime". So, Jonathan Winters knows that Bob is two people in one. So, he knows Howard and Bob with two heads the writer. Two of the most famous names in America sleep together.

Here's more proof. In one of Bob Hope's films he says to a woman that he's making it with that "if I die and come back you can say you made it with the both of us". The both of us being Bob and Howard as one. There he said it again. He is the two of us.

* * * *

#231 April 19, 1987

Hope talks about Moscow USSR and that our Embassy is being bugged by the Russians, there spies everywhere. He talks about current events and politics. Hope goes on to make this statement "that the Government of the United States can work out of a small place I know that they've been working out of my pocket money for years". Oh, that's a serious joke. He's using all his own money out of his own pocket for the Government for he is the Government. In one of Bob

Hope's movies he shows himself in the UN in a closet space running a bunch of secret tape recorders.

I have a quote from Howard Hughes that "My Father Won World War I and I won World War II and I'm working in Vietnam today with my newest equipment". (Helicopters).

* * * *

#232 May 25, 1987

This show is about Hope and the 40th Anniversary of the United States Air Force from Fort Bragg Arkansas. All about Aircraft. A great flying film history. Bing Crosby's the guest and he refers to Bob Hope as "Orville". I'm sure Bing referring to Hope as Orville is because of Hughes being an inventor and improving the airplane all the way up and into aerospace planes and Rockets. Bing Crosby had said in a movie that he and Orville Bob "will be rich and famous."

Hughes has been involved with the Airplane since the early 20s. Hope says, "I remember it well". "since bucket seats" (1922)

The rest of the show is the United States Air Force given an award to Hope for excellent service. The award is for the air transport system. (called MAPS). Hope designates the entire show to the Air Force and to the air transport system, thanks Stuart Symington the former Secretary of the Air Force under Harry Truman. He and Hope established the Military (air) Transport System. President Reagan himself live on the show paid tribute to Bob Hope and his efforts in three wars with the United States Air Force. Hope or Hughes. Pick one. Pick both!

* * * *

#233 September 17, 1987

This show opens with the title NBC investigates Bob Hope. A celebration of 38 years on NBC

Skit # 1 ... Bob opens up talking about split personalities, like the writer with two heads, like the two famous names that sleep together, and he makes this quote from his inner and outer self "if I die and come back as another person".......

Skit takes place in an NBC board room stating it, NBC may lose Bob Hope they want to "investigate the basement at NBC that a spy operation is working right out of the building", by Bob Hope. Interesting. Bob Hope is in disguise. Hope is running a spy network working right out of NBC and there's talk of all kinds of disguises. In the following dialog it is said that "Hope should be King or President because of what he has done for the people". Hope makes a speech about what he wants to do. "I divide all the money". Years ago, there was a movie out of Hollywood titled the man who would be King.

* * * *

#234 December 19, 1987

Bob opens the show talking about Missiles. What's Bob have to do with Missiles? Howard has a lot to do it Missiles. He talks about the range of the Missiles from 300 to 3,000 miles away, The USA and Hope are talking about Star Wars. Talks about the laser called SDI the Strategic Defense Initiative.

* * * *

#235 January 9, 1988

This show opens with a flight film showing jet planes in the Persian Gulf en route by aircraft carrier with film of the Christmas show on the aircraft carrier Midway. Hope jokes about Iran.

The first stop is the Philippines and Hope talks about special makeup due to the heat. He also travels to Diego Garcia and talks about things that are top-secret. Jokes about carrying a big makeup box. Then stops in Bahrain, then lands on the Okinawa carrier in the Persian Gulf. Don't forget the commercial during the Gulf War where in a TV commercial Hope says, "keep the oil flowing". Talks about Texaco being the sponsor of the show and that the Military must defend the strait of Harmuse. So, who is he Bob Hope? Comedian or Howard Hughes Billionaire Industrialist?

On this show Hope referred to the Kennedys as "the family". Note: Howard Hughes hated the Kennedys and the Kennedys hated Hughes since the 20s. Don't forget that television skit where Hope states that he was against JFK because JFK had a deal where if he got the Mob vote out of Chicago. Kennedy was to lay off the Mob. The Kennedy's did not lay off the Mob. Bob Hope says because of the breaking of that deal, he whoever he is said he "really turned his(JFK) head around didn't I ". You think Howard had anything to do with the assassination of John Kennedy. (over the deal, or not providing Air support for the Bay of Pigs invasion of Cuba.)

Later in the show Bob Hope talks about an "Inflatable Phyllis Diller doll". Note: both Howard Hughes and Bob Hope are very familiar with female inflatable dolls.

* * * *

#236 May 16, 1988

This is a tribute show and Bob Hope calls "Morocco Texas and that it is owned by the United States". It's Bob Hope's 85th Birthday and his 50th year on NBC.

* * * *

#237 September 8, 1988

Hope opens show for the H N N TV Network, titled: Hope News Network and puts out a monologue on current events. Then opens the show with a hint as to whom he may be.

Note: first there was a TV show in the 50s or 60s titled "I led three lives". My theory is that one life is Howard Hughes, Second Life is Bob Hope, and the third life, the Ayatollah Khomeini. Here's more proof to back up my claim.

Skit # 1 … With perfect makeup Hope comes on screen dressed as the Ayatollah Khomeini. A perfect walk on, stands in front of the camera and says, "do you know me"? Is That a crack or a joke, is it him as Khomeini? Hope says HE (Khomeini) has a night on the town in nightclubs and Bob Hope is quoted again saying "not everyone recognizes me". (I DID)!!! And right there in the skit he talks about great costumes and fabulous disguises. He certainly is a great character actor with great disguises pulling off great things around the world. Howard Hughes/Bob Hope is/was the Greatest Show on

Earth. Ironic that the television show Mission Impossible really was Mission Possible. It was done. My personal view is that it's greater than that. Like he led seven lives. I have Bob Hope in movies saying he has many different Masks, many different faces, many different noses and that he does his act as The Greatest Impersonator of people in the World, right in front of the people and they don't get it.

* * * *

#238 December 19, 1988

This show is a Christmas show from a cruise ship strictly entertainment

* * * *

239 January 29, 1989

This show is all about football. No skits no clues no quotes.

* * * *

#240 March 25, 1989

The show comes to you from the Bahamas where Hope says that he sent a card to Khomeini but didn't say what for.

* * * *

#241 May 24, 1989

The show comes from Paris France. One skit has Bob Hope at a firing line.

* * * *

#242 September 23, 1989

This is a Christmas show from Hawaii. All about Christmas and Football.

* * * *

#243 December 16, 1989

Another Christmas show from Hawaii.

* * * *

#244 February 17, 1990

Show comes you from Hollywood. Bob Hope is dressed as the "Joker" and as the Joker he says to Batman "I had a Mask like that". Would that be the Mask of the Lone Ranger? Or any of the many other Masks and disguises that Howard Hughes wears. Dialog in the script says, "Tear his face off."

Note: made in Hollywood there's a movie called the Mask. Other movies, The Invisible man, The Walking Dead, Spies like us, many movies all about Howard Hughes. The great Rupert!!

* * * *

#245 April 9, 1990

Show comes to you from Acapulco Mexico. Hope makes a comment to his wives. Wives, more than one? Hope or Howard? He says, "would you have married me if my Father hadn't left me a fortune"? Did Bob Hope's Father leave him a fortune or did Howard Hughes Father leave him an inheritance. Watch the movie Paleface and the Movie Son of Paleface for the answer. Those movies must be seen. Must be seen. Bob Hope is then quoted as saying "it's hell to be rich."

* * * *

#246 May 19, 1990

This show starts off stating that it's Bob Hope's 50th show for US troops. He talks about the show coming from the many airbases of the United States. The troupe takes off to Berlin and then to Moscow, then the United Kingdom and London. He speaks about the Royal Air Force and the opportunity to "talk about himself."

Bob talks about himself all right while in England he says, "I was born right here and went to America, I'm from Elton England, says he has "six brothers". To me that's the cover story, they got him covered.

Bob talks about the Berlin wall coming down. He was there, there's a photo of him sitting on it. Talks about Moscow and how the Embassy was bugged, says that he was "last in Moscow in 1958". He makes a crack about Moscow's weather and American businesses.

Note: in one of Bob Hope's books he is saying that he went back to London and when he was in London and being assisted by a Butler Hope says to the Butler "you know I was born in England" and the Butler responds and says, "I'll keep your secret". How About that! So, it's a secret! Throughout the show Hope speaks about the United States Air Force, its personnel, about rockets and about the space telescope Hubble. And Bob Hope knows all about that.

* * * *

#247 September 15, 1990

The show opens and it's Bob talking all about his new book, Don't Shoot it's Only Me. Hope talks Kissinger and about world leaders.

Skit # 1 … The skit is based on the book don't shoot it's only me. Bob Hope says that "he disagrees with Lincoln's quote that you can't fool all the people all the time". Bob Hope says, "you can fool all the people all the time". And you know why he can say that is because he as Howard Hughes with the Bob Hope face has fooled all the people all the time.

With this show being Bob's 41st year on TV he shows a History film of his Vaudeville days from 1923 and up.

* * * *

#248 December 15, 1990

The shows from Bermuda. Strictly entertainment. No clues no quotes.

* * * *

#249 January 12, 1991

This show comes to you from Saudi Arabia in the war zone before the start of the Gulf War. Hope is in Bahrain. Bob Hope the entertainer or Howard Hughes stands at the front of his troops again right in the desert with his troops.

* * * *

#250 April 6, 1991

Here we have Bob and Dolores Hope with the Generals with photos from home with President Bush, General Powell and General Schwarzenegger about the victory in the Gulf, with a victory party in Bob Hope's backyard. It's an All-Star show with the Military show, celebrating Victory in Iraq.

* * * *

#251 September 12, 1991

Not much information in this show but it does show the Russian coup with Yeltsin on a tank

* * * *

#252 December 12, 1991

This show was a very patriotic show about the United States of America. Variety entertainment.

* * * *

#253 March 14, 1992

nothing to be gleaned from this show.

* * * *

#254 May 16, 1992

strictly variety entertainment.

* * * *

255 November 28, 1992
nothing to be gleaned from this show.

* * * *

#256 December 18, 1992
This show comes to you from San Antonio Texas, deep in the heart of Texas from the Alamo.(1836). It is stated that Texas is the United States. On this show there are many Generals with everyone fully dressed and their saluting Bob Hope. Talk is about Texas and about its five Air Force bases, not to mention all the Army bases. Do we have to wonder any longer as to who he is and what he did? Does he just tell jokes? Here's a quote from Bob Hope "the names of the innocent have been changed to protect the joke". We should know by now that the jokes on the people. All the people all the time. Howard Hughes was Bob Hope in Make-up.

* * * *

#257 May 14, 1993
Bob Hope is 90 years old says he was born in 1903 in London. The fifth child. He says his name is Leslie Townes Hope. Says he came over to America, moved to Cleveland into his Uncles house which was full of Theater people. Hope shows an old film of his Vaudeville days and his makeup and disguise. He turns the show into tributes to the Presidents, He then congratulates his writers and many others and they're all saluting Hope.

* * * *

#258 December 15, 1993
This show is all reruns of skits previously seen.

* * * *

#259 May 11, 1994

Show starts off showing many reruns but there is a speech from Gen. Haig. The show is from West Point and Hope drops in as the Lone Ranger theme song plays, then the Superman song plays, and Hope reveals himself and arrives in a mini jet, talks about his birthday being 91, shows all past clips of shows. No new skits, same theme about spies, with an All-Star Hollywood cast.

* * * *

#260 August 27, 1994

This show is dedicated to Comedians and Hope brings on a lot of young Comedians. Pretty funny show. Just Entertainment.

* * * *

#261 December 14, 1994

The show is a complication of rerun clips and no skits, no quotes.

* * * *

#262 March 25, 1995

Could clean nothing out of this show. Entertainment.

* * * *

#263 August 5, 1995

Hope talks about the Presidents and he says and tells that "he should be President since 1941". That's what I've been saying, that as Howard Hughes he won World War II with his money, his equipment and with his power. He was President. He made all the calls. Hope goes on to say that "The Government was his sponsor". Did you ever wonder why Bob played golf with every President? Why he lived and stayed in the White House. He was always said to be the man behind the scenes. The Masked man. His problem was that his Cover Story that he was from England took away his real opportunity to run and be the elected President of the United States.

* * * *

#264 November 23, 1996 the DVD did not work.

* * * *

#265 April 30, 2002

This show is a show of stars with many beautiful Hollywood women on the show. The skit shows bloopers and outtakes. Bob is pointing to Santa clause and he says about himself "it's a little different when you got the Mafia on your side". There is Atlantic City connection again. (My Hometown)

* * * *

#266 No date

This show previewed 100 years of Hope and was a tribute to his career in Show Business Entertainment. He was the Beak, the Peacock. Clips of his life were shown. He was great! TV's most remarkable man died in 2003 at 100 years of age. If Howard 98 years of age.

It was a joke about his big cue cards and his constant Texas drawl saying well I want to tell you. This was a history show. 62 movies, 12 books, 9 albums, published comic books, plus 266 TV shows, it's all there.

My theory that Howard Hughes was Bob Hope in makeup was proven beyond any reasonable doubt. He said it, He wrote it, He told you, He showed it, He acted it, and I Found it!. I found out and with this book I told you so. 50 years of research. The Lone Ranger, Superman, the Beverly Hillbilly, Howard Hughes led three Lives as the Character Actor! Howard Hughes, Bob Hope, and the Ayatollah Khomeini. That makes three. There I said it again. And don't forget he did say that he had seven masks that he was 007 that he was the CIA.

The end

Thank you for reading this Book. I hope I have convinced you beyond any reasonable doubt.

Joseph Polillo

* * * *

My Theory is that HRH was Bob Hope, Secret President of the US, who had won WW 2, and running everything, holds all titles. Ran America, the Mob, the CIA. Does all Radio, TV, and Movies! My Theory is proven by what is said and shown in all of Bob Hopes Acts. Plus, with control of most oil of the world and much of the world's raw materials. and with great sums of money Hughes makes the calls. Howard Hughes ran NASA, Rockets and the United States of America.

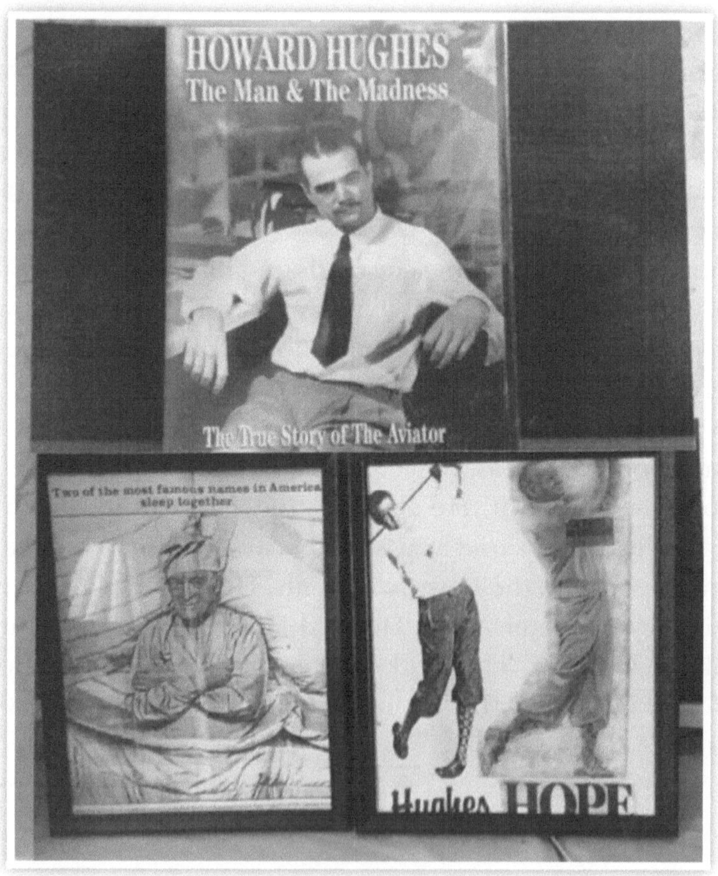

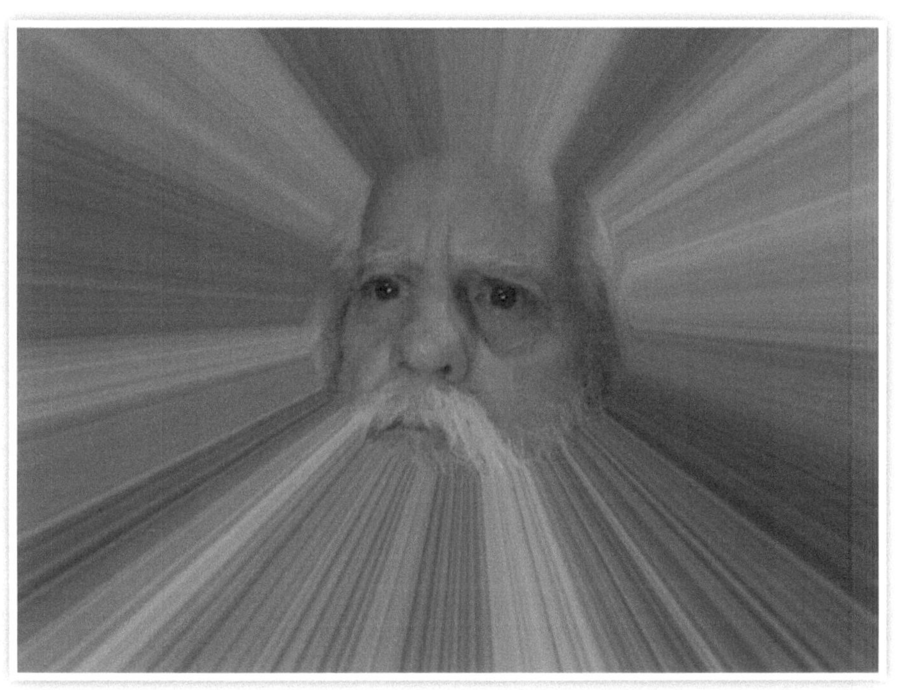

www.ingramcontent.com/pod-product-compliance
Ingram Content Group UK Ltd.
Pitfield, Milton Keynes, MK11 3LW, UK
UKHW041859190726
13854UKWH00002B/986

9 781639 500574